The politics of attack

Manchester University Press

CONTEMPORARY ANARCHIST STUDIES

A series edited by
Laurence Davis, *University College Cork, Ireland*
Uri Gordon, *University of Nottingham, UK*
Nathan Jun, *Midwestern State University, USA*
Alex Prichard, *Exeter University, UK*

Contemporary Anarchist Studies promotes the study of anarchism as a framework for understanding and acting on the most pressing problems of our times. The series publishes cutting-edge, socially engaged scholarship from around the world – bridging theory and practice, academic rigor and the insights of contemporary activism.

The topical scope of the series encompasses anarchist history and theory broadly construed; individual anarchist thinkers; anarchist informed analysis of current issues and institutions; and anarchist or anarchist-inspired movements and practices. Contributions informed by anti-capitalist, feminist, ecological, indigenous and non-Western or global South anarchist perspectives are particularly welcome. So, too, are manuscripts that promise to illuminate the relationships between the personal and the political aspects of transformative social change, local and global problems, and anarchism and other movements and ideologies. Above all, we wish to publish books that will help activist scholars and scholar activists think about how to challenge and build real alternatives to existing structures of oppression and injustice.

International Editorial Advisory Board:
Martha Ackelsberg, *Smith College*
John Clark, *Loyola University*
Jesse Cohn, *Purdue University*
Ronald Creagh, *Université Paul Valéry*
Marianne Enckell, *Centre International de Recherches sur l'Anarchisme*
Benjamin Franks, *University of Glasgow*
Judy Greenway, *Independent Scholar*
Ruth Kinna, *Loughborough University*
Todd May, *Clemson University*
Salvo Vaccaro, *Università di Palermo*
Lucien van der Walt, *Rhodes University*
Charles Weigl, *AK Press*

Other titles in the series
(From Bloomsbury Academic):
Anarchism and Political Modernity
Angelic Troublemakers
The Concealment of the State
Daoism and Anarchism
The Impossible Community
Lifestyle Politics and Radical Activism
Making Another World Possible
Philosophical Anarchism and Political Obligation

(From Manchester University Press):
Anarchy in Athens
The Autonomous Life?

The politics of attack

Communiqués and insurrectionary violence

Michael Loadenthal

Manchester University Press

Copyright © Michael Loadenthal 2017

The right of Michael Loadenthal to be identified as the author of this work has been asserted by him in accordance with the Copyright, Designs and Patents Act 1988.

Published by Manchester University Press
Altrincham Street, Manchester M1 7JA
www.manchesteruniversitypress.co.uk

British Library Cataloguing-in-Publication Data

A catalogue record for this book is available from the British Library
Library of Congress Cataloging-in-Publication Data applied for

ISBN 978 1 5261 1445 7 hardback
ISBN 978 1 5261 1444 0 paperback

First published 2017

This work is licensed under the Creative Commons Attribution-Non-Commercial-ShareAlike 2.0 England and Wales License. Permission for reproduction is granted by the editors and the publishers free of charge for voluntary, campaign and community groups. Reproduction of the text for commercial purposes, or by universities or other formal teaching institutions is prohibited without the express permission of the publishers.

The publisher has no responsibility for the persistence or accuracy of URLs for any external or third-party internet websites referred to in this book, and does not guarantee that any content on such websites is, or will remain, accurate or appropriate.

Typeset
by Toppan Best-set Premedia Limited
Printed in Great Britain
by CPI Group (UK) Ltd, Croydon, CR0 4YY

CONTENTS

List of figures vii
Preface viii
Acknowledgments x
Abbreviations xii

1 Concerning method and the study of political violence 1

2 Insurrection as history from Guy Fawkes to black blocs 32

3 Insurrection as a post-millennial, clandestine, network of cells 65

4 Insurrection as warfare, terrorism, and revolutionary design 96

5 Insurrection as theory, text, and strategy 134

6 Insurrection as values-driven theory and action 161

7 Insurrection as anti-securitization communication 198

References 226
Index 260

FIGURES

3.1 CARI-PGG's logo included in communiqués 83
3.2 Image circulated with "First communiqué of Wild Reaction (RS)" 85
7.1 Secondary–tertiary target audience concept map 212
7.2 Communiqué/attack–form/function concept map 219
7.3 Knowledge transmission concept map 222

PREFACE

On a chilly, rain-soaked April day in the nation's capital, I find myself trudging through the puddles looking for a post office. Now, while my use of the federal mail system is quite limited in these days of e-mail, digital document signing, and electronic bill paying, today I'm mailing my contract for the publication of my first book, this book.

As fate would find it, the contract reaches my desk while I am residing in Washington, DC, for some precariously contingent teaching work, residing in a colleague's Capitol Hill basement unit. Through the wonders of smartphone mapping, on my walk to the metro, I locate a post office only a few blocks from me. I traverse the various post-9/11 fortifications surrounding the Capitol area designed to blend into the landscape, past the cars being searched for bombs hidden beneath their chassis, past the officers hiding behind panopticonal, opaque glass screens, and eventually find myself inside of one of the main Congressional buildings; part of a series of such facilities connected to one another through a series of tunnels, elevators, and stairs and just adjacent to the south Capitol lawn.

I enter the building through the "non-members [of Congress]" door, submit myself and my possessions to an x-ray machine and metal detector, and am eventually cleared to enter and given relative free rein to explore. I begin by riding the "members-only" elevator down to the basement, sharing the ride with a man who from his age and dress I assume is a Congressman. His body language expresses his annoyance that a dripping wet, hooded, septum-pierced traveler is descending the elevator shaft with him.

After exploring the catacombs and long hallways of the lower level, I begin asking for the post office. When I eventually find it, its familiarity and unremarkability are the only things I note. It is nearly identical to every other post office I have ever encountered. I mail my package and wander around the building a bit. I pass the offices of various Representatives proudly displaying their state flags. I pass bubbly, expertly quaffed, intern-aged women and men, most of whom are too buried in their phones to even notice me. I overhear discussion of legislation, travel, last night's social events. Though the building is on the surface a public place, I feel like an outsider, like everyone must know I do not belong, and I imagine the buildings and its inhabitants exuding a small sigh of relief when I depart its doors without incident.

Upon leaving the building and re-entering the rainy Thursday morning, I am struck by how very odd the whole experience was. Here I am, an underdressed (to say the least), non-umbrella holding, non-badge displaying, non-member of Congress exploring the labyrinths of technocratic statecraft, looking to mail a package that – when abstracted to its most sensational – is chiefly focused on underground actors mailing explosives to the offices of politicians. This book contract, securing the publication and distribution of a foray into insurrectionary warfare, passed through the hands and x-rays of the US Capitol Police, and in that moment I am reminded of FBI press conferences where manila envelopes are held up to display improvised explosive devices intercepted en route.

I imagine my own package sitting in a bin, deep inside the federal building, already buried beneath other mail. Tick, tick, tick. It has yet to reach the world. Tick, tick, tick. I imagine it is waiting to explode. Tick, tick, tick. I imagine that we live in a world where ideas and arguments burst from the pages and into our consciousness.

This book is an examination of militant resistance, and while some will be quick to call bombs in the mail and the arson of property "terrorism", nothing we could do can ever approach the terror inherent in statehood. As the post-9/11, anarcho bathroom graffiti so often said, "The State is the only terrorist!"

As I remember my drenched walk through the vaults of centralized power, I think of my own manila package – one that I hope will be incendiary – and my own battles with the forces of domination. I think of the morning's events and I laugh just audibly enough that it makes my fellow hallway travelers notice, and maybe, just maybe, threatens their sense of security that has become such a hallmark of state control.

ACKNOWLEDGMENTS

This book would not have been possible without the kind efforts of a number of individuals. I would like to first thank my amazing dissertation committee, chaired by Richard Rubenstein, and joined by Leslie Dwyer and John Dale. Rich, without your patience, generosity, guidance, and support, none of this would have been possible. I would also like to thank the Contemporary Anarchist Studies series editors who provided feedback throughout this process. Thank you to Laurence Davis, Nathan Jun, Alex Prichard, and especially Uri Gordon, who was always a voice of encouragement. Additional thanks is due to the great team at Manchester University Press, especially Thomas Dark, Alun Richards, and Robert Byron. I would also like to sincerely thank Bruce Hoffman and Anne Routon at Columbia University Press for their support in my early quest to locate a suitable publisher.

I am thankful for the support of Solon Simmons who was a sounding board for some of my methodological conundrums, and William Leap who first introduced me to corpus linguistics. My most heartfelt appreciation and praise to my former-students-turned-research-assistants at Georgetown University who helped to compile the communiqué corpus. Thank you to Phoebe Wild who began the collaborative endeavor, Anna Colette Heldring and Annie Kennelly who joined us later, and Jessica Anderson who saw it through in its final stages. I hope these relationships were mutually beneficial and collaboratively non-coercive. My most humble gratitude to the staff at Georgetown's Program on Justice and Peace and the Center for Social Justice Research, Teaching & Service, who provided encouragement and office space during the writing phase. A special thank you to thank Kayla Corcoran who assisted me in constructing the figures contained in the final chapter. Last, but certainly not least, I am humbled to thank Georgetown's Andria Wisler, Randall Amster, and Mark Lance – dazzling scholars, friends, allies, and colleagues in the truest sense. I would also like to thank Gwyneth O'Neill and John Copacino at Georgetown's Criminal Justice Clinic for shepherding me through my first federal felony, for helping keep me out of prison, and for allowing us to stand tall in a new era of criminalized dissent.

I also must thank the various members of the North American Anarchist Studies Network who helped me locate some of the more obscure historical texts from anti-state attackers of centuries past. Thank you as well to the members of the Critical Studies on Terrorism Working Group who provided insight at various points in this process. I also could not have completed this project without the use of a number of key institutions whose libraries I plundered for texts on linguistics, discourse analysis, poststructural philosophy, guerrilla warfare, and anarchist histories. Thanks to the re-shelvers at the libraries of Georgetown, George Mason University, Northern Kentucky University, University of Cincinnati, and especially Donald Russell at Provisions in Fairfax, VA. I also must thank my friends Gary Hall and Michael J. Woods who provided me with bedrooms to hide away and write, Amanda Meister who took care of the wee ones during my doctoral defense, and the Washington Metro Area Transit Authority – without your constant delays and slow service I would have never been able to get so much reading done.

Of course I have to thank the clandestine window smashers and fire starters distributed throughout the world: Without you, these pages would be quite a different story. Thanks for always writing such passionate prose, and thank you to those who were diligent with their footnoting, cross-referencing, and attribution. Your eye for anal-retentive editing has not been overlooked.

I would like to thank my dearest kids, Emory Sheindal, Simon Bella, and Tevye Yosef who were willing to share their Daddy with this time-consuming enterprise, and who inspire me every day to be brave, take risks, and work towards a brighter future.

Finally, I would like to thank my partner and co-conspirator, the brilliant anthropologist, Jennifer Grubbs. Jennifer, thank you for listening to me talk about my work, helping to create time for me to write, dealing with the never-ending stacks of books strewn about, and for always encouraging me to be better.

ABBREVIATIONS

17N	Organization 17 November
ALF	Animal Liberation Front
BB!	Bash Back!
CARI-PGG	Práxedis G. Guerrero Autonomous Cells for Immediate Revolution
CCF	Conspiracy of Cells of Fire
CSS	Critical Security Studies
CTS	Critical Terrorism Studies
ELF	Earth Liberation Front
EMETIC	Evan Mecham Eco-Terrorist International Conspiracy
EZLN	Zapatista Army of National Liberation (*Ejército Zapatista de Liberación Nacional*)
FAI	Informal Anarchist Federation (*Federazione Anarchica Informale*)
F.A.I.	Iberian Anarchist Federation (*Federación Anarquista lbérica*)
FAI-M	Informal Anarchist Federation – Mexico
FARC	Revolutionary Armed Forces of Colombia (*Fuerzas Armadas Revolucionarias de Colombia*)
HRC	Human Rights Campaign
IED	improvised explosive device
IEF	Institute for Experimental Freedom
IID	improvised incendiary device
IRF	International Revolutionary Front
ITS	Individualists Tending Toward the Wild
OPCA	Obsidian Point Circle of Attack
OPCAn	Obsidian Point Circle of Analysis
PIRA	Provisional Irish Republican Army
RAF	Red Army Faction
RB	Red Brigades
RC-ALB	Revolutionary Cells – Animal Liberation Brigade
RS	Wild Reaction (*Reacción Salvaje*)
RZ	Revolutionary Cells (*Revolutionäre Zellen*)
TAZ	Temporary Autonomous Zone
TIC	The Invisible Committee
WTO	World Trade Organization
WUO	Weather Underground Organization

1
Concerning method and the study of political violence

Ah hell. Prophecy's a thankless business, and history has a way of showing us what, in retrospect, are very logical solutions to awful messes ... Things are certainly set up for a class war based on conveniently established lines of demarcation, and I must say that the basic assumption of the present set up is a grade A incitement to violence. (Vonnegut 1999, chap. IX)

When asked about anarchism's association with violence, I often reply by inquiring whether one would ask the same thing of a retail clerk, a stockbroker, a lawyer, a priest, an engineer, a taxpayer, a consumer, a liberal, a conservative – or any other identity attribute associated with mainstream society. Most assuredly, the scale of violence perpetuated by the day-to-day operations of capital and the state is grossly disproportionate to anything in the anarchist lexicon, with upwards of 100 million deaths from wars alone during the twentieth century. I daresay that the sum total of people killed or physically injured by anarchists throughout all of recorded history amounts to little more than a good weekend in the empire ... Are anarchists violent? Sometimes, but more so when they are participating in the casual, invisible, structural violence of modern life than when they are smashing its symbols of oppression. (Amster 2012, 43–44)

An anarchist group has claimed responsibility for an arson attack on North Avon Magistrates' Court ... police are investigating the on-line claims but say they do not have the evidence to link it to other attacks carried out on buildings owned by "establishment" bodies, including the police, the Army and various banks. In a post on the 325. nostate website, people naming themselves as the Informal Anarchist Federation, said: "10 camping gas canisters were enough to devastate the front lobby, with a homemade napalm mixture as the detonator. We chose the early hours to avoid any injuries." (*The Bristol Post* 2014a)

Introduction

Throughout the past decade and a half, scholarship focused upon the study of political violence, specifically that which can clearly be labeled as *terrorism*, has rapidly increased (Ranstorp 2007; Silke 2009). With the powerful aftereffects of the 9/11 attacks, interest in those pursuing political, social, and religious objectives through violence found an obvious place in the academy. Largely, this scholarship was dealt with through the fields of Terrorism Studies and Social Movement Studies, as well as interrelated disciplines such as Criminology, Security Studies, and Sociology. While these fields have often overlapped through interdisciplinary pursuits, each has its own epistemological presumptions, methodological tendencies, and canonical truths.

For the study of political violence, and especially clandestine political violence which is the subject herein, one is often positioned at the crossroads between interpreting the subject as a *terrorist* or a *social movement* and, as such, is led towards those corresponding disciplines, literatures, and presumptive groundings. Keeping in mind the poststructuralist assertion that the production of knowledge – especially that which is involved in the formation of political policy – is never a neutral endeavor (Foucault 1980, 98), the collection of evidence and the construction of arguments is inherently the culmination of intentional decisions. When faced with these choices, held up against the subject of post-millennial, anti-authoritarian, insurrectionary networks, such concerns are paramount. Those who choose to pursue study through the literature of Terrorism Studies, are likely to be burdened with not only the state-centric bias of background literature, but also the field's lack of theorization and its focus on *counter*terrorism (della Porta 2013, 282) and other securitization implementations. Those who choose to examine such networks as social *movements*,[1] a field that bases its focus on manifestations of social protest, also face difficulties as this field has often remained apart from *radical* politics within *militant* and *violent* protest, and has a corresponding theorization abyss regarding these borderlands.

Since the end of the twentieth century, an explosion of anti-state networks of clandestine militancy have emerged throughout the world. Through thousands of attacks, revolutionaries have been constantly at war with the status quo, targeting localized manifestations of state and capital in an attempt to create a venue of conflict that can bring about system-level change. Though distributed globally and irregularly active, these networks attack with frequency and vigor, making them a top priority for law enforcement. In one locale, Bristol, England, a city of around half a million residents, insurrectionary anarchist networks have been responsible for "over a hundred offensives dating [from] 2010 [to December 2014]" (Bevan 2014, pts. 00:44–00:50) according to the lead investigating officer. According to sympathetic activists, this number may be far higher, as those compiling local communiqués were able to locate more than 60 attacks in a two-and-a-half year period (Bevan 2014). These attacks, many of which involve arson, are said to have caused approximately £20 million (~$31 million) in damage. The vast majority of these attacks have been claimed via online communiqués through anonymous monikers such as the Informal Anarchist Federation (FAI). The FAI moniker has been adopted so frequently that, despite not having a centralized structure or "members," the entity was declared to be a terrorist organization by the European Union in 2009.

In only a few years, in the city of Bristol alone, the clandestine political networks under examination were responsible for the £18 million arson of a police firearms training center, the burning of UK Border Agency vehicles and personal vehicles belonging to a Mayor and other local politicians, sabotage targeting a local commuter rail service, and the arson of industrial infrastructure, which resulted in a loss of radio and TV service to more than 80,000 homes (Channel 4 News 2013; Malik 2012; 2013). Other Bristol-area targets struck in the last few years include private security company G4S and the zoo. This brief look at Bristol is meant to provide insight as to the *scale* of the subject. The international, insurrectionary milieu – the subject of this book – is deserving of attention even if one only judges them on the basis of their destructive capabilities. Though modern attackers are not successfully assassinating heads of state, as was somewhat commonplace in late nineteenth and early twentieth century, they are dispatching bombs to European Prime Ministers, burning down Mexican Walmarts, and carrying out thousands of costly attacks targeting governmental, financial, commercial, and other sites. Furthermore, since there have been very few arrests of this movement, we know relatively little about the participants. Because of this reality, in order to understand the insurrectionary arsonists, bomb makers, and saboteurs, we must examine their frequent articulations of critique – the communiqué.[2] Despite often failing to do this, the need for such forms of analysis have been expressed in mainstream press reporting, for example this article from *The Bristol Post* which states:

> To understand why these attacks are happening, for what reason, and how these individuals identify politically, it's recommended to read their words and statements for clarity. Each attack is by a unique established group of individual/s, with a diversity of anonymous cloaks, presenting varying ideological viewpoints. The beauty of the insurrectionist movement you might say. (2014b)

While these attacks, and the communiqué/claims of responsibility that accompany them, have received nominal attention in the (counter) Terrorism Studies literature, very little focus has been paid to their political ideology and socio-political critique. Moreover, the interaction between "radical social movements" (Koehler 2014, 2) and their broader contexts (e.g. social, political, ideological) is under researched.

The following introductory chapter will examine a number of key issues of central importance to the book. First it will discuss the object of analysis – the communiqué – as a method for delivering critical analysis typically reserved for more formalized texts. This approach begs the question: "Can one read a claim of responsibility (i.e. a communiqué) in the same formalized manner as one would read *The Communist Manifesto* or *The Federalist Papers*?" This discussion will also survey the available literature that focuses on the study of communiqués, identifying weaknesses and necessary corrections to this reading. Second, this chapter identifies some initial difficulties arising from the study of these objects, specifically problems relating to verifiability, triangulation, determining credible authorship, and the inherent subjectivity in historical interpretation. Finally, this chapter discusses the limitations and scale of the study, establishing two key questions, which are pursued throughout the remaining chapters. These questions aim to guide the reader to evaluate two central claims: (1) Modern insurrectionary networks are informed by, and act to, constitute an "insurrectionary canon," and (2) Due to the poststructural influence on the modern insurrectionary critique, the milieu will resultantly carry forth an expanded understanding of structural violence and inequality.

A feminist method for studying violence

While a more complete discussion of ethically-embedded, critical modes of inquiry is pursued at the *conclusion* of this chapter, a brief discussion of ethics is warranted before proceeding. A methodological positioning informed by feminist ethics permeates the proceeding discussions. The feminist methodology and ethic of research (Mies 1983; Cook and Fonow 1986; 1991; Maguire 1987; Harding 1988; Lather 1988; Kirby and Kate 1989; Collins 1991; Reinharz 1992) adds a great deal, including a reading of identity politics, standpoint theory, action-orientated research, and embedded, emotive and sincere participatory involvement. From among these tendencies, this inquiry seeks to maintain a single goal, namely that research generates a reciprocally positive impact for the subject (Oakley 1981), and in this manner, the respondent community is not seen as a vessel containing knowledge to be taken, but rather as a partner in a collaborative endeavor to engage in knowledge building, *not* knowledge production. In the present discussion of insurrectionary anarchism, this involves the construction of knowledge for social action and not further criminalization, and remaining accountable to the community of activists and scholars whom the movement is based around.

Feminist methodology seeks to subvert traditional power relationships and ethical pitfalls, and according to one scholar, challenges four concerns otherwise recurrent in field research:

1.) The increased salience of race/ethnicity, gender, and class in the research relationship; 2.) the objectification of research subjects; 3.) the influence of social power on who becomes a research subject; and 4.) problematic assumptions in the conventional analytic approaches. (Sprague 2005, 121)

In practice, the following analysis attempts to destabilize the "othering" (Letherby 2003, 20–24; Sprague 2005, 125) of the subject, which tends to portray the researchers' position as normative. In this manner, it becomes the task of a constructed taxonomy to position urban guerrillas among a wider socio-political movement, and through placement within such a continuum, such "violent" actors can be understood as similarly rational actors choosing to pursue a less popular – albeit illegal – form of protest. This also means that as a researcher, one can position themselves *within the research* as not only an observer, but a participant (Cole 1990, 159–166; Letherby 2003, 8) in the subject community. Such an approach can allow one to "understand the kind of questions that needed answering" (Cole 1990, 162), as well as the process of knowledge construction for the respondent community. This approach is far from mainstream, as most often, political actors adopting counter-state and violent strategies are viewed within the exoticized lens akin to the primitive savage of the colonial, anthropological, village subject. This tendency is (as can be expected) further exaggerated in mainstream journalistic accounts of these movements, which often carry sensationalist headlines such as "Meet the Nihilist-Anarchist Network Bringing Chaos to a Town Near You" (Hanrahan 2013). By de-sensationalizing the violence, and instead focusing on the movement's political discourse, one hopes to shift the readers' attention away from the frequency of the bombs, and towards the validity of the critiques.

Furthermore, one of the methods of subverting the pitfalls of traditionally unethical scholarship is to be found in emphasizing the subject's perspective, and allowing the knowledge holder to determine the research agenda and its analysis (Sprague 2005, 141). This is a contribution of post-1970s feminist methodological battles and a notable aspect of my methodological pursuit. Taken as a whole, a feminist methodological approach to qualitative investigation is adopted precisely because it addresses issues of power within the realm of research (Letherby 2003, 114). It does so in a practically applicable manner aimed at subversion and the development of new methods of investigation that exist as counter forces to traditionalism, knowledge banking, and the expropriation of stories from an *othered* subject. Therefore it is the aim of the proceeding discussion to not borrow the sexy dynamism of insurrection to construct an engaging argument, but rather to move beyond the discussion of these networks as merely the producers of fires and explosions and instead begin to understand them as social critics, "organic intellectuals" (Gramsci 1971b, 9), and philosophical practitioners.

Communiqués as political theory

> I say to you: that we are in. a battle, and that more than half of this battle is taking place on the battlefield of the media. And that we are in a media battle in a race for the hearts and minds ... And that however far our capabilities reach, they will never be equal to one thousandth of the capabilities of ... that [which] is waging war on us. (al-Zawahiri 2005, 10)

Communiqués are seen as an essential communicative component of insurrectionary attack. Following each incident of political violence – from a broken bank window to an assassinated nanotechnologist – the act is explained, "infused with meaning" (Hodges 2011, 5) via a text meant to expand the discourse on revolutionary struggle. This site, that of the communiqué, demonstrates the social construction of *both* the act (of "terrorism") and the discourse (*on* "terrorism"). Both the event (i.e. the attack) and the object (i.e. the communiqué) are socially constructed phenomena (Stump and Dixit 2013, 108), serving to apply meaning and context for a wider audience. These explanatory frames discursively embed the act of anti-social violence, and have key functions within the construction of consequent discourses and attacks. To borrow an explanation from the bomb throwers themselves, "through the communiqués that accompany attacks we can begin an open debate on reflections and problems that, even if viewed through different lenses, are certainly focused on the same direction: revolution" (G. Tsakalos et al. 2012, 15). Such "requisite revolutionary discourse ... following[ing] bombings against targets that serve domination" (G. Tsakalos et al. 2012, 11) typically takes the form of a written communiqué posted and circulated through a network of websites. These websites form a repository for the collection of communiqués and the establishment of a corpus. This communiqué corpus constitutes the central "data" for this book and its discussions.

Surveying communiqué collections

Academic and popular press books dealing specifically with communiqués as subject – often reprinting entire documents – have been sparse, interdisciplinary, and seemingly on the rise. Notable examples include edited volumes such as *Europe's Red Terrorists: The Fighting Communist Organizations* (Alexander and Pluchinsky 1992), *Speaking Stones: Communiqués from the Intifada Underground* (Mishal and Aharoni 1994), *Our Word Is Our Weapon: Selected Writings of Subcomandante Marcos* (Marcos 2002), *Voices of Terror: Manifestos, Writings and Manuals of Al Qaeda, Hamas* ... (Laqueur 2004), *What Does Al-Qaeda Want?* (Marlin 2004), *Sing a Battle Song: The Revolutionary Poetry, Statements, and Communiqués of the Weather Underground 1970–1974* (Dohrn, Ayers, and Jones 2006), *Earth Liberation Front 1997–2002* (Pickering 2007), the multi-volume series, *The Red Army Faction: A Documentary History* (Moncourt and Smith 2009a; 2009b), *Creating a Movement with Teeth a Documentary History of the George Jackson Brigade* (Burton-Rose 2010), *Queer Ultraviolence: A BASH BACK! Anthology* (Eanelli and Baroque 2012), and studies utilizing communiqués comingled with other forms of texts such as *The Road to Martyrs' Square* (Oliver and Steinberg 2006) which documents Palestinian militant culture through communiqués, video transcripts, graffiti, and other ephemera. Additionally, there appears to be an increasing number of studies that apply a linguistic or discursive analysis to politically violent ephemera, such as farewell correspondences from suicide bombers (e.g. S. J. Cohen 2016) and jihadist magazines (e.g. Ingram 2015; Novenario 2016).

Yonah Alexander and Dennis Pluchinsky's book provides one of the more comprehensive approaches to the examination of communiqués. Alexander and Pluchinsky (1992, x) focus on nine European "fighting communist organizations [FCOs]," and in speaking to their book's limitations note:

> This book was not designed to be an all-inclusive, detailed study of the European FCOs. To the authors' knowledge, no such study exists. The intent was to compile a brief collection of documents (attack communiqués, ideological tracts, interviews, policy statements, etc.) ... so that the reader can obtain a general understanding of how these groups think and view the world about them.

While the aforementioned books contain very valuable exhibitions of primary source materials, with exceedingly few exceptions, the communiqués are not *analyzed* thoroughly and are often simply *presented*. The texts are far more descriptive in nature, not analytical. Typically the volumes are nearly entirely the words of the non-state actor with a brief introductory frame written by an editor. While some are careful to discuss the texts in relation to actual events (e.g. Moncourt and Smith 2009a; 2009b; Burton-Rose 2010), the texts themselves are rarely the focus. In none of the volumes surveyed is the political critique of the non-state actor held up as legitimate theory to be evaluated. Instead, it is often showcased in an exotic manner, or in the case of Laqueur's edited volume, displayed as the writings of various "terrorists."

Additional books cataloging the political writings of individual practitioners of political violence are quite common, such as those containing the words of Islamist figureheads Osama bin Laden (2005) and Sayyed Hassan Nasrallah (2007), Marxist guerrilla leader Ernesto "Che" Guevara (1997), the Red Army Faction's Ulrike Meinhof (2008), "New Afrikan" militants Jalil Muntaqim (2002), Kuwasi Balagoon (2003), and Russell Maroon Shoatz (2013), anarcho-primitivist "Unabomber" Theodore Kaczynski (2010d), and Animal Liberation Front activists Walter Bond (2011) and Rod Coronado (2011). In these person-specific compilations, the original (and translated) works are presented with very little commentary and often no analysis. There are also frequent personal narratives, memoirs, autoethnographies, and autobiographies from individual actors that often portray life events but exclude formal political statements. Examples from the revolutionary left include those by North American militants Ann Hansen (2002) and David Gilbert (2011), West German urban guerrilla Bommi Baumann (2002), 1960s student protest leaders and Weathermen Mark Rudd (2010) and Bill Ayers (2009), American Indian Movement political prisoner Leonard Peltier (2000), Palestinian airplane hijacker Lelia Khaled (1973), Revolutionary Armed Forces of Colombia (FARC) guerrilla María Eugenia Vásquez Perdomo (2005), and Black Panther Assata Shakur (2001), as well as a semi-autobiographical, first-hand account from Basque ethno-nationalist militants (Agirre 1975), Italian Red Brigade militants (Giorgio 2003), and Americans who joined Spanish Republicans to challenge fascism in the 1930s (Orwell 1980; Bailey 1993). Many more have been published digitally, including autobiographical accounts of 1996 Olympic Park bomber Eric Rudolph (2015) and American-born jihadi leader Omar Hammami (2012).

Communiqués as political texts are an under-theorized site for critical inquiry. Despite their prominence in the ephemera of clandestine networks of political violence, their compilation, interpretation, and analysis has been lacking. Some scholars (e.g. Harrison 2013) have focused on the development of methodologies for interpreting the ideological predilections of political manifestos. Though these works are instructive in a general sense, their focus on *ideology* and *parties* make them ill-suited for discussing anti-ideological, anti-political (i.e. those that reject politics as a method of social change) movements. Insurrectionary theorists posit that the foundational basis, whether anarchist or other, is never stoic or fixed but rather a "non-essentialist, non-ideology" (Rodríguez 2011b) enacted diversely by diverse actors. This makes demarcating what *is* and *is not* "insurrectionary" a difficult taxonomic task. In Sarah Harrison's (2013, 55–56) study, the author focused on the discourse of right-wing political parties, identifying the frequency of select words and coding these keywords for thematic analysis.

Similar studies have been coordinated by the Manifesto Research Group/ Comparative Manifestos Project (2014) which has conducted "quantitative content analyses of parties' election programmes from more than 50 countries covering all free, democratic elections since 1945."

Not all acts of political violence – clandestine or otherwise – are claimed via a written communication. Some are claimed via video releases, audio transmissions, graffiti, or telephone calls, and still others are unclaimed. Research suggests that only approximately 14% of terrorist attacks occurring in the period 1998–2004 were followed by claims of responsibility, and that the rate is declining – with 61% of attacks claimed in the 1970s and 40% in the 1980s (Wright 2011). The issuing of communiqués following acts of violence is often dependent on the modus operandi of the movement (A. M. Hoffman 2010). Animal Liberation Front (ALF) and Earth Liberation Front (ELF) attacks are nearly universally claimed via a written communiqué – in approximately 93% of attacks (Loadenthal 2010, 89 (chart 3.3)) – which are then compiled and circulated by aboveground support networks such as *Bite Back Magazine*, the North American Animal Liberation Press Office, and the international, translation, and counter-information network "of the new generation [of] incendiary anarchy and global anti-civilization attack" (K. Cohen et al. 2014, 251) embodied in websites such as 325.nostate, War on Society, and others. Comparatively, in attacks by Palestinian paramilitary organizations (1968–2004), 56% were claimed (A. M. Hoffman 2010, 621), while in other conflicts, especially those where non-state factions are less competitive in their battles for supporters, the rate is often much lower. In Provisional Irish Republican Army (PIRA) and affiliated attacks, since the paramilitary is seen as having fewer competitors than the various Palestinian factions, attacks in England (1973–1998) were claimed in less than 15% of cases (A. M. Hoffman 2010, 624). This has led some to conclude that anonymous, unclaimed attacks are actually the norm (Abrahms and Conrad 2016, 2), which is *not* the dominant trend in attacks by insurrectionary anarchists under discussion.

In examining the post-millennial clandestine attack networks that drew inspiration and modeling from the millennial anti-globalization, counter-summit protests, it is no surprise that the militant edges of this movement are communiqué-rich sources. In a lengthy piece of strategic writing authored by anonymous individuals "somewhere in the [American] Mid-West" and affiliated with the direct action network Anti-Racist Action, the authors instruct:

> It is important that all ... [militant street] actions be followed with a comprehensive communiqué ... This communiqué should discuss the action in terms of why it occurred, why specific conflicts/tactics developed and how this immediate struggle is connected with the broader Anarchist movement towards a liberated and creative world ... Such

communiqués are important in regards to reaching out to the broader populace, as well as in debunking the demonization of our activities as can be expected to emanate out of the corporate press. (G-MAC and People Within The ARA 2002, 220–221)

This commentary speaks to the reliance on communiqués as a speech act, and specifically as a means to self-report, spread propaganda, and challenge divergent accounts from media and liberal/sectarian sources. What explains the underground attackers' preference for reporting via communiqués? Maybe it is that the communiqué structures a particular speech device and, in doing so, facilitates direct communication between a previously silenced entity (i.e. the attacker) and an often-curious recipient (i.e. the public).

The challenges of collecting communiqués

On a practical level, the collection of communiqués allowed for the construction of an approximated incident-based dataset: a historical recounting of the politics of direct attack as told through the broken windows, slashed tires, and burnt storefronts so eloquently rationalized through the texts. The construction of such a dataset begins with the development of strict in-group/out-group rules for inclusion and exclusion. The construction of this rule set requires a more generalized familiarity with the content hosted on the website network surveyed. In discussing the analysis and mapping of "radical violence in social media," researchers from the Swedish Defense Research Agency make the same observation, writing, "in order to develop relevant keywords that actually indicate radicalism, an in-depth knowledge of the milieu in question is required" (K. Cohen et al. 2014, 251). After familiarizing myself with its content over the course of years of reading,[3] broad parameters are established, tested, and then refined and recorded in a decision tree. Only incidents that were claimed via a communiqué and posted to the surveyed hubs were included. Similarly, communiqués that did not *claim responsibility* but offered more general critique, theory or debate were excluded.

This was by no means an easy task. The nature of clandestine, decentralized, and internationally-dispersed cells offers methodological challenges beyond simply the frequent inability to triangulate data and reach respondents to follow. In their discussion of the Revolutionary Cells (RZ) – a German, moniker-driven, direct action network operating between the 1970s and1990s – Moncourt and Smith (2009b, 2:221) discuss similar problems stating:

> The Revolutionary Cell [RZ] seemed unstoppable in 1982, but tabulating their activity poses a methodological problem, as anybody could carry

out an attack – from breaking some windows to planting a bomb – and claim it as an RZ action. Limiting the account to major actions is both arbitrary and unavoidable in a study not itself devoted to the Cells; nonetheless, readers should keep in mind that these major attacks [e.g. bombings, shootings] were accompanied by a much greater number of low-level actions [e.g. vandalism, sabotage], even if most of these are now largely forgotten.

It is precisely because of such cautionary methodological tales of woe that this study was constructed around the communiqué. Within these means, the presence of the primary source document equates to inclusion, not the subjectively judged "severity" of the attack. Thus, while the dataset will contain discussions of bombs, bullets, and Molotovs, to a larger degree it is the story of painted walls and broken windows. The history of the modern insurrectionary attacker mirrors that of the RZ, in that the frequency of revolutionary vandalism is overshadowed by the spectacle of tactics more easily understood as *terrorism*, namely those involving fire, explosives, and guns.

Furthermore, by including the entirety of attacks claimed by communiqué, and not sorting for those which are high profile, one allows the incident-based history of the movement to speak more for itself, rather than reflect the careful manipulation of inclusion and coding methods to serve political, securitization or rhetorical ends. In an analysis of 27,136 incidents of so-called "eco-terrorism" occurring between 1973 and 2010,[4] I discovered that the tactical coding of these incidents by state-funded and allied scholars allowed incendiary devices to be regarded as explosives, animal releases to be recoded as theft, and the frequent gluing of locks, slashing of tires, breaking of windows, and sabotaging of machinery to be nearly uniformly disregarded (Loadenthal 2010, 2014b).

Opaque truths and verifiability

In the deciphering of textual authenticity that is necessary in interpreting opaque online reports, one must acknowledge that misrepresentation, exaggeration, and outright fictitious incidents will most certainly occur. First, establishing authorship is difficult if not impossible in a variety of cases. Communiqués, letters, and other forms of text are written, published, and distributed, and those behind them are unknown. If ten texts are posted, it is difficult to determine if these are the work of a single author, ten independent authors, or possibly scores more writing collaboratively. While there are investigative linguistic techniques that can be used to identify and compare lexical features, word classes, and syntax – such as the frequency of words, parts-of-speech, and sentence constructions respectively – these methods are "not mature enough" (K. Cohen et al. 2014, 252) and outside the intent of this book.

Determining authorship remains a challenge for the analysis of online and anonymously authored texts, but does not present a particular challenge for this inquiry as establishing such points of identification are not necessary. The intent here is not to determine the identity or size of a given milieu, but rather its collectively-constituted universe of ideas. The linking of individual texts to individual or group authors would require extensive social network research, mapping, and triangulation, and because such an effort could easily be used by law enforcement for intelligence gathering and repression, it is avoided. Furthermore, identifying authors of anonymous communiqués disrupts the intended function of the text. The decision by an attacker to communicate via a moniker, pseudonym, or remain anonymous, is a conscious decision and the result of many calculations. In this sense we can consider each new articulation of identity – from the formal "FAI" or "ALF" to the playful "some insurrectionary anarchists" – as a new author, even if the new persona is embodied in a prior writer. It can be assumed that individual authors have written under a variety of pseudonyms, and that documents seemingly representing a multitude of voices are written by a single individual.

These sorts of challenges with reliability are not confined to the postings of anti-state revolutionaries, as both traditional non-state actors (e.g. the Taliban) and state security forces (e.g. Department of Defense) have intentionally falsified reports. Often, official accounts of counterterrorism operations are falsified to demonstrate strength to one's opponents, weakness of the enemy, or to reframe skirmishes and otherwise muddy the waters of accurate narration. Such acts of narrative reframing can be used to retell a stone throwing demonstration against the military into a "terrorist attack", or to reframe as "armed clashes"' the invasion of a village (Loadenthal 2013). To cite one example, National Public Radio's correspondent Leila Fadel states that when investigating Egyptian counterterrorist operations targeting jihadi insurgents, the state was found to have misrepresented itself, and engaged in outright false reporting. According to Fadel, "We found that a lot of that huge military operation was actually quite fictional. We couldn't really find evidence of these major attacks. A lot of the reports of militants being killed were really exaggerated" ("With Egypt's New Choices, The Burden Of Democracy" 2012).

This problem of reliability is not reserved to armies and arsonists. Consider the frequent revisions the nation was treated to in US President Obama's retelling of the killing of Osama bin Laden (Hersh 2016). Since the SEAL team responsible for his assassination, and the soldiers charged with dumping his body into the sea, are few in numbers and discouraged from public comment, the citizenry is largely unable to access information regarding the historical event. Instead, the population is forced to accept the state narrative or enter into the ill-fated world of the "conspiracy theorist." Similar problems exist in establishing fact regarding US drone strikes in Syria, Iraq, Pakistan, Afghanistan, Yemen, Libya, and Somalia; such accounts offer a single state-produced narrative which one is forced to accept, as comparative data sources are often unavailable. This is particularly relevant when questioning fatalities and victims' status as combatants or civilians. When civilian eyewitness and NGO data is available, their reporting often shows disagreement between state accounts and those from local media, eyewitnesses, and foreign governments. For example, we can examine the wildly differing accounts of a January 2009 airstrike in Sudan, which targeted a convoy allegedly transporting weaponry to the Gaza Strip. According to media accounts, 39–41 people were killed in the airstrike (Harel, Melman, and Ravid 2009), yet according to the Sudanese Defense Minister, Abdel Rahim Mohamed, 119 were killed including "56 smugglers and 63 smuggled persons from Ethiopian, Somali and other nationalities" (Reuters 2009; BBC 2009). Here we see once again that the consumers of information, even those that attempt to triangulate and verify their sources, are left with stark choices: accept either the state or the non-state narrative, both of which are inaccessibly unverifiable.

This problem with data validity is additionally burdened by analysis that often accompanies reporting of acts of political violence, especially if those reports are found within security literature such as annual Federal Bureau of Investigation (FBI) reports, INTERPOL papers, or government-funded attack databases, such as the Global Terrorism Database maintained by the National Consortium for the Study of Terrorism and Responses to Terrorism, a university-affiliated research project of the Department of Homeland Security. The complexity of political violence, its various strategic and tactical tendencies and intersecting but separate histories, are far beyond the scope of what most desire in seeking to contextualize an attack. Most data consumers simply want to know if the attacker is "right-wing" or "left-wing," "Communist" or "jihadist," "anti-government," "pro-militia," etc. Surely these are truncated categories to the point of being cartoonish, but despite these limitations, contextual data surrounding political attacks against the state are often not available. When such narratives *are* located, they routinely are penned by either the direct producer of violence (e.g. the one sending the mail bomb) or the recipient entity (e.g. the Office of the Prime Minister). From both perspectives, inflated, bombastic, and misleading description can be employed to craft simple narratives from complex events.

One of the explanations for fantastical explanations for significant events – like the US's assassination of Osama bin Laden – can be found in the study on conspiracy theories and narrative. In a 2014 study published in the *American Journal of Political Science*, the authors explain:

[Americans have a] natural attraction towards melodramatic narratives as explanations for prominent events – particularly those that interpret history [in terms of] universal struggles between good and evil ... For many Americans, complicated or nuanced explanations for political events are both cognitively taxing and have limited appeal. (Jacobs 2014)

This sort of logic can not only explain the difficulty in distinguishing falsehoods from truths in an age of unprecedented information availability, but also the challenge of pushing discussion of political violence towards an arena of nuanced, well-informed, and engaged analysis. It is much easier – and more dramatically appealing – to present clandestine revolutionaries as caricatures of themselves; to reinforce old tropes of the bomb-throwing anarchist hiding around the corner.

Arsonist theorists and "primitive rebels"

In developing political theory as derived from communiqués and other claims of responsibility, it is important to note the revolutionaries' tendency toward "organic intellectualism." Antonio Gramsci, the Italian Marxist, offers this concept, writing, "all men are intellectuals ... but not all men have in society the function of intellectuals ... Everyone at some time fries a couple of eggs or sews up a tear in a jacket, we do not necessarily say that everyone is a cook or a tailor" (1971b, 9). In this manner, the production of high theory through non-academic, non-traditional settings is commonplace in the activist-academic community, as well as from activists "in the streets." Sandra Jeppesen (2011, 151–152), an anarchist academic, speaks to this tendency writing:

> Among anarchists there are many "organic intellectuals" who produce theory and action in written and dialogical texts that are not primarily academics, including zines, blogs, workshops, teach-ins, counter-summits, Indymedia web sites, and other anarchist spaces ... Thus, in considering post-anarchist[5] theory, we need to extend that space that we investigate as post-anarchist or we risk seeing only a partial picture that looks neither beyond the male European classical anarchists to contemporary anarchist thinkers ... [and] current social movements in which anarchists are playing agenda-setting roles.

This "theory and action in written and dialogical texts" is part of a larger anarchist pedagogy based in developing ephemera, theory, and inter-movement histories. Another way to think of these extra-academic knowledge products is that of "guerrillas texts" described as "irregular non-uniform anti-authoritarian texts combating a much larger normalized authoritarian system of textual production that tends to be capitalist, patriarchal, heteronormative, racist and/or ableist" (Jeppesen 2010, 473). Therefore the anonymously-authored texts that make up the object of analysis throughout this book can be understood as not only the products of anarcho-organic intellectuals, but texts which are in themselves "subterranean at times, like manifestos, zines or direct action communiqués, breaking out as 'surface extensions' in many directions, like books by independent publishers or pamphlets distributed at protests" (Jeppesen 2010, 474).

While discussing the histories, action, and ideas of a social movement, one inherently adapts an often unspoken framework that influences the construction of arguments and the ordering of events within a politicized logic. It is therefore important to attempt a transparent process when constructing histories, and it is equally important to point out when others are not meeting this standard. There is an inherent subjectivity hidden within historical interpretation, and when one's history prejudices one against an even-handed analysis of a subject, this bias should be acknowledged. I have attempted to do this by engaging as an "anarchist academic," publishing this book within a series on anarchism. I have not hidden my affinity for anarchism's critiques nor associations with anarchist movements.

To cite a counter example of a foundational, social movement text which is at odds with the present discussion, we can examine historian Eric Hobsbawm's 1959 book, *Primitive Rebels: Studies in Archaic Forms of Social Movement in the 19th and 20th Centuries*. In this book, Hobsbawm (1971, 2) develops the archetype of the "primitive rebel," which he describes as a "pre-political ... blind and groping" mass of individuals struggling from poor and/or rural areas in a battle against domination.[6] Hobsbawm speaks deploringly of these masses and their agitation, thus earning them the apolitical term *primitive* and the slightly less despairing term, *rebels*. Hobsbawm speaks of "social bandits," best understood though the Robin Hood (1971, 4, 13–27) character, who emerge from the masses to carry out illegal acts against those in power in an attempt to redistribute wealth and control to the poor and marginalized. While one may find such character portrayals admirable, Hobsbawm deplores them as having "next to no organization or ideology ... totally inadaptable to modern social movements" (1971, 5).

Hobsbawm's criticism reaches beyond his rejection of Robin Hood-styled banditry, and the *primitiveness* of unorganized mobs, and appears overly despairing of a political and social framework the author found counter to his own. Hobsbawm's portrayal of spontaneous, collective violence, such as riots, has been called "anti-class struggle" (Young 2001, para. 30), as critics accuse this bias of existing "at the heart of all his written work as a labor historian." This is largely due to Hobsbawm's expressed preference for social change through organized labor (i.e. union activism) and his dismissal of "the spontaneous militancy of primitive rebels, bandits and ... working-class militants" (Young 2001, para. 23). These later methods of contestation are seen as un-political, inherently unsuccessful, and thus largely irrelevant in the historical record outside of demonstrating their unsuccessfulness.

Hobsbawm explicitly addresses anarchist militants, focusing on those active in the Spanish Civil War of the 1930s. Despite the establishment of collectivized, anarchist-styled lands, trade unions, factories, social services, organizational bodies, and militias occurring in conjunction with a highly asymmetric war against the fascists of Francisco Franco, Hobsbawm laments the militants' efforts, writing: "anarchism was and is helpless ... Nothing is easier than illegal organization in a unanimous village ... but when the millenarian frenzy of the anarchist village subsided, nothing remained but the small group of the ... true believers" (1971, 91). This portrayal stands in contrast to the findings of other scholars (Bookchin 2001; Peirats 2011) specifically examining the anarchist experiment in Revolutionary Catalonia. In typical accounts, scholars have concluded that its failure was not the fault of *anarchism* but rather of reformist efforts on the left and direct repression from the right. Hobsbawm later writes, in reference to Revolutionary Catalonia, "anarchism is thus a form of peasant movement almost incapable of effective adaptation to modern conditions ... thus the history of anarchism, almost alone among modern social movements, is one of unrelieved failure" (1971, 92).

Hobsbawm's prediction for mass-based organized labor and his rejection of anarchism's "spontaneous and unstable rebelliousness" (1971, 92) is obviously influenced by his efforts in conjunction with the German Communist Party which he joined in 1931, the Communist Party of Great Britain which he joined in 1939, and his consistently vocal support for Joseph Stalin's Popular Front (Young 2001, para. 4). Hobsbawm assumes in his method of argumentation that socialist-inspired forms of organized labor consistently led the charge for reform, and that forms of resistance from the "inarticulate" (1971, 2) are meaningless. This stands in obvious contrast to the insurrectionary position that favors the spontaneity, anti-reformist, and unorganized nature of mass revolt and struggle and rejects the glorification of "workerism" and "workerists."[7] Additionally, Hobsbawm's criticism of loosely assembled, spontaneous outbursts of anti-state anger (i.e. riots) as lacking merit represents one side of a debate, with insurrectionary-sympathetic writers, on the other side, often speaking of the potential strengths of these types of outburst.

This discussion of Hobsbawm is meant to partially unearth the political subjectivities that inform our collection and interpretation of historical data. Certainly one cannot escape their own subjectivity, especially in matters of historical interpretation as read through politics. Therefore I would be remiss to avoid noting that my own reading of history, the reading of history contained herein, is understood through my embracing of the anarchist tradition. As Hobsbawm was in favor of large, mass-based forms of protest by organized labor, this was likely the result of his positive experience with such movements for socialism. However normal this appears, it becomes problematic when Hobsbawm uses this position not only to speak of the possibilities contained in Stalinist socialism, but the child-like sensibilities of those who operate with more fluidity and less predictability. For Hobsbawm, these rioters, peasant insurgents, social bandits, and illegalists are the short-sighted, illogical, non-strategic masses, and it is only through the centralism of Communism that one can effectively wage such battles. As a result, Hobsbawm's notions of social change do not align with that of his subject and, as a result, he tosses them aside. Noting the failures of Hobsbawm, the current examination of insurrectionary anarchism is not meant to inscribe this author's anarchism atop the subject; to judge its successes or failures with strategy or message and offer a complementary or critical alternative. Rather the intent here is to explore insurrectionary theory through its own framework, which while informed by anarchism at its roots, embodies a new articulation of its own ilk.

New methodologies of critical inquiry

> What's on trial is the option of armed struggle against the murderous machine of power. Today, anyone who does not understand the necessity of armed anarchist action against the tyrants of our life, is either extremely naïve or a cop ... Our voices and ideas are more powerful when they come from the barrel of a gun. (Economidou et al. 2016)

The exploration of radical political actors can serve a variety of functions. One can analyze patterns of attack and target selection for the creation and refinement of methods designed to identify, disrupt, and capture combatants. Conversely, one can examine the lived realities that produce combatants and seek to analytically apply these criticisms to subjects as grandiose as structural violence (Galtung 1969). This book is most certainly the second form of inquiry. In doing so, the analysis begins from the fields of Peace/Conflict Studies, not International Relations, and leans towards anarchism and poststructuralism (i.e. post-anarchism) rather than realism or neoliberalism. This is not to claim ideological blankness, but rather to assert my a priori framework. If one were to pursue the study of political violence through the preeminent field of Terrorism Studies, emboldened by the boom in scholarship post-9/11, then one would likely investigate how best to secure the homeland from attackers, and in doing such "agenda setting" (M. Crenshaw 1990, 17), present the subject as one of securitization, not investigation (Jackson et al. 2011, 13). This manner of scholarship has been critiqued for its avoidance of empirical measures to study terrorism. When *counter*terrorism is the focus, such a pattern is even more striking, as according to one study (Lum, Kennedy, and Sherley 2008) "only 3 percent of articles from peer-reviewed sources appeared to be rooted in empirical analysis" (Biglan 2015).

In their discussion of "the terrorism industry" the authors of *Terrorism: A Critical Introduction* cite the failure in scholarship embodied in traditional/orthodox Terrorism Studies.

> ... the orthodox terrorism field has developed a long-term material interest in the maintenance of terrorism as a major public policy concern ... [and] in order to protect its privileged position, the field has developed a number of subtle gate-keeping procedures which function to ensure that scholars or critics who do not share dominant views and beliefs are marginalized and denied access to policymakers and the main forums for discussion. (Jackson et al. 2011, 13)

Such a demarcation has been developed to separate research on political violence associated with securitization and counterterrorism, and that which establishes other aims. To borrow again from the book's authors, in attempting to separate oneself from this trend, they define traditionalist scholarship as that which embodies "the failure to recognize that 'terrorism' is a label given to acts of political violence by outside observers, and that the designation of what constitutes terrorism has historically changed according to political context" (Jackson et al. 2011, 15).

Scholarship examining social movements, including those movements that challenge through force, is essential, yet must be carried out apart from the discourse on securitization found prevalent in Criminology (orthodox) Terrorism Studies and Security Studies. This securitization focus limits the types of scholarship that is produced. In the preface to their multi-volume exploration of Germany's Red Army Faction (RAF), the authors write:

> We felt our work was unique, as English-language studies of the RAF were almost uniformly written from a counterinsurgency perspective, the goal being to discredit the guerrilla and to deny it any recognition as a legitimate political force; in short, to deprive us of its history. (Moncourt and Smith 2009b, 2:XVI)

It is precisely this notion that has motivated the subsequent examination of insurrectionary texts. While very little scholarship addresses this milieu at all, that which does focuses on securitization (Marone 2014) and sensationalism (Hanrahan 2013; Winfield and Gatopoulos 2010), presenting a broad and diverse social movement as a secretive conspiracy of inter-linked and orchestrated actors.

In order to interrogate this understanding of this portrayal, one must first establish what is meant by a *movement*, and more specifically, a (radical) social movement. Political theorist Daniel Koehler offers a definition of "Radical Social Movement[s]," building off the concept of a "social movement" as defined by Sociologist Mario Diani (1992, 13). Koehler's (2014, 4) defines radical social movements as:

> Networks of informal interactions between a plurality of individuals, groups and/or organizations having the character of a counterculture with the primary goal to influence (positively or negatively), fundamentally alter, or destroy a specified target society on the basis of a religious or political ideology, using all available means, legal and illegal, including the strategic use of violence, to fulfill and realize the ideologically corrected or purified version of the target society.

This description bodes well for the current study, as in reality the insurrectionary model is a tactical and strategic sub-trend within a much larger social movement against the state and capital. Though some scholarship has sought to describe non-state actor networks as akin to "countercultures" where individuals "associate with each other through shared definitions of what is wrong with the status quo and where to look for a better alternative" (Hemmingsen 2014, 7), as insurrectionary action is the sum total of a variety of transnational counterculture *networks*, it is best understood as a *movement* which draws its constituency from a variety of cultures, both mainstream and counter. It is bound by shared politics as well as overlapping, associated social circles. This *social* aspect separates it from the authoritarian, militarized conflicts mobilized at the community level (e.g. ethno nationalist/diaspora communities, separatist movements) and enforced through regimented fighting forces, broad-based social service provision, and participation in the political sphere. In this manner, it is more RAF than FARC,[8] more Weather Underground Organization (WUO) than PIRA, despite frequent portrayal to the contrary. In other words, while these latter examples (i.e. FARC and PIRA) maintain networks of fighters that may drain supporters from larger social networks, the organizations are firmly integrated into the society through more dominant institutions such as formalized paramilitary brigades, direct service provision (e.g. education, healthcare), and interaction with state-level politics.

While scholarship (both academic and state) has been keen to analyze the internet activities of violent non-state actors such as those affiliated with the global jihad (e.g. National Coordinator for Counterterrorism 2007; United Nations Office on Drugs and Crime 2012; von Behr et al. 2013; Drissel 2014; Klausen 2014; Torres-Soriano 2014), little attention has been directed at similar online outreach and organizational efforts by those challenging the state at a more fundamentally existential (and secular) level.

This has created a noticeable gap in the literature. Though the precise cause for this exemption is unclear, it is likely influenced by the various venues of conflict. In the majority of cases, insurrectionary political violence occurs outside of the "traditional" physicality of the exoticized and Orientalist (Said 1979) "East" (e.g. Afghanistan, Pakistan, Iraq, Syria, Palestine, Iran, Somalia ...) but rather in largely "Western" nation-states (e.g. US, UK, Spain, Italy, Sweden, Greece, Argentina). In other words, while traditionally terrorism is something done *to* the West by a sub-state, *subaltern*[9] (Gramsci 1971a, 202; Spivak 1988), Oriental actor, insurrectionary violence is often located and produced by the so-called First World. In the present discussion, this seemingly unnatural turn away from the Arabian battlefields has likely contributed to the scant examination of insurrectionary violence in traditionalist Security and Terrorist Studies discourses.

This may also be due to unfamiliarity and discomfort with discussing violent outbursts outside of standard explanatory frames – lack of political opportunity, authoritarian political regimes, abject poverty, and religious fanaticism. In other words, it may be precisely because of the insurrectionary critique that its actions are not examined; as to assess its "findings" could serve to challenge the nature of power which establishes the legitimacy of the scholarship and knowledge construction. This sort of (often avoided) approach functions to focus the readers' attention toward structural criticisms such as rejections of the nation-state, capitalism, eco-cide, speciesism, patriarchy, militarism, and the like. There is of course exemplary scholarship examining the insurrectionary tendency and, although scant, these works must be recognized. Many are the product of insurrectionary proponents (e.g. CrimethInc. Ex-Workers' Collective 2009; IEF 2013; Casper/CrimethInc. and Graeme/IEF 2014), anti-authoritarian theorists (e.g. Williams and Thomson 2011; Nomad 2013; Wood 2013; The Institute for the Study of Insurgent Warfare 2014), politically-aligned public events (e.g. Ariel et al. 2014), and traditional (critical) academics (e.g. Noys 2011).

In order to build an analytical model to further explore these networks of non-state actors, I have adopted the frameworks developed within the so-called *critical* turn in social science analysis: a collective of evolving interdisciplinary fields which have influenced arenas such as poststructuralism, Justice and Peace Studies, Feminist Theory, and elsewhere. While the preceding discussion was meant to describe how one can descriptively establish *what* a movement consists of, and subsequently *where* and *why* that movement's ideological boundaries exist, these intermediate goals are subservient to a larger methodological task of exploring new manners of critical inquiry adopted from feminist theory, Critical Security Studies (CSS), Critical Terrorism Studies (CTS), and the mixing of these disciplines through hybrid mechanisms such as feminist security studies (Wibben 2011) and human security (Tadjbakhsh and Chenoy 2007).

This book is seeking to incorporate aspects of two broadly inter-related fields, namely that of CSS and CTS. The often linked fields of Terrorism Studies and Security Studies have witnessed a boom following the more generalized rise in university study directed at Islam, political Islam, Islamic terrorism, and Middle Eastern politics following the 9/11 attacks. Subsequently, new approaches have been developed and taxonomized under a host of "critical" fields including *Critical* Terrorism Studies and *Critical* Security Studies which attempt to problematize and clarify a *methodology* for those seeking to investigate political violence and its responses through a non-orthodox, non-realist lens. Recurrent throughout both of these emergent fields is what is often referred to as the *critical turn*, characterized by (at least) four key components:

1) Social and political life is messy: our analysis must reflect our belief that we cannot identify any single unifying principle in social and political life; methodological pluralism is a hallmark of this belief.
2) Agency – the capacity to act – is everywhere: it can be found in individuals, groups, states, ideational structures, and non-human actants.
3) Causality is emergent, rather than efficient: analyses set out the conditions of possibility for a set of politics, identities, or policies, rather than a single or complex source.
4) Research, writing, and public engagement are inherently political: we understand politics in its broadest sense to mean questions concerning justice, power, and authority; critical scholarship means an active engagement with the world (Salter 2012a, 2).

A great deal of this book's approach speaks to the first critical component, that of methodological pluralism, as well as issues of agency. However important such components are, I have chosen to adopt a *critical* framework precisely because of component number four: the inherently political project of research, writing, and public engagement. To this end, CSS begins its pursuit by problematizing the concept of securitization itself, as "no neutral definition is possible" (Smith 2005, 27). This should be understood as a single appeal within a larger set of analytical features such as the *critical* turn away from knowledge extraction and towards knowledge construction, away from detachment and towards engagement and away from expertise-ism and towards participatory research that engages marginalized knowledge and subjects (Scheper-Hughes 1995; A. Doucet and Mauthner 2006; Blakely 2007; Hesse-Biber 2011). These contributions – largely adapted from feminist interventions in the study of methodology – redefine the venue of research as inherently political; seeking social change by operating at the margins of subjugated knowledge. In their discussion of methodology and epistemology, A. Doucet and Mauthner (2006) state this clearly, noting that a feminist method may not be a *distinct* approach, though it functions to overlay this emancipatory political project atop knowledge building.

As other approaches do, CSS carries with it a set of proscriptive presumptions including the validity of ethnography and discursive investigations as form of security-themed investigation. CSS diverges from orthodox Security Studies in its validation of the "ethnographic turn" (Salter 2012b, 51–57) and the "discursive turn" (Salter and Mutlu 2012, 113–119), elaborating these tendencies within the field. Concerning ethnographic tendencies within CSS, the framework suggests that respondent "cultures" must be experienced to be understood (Salter 2012b, 56–57) and that even in the realm of studies concerning policing, national security, and statecraft, issues such as reflexivity, critical engagement with "expertise," and one's relationship to the security state must be acknowledged and confronted. Questions such as "What constitutes *security*?," "Can security have emancipatory functions?" (Alker 2005, 189–213; Toros 2012, 35–40), and "What is the implied narrative in traditionalist conceptions of security?" (Wibben 2011, chap. 4) are indeed relevant at the onset of a research project. Such concerns separate *Critical* Security Studies from a non-critical method in radical ways of direct relevance to this book. For example, the relationship between knowledge construction and securitization, policing, and intelligence gathering is a tricky collaboration at best.

Examining CSS's *discursive turn*, one returns to the Foucauldian emphasis on the socio-political power issues recurrent in language and storytelling, as in order to accomplish "serious discourse analysis ... the researcher must hold a certain degree of linguistic and cultural fluency" (Salter and Mutlu 2012, 116). For example, in describing the political posturing of actors, it is necessary to maintain a distinction between those acting with anarchist, communist, communizationist, insurrectionary, autonomist, primitivist, and related political self-identifications. The flattening of the radical subject as one of "extremists," "revolutionaries," "militants," or, worse yet, "terrorists" not only does a political disservice to the production of nuanced description, but also fails to acknowledge the diversity of tactical, strategic, and theoretical visioning of these networks.

Occurring directly alongside CSS is the field of CTS. Similar to the acknowledged contributions of CSS, CTS repositions the role of the researcher, respondent, and state in a newly theorized manner. Thus, CTS is adopted as a guiding framework precisely because it confronts and seeks to destabilize a state-centric analysis as well as the "objective features" of world politics (Stump and Dixit 2013, 3). In yet another useful presumption of CTS, the contestability of the definition of "terrorism" is seen as banal, an intellectual task quite controversial in fields such as International Relations, Security/Terrorism Studies, and Government. Like CSS, CTS similarly maintains a focus on ethnography and discourse, and bases its analysis appropriately within critical theory and feminist/postcolonial approaches

(Stump and Dixit 2013). Lastly, CTS has an explicit focus on confronting the "big T" truth of Terrorism Studies (Stump and Dixit 2013, 160), as well as pursuing research of radical actors with a focus on ethics, non-linear causality, and, to borrow from the feminist tradition, *applied* research. Such concerns have an obvious place in the designing of research in the manner previously laid out and, as such, the combined methodological proscriptions from feminism, CSS, and CTS amount to a potentially emancipatory[10] framework for critical inquiry beyond the search for absolutist truth.

Duel use and re*turn*ing to the principal of "do no harm"

In designing a method of inquiry for exploring the object of the communiqué and the subject of insurrectionary theory, careful attention was paid to the sorts of questions which were relevant for the extrapolation of critical theory but not useful for securitization through social network mapping, behavioral analysis, and other forms of intelligence and information processing. Certainly a tactical analysis, broken down by target and country and cross-referenced for moniker, could be enlightening, but the danger it may pose to those it represents may be far greater. This inverts the concern held by security theorists regarding "dual use" technologies – goods and methods designed for one purpose yet employed for another. For example, GPS technology, civilian drones, encrypted peer-to-peer text messaging, and enhanced optics have obvious military applications yet are largely understood to be the products of civilian hobbyists including hikers, bird watchers, aviators, and photographers.

In recent years, the household pressure cooker has become inextricably recast as a dual use technology following its use in the construction of explosive devices including those targeting the Boston Marathon in 2013 and the attacks in New York in 2016. This can also be said of box cutters post-9/11, or even diesel fuel and fertilizer following its use in the truck bombs built and detonated by Timothy McVeigh to target the Oklahoma City Federal Building in 1995. In all of these cases, objects were repurposed outside of their original intent, and utilized to meet the practical needs of the attacker through accessible technologies. It is important that those partaking in research *on* and *for* social movements engage in the process of knowledge construction in a way that does not make such repurposing easy for state forces seeking to extract actionable intelligence from research meant to exist in solidarity with the subject.

In designing research aimed at social action, it is essential that authors and researchers understand the potential dual use of their own work, and ensure that their efforts are not co-opted to serve the larger state projects of policing, securitization, and the criminalization of dissent. Therefore, *how* knowledge is constructed and *for what purpose* are central concerns in design, implementation, and the eventual dissemination of results, as data collected for one purpose can readily be *re*purposed by security and intelligence services for alternative means. It is therefore the responsibility of the researcher to ask the right questions, collect only the necessary types of data, and avoid using academic efforts to foster insecurity amongst the subject community. On a practical level this may involve the anonymization of respondents, securely recording and storing data using strong encryption, and not using one's privileged or "insider" knowledge of a social milieu to elucidate what otherwise may have remained opaque to police and intelligence services.

Such key research design decisions establish the intent of the inquiry, and ask key questions: When one speaks of securitization, *whose* security (e.g. the state v. the social movement) are we protecting (Wibben 2011; Smith 2005, 27–62)? This decentering of the state as an object of analysis subverts traditionally securitized discourses allowing for the exploration of alternative political frames. As someone conducting research on clandestine, illegal, and anti-state actors, the expropriation of my work for generating actionable intelligence is more than obvious. In this manner, it becomes the burden of the researcher to maintain a methodological focus on generating reciprocal (not juridically detrimental) results for my respondent community. Moreover, my choice of subject and method is informed by Nancy Scheper-Hughes' call for a "militant anthropology" wherein scholarship remains engaged with social struggle and avoids the artificial appearance of a detached spectator, instead embracing a "participation in the struggle" (1995, 414). Scheper-Hughes asserts this desire in no uncertain terms, writing, "I have to pause and reconsider the traditional role of the anthropologist as neutral, dispassionate, cool and rational, objective observer of the human condition" (1995, 410). While this does not mean that my work necessarily helps to advance illegal activities of anti-statist revolutionaries – though ideally it would – it may serve to elaborate the politics of their analysis, or at the very least serve to nuance a reader's interpretation of their method of attack. At the very least, I seek to insulate the respondent community from harm provoked through the process of inquiry.

This manner of scholarship – where someone seeks to elevate a subterranean discourse to the level of critical inquiry – is quick to be labeled as recuperation, wherein the politics of dissent are utilized to further refine the technologies of statecraft. In the analysis of recuperation offered by Situationist Guy Debord (1967, 2, 10), critical notions (e.g. theories of revolutionary change) are defanged through their inclusion in social discourses, and after being sanitized of revolutionary potential, reintroduced back into mainstream society devoid of their destabilizing power. In this process, radical notions are co-opted and commodified before being allowed to carry forth and, in doing so, aid the process of statecraft through allowing the systems of domination to appear more malleable than they actually are. I have argued that the present study does *not* serve recuperative purposes precisely because the state is not concerned with incorporating the insurrectionary critique into its framework in the same way that riotous protest culture is used to sell consumer products.[11] Instead, this book seeks to apply a radical critique to the social order and to unearth these ideas for greater consumption.

While there is certainly law enforcement interest aimed at insurrectionary action, their focus is on *stopping* acts of illegal activity, *not* understanding the critique offered through communiqués that accompany these incidents. If one could suspend logic and presume that state authorities *did* in fact give concern to how insurrectionary theory understands notions of identity, power, and structural violence, or the political and cultural histories that preceded them, then the same inquiry would conclude that anti-system violence can be prevented when structures no longer replicate the critiqued ills, namely inequality, alienation, domination, etc. Therefore, interactions with the previously subterranean material should be not seen as a manner of potential recuperation, but a site of potential conflict transformation (J. P. Lederach 2003), where "talking [with communiqués]" can be used as a "less harmful" (Toros 2012, 4–6, 46) method to prevent violence. Borrowing from the work of CTS scholar Harmonie Toros, the approach adopted herein seeks to support a form of "talking with terrorists (sic)" through exercising texts from among the ephemera of the internet and critically engaging with the ideas offered by a non-state actor. This form of talking is not to be confused with notions of negotiation or compromise – asking the aggrieved parties to put aside their anger in favor of a social peace – but rather a method to allow the texts to dialogue with the society at the level of discourse, and beyond its own in-group/out-group distinctions. While negotiation is focused on meeting the needs of opposing parties, dialogue in this manner is focused on understanding (Toros 2012, 53), not winning a negotiated peace. Of course, the insurrectionary attack itself is also a form of *talking* yet its method of speaking disqualifies it from the arena of state-centric conversation as the state proudly claims to "not negotiate with terrorists."

In maintaining the aim of the research, it becomes dangerous to assume that potential respondent knowledge is of no use to intelligence and law enforcement, and thus there is an increased burden on the researcher for operationalizing issues of anonymity, *informed* consent, and respondent engagement. This is the primary reason why exchanges with clandestine authors were not included. All documents examined were obtained on public forums in widely circulated hubs of radical information. Furthermore there is a history of academic inquiries involving illegalist respondents ending in Federal Grand Juries where state authorities coerce individuals into providing information on respondents thought to be affiliated with clandestine networks or face prison. This can be seen in the cases of Rick Scarce, Professor of Sociology at Skidmore College, indicted in 1993 for his presumed knowledge of an ALF raid on a vivisection laboratory, as well as Scott DeMuth, a graduate student at the University of Minnesota, indicted in 2009. DeMuth refused to provide investigators with the names of activists he interviewed for his graduate work and was sentenced to six months in prison for conspiring to violate the Animal Enterprise Terrorism Act. One is reminded of the Latin phrase "*primum non nocere*," "first, do no harm." In this spirit, and for the development of an *anti*-securitization analysis, this book aims to endanger no one except the target of insurrectionary attack, by bringing attention to their critique – the critique they are waging war to offer.

In sum, the design and methodological intent of this book seeks to excavate and elevate marginalized voices – the voices of those relegated to the label of terrorists or extremists – and to embrace a "militant" form of inquiry which is counter to the project of securitization, avoids the creation of dual use knowledge, remains embedded and action-orientated, and works to construct knowledge for revolutionary ends, not extract it for detached analysis and intelligence gathering.

Questions and intent

This book is designed to examine post-millennial, clandestine actors, organized into networked federations, sharing a politic that is anti-state and that advocates direct attack in response to structural violence. From this point on, those inhabiting such a milieu will be identified as "insurrectionists" and would include the FAI, International Revolutionary Front (IRF), Conspiracy of Cells of Fire (CCF), and a variety of individuals and unknown cells showing ideological affiliation. This inquiry seeks to answer several central questions: What precisely is the contemporary insurrectionary tendency? How can it be historicized? And what application does this framework offer for understanding conflict?

These questions will be pursued alongside a larger focus on issues of canonization and the formation of (capital T) *Theory*. One can think of this as a bifurcated hypothesis, the first of which contends that modern insurrectionary networks of attack are informed by, and act to, constitute an "insurrectionary canon": an indispensable body of written work that the milieu consumes, interprets, and reacts to in voice and action. The second hypothesis states that because of the poststructural influence upon the modern insurrectionary critique, the latter will resultantly carry forth an expanded understanding of structural violence and inequality. This inquiry centers on how the social movement tendency establishes conceptions of power, hierarchy, violence, and community. Their political framework will be discussed vis-à-vis poststructural theory, as I hypothesize that the insurrectionary and poststructural theories share important components such as a deterritorialized subject, boundless arenas of expansion, and a focus on *power and domination*, not simply their local manifestations. In seeking to draw out the theoretical traditions of this community, I hypothesize that one can construct a political framework that is no less rigorous than competing orthodoxies (e.g. Marxism, Leninism, Trotskyism, 'classical' anarchism, anarcho-syndicalism, primitivism, etc.) despite the community's lack of consistent, canonical texts.

While the bounds of Marxism are easy to trace through the works of its namesake and those of Frederick Engels, V. I. Lenin, Rosa Luxemburg, Antonio Gramsci, and others, the contemporary insurrectionist tendency is not often viewed in such a manner. The format of the insurrectionists' communication has inherently limited its academic consumption. As the movement has been slow to produce book-length treatises and academic journal articles, its communiqués, zines, pamphlets, posters, and websites have been relegated to the trash heap of revolutionary ephemera when, in reality, they collectively form a precise theoretical cannon – that remains unbounded and open – establishing ideological fence posts to create a well-defined in-group/out-group community of ideas. This insurrectionary tendency deserves our attention if for no other reason than its destructive and disruptive capabilities. The activity of these groups has led many governments to designate entire portions of the left as "terrorists" and throughout their short, half-century history they have caused tens of millions of dollars in damage to property. It is precisely this rhetorical reality that should motivate critical investigators, because if those who share some manner of affinity do not conduct such an inquiry, it will eventually become the sole purview of the state and its counterterrorism framework.

These hypotheses were chosen for their specific applicability to developing theories concerning ideological construction, discursive formation, and structural violence. The integration of critical theory for the understanding of political violence is central. Since the violence is meant as commentary, or reaction to problems at the level of the entire society (e.g. poverty, pollution, police violence), the nature of the explanation is often based in notions of a social order. Critical theory is meant to "isolate and critique those rationalizations of society which are advanced as self-evident truths, but which may be ideological mystifications" (M. Hoffman 1987, 236). Such "evident truths" – the validity of the state, the wage–labor exchange system, or the commodification of animals for food – can be called into question if such a critical theory is applied to insurrectionary action. Through an interrogation of the textual basis for this revolutionary tendency, one can more freely interact with the ideas presented, understood as distinct from the vehicles that delivered them. In other words, through a deep reading of insurrectionary communiqués, we can interact with the milieu's analysis and reasoning without the burdensome rhetoric of terrorism and anti-social violence muddying the waters.

Despite the fact that theory is delivered in the form of a document claiming responsibility for a criminal act, in attempting to develop a canon from these texts, we are acknowledging their legitimacy as objects of analysis, something typically denied when politics is delivered via violence. By suggesting that insurrectionary theory has conceptual lessons akin to those of Marxism, poststructuralism, or Queer theory, the attention of the reader shifts to *what* the actors say, not through the lens of which criminal act (e.g. broken window, graffitied storefront) they chose to speak through. This dual hypothesis approach is thus designed to "test" both the applicability of insurrectionary theory to central questions of conflict analysis (e.g. structural violence, inequality), as well as its discursive construction from among the critical tradition of poststructuralism. This hypothesis testing approach can be understood as akin to a philosopher's test of a logical proof in more ways than it resembles a scientific hypothesis.

The importance and implications of this research rest in a number of key areas. First, it is essential that the theoretical and political ideas of this movement enter into the public arena of intellectual debate, and not be simply excluded on the basis of the group's choice to adopt "violence" as a means. The community's choice to utilize non-traditional, non-state sanctioned methods is well informed by their politic and intrinsically linked to its understanding of structural reality. These theoretical contributions – which up until now have been overlooked – can serve to advance an expanded analysis of structural and systemic conflict, further helping one understand how discourse is constructed through an exchange of texts. The theoretical contributions of the insurrectionary tendency – derived from anonymously penned communiqués – can serve to advance the development of transformative strategies aimed at confronting persistent, system-level conflicts, such as those dealing with growing wealth gaps, racial inequality, patriarchy, ecological degradation, and other associated ills.

Conclusion

The book's scope is limited to a difficult to define, yet demonstrably separate, segment of the wider anti-state, anti-capitalist, quasi-anarchist milieu. This internationally decentralized community of autonomous cells and networked groups has been called:

> The Black International ... the affinity groups of anarcho-individualists and nihilists ... promot[ing] informal organization, affinity between cells

and the uniqueness of each individual ... [an] invisible community where the desires of attack against our era, meet ... [known as] New Anarchy and the Black International. (CCF-FAI/IRF Imprisoned Members Cell 2013)

This neo-insurrectionary community, the "anarcho-individualists of praxis" (Polidoros et al. 2014), borrow and reinterpret a variety of previous manifestations of resistance including those advancing "propaganda of the deed" in the late 1800s, illegalist anarchists from the first half of the 1900s, the armed guerrillas of the latter half of the 1900s, and the populist anti-capitalist and anti-globalization movement of the late 1990s. These intersectional histories will be explored in depth in Chapter 2 and Chapter 3, but prior to proceeding, it is important to develop some broad groupings.

The groups under examination, while emerging from the wider anarchist milieu, are keen to differentiate themselves. Many cells have firmly declared themselves to be outside of the anarchist community, as this tendency, according to the anonymous communiqué authors, has been co-opted by sectarian leftists, populist movements, and so-called "civil anarchists" (Anonymous 2013d) who seek to resist within the confines of the state's laws. These distinctions are made consistently throughout the literature, as a collective of imprisoned members of one insurrectionary network state:

> Especially today, we believe that simply stating that we are "anarchists", in order to speak through a communique or an action, is inadequate and problematic. We choose to separate our positions from the "anarchists" who cooperate with the leftist grassroots labor unions, use Marxist analyzes, unionize their misery, slander direct actions, fantasize workers' communes, participate in residents' local committees and transform anarchy into a social therapy. (CCF-FAI/IRF Imprisoned Members Cell 2013)

Therefore, while it is important to understand the development of these networks from within the broader anti-capitalist and anti-statist left, the insurrectionary tendency must be understood as distinct yet intersectional, complementary yet oppositional. Therefore, at its most basic level, it is essential to ask: When the term "insurrectionist" or "insurrectionary anarchism" is used in the subsequent discussion, what does it mean? For the purpose of discussion, one can think of insurrectionary anarchism in the following terms, provided by the influential anarchist collective known as CrimethInc. In their radio show discussing the insurrectionary tendency within contemporary anarchism, the presenters state:

> By definition, an insurrection is an act of revolting against a civil authority or government. So, an insurrectionary anarchist would be an

anarchist who is in favor of revolts against civil authority or government, or more specifically, one who believes that smaller revolts against authority will lead to larger revolutions. (CrimethInc. Ex-Workers' Collective 2013)

This definition is adequate to begin our exploration of the pre-modern history, while keeping in mind these broad tendencies that are recurrent throughout the milieu, namely those of un-civil rebellion against capitalism and the state.

Notes

1 This approach is adopted frequently by scholars in relation to right-wing (e.g. Neo-Nazi, white supremacist, neo-fascist) movements (e.g. Ezekiel 2002; Adams and Roscigno 2005; Dalgaard-Nielsen 2008; Zeskind 2009; T. Morris 2014).
2 Throughout this book, a diverse set of communiqués and other primary source documents constitute the insurrectionary corpus under examination. This corpus was assembled by collecting all English-language claims of responsibility posted to the five most prominent websites distributing insurrectionary communiqués, deemed to be: http://325.nostate.net/, http://waronsociety.noblogs.org/, http://actforfree.nostate.net/, https://interarma.info, and http://en.contrainfo.espiv.net/. Through these parameters I identified 962 communiqués, from 36 (Argentina, Australia, Belarus, Belgium, Bolivia, Brazil, Canada, Chile, Costa Rica, Croatia, Czech Republic, Denmark, Ecuador, Egypt, Finland, France, Germany, Greece, Indonesia, Italy, Luxembourg, Mexico, Netherlands, Peru, Philippines, Poland, Portugal, Russia, Spain, Sweden, Switzerland, Turkey, Ukraine, United Kingdom, Uruguay, United States). The final set of texts included 428,219 words, appearing 21 February 2008 to 30 June 2014. Beyond familiarizing myself with the communiqué corpus, I also gathered and systematically annotated letters from prisoners, non-communiqué analyses, proclamations, announcements, condemnations, reporting on current events, and other documents posted on the same sites, during the same time period. This second corpus totaled an additional 488,202 words. These texts were analyzed through both Corpus Linguistics and Critical Discourse Analysis. The results, which also inform this book, are being published in a series of articles beginning with Loadenthal (2016b).
3 This speaks to my own positionality vis-à-vis the subject. Prior to deciding to pursue a study of these materials, I regularly read insurrectionary and sympathetic communiqués for years through many of the websites featured here. Also, while writing my Master's dissertation, I systematically read thousands of communiqués written by the ALF/ELF and affiliated activists.
4 In this study, each of the +27,000 incidents (i.e. attacks) was coded for 22 variables, and statistically analyzed for patterns focused on targeting, tactics,

moniker, location, date, and method of communication. This was done under the supervision of the Centre for the Study of Terrorism and Political Violence. Some of these findings, and an expanded discussion of data collection and analysis methods, are available (Loadenthal 2016a).
5 Post-anarchism is a growing literature (Rousselle and Evren 2011) that utilizes poststructuralism to inform anarchism.
6 Hobsbawm's depiction can be understood as a negative interpretation of Hardt and Negri's (2001, 61, 411; 2005) "multitude" – a more sympathetic and possibility-laden imagining of a non-unified, politically-revolutionary, affective mass of individuals in resistance. This notion can be linked to earlier conceptualizations including those appearing in Niccolò Machiavelli's *Discourses on Livy* (1517), Thomas Hobbes' *On the Citizen* (1642), and Baruch Spinoza's *Theological-Political Treatise* (1670).
7 This term is used throughout insurrectionary texts (e.g. Bonanno 1988; 1998a; Anonymous 2003).
8 Throughout this book, comparisons are made between the insurrectionary milieu and "traditional" armed, non-state actors such as PIRA, FARC, and Hamas. While such a comparison could be made based on any number of non-state actors, these groups are chosen for consistency, and because their discussion in the Terrorism Studies literature is archetypal and common.
9 The notion of the *subaltern* as it applies to postcolonial and feminist approaches to the study of terrorism is explored in Stump and Dixit (2013, 74)
10 Harmonie Toros (2012, 35–40) provides a discussion of "emancipation" as it relates to Critical Terrorism/Security Studies.
11 For shockingly obvious examples of this, see Axe body spray's "Anarchy" campaign, the fictionalized ITS-styled group in *Transcendence* (2014), as well as films based explicitly around anti-authoritarian/anti-capitalist struggles such as *This Revolution* (2005), *Battle in Seattle* (2007), *The East* (2013), and faux-rioting music videos such as Kanye West and Jay-Z's "No Church in the Wild" (2011), and 2 Chainz's "Riot" (2012). One could also make the point to MasterCard/Virgin offering a Sex Pistol's themed credit card (2015) or Forever 21 selling Blank Panther t-shirts.

2
Insurrection as history from Guy Fawkes to black blocs

This is how the new anarchist urban guerrilla was born, this is how the Conspiracy of Cells of Fire continues to exist. Our attacks deliver blows to the system's officials and symbols, destroy temples of money, torch political party offices, attack private security guards and security companies, place bombs at jails, courts, detention centers, fascists, at the Parliament, police stations, churches, houses of ministers, we send explosives to embassies and heads of states, blow up military vehicles and militaristic targets, burn newspaper offices and journalists' cars, we choose to live in the lawless side of life, away from the aesthetics of money and the morality of authority, against the technological shackles of the digital world and the herd of slaves, against the culture of compromise and the civilization of animal and natural exploitation. (Polidoros et al. 2014)

History, genealogy, and subjectivity

To define the insurrectionism is to observe its "broad umbrella spaces" (Juris 2004, 68) which collectively form a critical framework. While more traditional, modern anarchism – embodied in anti-globalization activists opposing multilateral trade talks – is based around a politic of collectivism, civil disobedience, direct action, and voluntary association, the illegalist-infused insurrectionary approach is based around a complementary but tangential set of features. These tendencies appear more negative and less utopian then those strands of anarchist resistance seen in the past; borrowing from the centuries of nihilism, individualism, and freedom-centric egoism. These tendencies position themselves within a generalized spirit of aggression and revolt; the fostering of social war on all fronts.

While these individuals envision an egalitarian, communist-like future, they aim more towards tearing down than building up. The critique is boundless and aimed at any and all manifestations of domination and power including any spokes linked to religion, governance, economy, and ecocide, as well as the more central hubs of capitalism and the state. Individuals' motivations to immerse within this clandestine milieu often point to social and economic inequality and a "widely shared sense of injustice" (della Porta 2013, 238), a common motivational feature for the production of political violence. The emphasis of the insurrectionary, nihilist-infused anarchism is on creating war-like conditions for opposing capitalism, the state, and that which perpetuates structural violence (e.g. racism, poverty, speciesism, gender roles). The "insurrectionary turn" in contemporary, revolutionary politics is largely due to a poststructuralist influence, and as such is well suited for analyzing power and domination. The poststructural influence has allowed insurrectionary anarchism to become unlinked from the structural Marxism which birthed it, and instead, the decentralized networks of attack being seen today are boundless, ribosomal occurrences defined only by a shared banner of total liberation and a rejection of traditional populist social movements, mediation through representation, and reformism.

A genealogical account of discourse

The approach to history adopted in this book is informed by Michel Foucault's notion of "genealogy" (1971, 1977, 1980) which, according to poststructural anarchist philosopher Todd May (1994, 90), "seeks to trace the emergence of its object, be it a discourse, a practice, or a concept," in this case, insurrectionary anarchism. This genealogical history of insurrection is an assemblage of events, ideas, and individuals from among a broad historical record, united in a shared ethos and praxis of illegality, aggression, spontaneity, informality, and clandestinity. While a machinegun-toting French bank robber of the 1910s may look nothing like a modern Mexican mailbomb-sending anarchist, they both can occupy a shared historical narrative. The process of excavating a semi-linear narrative from centuries of history experienced across the world is inherently incomplete, and its retelling rife with gaps, discontinuities, and subjective choices. In trying to explain the amorphous object of *insurrectionism* the following historical accounts attempt to cherry pick moments of rebellion which can be read as *insurrectionary*. In these moments which have been curated for narration, individuals and small groups of anti-state dissidents self-organized and attacked their enemies directly, without the mediation of politics, formal organization or partisanship. Their stories constitute the history of insurrectionary politics and theory. Though the attackers may not have self-identified as engaging in insurrectionary struggle, their actions are often recalled in the imagery, textual accounts, and imagination of twenty-first century proponents of anti-state violence.

The history of insurrection is the history of unmediated attacks against the systems of power. To develop such a history – and not the history of another idea or tendency – is to foster a taxonomy, a set of rules for inclusion and exclusion and, to again borrow from Foucault, establish *knowledge* (i.e. power/knowledge) through acknowledgment and inclusion. In Foucault's (1980, 78) own words, when historicizing sexuality, "I have sketched a genealogical history of the origins of a theory and a knowledge of … the various techniques that relate to it." In the establishment of a chronological record, one determines the discursive borders of the insurrectionary tendency through retroactively labeling diverse forms of resistance through a modern framework. This historical record is thus dependent on one's understanding of the discursive tradition, its origins, and its strands of contributive thought. The resulting genealogy of insurrection "recognizes that its knowledge is value-laden and contextually situated" (May 1994, 94) within one's understanding of this milieu. This is especially important as Foucault (1980, 83) notes, "historical knowledge of struggles … [are often] … buried [and] subjugated" as illegitimate knowledge precisely because they are seen to be "hostile" to systems of power. The excavation of this genealogical account is key *prior* to any nuanced discussion of tactics, strategy or ideology. It is essential to understand the history that formed a set of ideas before exploring the ideas themselves. This historical and evolutionary lens allows the reader to consider the political developments in context and within a broadly temporal ordering. Therefore, the structuring of this book is intentional: first comes history (Chapters 2 and 3), then strategy (Chapter 4), then theory (Chapters 5 and 6), and finally interpretation (Chapter 7).

The book seeks to trace the borders of this neo-insurrectionary tendency, to see where its adherents converge and dissent. Though this task is descriptively difficult based on the fluid and amorphous nature of such moniker-based networks, one can begin by mapping the history of these illegalist and militant tendencies prior to examining the texts generated by individual, cell-level actors claiming ideological affinity. The following historical account will trace the trajectory of illegalist anarchism, individualistic attack, and *propaganda of the deed* before arriving at the modern history of clandestine, insurrectionary guerrillaism. This history is key as it demonstrates not only the genealogy of anti-state, direct attack, but also establishes a lineage of martyrs whose names are often invoked in the present era of internet communiqués. From the shooting of monarchs to the placement of bombs to kill the bourgeoisie, the history of illegalist, nihilist, and insurrectionary anarchism prior to the twenty-first century paves the way for the post-9/11, networks of the "Black International … anarchists of praxis" (FAI/IRF Nicola and Alfredo Cell 2013).

What's so new about insurrection?

This book begins with the premise that modern insurrectionary methods are a new phenomenon which occurred around the turn of the twenty-first century. These contemporary insurrectionary networks may resemble unmediated attackers of the previous century but, in the modern era, they carry out attacks against state and capital and report this via online communiqués. However, while the monikers are millennial, and the methods inherently modern, this is not to suggest that such ideas, tactics, and strategies were birthed recently. Certainly the break between pre- and post-2000 methods of organization and attack is somewhat artificial, and just as the present reality will inform the attacks yet to occur, the (post)millennial, clandestine, insurrectionary, anarchist networks are a *continuation* of centuries of progression and militancy. I adopt this approach to separate "*old*" eras from that which is "*new*"; to single out those who meet, plot, and share *online* versus those militants of a century past who commingled in smoky union hall meetings or atop the orator's soapbox. I use the term "*new*" simply to distinguish those modern networks facilitated by global, synchronous, digital communications versus those of eras prior whose social networks were limited and dictated by physical proximity and social circle.

The modern insurrectionary tendency has reimagined the model of the leftist *urban* guerrilla popularized in the 1960s and 1970s through both "Third World" and metropolitan struggles. This era, and on into the 1980s, saw the rise of such armed anti-imperialist internationals (Ashley et al. 1970, secs. 1, 6) as the RAF, RZ, and Movement 2 June in Germany, Action Directe in France; First of October Anti-Fascist Resistance Groups in Spain; Fighting Communist Cells in Belgium; the Red Brigades (RB) in Italy; 17 November in Greece; Dev Sol (Revolutionary Left) in Turkey; the Popular Forces of 25 April in Portugal; the Fuerzas Armadas de Liberación Nacional in Puerto Rico; or WUO, Symbionese Liberation Army, New World Liberation Front, May 19th Communist Movement, and United Freedom Front in the United States. Such armed formations are distinct from their ideological compatriots operating in largely rural "Third World" environments, such as 19th of April Movement in Colombia, the Tupamaros National Liberation Movement in Uruguay, the Túpac Amaru Revolutionary Movement and Shining Path in Peru, and various armed insurgencies throughout South/Central America, the Middle East, Asia, and Africa. The majority of these groups were based around majoritarian Marxist, Leninist, and/or Maoist frameworks, yet their histories provide some clarity to the realities through which modern insurrectionary struggle emerged in the metropolis.

While these groups are obviously quite different in terms of tactics, strategies, message, ideology, and every other such measure, they share characteristics of being anti-capitalist and often anti-state, urban-based, pro-armed struggle, and active in the late twentieth century. Their inclusion within a historical discussion is meant to speak to their contemporariness, that fact that they all emerged and fought in a similar era. While we can continue to discuss such unique collectives within a single lens, we must avoid considering them the same, or risk misunderstanding their particular formations as informed by ideology, strategy, and approach. In an early work critical of orthodox approaches to terrorism, Joseba Zulaika and William Douglass (1996, 23) warned of "homogenization and trivialization of vastly different social realities under the buzzword of 'terrorism'," and I would expand that to encourage a detailed examination of particular groups open lumped together in categorically cumbersome manners. Groups form, act, and decline for a variety of reasons and, while active, carry out violence through vastly divergent realities. For example, the conditions that led to the formation of insurrectionary anarchist cells in Greece are different from the conditions that generated similar results in Mexico. This should be obvious to the reader. Therefore, the task of the historian becomes distinguishing what degree of similarity provides utility for comparison, and what distinct features deserve discussion in order to understand the subject as a distinct, novel entity. In this case, what distinguishes the insurrectionary subject from the urban guerrillas of decades past is their anarchist-derived framework, and their use of specified online communiqué repositories.

The post-2000 rise of the anarchist urban guerrilla under examination did not emerge anew, but rather is the outgrowth of centuries of militant struggle, which found a new form of internationalism and tactical mimicry with the aid of online communities. To clarify this point, it is helpful to briefly explore the case of Greece, which was home to armed movements in the previous century and is one of the "homes" of insurrectionary attack in the twenty-first century. Since the mid 1970s, Greece has witnessed strikes by urban, anti-statist, anti-capitalist guerrillas, most centrally Revolutionary Organization 17 November (17N), followed by Revolutionary Struggle, which emerged in 2003. When Revolutionary Struggle declined, CCF was primed to fill this vacuum. As one author explains, "CCF's ambition is to be the avant-garde of the militant anarchy in Greece, seeking to embody the most elevated principles of protest action in what is perceived as a critical moment for the anarchist revolutionary movement" (Kassimeris 2016, 3). Therefore, the *"emergence"* of the CCF is not an emergence at all, but instead a modern articulation, rebranding, and reconstitution of a preexisting social milieu (i.e. former members and sympathetic supports of 17N and Revolutionary Struggle) infused with a new, militant form of internationalism aided by the transnationalism of digital communities.

In the UK, prior to the emergence of FAI cells, the state saw the birth of the Angry Brigade in 1970, and the ALF a few years later. Both the Brigade and the ALF advocated anti-authoritarian, anarchist-aligned strategies of direct attack (e.g. vandalism, sabotage, arson, etc.), carried out through small, clandestine cells, and utilizing available technologies and accessible, *soft* (i.e. unguarded) targets. Though the groups varied in form, strategy, and image, North American groups like the George Jackson Brigade, United Freedom Front, Symbionese Liberation Army, and Direct Action 5 echoed strategies later adopted by insurrectionary networks. Across the ocean in Europe, similar groupings thrived, such as the 2 June Movement, RAF, RZ, RB, and others. These groups often arose suddenly, attacked in bursts of activity, and then were either repressed or dissolved. The emergence of anti-authoritarian networks in the 1970s and 1980s occurred in tandem with the decline of Marxist-Leninist groups and the fall of the Soviet Union. After the official end of Sovietism, groups populating the Latin American and European countryside faded further. The groups that took the place of the red hatted, bandoleer-wearing Leninist cadres were more decentralized, horizontal, and would prefigure the insurrectionary moniker networks that developed in the proceeding decade. The insurrectionary networks embodied in the FAI continue within this history of illegal, anti-state attack, yet constitute a new form; that of the internationalist, freely forming, moniker-based network engaging in a semi-transparent discourse through the exchange of digital texts, not party platforms. Insurrectionary anarchism practiced by clandestine cells independently carrying out attacks and subsequently discussing them online is thus a uniquely modern articulation of the historical tradition of those advocating propaganda of the deed, and the Marxist-Leninist militant organizations of the nineteenth century.

With these pre-histories in mind, it becomes obvious that to speak of a historical break – a point of demarcation at the turn of the millennium – is a somewhat arbitrary genealogical method for segmenting periods of history for the sake of discussion and interpretation. However arbitrary, the segmenting of these eras coincides with a larger discourse (e.g. Kaldor 2001) focused on globalization and the challenges it produced to governance, sovereignty, culture, and identity in an era of deterritorialization. The historical borders established by a pre/post-2000 periodization is to create a reference point for the era in which previous styles of anti-state attack began to be carried out with the aid of a globalized digital mode of communication. In the early twentieth century, an attacker still possessed the ability to attack a target with a bomb and claim responsibility with a written communiqué; however, news of that strike would not reach a global audience of ideological supporters instantaneously. The advent of the internet allowed for these networks to develop and interact in unprecedented ways. Thus, while the "style" of anarchism is not unheard of, the cell-based, moniker-driven, communiqué-posting tactical array is new.

The remainder of this chapter develops a multi-century historical trajectory that arrives at the development and expansion of modern, global, insurrectionary networks. Though the vignettes may appear fractured, they collectively constitute a history of anti-statism based in the deployment of political violence. The individuals profiled are those that are most often invoked in the modern insurrectionary narrative. From the French bank robbers to the Italian assassins, these events form the history of direct attack. In other words, in choosing to include and exclude specific individuals and events, those that were selected for inclusion reflect the tendencies carried forth from the annuals of the past into the present. Because this backgrounding temporarily suspends the book's central goal of understanding insurrectionary action through the object of the communiqué, it can be read as an addendum, a necessary precursor to the development of ideological borderlands.

Finally, by design, this global history functions to flatten a great deal of national, cultural, and historical-temporal differences in order to draw lines of similarity for the purposes of examining a particular political tendency. There is a tremendous amount of difference between these locales in terms of culture, custom, law, traditions, yet in order to tell the story of insurrection, a degree of linear thought is forced upon a non-linear world. The individual settings – from seventeenth-century England to modern-day Mexico – emerged through their own multi-century histories of social change; of reform, revolution, counterrevolution, uprisings, and repressions. What accounts for increased insurrectionary tendencies in a nation like Italy, Greece or Chile (e.g. clandestine networks to counter fascist movements) may not explain why aesthetically similar attacks and groups are seen in Indonesia or Canada. These histories of colonialism, national revolution, war, and shifts in custom constitute a political culture that is likely to inform and scaffold the development of insurrectionary politics. Therefore, this historical account is not meant to imply that the emergence of insurrectionary actors in nineteenth-century Europe led to similar movements a century later in the Americas, but rather to demonstrate the recurrence of this tendency as seen through a variety of snapshots.

Introducing a past history of insurrectionary attack

Insurrectionary anarchism is primarily a practice, and focuses on the organization of attack. (Anonymous 2003)

[The vanguard] is the most politically conscious section of the society which is responsible for leading and making a revolution. (Maziotis 2014)

Armed propagandists

On 26 October 1605, a letter arrived to the Baron of Monteagle informing him that in ten days, Robert Catesby, Guy Fawkes, and nine co-conspirators would attempt to blow up the House of Lords during the annual State Opening of Parliament. The bombing was to target King James and provoke a Midlands revolt against the regent. Fawkes was captured the day before the planned explosion – set to occur on 5 November – in the presence of 36 barrels of gunpowder to be used in the bombing. Catesby was shot and killed resisting arrest by the Sheriff of Worcester, and eight captured conspirators, including Fawkes, were sentenced to be hanged, drawn, and quartered. One man was hanged, castrated, disemboweled, *and then* quartered. Fawkes avoided public torture by leaping from the gallows once his rope was tied, killing himself. Catesby and a second man who avoided trial were later exhumed and decapitated, their heads displayed on spikes at the House of Lords. The attempted bombing, known as the Gunpowder (Treason) Plot, is eulogized in the late seventeenth-century folk rhyme:

> Remember, remember! The fifth of November,
> The Gunpowder treason and plot;
> I know of no reason, Why the Gunpowder treason,
> Should ever be forgot!
> Guy Fawkes and his companions, Did the scheme contrive,
> To blow the King and Parliament
> All up alive. Threescore barrels, laid below,
> To prove old England's overthrow.

This short vignette is provided to position Fawkes and his co-conspirators as one of the oldest, yet contemporarily relevant, actors striking unilaterally against the state. The Gunpowder Plot served as the basis for the 1980s graphic novel, *V For Vendetta*, which features an insurrectionary-styled protagonist – named V – who wages an armed campaign against the state through the use of guerrilla warfare. This text became a film in 2006, and though Fawkes (and V) was far from a self-declared insurrectionary anarchist, his example of attack without mediation, and a rejection of traditional politics, earned him a place in the insurrectionary hall of heroes.

More than two and a half centuries later, the historical precedent for the modern insurrectionary campaign of arson and explosives can be found around the eighteenth century, when anarchists carried out demonstrative acts of violence and termed it "propaganda of the deed." This concept of individuals or small groups acting as a form of performative *propaganda* is key to understanding modern insurrectionary violence. This strategy is explained in relation to one European nation:

The anarchist belief in violent direct action, formulated in the policy of "propaganda by the deed" (rather than by the word), reflected the particular bitterness of these struggles. Propaganda by deed was translated into action in three forms: insurrection, assassination, and bombing. The insurrectionary method ... was not tried out in France. Instead, assassination became the principal weapon of revenge against the bourgeoisie and the figureheads of the State. (R. Parry 1987)

Propaganda of the deed carries with it the presumption that "the population bearing witness to these acts would both see the fallibility of power AND would rise up to fill this void" (Aragorn! 2009, 25). This belief is rooted in anarchism's inherent positive view of human nature (i.e. people yearn for greater freedom and naturally oppose domination) and its understanding of a progressive route from the oppression of present to the liberated territory of the future. As a strategy, propaganda of the deed does not presume to in itself bring about radical social change. The early anarchist thinker Peter Kropotkin stated that "a few kilos of dynamite could not demolish the historical structures [of oppression] created over thousands of years" (quoted in Schmid and Graaf 1982, 14) and thus understood these attacks as forms of propagandistic communication, not substantive methods of socio-political change. In this manner, political violence can be understood as a manner of demonstrative communication; an opportunity for an individual to live a set of beliefs while engaging in an inherently political dialogue with the general public. Propaganda of the deed functions to enact social struggle through spectacular displays – of broken windows, burned buildings, and buildings cordoned off by police.

These manifestations of individualistic resistance reached an apex in the latter decades of the nineteenth century and raged throughout the world in the early days of the new century. This global period, from approximately 1878–1901, saw knife-wielding and bomb-throwing anarchists assassinate a host of world leaders and local enemies. Some scholars have linked this era to contemporary discussions of political violence and terrorism, terming this period the "classic age of [anarchist] 'lone wolf' or leaderless terrorism" (R. B. Jensen 2013). The most well-known group of this era is often the Russian Narodnaya Volya [*The People's Will*] (~1878–1887) who successfully assassinated Tsar Alexander II. The group, which offered a nihilist-infused anarchism, maintained cells in more than 45 cities with membership of around 500 people. Between 1879 and 1883 more than 2,000 members of Narodnaya Volya were brought to court in a series of more than 70 trials. Notably, the concept of propaganda of the deed has remained salient into the contemporary and, in 2011, one group of Mexican attackers decided to label their cell the "Revolutionary Action Brigade for Propaganda by the Deed and Armed Action." Both the attackers of the nineteenth and twenty-first centuries acted from a nihilist position, rejecting the moral authority that opposes attacking people as part of a social contract (O'Goodness 2013, pts. 8:30–11:20). A common strand throughout these nihilist attackers which separates them from more traditional, aboveground, social-movement minded anarchists is that while the former advocates the killing of its targets free from a moralizing logic, the latter tend to prioritize prefigurative politics which match the methods of struggle to one's desire for a future society including its associated morals.

During the late nineteenth century, there was a common assertion linking anarchism to terrorism. While prior eras of struggle helped to establish this understanding, the actions of two Russian anarchists – Sergey Nechayev and Mikhail Bakunin – cemented these beliefs. Nechayev, often associated with anarchism's nihilist tradition, helped to inaugurate the "prototype of modern terrorism" (Schmid 1988, 74), drawing inspiration from fellow Russian Dmitry Karakozov who infamously was the first Russian revolutionary to attempt killing a tsar. On 4 April 1866, Karakozov fired at Tsar Alexander II in a Saint Petersburg park but failed to kill him and was arrested and executed several months later. Nechayev would later write "The Revolutionary Catechism" (possibly in conjunction with Bakunin), which advocated the formation of clandestine networks modeled after secret societies. "Catechism" has been regarded as the text that "inspire[d] the [nihilist] movement-in-waiting into a movement-with-teeth with dozens of [armed] actions against the Russian state" (Aragorn! 2009, 7). The release of this influential text also served as a historical marker separating nihilism's foundational period (1860–1869) from its "revolutionary period" (1870–1881), directing nihilist thought away from pure philosophy and towards revolutionary action (Aragorn! 2009, 6–7, 11). This urging for revolutionaries to head underground would lead to Bakunin's expulsion from the First International by the Marxists who accused him of fomenting a conspiratorial "secret society" within the association (Rubenstein 1987, 141). The echoes of "Catechism" would be felt a century later when the Black Panther Party, and leader Eldridge Cleaver in particular (A. Parry 2013, 15), studied and circulated the text, even reprinting it for sale as a pamphlet advertised in the Party's newsletter (Faraj 2007, 34). Though they were not the first, the secretive means through which Nechayev and Bakunin were seen to operate cast them infamously as anarchist terrorists aimed at fomenting revolution through individualistic acts of anti-state violence.

Several years before the outbreak of anarchist-led attacks against the state, Louis Auguste Blanqui, a leader of the 1871 Paris Commune, furthered a strategic framework of elite vanguardism that would be instrumental in inspiring former communards-turned-illegalists.[1] After the destruction of the Paris Commune, Marxism and anarchism began down divergent paths, leaving Blanquism to rot on the vine. Its influence, however, reverberated throughout the leftist discourse, though often unacknowledged. It is Blanqui's theories that help formulate the Bolshevik-Leninist notion of an "elite Party leadership" (Meltzer 1969) and subsequent notions of an armed, military-styled vanguard devoid of support from the industrial proletariat. Blanquism succinctly explained is the fomenting of a libertarian socialist "coup d'état" (Gillespie 1986, 13) by small groups or highly organized, professionalized, and clandestine cooperating conspirators. In the temporary, revolutionary period, the socialists would establish a form of dictatorship, allowing for its forces to seize power and use its position to implement socialism. Once socialism was established, the dictatorship of the minority would be dissolved and power handed back to the people. In this sense, the Blanquist framework is preoccupied with the methods of revolutionary change and not post-revolutionary reconstruction. The socialist revolution and toppling of the bourgeoisie can be understood as an end in itself even prior to the formation of socialism. Blanqui, diverging from Marx, did not believe that the proletariat had a large role in the socialist revolution, nor would they naturally form a revolutionary consciousness. Moreover, Marx and Engels rejected the premise that individualistic acts of violence (e.g. terrorism as strategy) could be the fire that ignited the historically inevitable revolution (Gillespie 1986, 30).

Nearing the beginning of the twentieth century, anti-capitalist and otherwise revolutionary insurrections were occurring in a variety of locales. While the subsequent history will focus on the European continent, a great deal of activity was simultaneously erupting in less-chronicled battles. In a rarely cited example, Francisco Zalacosta – the student of Greek anarchist Plotino Constantino Rhodakanaty – organized armed peasant revolts in central Mexico. Some of these orchestrated insurrections involved up to 1,500 armed fighters simultaneously, and occurred throughout several states, focusing on lands seized by railway speculators (MacLachlan and Beezley 2010, 130). This period involved "a few hundred men, sack[ing] and burn[ing] haciendas across several states for more than a year and a half" (Beezley 2011, 82). Other historians describe the effort as a "running battle with government troops" (Marshall 2010, 510) as Zalacosta's fighters spread and took over several towns in southern Mexico. By 1871, the movement was reinvigorated when former participants of the Paris Commune arrived to assist. In 1878 Zalacosta formed those in revolt under the *Gran Central Comunero*,[2] spreading the peasant revolts until 1883 when the movements were successfully repressed under the direction of President Porfirio Diaz. Zalacosta's network would spawn 62 national sections, a journal, and an 1879 reunion attended by 5,000 (Poole 1977, 10). Zalacosta himself would be executed by the state in 1880 (Hart 1987, 41). The Mexican uprisings spread the logic of insurrectionary struggle through example throughout the countryside, drawing support from the widespread anger at displacement and land confiscation.

While Zalacosta was forming the *Comunero* to spread rural revolt, propaganda by example was picking up steam in Europe. In 1878, Sergei

Kravchinski – later known as "Stepniak"– stabbed and killed the chief of the Russian secret police in Saint Petersburg (Joll 1964, 122). Stepniak later wrote a manual of guerrilla warfare, and joined with Errico Malatesta and approximately 30 others who took to the mountains to try and organize armed revolt in the Italian villages. The revolutionaries seized two southern villages, destroying symbolic capital, and called for an end to the monarchy. Similar efforts were carried out throughout the world. Two years prior, in 1876, the Berne Congress of Bakuninists "enthusiastically adopted" Malatesta's proposal for the carrying out of "insurrection deeds as the most effective means of promoting 'the principals of socialism'" (Buttermorth 2010, 125–126). Two weeks after the Congress, French socialist Paul Brousse would coin the phrase "propaganda by deed."

Returning to 1878, Giovanni Passannante, a 29-year-old cook, stabbed the new Italian king, Umberto I, in Naples with a knife that bore the inscription "long live the international republic!" (Joll 1964, 123). Also injured in the attack was the Italian Prime Minister. Supporters of the King organized a parade to celebrate the monarch's survival, but a bomb thrown into the procession killed four and injured ten. Twenty-two years later, a second anarchist, Gaetano Bresci would finish the job and successfully assassinate King Umberto. Following the King's death, American anarchist James Ferdinand Morton, Jr. (1900) wrote:

> All through the [American] South, men are hung, shot, tortured, and burned at the stake on the flimsiest pretexts; and the dastardly murderers invariably escape unpunished. These are only negroes. In Pennsylvania, and elsewhere in this free land, unarmed men, marching in peaceful procession on the public highway, are shot down like dogs by the hirelings of capital; and their death remains unavenged. These are only workingmen. But when the bullet or dagger strikes down one solitary man who sits on a throne, a parasite whose hands are red with the blood of his fellow-men, whose coffers are filled with the wealth wrung from the exploited and starving wage-workers, all the world cries out in horror. For he is a king.

Two days after the King's parade was attacked, another bombing occurred, this time a hand-thrown device in Pisa targeting a celebration of the Queen's birthday. Such acts of individualistic attack prefigure the contemporary notion of the "lone wolf"; the ideologically-motivated yet organizationally-detached individual. In these nineteenth-century examples, attackers likely drew inspiration from local, regional, and global struggles, yet chose distinctly accessible targets for striking.

The attempts on King Umberto's life in 1878 came only months after similar attacks targeting the German Emperor by August Reinsdorf – the "father" of German anarchism (Schaack 1889, 96–98) – and the King of

Spain by Otero, all linked to illegalist-insurrectionary anarchists. In 1892, Paulino Pallás, a Spanish anarchist, attempted to kill General Martinez Campos of Catalonia by throwing a bomb into the Alcantara Theater, shouting "Long live anarchy!", during annual May Day celebrations. A crowd of demonstrators cheered and applauded the action which was seen as an attempt to "register protest" for the death of four comrades, not kill the General (Esenwein 1989, 185). Later, a friend of Campos's assailant, Santiago Salvador, furthered the plan for vengeance by allegedly throwing a bomb into a Madrid theater killing 20–22 people. This bombing and a subsequent explosion targeting a religious procession – which injured 60 and killed 12 – were condemned by anarchists and believed by some to be the work of police provocateurs (Joll 1964, 130). Others have argued that Jean Girault, a French anarchist who left Spain for Argentina following the attack, carried out the religious procession bombing (R. B. Jensen 2013, 88). One year after the attack on General Campos, in 1893, Auguste Vaillant attacked the Parisian Chamber of Deputies with a hand-thrown, shrapnel-laced, powerful improvised explosive device (IED). When he was captured, convicted, and executed, his last words were "My death will be avenged!" (Joll 1964, 132). Six months later, French President Sadi Carnot – who had denied Vaillant leniency – was stabbed to death in Lyon by 21-year-old anarchist, Santo Geronimo Caserio. Within a few years, other anarchist-led assassinations targeted US President William McKinley, and the Empress Elisabeth of Austria who was stabbed by Italian Luigi Luccheni. Between 1892 and 1894, Paris alone witnessed 11 major explosions, as well as the assassination of President Carnot, all linked to anarchists (Joll 1964, 136). In 1897, Italian anarchist Michele Angiolillo Lombardi shot and killed the Spanish Prime Minister Antonio Cánovas, and was executed (*New York Times* 1897). It is worth reminding the reader that for those of the era, *anarchism*, not Marxism, jihadi Islamism or another framework was the dominant association with occurrences of terrorism. While anarchist analysis and social struggle has never garnered the sympathetic praises of the state – nor did it seek to – it was this period of frequent attacks that guaranteed its designation as existing violently at odds with positions of power.

Around the same time, in 1882, German anarchist Johann Most arrived in the US by way of Austria and England. Most was heavily influenced by the writings of Bakunin and Blanqui, and while in the US began the German-language anarchist paper *Freiheit*. In 1885, Most published a pamphlet which would be influential within the illegalist propaganda of the deed-brand of anarchists entitled "Science of Revolutionary Warfare: A Little Handbook of Instruction in the Use and Preparation of Nitroglycerine, Dynamite, Gun-Cotton, Fulminating Mercury, Bombs, Fuses, Poisons, etc." As the title suggests, the pamphlet provided instruction for the manufacturing of weaponry.

This sort of manual would prefigure similar attempts to distribute tactical information for the construction of explosive and incendiary devices by anarchist direct action networks, including the ALF, ELF, CCF, and others. The inability of independent actors – those operating without the support of an organizational structure based in a division of labor – to acquire technical materials such as explosives can limit their ability to act in specific manners. Therefore the distribution of tactical manuals serves to facilitate more militant forms of contestation by making more deadly means accessible and adoptable. On 5 March 1886, after finding himself unable to acquire a bomb, 27-year-old anarchist Charles Gallo took prussic acid to the Parisian stock exchange and, after reaching its gallery, threw the bottle of acid and fired three rounds from a borrowed revolver. Gallo is preserved in the annuals of revolutionary history through his closing words to the court upon sentencing:

> Long live revolution!
> Long live anarchism!
> Death to the bourgeois judiciary!
> Long live dynamite!
> Bunch of idiots! (Duncombe 1997, 204)

The year 1886 also offered the Haymarket bombings, one of the most commonly referenced moments of anarchism's past.

On 4 May 1886, anarchists organized a rally in Chicago's Haymarket Square. After a series of fiery speeches, police arrived in a large contingent and ordered the speakers to halt. As the police lines advanced on the podium, a dynamite-filled bomb was thrown, killing a police officer and wounding six others (all of which later died from their injuries). The explosion triggered an exchange of gunfire between police and demonstrators, though it is widely debated who fired first. Four demonstrators were killed in the fighting and 60 police officers were injured. The incident would usher in a stern repression of leftist and pro-labor activists (i.e. the Red Scare). This included the arrest and conviction of eight individuals said to have been involved in the attack, all of who were condemned to die. One of the defendants – Oscar Neebe – was sentenced to 15 years, two defendants – Samuel Fielden and Michael Schwab – were able to have their sentence commuted, one committed suicide,[3] and George Engel, Adolph Fischer, Albert Parsons, and August Spies were hanged. The arrest, trial, and conviction of the Haymarket anarchists is an often invoked rallying cry in the present, extolling the honor bestowed among revolutionary martyrs. Contemporary anarchists often adopt the name, and the image of the martyrs is frequently reproduced as part of propaganda and outreach efforts.

Between 1892 and 1894, French illegalist Émile Henry carried out a series of deadly attacks including the bombing of a Parisian police station, a café, and mining company, as well as the shooting of three police officers. The café bombing is noted as a turning point in the modern history of political violence, "the day that ordinary people became the target of terrorists" (Merriman 2009, 5). This manner of discourse has been reinvigorated with the attacks of Mexican eco-insurrectionary groups (e.g. Individualists Tending Towards the Wild) targeting scientists and members of the technocratic and academic world. In 1892, famed anarchist Alexander Berkman attempted to assassinate Henry Clay Frick in the US for his role in anti-union activity leading to the death of nine unionists. After failing to construct a working bomb – once again demonstrating practical barriers to tactical choice grounded in efficacy or ethics – Berkman acquired a handgun and traveled to Pittsburgh to confront Frick. After bursting into his office, Berkman fired twice before being tackled and stabbing Frick with a dagger hidden in his pocket. Frick survived, and Berkman's actions were condemned by a host of radical thinkers, including Most who wrote an essay entitled "Reflections on Attentats," arguing that the "propaganda of the deed" strategy was predestined for misunderstanding in the American context. Such debates as to the efficacy of individualistic attack will remain a mainstay of inter-movement debate into modernity.

Criticism was also levied inward – showing an evolution of thought – as Berkman (1929, 6) would comment 37 years after the shooting of Frick:

> ... many Anarchists who at one time believed in violence as a means of propaganda have changed their opinion about it and do not favor such methods any more. There was a time ... when Anarchists advocated individual acts of violence, known as "propaganda by deed." They did not expect to change government and capitalism into Anarchism by such acts, nor did they think that the taking off of a despot would abolish despotism. No, terrorism was considered a means of avenging a popular wrong, inspiring fear in the enemy, and also calling attention to the evil against which the act of terror was directed. But most Anarchists today do not believe any more in "propaganda by deed" and do not favor acts of that nature.

A few years after Frick's shooting, in 1901, propaganda of the deed once again received international attention when Leon Czolgosz, a man who had attended a lecture of famed anarchist Emma Goldman's, assassinated US President William McKinley. After McKinley's shooting, several anarchists were arrested in connection, including Goldman and Most. The killing of McKinley, in conjunction with the public's reaction to the Wall Street bombing of 1920 which killed 30 and injured more than 140, effectively ended 20 years of illegalist, insurrectionary-styled attacks by anarchists and, in the US, ushered a series of anti-anarchist/leftist/immigrant legislations that were rapidly passed by Congress.

The Bonnot Gang

Across the Atlantic Ocean, the turn of the century saw similar activity throughout Europe. This history of illegalism is embraced by contemporary insurrectionary networks both in terms of its spirit of disregarding the state, and its focus on directly meeting the needs of revolutionary communities. Between 1911–1912, a collectivity of around 20 anarchists, known popularly as *La Bande à Bonnot* [The Bonnot Gang], carried out a series of attacks in France and Belgium within the illegalist (i.e. criminal) anarchist tradition. Their activities, despite pejorative portrayals, were distinctly revolutionary as they understood their efforts as "attacking the economy through the direct individual reappropriation of wealth" (Imrie 1994). Most members of the Gang were French, a few Belgian, and all frequently unemployed. The members were born during a period when France experienced an exasperation of class tensions, and many were further radicalized by the suppression of the 1871 Paris Commune, which involved the death of 17,000–30,000 communards. Following the offer of amnesty issued in 1880 to past communards, thousands of anarchists and other leftists returned to France from exile.

This period saw the wide expansion of anarchist groups in the country with an estimated 2,500 "active" members whose groups adopted violence-laden and militant names including "Dynamite," "The Sword," and "The Terror of La Cioat" (R. Parry 1987, 9–10) signaling what was to come in the following years of revolutionary, illegalist activity. This upsurge of offensive attacks by anarchists was seen throughout Europe. The addition of dynamite to the revolutionary arsenal saw a peak a few years prior in 1892 when more than 1,000 bombings were reported to have occurred throughout Europe. With the Bonnot Gang, explosions gave way to guns and getaway cars. The individualists that formed The Gang were involved in the anarchist periodical *L'Anarchie* (Rodríguez 2011a, 8) and scholars have been careful to describe them "not [as] a close-knit criminal band in the classical style, but rather a union of egoists associated for a common purpose" (R. Parry 1987, 5). Other historians have argued "those who grew-up with the Bonnot Gang [considered them] as some sort of modern Robin Hood and his Merry Men" (Meltzer 1969, para. 13). The core of the Gang centered around Jules Bonnot, Raymond Callemin, Octave Garnier, Élie Monier, André Soudy, and René Valet[4] who utilized automobiles and semi-automatic firearms in their attacks. The group carried out its first attack in December 1911 – a robbery targeting a Parisian bank. The robbery was the first in history to use an automobile as a getaway mechanism, and the robbers successfully got away with over 5,000 francs. The same month, the group robbed a gun store in Paris, and days later entered the home of a prominent businessman and killed him and his maid, stealing approximately 30,000 francs. Several other robberies occurred in this time period, resulting in the deaths of two police officers.

In March 1912, the Gang stole an automobile in Paris, killing the driver, and used the car to rob a bank, shooting three bank workers in the process. By May, French police had arrested 28 members and associates of the gang while at least three of the founding members remained at large. After shooting two officers and escaping an attempted arrest on 24 April 1912, Jules Bonnot was killed on 28 April, in a police raid that involved nearly 500 officers and the eventual dynamiting of the building. On 14 May 1912, two other members – Garnier and Valet – were killed in a similar raid, this time involving 300 police and 800 soldiers and a similar use of explosives. In February 1913, 14 Bonnot Gang members were tried and ten convicted. Following the trial some members were imprisoned, Édouard Carouy committed suicide, and Caillemin, Monnier, and Soudy were executed. Four individuals were found not guilty. Following the disassembling of the Bonnot Gang, French police led a series of anti-leftist raids similar to those organized by the FBI (i.e. The Palmer Raids) less than a decade later.

Of course the Bonnot Gang did not comprise the entirety of the illegalist tendency of the time, and even limited to the French state, other illegalists were quite active. Around 1900, Marius Jacob organized anarchists in Paris explicitly for criminal activity, calling his group the "workers of the night" (Rodríguez 2011a, 7) or "Banda Abbeville." The "workers" operated in France, Italy, and Belgium and carried out highly successful burglaries and subsequent sale of stolen goods. As Jacob had a radical, anarchist politic that predated his criminality, the group focused its theft on bourgeoisie and government-affiliated individuals, and some members, on Jacob's urging, donated 10% of their criminal earnings (Imrie 1994). The group avoided the violence typically associated with armed robberies and instead functioned quietly through prowess not force. According to contemporary illegalist anarchist Gustavo Rodriguez (2011a, 8), in a talk given in a Mexican squat, the "workers of the night" had a code:

> ... only use the weapons to protect our life and our freedom from the police, only steal from those considered social parasites; entrepreneurs, bankers, judges, soldiers, nobles and clergy, but never to those who do noble and useful professions; teachers, doctors, artists, artisans, workers and so on. And set aside a percentage of the money recuperated for propaganda of the anarchist cause.

Jacob may have been involved in up to 150 burglaries (Rodríguez 2011a, 8), though by his own account, he was only a part of 106, earning five million francs (Imrie 1994); 29 members of this network were arrested in 1903 and, after a trial, 16 were convicted including Jacob. Ten of the accused, including Jacob's mother, were acquitted. The illegalists accordingly occupy a special place of heroic martyrdom in the pre-modern insurrectionary history as their example serves to inspire those seeking direct confrontation with the forces of state and capital.

The example of the Bonnot Gang specifically, and illegalist anarchists more generally, is important for understanding the modern insurrectionary tendency. These twentieth-century actors put into practice the anarchist politic of unmediated attack and revelled in the criminal and anti-bourgeoisie, anti-capitalist, and anti-state nature of their violence. The groups embraced structural and strategic leanings towards informality, temporality, decentralization, the use of easily repeatable methods of attack based around dual-use technologies, and their non-apologetic statements and speeches – typically delivered while in the custody of judicial or security forces – mirrors the unrepentant statements made by contemporary imprisoned insurrectionary anarchists whose prison and court statements are regularly hosted and distributed by online networks. In consuming modern insurrectionary texts, one cannot avoid coming across these statements from imprisoned militants who use their prison pulpit to promote their lack of remorse and continued commitment to insurrectionary means and messages.

Galleanists and the (original) F.A.I.

> Italian apostles of Anarchism ... impressing characters all of them, clear minds and pure consciences. But their activity here, however intense, was more or less of a short duration. Galleani's on the contrary, spread over most of twenty years and was marked by the continuous progress of his mind and of the revolutionary movement as well. (Schiavina 1974, para. 2)

Italian anarchist Luigi Galleani was trained as a lawyer but never practiced, instead choosing to organize among anarchists, including involving himself in campaigns to resist Italian colonization in Ethiopia. He was imprisoned in Italy in the 1890s but later escaped. While traveling through France, Switzerland, Egypt, and England he was imprisoned several times, deported twice, and though it proved unsuccessful, was the subject of an attempted extradition by Egypt to face criminal changes in Italy. Galleani arrived in the US in 1901 and lived in Patterson, New Jersey, and Barre, Vermont, both areas with large Italian immigration and active militant anarchist communities. Galleani was active in the US and eventually deported back to Italy in 1919. Galleani argued that individual acts of violence – including expropriation (1925, 23–25, 30, 63, 77–79) – against the state and capital constituted "'a necessity and inevitable medium' by which a just society might be achieved" (Shone 2013, 200), and from 1914–1931 Galleanist anarchists[5] carried out a series of assassinations and bombing attacks targeting government, business, and religious sites. In his work as editor and propagandist, Galleani used his platform to defend and explain the actions of illegalist anarchists such as Czolgosz (McKinley's assassin) and Bresci, the second assassin to target Italian King Umberto. Galleani saw Umberto's assassination at the hands of Bresci as a global event awakening a revolutionary moment (Shone 2013, 201–202). Galleani's mark on the history of political violence is far wider than the actions of the individual, and his presence in the wider anarchist milieu is instructive for understanding the role of the individual in a social movement's direction. Though anarchist networks are *not* based around leadership, the roles played by some personalities certainly serve to inspire and coalesce the actions of others. In the modern discussion, Galleani could be compared to Alfredo Cospito, or other imprisoned insurrectionary proponents who, though maintaining individual prominence, are not seen as leaders, decision makers or sites of centrality.

Four years after arriving in the US, in 1905, Galleani published a pamphlet – "*La Salute è in Voi*" [The Health is Within You], which Emma Goldman may have translated into English – that instructed anarchists in the manufacturing of explosives. Such methods of spreading information were used by Johann Most, who in 1885 published "Science of Revolutionary Warfare," also a pamphlet-length anarchist how to manual dealing with explosives and poisons. Similar tactical manuals were uncovered in police raids in 1911 targeting future members of the Bonnot Gang. In one such police search, two manuals were discovered – "How to Use the Blowtorch" [to break into safes], and "Revolutionary Manual for the Manufacture of Bombs" – along with counterfeit money, binoculars, maps, nitroglycerine, and various surveying, chemistry, drafting, and mechanical tools (R. Parry 1987, 71). Galleani's pamphlet was utilized by those who bombed the home of John D. Rockefeller (4 July 1914) in retaliation for the industrialist's role in the repression of miners in Colorado (Tejada 2012, 103). Galleani's manual was also found in the home of anarchists attempting to bomb St. Patrick's Cathedral in New York who were arrested when undercover police agents embedded in their group emerged.

In 1916, Galleanist Nestor Dondoglio, in his role as a chef, added arsenic to the soup of 100 guests attending a banquet in honor of an Archbishop. The attendees, who were leading figures in business, industry, and government, all survived with the help of a doctor who was on site attending the event. The same year, Galleanist Alfonso Fagotti stabbed a police officer during a demonstration-turned riot in Boston, and the day after, Fagotti (or an associate) detonated a bomb in a city's police station. Though it could never be conclusively linked to Galleani or his network, as the city of San Francisco held a parade for Preparedness Day, a bomb concealed in a suitcase detonated (22 July 1916), killing ten and wounding 40. The bomb's construction, particularly its use of metal shrapnel additives, resembled previous and future devices used by Galleanists. It is thought to have been built by Mario Buda. Buda is also thought to have built the IED that detonated at a police station in Milwaukee (24 November 1917) killing nine officers and one civilian. The bomb had originally been placed in a church, presumably to target Reverend August Giuliana, who was involved in activities seen as anti-anarchist. On 30 December 1918, a series of at least three bombs detonated in Philadelphia targeting the homes of a judge, the Acting Police Superintendent, and the President of the Chamber of Commerce. Each bombing was accompanied by anarchist flyers left on site. Two months later, in February 1919, four Galleanists were killed while attempting to place a bomb at the American Woolen Company whose workers were on strike.

Galleani's 1919 deportation back to Italy occurred at a time when the US was witness to frequent bombings by leftists. In April of 1919 alone, 36 dynamite bombs in the US were mailed to government officials, servants of the court, and prominent businessmen, and on 2 June 1919, nine shrapnel-packed pipe bombs exploded nearly simultaneously across seven US cities – New York, Boston, Pittsburgh, Cleveland, Patterson, D.C., and Philadelphia (Shone 2013, 203; Federal Bureau of Investigation Philadelphia Division n.d.). Like previous Galleanist bombings, flyers were left at the scene speaking of class war, violence, and retaliatory justice. The June 1919 bombings targeted, among other sites, the home of US Attorney General A. Mitchell Palmer, a man who would later lead the anti-anarchist "Palmer Raids," and aid the creation of the FBI's counterintelligence program targeting leftists. Palmer's bomber, who was killed in the attack, was identified as Carlo Valdinoci, an associate of Galleani. When Galleani was deported several weeks later, the newly formed FBI/Department of Justice's General Intelligence Unit – run by future FBI innovator J. Edgar Hoover – linked Galleani as central to the attacks.

Following Galleani's deportation, possibly the most (in)famous case of anarchist history unfolded in the US state of Massachusetts. On 15 April 1920, a factory worker was robbed and murdered. The crime was blamed on two Italian anarchists, Nicola Sacco and Bartolomeo Vanzetti. While it is likely that Sacco and Vanzetti were followers of Galleani (Avrich 1996; Watson 2008) and committed anarchist militants, it is unlikely that either was involved in the robbery-murder. Sacco and Vanzetti were arrested, tried, and executed and their death became a rallying cry for anarchists further enraged by a miscarriage of justice linked to the state's fear of revolutionary change and its discrimination of Italian immigrants. Numerous attacks were carried out in the two martyrs' names. For instance, days after their arrest, an unknown assailant – thought possibly to be Mario Buda, a colleague of the two arrestees and known Galleanist – placed a bomb outside of the J.P. Morgan building on Wall Street. The bomb killed at least 33 people. This method of honoring fallen comrades would prefigure a similar tendency in the twenty-first century. In these modern incarnations it is exceedingly common for strikes against the state and capital to be "dedicated" to a specific ally – often one who has been recently captured or who is serving a prolonged prison sentence – and for the rejection of their carceral status to be used to mobilize a rageful response.

Other prominent illegalist anarchists of the late nineteenth century include Giuseppe Ciancabilla, who immigrated to the US in 1898 with Galleani and settled in Patterson with other Italian anarchists. He worked as an editor of numerous anarchist publications including those affiliated with poet Pietro Gori and Malatesta, also working to translate the works of prominent anarchists including Peter Kropotkin. Ciancabilla is routed squarely in the modern insurrectionary tradition and paves the way for such tendencies in his essay "Against Organization" (1890), writing:

> … we don't want tactical programs, and consequently we don't want organization. Having established the aim, the goal to which we hold, we leave every anarchist free to choose from the means that his sense, his education, his temperament, his fighting spirit suggest to him as best. We don't form fixed programs and we don't form small or great parties. But we come together spontaneously, and not with permanent criteria, according to momentary affinities for a specific purpose, and we constantly change these groups as soon as the purpose for which we had associated ceases to be, and other aims and needs arise and develop in us and push us to seek new collaborators, people who think as we do in the specific circumstance.

This rejection of programs and emphasis on free, temporary, and informal association would eventually mark the insurrectionary networks that proliferated in the twenty-first century.

This early twentieth-century manner of practice embraced individualism, while coordinating collective, militant action. Individualists of this ilk included Abele Rizieri Ferrari, who wrote under the nom de plume Renzo Novatore. Novatore was a famed Italian poet and philosopher of the illegalist school, inspired by individualist Max Stirner. Both Novatore and Stirner continue until the present to inspire insurrectionary, nihilist, and individualist tendencies found in anarchism, and sympathetic leftist presses frequently publish their works (e.g. Novatore 2000; 2012; Stirner and McQuinn 2012). In 1920, Novatore wrote his famed essay "My Iconoclastic Individualism," wherein he writes:

... Individualism is neither a school nor a party, it cannot be "unique", but it is truer still that Unique ones are individualists. And I leap as a unique one onto the battlefield, draw my sword and defend my personal ideas as an extreme individualist, as an indisputable Unique one, since we can be as skeptical and indifferent, ironic and sardonic as we desire and are able to be ... Individualism, as I feel, understand and mean it, has neither socialism, nor communism, nor humanity for an end. Individualism is its own end. (1920)

Other prominent illegalist, insurrectionary forebearers of the time include Bruno Filippi, an Italian individualist anarchist inspired by Stirner and publisher of *Iconoclasta* together with Novatore. Filippi was involved in the Italian Red Biennium, a two-year post-war period (1919–1920) of social protest involving mass strikes, workers demonstrations, factory occupations, the creation of workers' councils, and guerrilla warfare in cities and the countryside. Bruno died during this revolutionary period while attempting to detonate a bomb targeting the city's elite during a reunion. Comrade Novatore (1916, 8) eulogized him in an article speaking of the slain anarchist in a "fruitful embrace with death because he madly loved life."

Also from Italy was Severino Di Giovanni, who resided in Argentina after Mussolini's rise to power caused him to leave Europe. In Argentina, Giovanni organized against fascism and in support of Sacco and Vanzetti. In 1925 he founded *Culmine*,[6] an anarchist periodical advocating propaganda of the deed through direct action. Giovanni carried out a series of bombings including targeting the US embassy in Buenos Aires hours after Sacco and Vanzetti were sentenced. Other bomb attacks targeted a statue of George Washington, the Ford Motor Company, a tobacco company who had proposed selling a Sacco and Vanzetti cigarette, the headquarters of Citibank, the Bank of Boston, and the Italian consulate. The consulate bombing killed nine Italian fascists and injured 34, making it the deadliest bombing ever to occur in Argentina. Giovanni was also involved in several assassinations and attempted assassinations targeting a member of Mussolini's secret police, a federal police officer in charge of investigating bomb attacks, the president of the Fascist Committee of La Boca, and US President Herbert Hoover. After the bomber targeting Hoover was arrested, Giovanni entered a period of inactivity, returning his attention to *Culmine*. While evading arrest at a printing shop, Giovanni shot and killed a cop and injured a second. In a subsequent gun battle in which two anarchists were killed, Giovanni was arrested. He was tried by a military tribunal and executed by firing squad. He shouted, "Long live Anarchy!" before being shot eight times. Giovanni embodied the insurrectionary illegalist tradition of direct attack, propaganda of the deed, and direct action. He believed in retaliatory violence, symbolic violence, and asymmetry as a model of warfare.

One of the most famed periods of militant anarchism also occurred in this time between the end of World War I and the start of its predecessor. Towards the end of the 1930s, the Civil War in Spain was ending. Throughout the conflict between the Spanish Republicans and the fascist General Francisco Franco, anarchist activity was in large part managed via the *Confederación Nacional del Trabajo* [National Confederation of Labour] (CNT), an anarcho-syndicalist union active since 1910. The CNT would eventually form an alliance with the *Frente Popular* [Popular Front] – a collation of Marxist-Stalinist factions – which would foster dissention amongst the anarchists. Within the CNT was a second organization, the *Federación Anarquista Ibérica* [Iberian Anarchist Federation], which, similar to the modern network, adopted the moniker F.A.I.[7] The F.A.I. is the clearest pre-model for the *affinity group*, wherein small groupings of comrades freely assemble on a temporary basis when their interests align. The F.A.I. began in secret in 1927 in response to the CNT's push towards trade unionism and libertarian communism and away from militant agitation and anarchism. Though it was still young, by the early 1930s the F.A.I. was exerting significant influence over the larger CNT. This caused some rifts within the CNT, with more moderate factions breaking away eventually forming the Catalan *Partit Sindicalista* [Syndicalist Party] or joining other factions within the Popular Front such as the *Partido Obrero de Unificación Marxista* [Workers' Party of Marxist Unification].

The militant revolutionary spirit of the F.A.I. adopted familiar methods including armed expropriations, organizing general strikes, and direct attacks against the fascist forces. The disagreement between the CNT and the F.A.I. can thus be understood to embody several forms: one in terms of structure (e.g. mass-based, formalized syndicalist trade unionism v. clandestine anarchist militant affinity groups), and the other in terms of spirit (e.g. labor-centric unionism v. anti-state illegalism). This disagreement between those in favor of large, horizontal organizations and those advocating underground networks of aggressive militants foreshadowed the rifts that would be highlighted later between so called "classical" anarchists and those advocating insurrection. Importantly, when the fascists defeated the Republicans in 1940, the Franco regime went on to execute up to 200,000 dissidents, and many CNT-F.A.I. members fled internationally. Some, such as Francisco Sabaté Llopart (aka El Quico or simply Sabaté), fled to France and aided the French Resistance to Nazi occupation. After Sabaté and others finished fighting in France, many would return to Spain under Franco and carry out anti-state attacks including assassinations, prisoner releases, and armed expropriations to fund revolutionary activities. These methods were drawn from past experiences with militant guerrillaism and would prefigure decades of inspired anarchist attack. In other countries, such as Italy and Chile, similar fights against authoritarian regime would help to form networks of anarchist militants, some of which would later constitute the insurrectionary milieus.

In the years between the World Wars, global anarchist violence seemed to decline, ending the so-called "first wave of terrorism" (~1880–1920), often termed the "anarchist wave" (Rapoport 2002). This broadly defined post-World War I, pre-millennial century saw anarchists take up arms against Franco in Spain, though anti-statism ceased to be the predominant source of global non-state, political violence. While anarchist influence was widely seen in terrorism's third wave – the "New Left" wave (Rapoport 2002) embodied in the Weather Underground and other opponents of the Vietnam War – it would cease for a time to be explicitly affiliated with militant attacks against the centers of power. Anarchism remained a potent social force throughout the twentieth century, entering its "classical period" of thought marked by collectivist thinkers such as Emma Goldman; however, its armed tendencies, especially those prioritizing networks of armed attackers, would lie largely dormant until the eve of the twenty-first century.

The twenty-first century: from Chiapas to 9/11

The postindustrial shifts in the economy, the globalization of markets, the decline of a large industrial working class in core capitalist nations, and the questioning of modern forms of culture all set the stage for new types of social movements ... [These movements] did not have a clear-cut class base, as had large working-class socialist movements. They organized in the name of the public ... or the marginalized, as well as women and youth ... activists included educated middle-class young people as well as more marginal people ... Together they provided a support base for some of the new social movements and the increasingly decentralized forms of critical resistance ... The new social movements did not seek to capture the state or use it to carry out reforms; rather, they harassed it, sniped at it with local actions, worked around it, and showed their contempt for it ... the new movements were self-consciously local, decentralized, antibureaucratic, and antihierarchical. (Garner 1996, 99–100)

Indians and elves

On 1 January 1994, the Zapatista Army of National Liberation (EZLN), made up of only 3,000 revolutionary, indigenous fighters, led an uprising against the Mexican state, while freeing prisoners and destroying military and police property. Following their surge, the Mexican army counterattacked EZLN forces, and fighting lasted for ten days. The EZLN's armed insurrection was timed to coincide with activation of the North American Free Trade Agreement, and through subsequent, lengthy texts, the movement expressed an anarchistic rejection of neoliberalism, "free trade," and capitalism at large (e.g. Marcos 1996; 2002). This action brought an anti-globalization, anti-capitalist sentiment to an international audience in a violent outburst not seen from anti-statists in decades. With lightning speed, a relatively unknown non-state actor successfully took control over the state of Chiapas, establishing counter-institutional infrastructure and preventing Mexican incursion. The Zapatistas set up 38 autonomous municipalities – local forms of decentralized, horizontal, participatory democracy with distinct anarchist, Marxist, and libertarian-socialist influences. They established hospitals and schools, factories and militias. The EZLN spoke for the rights of the marginalized; the indigenous, the poor and the citizens of the "global south" resisting neoliberalism and transnational capital accumulation.

The final years of the twentieth century saw the explosion of new networks of attack directly confronting state and capital. Zapatismo, the "ideology" of the EZLN, served to inform anti-capitalists internationally who in turn informed the EZLN through exchanges of ideas and shared experiences. This cross-pollination and the physical proximity provided by foreign activists' forays into Chiapas served to incorporate the Zapatistas into a global discourse of justice and anti-capitalism. Two years after the EZLN uprising, on Columbus Day, the first act of the ELF was claimed in the US. Though the network had briefly emerged in the UK in 1992 as a splinter faction from the Earth First! network (Joosse 2007, 354), on the night of 14 October 1996, clandestine ELF activists carried out three simultaneous acts of sabotage targeting a Chevron gas station, a public relations office, and a McDonald's restaurant (Molland 2006, 55). The targets had their locks glued shut and their walls defaced with political messages including the three-letter calling card moniker: "E.L.F." The ELF emerged during a roughly ten-year period (1994–2004) of global anti-capitalist and anti-globalization demonstrations and direct actions and would invigorate and heavily influence the organizational tendencies of many to follow.

The ELF, like its parent "movement" the ALF, utilize decentralized activists (in cells and as individuals) carrying out thousands of acts of property destruction to economically sabotage targets and industries. These attacks on property have at least two broad purposes as explained by Peace Studies advocate and anarchist Randall Amster: "The basic premise [of the ELF] is that economic sabotage can educate the public by highlighting unjust enterpriseism while at the same time conveying a spirit of empowered resistance through direct action" (2012, 76). These decentralized forms of collective communication make bold claims such as, "we oppose genetic engineering," or "stop urban sprawl." In this manner, the ELF/ALF and insurrectionary cells are nearly identical. Without the need for specialized communications bodies – though aboveground press offices have supported both the ALF and ELF at times – cells can sufficiently initiate campaigns through an action followed by a communiqué. An attacker can strike, report why a particular target was chosen and, within the same text, open debate regarding tactics, strategy, targets, etc. For the clandestine calls of attackers, the medium and the message are simultaneous and symbiotic. Everyone can communicate with the world through spectacular action, yet no one is constrained through the need to function via communicative bodies or coordinating entities.

Both the ELF/ALF and Zapatistas are modeled around anti-authoritarian principals and are prominently anti-state and anti-capitalist. They represent a new wave of movements, which while *philosophically* rooted in the Marxism of the 1970s, have since abandoned the red concept of historical materialism and its tendencies towards vanguardism, centralism, and hierarchical command structures. These movements did not agree with Marx who contended that although capitalism must be confronted – precisely why Marx along with Bakunin founded the First International – the system naturally contained within itself the contradictions that would lead to its demise. Rather, these post-Marxists understood that capitalism must to be confronted and destabilized, establishing alternative forms of organization as demonstrated through radical praxis. It was partially their confrontational, anti-reformist, anti-politics approach that led to the ELF/ALF networks being labeled "the most active criminal extremist element in the United States" (Lewis 2004) and the "number one domestic terrorist threat" (Schuster 2005). In developing this history of contemporary, clandestine networks, it is important to understand the evolution and internationalization of the ELF/ALF, as their tactics, strategies, and internet-aided, moniker-based communication style would mark the new era of insurrectionary struggle.

"Anti-globalization" and the black bloc

The rising tide of anti-capitalist anti-authoritarianism reached another global crest when, on 30 November 1999, 50,000–75,000 demonstrators marched in downtown Seattle against the third ministerial of the World Trade Organization (WTO). Following the first day of marches, direct actions, and rioting, more than 600 demonstrators were arrested. The protestors were so disruptive, and the police response so violently disorientating to the city's operation, that the opening trade talks were postponed. When the talks resumed as activists continued to demonstrate outside, they quickly collapsed on their own, and the three-day ministerial was concluded two days early. In response, the demonstrators declared victory. The so-called "Battle of Seattle" gave international attention to black masked anarchists defacing and damaging corporate property, and a multitude of diverse global justice activists engaged in pitched street battles with heavily armed, quasi-militarized police.

While movement historians are careful to point out that the majority of demonstrators assembled did *not* identify as anarchists per se,[8] "anarchist values and methods in fact played an integral part in the highly drilled non-violent demonstrations that shut down the WTO Seattle meeting" (Gabay 2010, 121). The demonstrations, which came to be known in the activist vernacular as "N30," ushered in a multi-year global movement of mass convergences coinciding with meetings of multilateral organizations. In the US alone, large-scale demonstrations were held opposing and disrupting meetings of the WTO, World Bank, International Monetary Fund, Group of Eight, Organization of American States, World Economic Forum, and others. These convergences were unique not only in their mass, but also in their focus on prefiguration and organizational practices derived from a larger anti-authoritarian praxis (i.e. horizontality) with a focus on participatory decision-making (Feigenbaum, Frenzel, and McCurdy 2013, 153) and direct action.

For years following N30, nearly every global multinational meeting was met with thousands of demonstrators, including a large section of militant anarchists. This era saw the importation and rapid adoption of the black bloc tactic,[9] which finds its historic roots in the *Autonomen* movement of West Germany that stood in defense of political squatters, in opposition to neo-Nazis, and in support of the urban guerrillaism offered by the RAF and RZ. This Autonomen movement rose in visibility in conjunction with similar movements contesting space in other European (and non-European) locales such as Denmark, which also witnessed a post-Soviet Union rise in movements to occupy and hold vacant spaces (i.e. squats) (Karpantschof 2014). Autonomen "ideology" embraced an intersecting patchwork of influences, including anarchism, Marxism, radical feminism, and an environmental, workers' rights framework (Dupuis-Déri 2014, 24). At pro-RAF assemblies, marchers armed with clubs would wear black leather jackets, motorcycle helmets, and black facemasks, protecting their lines with wide banners. According to Francis Dupuis-Déri (2014, 60), a Canadian political scientist who authored a comprehensive history of the modern black bloc, there has been a consistent association between such tactics and the insurrectionary tendencies of thinkers such as Alfredo Bonanno, The Invisible Committee (TIC), and Tiqqun.

From 1999–2001, the global wave of mass demonstrations continued. What began in the US as opposition to multinational trade talks, saw the diffusion of these social networks and political projects into other areas. The 2000 Republican and Democratic National Conventions, and the inauguration of President George W. Bush, saw similar mass convergences, similar uses of direct action street confrontations, and similar black blocs. In April 2001, demonstrations were held against the Free Trade Area of the Americas in Quebec City. In the first two days of actions, up to 20,000 militants, largely anarchists, attacked the security perimeter of the conference, tearing down hundreds of feet of fencing and barriers. Affinity groups of black bloc anarchists were able to smash bank windows and confront riot police lines with projectiles and charges. In their recounting of the demonstrations in Quebec City, known as "A20," veteran black bloc activists and authors of *The Black Bloc Papers* write:

> All and all Quebec marked a turning point. Although it did not have the immediate psychological impact on the general North American population as did Seattle, it did result in the further militant radicalization of the actively involved social protest population ... In the days of protests more than 450 were arrested ... All told, there were 75–100,000 social protesters pitted against approximately 10,000 Provincial and Federal police, primarily stationed behind a protective barrier. In the clashes at least one cop was seriously injured with another 71 treated in hospitals. On our side at least 100 required medical attention. In all the State fired 5,000 tear gas canisters in order to repress the voice of the people. (Van Deusen and Massot 2010, 131)

A20 truly did mark a turning point for this global wave of anti-capitalist, anarchist movement. Five months after the demonstrations, a non-state actor of a different nature changed the trajectory of global politics in ways still reverberating more than a decade later.

From the EZLN in Chiapas, through the clandestine saboteurs of the ELF, up through the "summit hopping" black blocs, all of the warriors wore masks. All opposed the state and capitalism as core principals of their philosophical, organizational, and political frameworks. Thus the EZLN, ELF, and the more generalized anti-globalization movement are reacting to similar tendencies under neoliberalism, namely "the command and control character of everyday life under globalization: its standardization, routinization, constant surveillance, performativity, and military style discipline" (Becker 2006, 24). These shared rejectionist positions allowed a multitude of influences to co-constitute the post-millennial insurrectionary tendency, which drew a great deal from these autonomous networks of anti-capitalist collectivities.

The Al-Qaeda effect and the diffusion of the rioters

On 11 September 2001, three airplanes were hijacked and flown in suicide missions attacking targets inside the US. The 9/11 attacks would rapidly lead to the US initiating two foreign wars, and a similarly rapid (and correlated) decline in the global counter-summit protests. The post-9/11 derailing of the anti-globalization movement can be encapsulated in the events of 29 September 2001. Following the attacks, the scheduled fall IMF/World Bank meetings were canceled. In response to the canceled meetings and out of "respect" for the victims of the attacks, most liberal and progressive social movement bodies canceled their planned protests of the economic summit in DC. While this cancelation severely restricted the number of attendees, unpermitted anarchist-organized marches and direct actions organized by the Anti-Capitalist Convergence carried on while other groups hosted a permitted rally. This march was in response to the group's revised "Call to Action," distributed only nine days after the 9/11 attacks. This document called for a "march against the growing capitalist war" and invited "all those interested in creating a world free from terror, hate, racism, poverty and war to demonstrate our unity and vision for a better world" (Anti-Capitalist Convergence DC 2001). The day of the march, the front banner read, "No War But The Class War," and through careful messaging, the group reframed their protest to oppose not only the policies of neoliberalism embodied in the meetings, but also nationalism, militarism, and war. This forced, reactionary reframing and the poorly attended street demonstrations functioned as a clear indication that the era of anarchist-led, militant summit hopping was over.

Beyond the impact on oppositional social movements, the September attacks also had wide reaching effects on US foreign and domestic policy. Following 9/11, policing and intelligences forces such as the FBI shifted their domestic policy aims from "policing" to "national security" (Hudson 2014), accompanying a newly invigorated rhetoric of (counter) terrorism-dominated media and political discourses. Militant activists fighting police in masks suddenly and irrevocably were reframed from engaging in revolutionary struggle to plotting dangerous, extremist, terrorism. Of course a global movement did not simply stop on a dime. Demonstrations, including those with large militant components, continued on irregularly for several years – eventually finding a new focus with the 2009 university occupations and Occupy Wall Street movements of the next decade.

What is undeniable is that tens of thousands of people who for several years prior had been involved in campaigns of semi-regular protest gatherings had now ceased to assemble for mass marches, convergences, and "summit hopping." There existed a certain surplus of labor from all segments of these diverse resistance movements. This included street medics, Indymedia journalists, communications and tech specialists, action organizers, tacticians, and trainers, previous and future participants in black blocs, and collectives penning theory. If 75,000 marched in Seattle, and 100,000 in Quebec City, did this mass movement's committed and interlinked participants simply abandon radical politics? It is likely that the wave of clandestine networks of anti-capitalist attack that occurred throughout Europe, Asia, and the Americas following 9/11 were populated by individuals and networks developed during these prior waves of summit protests and mass convergences.

Maybe a large portion of ELF activists and insurrectionary attack cells are made up of seasoned activists who were disheartened with the experiment seen in the anti-globalization, global justice movement? This theory has been proposed by, among others, the anonymous authors of *The Coming Insurrection*, who spoke of the post-summit period writing: "In all the affinity groups they spawned and left in their wake, we glimpsed the conditions that allow social movements to become a locus for the emergence of new communes" (TIC 2007, 121). This possibility has been supported by at least some anecdotal accounts given by members of "the family," the largest ELF cell ever exposed. Through interviews and police accounts, it is reported that four of the ten group members participated in the Seattle WTO black bloc[10] and planned acts of property destruction to coincide with the trade summit. Some of the 200,000 activists who were witness to violent confrontations surrounding the 2001 anti-G8 demonstrations in Genoa likely had connections to past and future "members" of the FAI which rapidly expanded a few years later. Seven years later, in 2008, when Greece underwent widespread social upheaval with mass anarchist involvement, international activists frustrated with the failures of the previous decade traveled to Athens and other cities to network, organize, and act. After the police's killing of a teenage boy, riots erupted in several Greek cities that included direct attacks on police and frequent destruction of property. The throwing of stones and Molotovs was broadcast from Greece to sympathizers globally, and (often-militant) solidarity demonstrations occurred in more than 70 cities around the world. This series of events once again captured the attention of North American anarchists as "activists [who] once drew inspiration from the Zapatistas of Chiapas ... now drew it from the student rebels of Athens ... the common link, to be sure, is a pervasive spiriting of taking charge, of acting as if one were already free, of rebellion and insurrection" (Williams and Thomson 2011, 266). This pre-9/11 period was a key time for cross-fertilization among a variety of struggles around the world. While the targets of the movements varied, they remained (to differing degrees) critical of state power and sought to "transform the social experience" (Papadopoulos, Stephenson, and Tsianos 2008, 71) through assembly and action.

9/11 had the effect of disrupting the cascading crowds of increasingly well-practiced networks mobilized to resist global capitalism. When the mass convergences ceased, a vacuum was created for former summit-hoppers, local organizers, and newly inspired and radicalized leftists to fight the state. Just as the tactics of the black bloc had migrated from German Autonomen and deterritorialized throughout the broad left, so too would the methods of the ELF/ALF intersect and cross-pollinate with new, previously unheard of, clandestine networks. Groups such as the Greek CCF would emerge in one country to attack and, soon after, strike in other nations. In this way, the new social movements of decentralized saboteurs, arsonists, and vandals would for some resemble the images of al-Qaeda or the Islamic State. In a poignant enacting of postmodernism, while nations were made to fear hidden cells of Islamist suicide bombers plotting to kill civilians, similarly hidden cells of insurrectionary anarchists were conspiring to bring down capitalism and the state through an old form of war. While jihadists chose the path of terrorism for the recreation of an Islamic empire, the insurrectionists chose urban guerrilla warfare as a path to freedom, autonomy, and liberation.

Conclusion

The varied anti-capitalist networks that sprang up around the world to resist shared a great deal in term of politics and form. All emerged during the period marked as "postmodern" and, in this sense, were interpreted by some through this lens. Borrowing from Deleuze and Guattari and their opus *A Thousand Plateaus: Capitalism and Schizophrenia*:

> The EZLN, suddenly emerging to occupy towns, their infiltrators just as suddenly disappearing and dissolving Mexican army units, and then fading into their jungle redoubts are rhizomes ... the anonymous and autonomous cells of the ELF erupting in sudden arson attacks across the United States and as rapidly disappearing are rhizomes ... Rhizomes threaten an established order; they often operate unseen; they are irrepressible and cannot be eradicated as their root stem allows for proliferation at each of its nodes. (Becker 2006, 6)

The rhizome, as described by Deleuze and Guattari (1987, 3–25), represents "a spreading, underground, decentered network of roots that appear aboveground as sprouts and thickets like blackberry bushes or bamboo" (Jeppesen 2010, 474). According to the rhizomatic interpretation,[11] these new emergent networks of resistance are easily multiplied, difficult to isolate and decapitate, and embody "irreducibility ... to any ultimate organizing principle" (Becker 2006, 8). In this manner, even if a spokesperson, cell, collectivity of cells or other segment of a network is compromised, captured, killed or otherwise neutralized, the remaining portion "shoots off in other directions continuing to proliferate" (Becker 2006, 8).

Therefore, while the post-NAFTA movements against neoliberalism and state power have shared a great deal which is observable and pronounced, it is likely that what they most intimately share is their reproductive logic; the organically-evolved, situational methods by which they emerge, exist, expand, die, and repopulate. For the EZLN, while a specific physical site such as a mountain-top autonomous municipality may fail, another site expands as the mass of Indians simply reallocate their presence. In the rare instances when ELF cells have been penetrated, disrupted, and captured, network energies shift in new directions, a portion of which rallies to support the captured comrades. In this sense one of the most distinguishable features of these networks is their fluidity, their leaderlessness, and their rapid adaptability.

Notes

1 Though numerous illegalist anarchists are (in)famous due to their linkages to specific acts of political violence, the tradition includes many lesser known individuals. These include French illegalists Clément Duval, François Claudius Koenigstein (aka Ravachol), and Alexandre Jacon (aka Marius Jacon). Other noted illegalists include Italians Vittorio Pini, Gaetano Bresci, and Gino Lucetti; Spaniards including Buenaventura Durruti and Francisco Sabaté Llopart (aka El Quico); and Indian socialist-anarchist Bhagat Singh who played a major role in India's anti-colonial struggle.
2 The *Communero* (sometimes written as *Gran Comité Conmunero*) would issue the *Ley del Pueblo* [law of the people] in 1879, which, much like the EZLN declarations around 1994, called for the distribution of nationally-owned and privately-owned lands to landless Mexicans.
3 Louis Lingg committed suicide (10 November 1887) the day prior to his scheduled execution, while in police custody. He did this by igniting a blasting cap in his mouth, which had been smuggled into the prison. Four days prior, four IEDs were discovered in his cell.
4 Other known members of the Bonnot Gang include Jeanne Belardi, David Belonie, Jean De Boe, Édouard Carouy, Eugène Dieudonné, Anna Dondon, Antoine Gauzy, Pierre Jourdan, Berbe Leclech, Henriette Maîtrejean, Marius Metdge/Medge, Charles Reinart/Renard, Victor Kibalchich (aka Victor Serge), Alphonse Rodriguez, and Marie Vuillemin.
5 Galleanist anarchists of the time include Frank Abarno, Pietro Angelo, Gabriella Segata Antolini, Luigi Bacchetti, Mario Buda, Carmine Carbone, Andrea Ciofalo, Ferrucio Coacci, Emilio Coda, Alfredo Conti, Nestor Dondoglio (aka Jean Crones), Roberto Elia, Alfonso Fagotti, Luigi Falzini,

Frank Mandese, Riccardo Orciani, Nicola Recchi, Nicola Sacco, Andrea Salsedo, Giuseppe Sberna, Raffaele Schiavina, Carlo Valdinoci, and Bartolomeo Vanzetti.

6 In the modern internet age of internationally-distributed insurrectionary communiqués, one of the main Italian language hubs for such material is similarly named *Culmine* and is available at https://culmine.noblogs.org/.

7 For the purposes of differentiating the Informal Anarchist Federation from the Iberian Anarchist Federation, the former will be written as "FAI" and the latter as "F.A.I."

8 The AFL-CIO assembled between 25,000–50,000 street demonstrators against the WTO, probably few of whom identified as anti-authoritarian or anarchist.

9 Conservatively, between 1999–2001, there were black bloc actions in Seattle, WA (Nov 1999), Washington, DC (April 2000, Jan 2001), London, England (1999), New York, NY (May 2000), Windsor, Ontario (June 2000), Philadelphia, PA (Aug 2000), Los Angeles, CA (Aug 2000), Prague, Czech Republic (Sept 2000), Boston, MA (Oct 2000), St Louis, MO (Oct 2000), Montreal, Quebec (Oct 2000), Cincinnati, OH (Nov 2000), Quebec City, Quebec (April 2001), Gothenburg, Sweden (June 2001), and Genoa, Italy (July 2001).

10 According to a government sentencing memorandum (Immergut et al. 2007, 100, 110, 116, 124), Nathan Block, Joyanna Zacher, Suzanne Savoie, and Daniel McGowan participated in the N30 black bloc. This is confirmed by one former ELF cell member in a 2011 documentary film (Curry 2011).

11 This approach is used to describe, among others, the EZLN (e.g. Khasnabish 2008, 19–20).

3
Insurrection as a post-millennial, clandestine, network of cells

> Revolt needs everything: paper and books, arms and explosives, reflection and swearing, poison, daggers and arson. The only interesting question is how to combine them. (Anonymous 2001a, 29)

Is *insurrectionism* even anarchism?

Prior to developing the history of the modern insurrectionary subject in this chapter, it is necessary to consider the historical and ideological tradition it is being descriptively embedded within, and to decide if *insurrectionism* is indeed anarchist in any meaningful way. As insurrectionary theory is at odds with the notion of (capital I) Ideology, and is practiced with far more egoistic individualism then prefigurative collectivism, is it correct to portray insurrectionary anarchism as a strand within the larger anarchist tradition? Is insurrectionary theory and practice a branch from anarchism's aged tree, or is it something else entirely? If we examine the notions of anarchism offered by the highly influential agitprop collective CrimethInc. in what is likely their best known work, *Days of War Nights of Love*, the authors instruct the reader to not think of anarchism as a "word order" as one would Sovietism, Marxism, or Republicanism, but rather to "think of anarchism as an individual orientation to yourself and others, as a personal approach to life" (CrimethInc. Ex-Workers' Collective 2001, 34). Contemporary insurrectionists have repeated such charges, reminding us that Bonanno himself argued that "Anarchism isn't a definition that, once reached, can be guarded jealously ... safe and conserved" (Rodríguez 2011b). This highly open and individualistic approach to anarchism's orientation encourages one to "think for yourself", reject hierarchy, law, national authority, and domination and to oppose "governments, bureaucracies [and] police" (CrimethInc. Ex-Workers' Collective 2001, 34–35).

Throughout the nineteenth- and twentieth-century periods of anarcho-illegalism and propaganda of the deed, a history of attacks paved the way for the international, digitally linked networks of today. While large anarcho-syndicalist organizations such as the Industrial Workers of the World marched for labor in the twentieth century (to speak nothing of the Spanish Civil War), and mass-centric black blocs confronted delegates and police barricades a century later, anarchism has always shown a duality of large-scale, movement-centric convergences, and individualistic rage carried forth through spontaneous attack. There have always been those who sought to organize the peasants and build the workers' councils, just as there have always been those who chose to shoot the banker, bomb the President, and rob the rich to increase the social tension.

Noting this patterned dual history, anarchist theorist Murray Bookchin took on this question in a well-known essay titled, "Social Anarchism or Lifestyle Anarchism: An Unbridgeable Chasm." In it, Bookchin (1995) argues that for 200 years anarchism has wrestled with two tendencies, "a personalistic commitment to individual autonomy and a collectivist commitment to social freedom." The individualist anarchism that Bookchin describes is infused with notes of escapism, bohemianism, mystical primitivism, and is opposed to the social, movement-making and institution-building collectivism embodied in "classical anarchist" thinkers such as Peter Kropotkin and Pierre-Joseph Proudhon. In understanding this history, social movement anthropologists note that anarchists choosing to employ physical violence have chosen to do so outside of an organizational framework, often as individuals (Graeber 2009, 254), and in this sense, looking backwards, those who chose to "be done with waiting" (Bonanno 1977, chap. 11) are insurrectionary forebearers precisely because of their individualistic and anti-social nature. While not speaking of insurrectionary theory explicitly, Bookchin's portrayal of anti/non-social anarchism can be likened to the insurrectionary subject at hand, which we will now compare to "social" anarchism in the discussion that follows.

Tendencies towards *mass* have always been peppered with smaller formations, often engaging in the most militant forms of politics. Since the insurrectionary internationalization of bombs and broken windows is so unlike the mass-centric anarchism of 1920s labor agitation, or 1990s anti-globalization movements, one may begin to wonder how contemporary insurrectionary activity actually resembles *anarchism* in a wider sense. Moreover, as the insurrectionary project is boastfully "against ideology" and "anti-political," what makes its attachment to *anarchism* – a heavily political and ideological term – an apt descriptor?

Anarcho signposts

In order to evaluate if insurrectionary action shares enough with its predecessors to continue the utility of the nomenclature, it is helpful to examine conceptualizations of anarchism originating in the time period of increased insurrectionary attack. This discussion will be pursued through two arenas: the first empirical-historical, and the second ideological. Insurrectionary anarchism can be understood as a tendency within anarchism's larger history, sharing the framework's chief concern of the destruction of state and capitalism through direct action, voluntary association, horizontality, mutual aid, and illegalism. Drawing from poststructuralism and Queer theory, contemporary insurrectionism challenges power through its multifaceted manifestations, and seeks to target its direct embodiments when possible. In assessing how anarcho is anarcho-insurrectionary action, their targets of attack – including police infrastructure, banks, and corporate property – demonstrate how the clandestine networks materialize their critique of the existent. The pattern of attacks followed by communiqués externalizes and clarifies the cells' critiques, demonstrating their analytical and epistemological roots in classical anarchism.

In a 2016 communiqué authored by a Grecian CCF/FAI cell, the authors clearly identify the efforts of these collectivities as within the anarchist tradition, writing:

> Anarcho-nihilism, anarcho-individualism and in general the more offensive anarchist heresies, are not "accidents" in the history of anarchy, but on the contrary, they are the most promoted parts of it.
>
> These trends can now constitute an autonomous political movement ... [A movement] that recognizes the political kinship of the groups and individuals who take part and meet in 5 basic characteristics: First of all, we are anarchists regardless of our particular mentions (nihilists, insurgents, individualists etc) ... We organize based on aformalism and coordination of groups and individuals of political kinship. Secondly ... we attack with actions against the state of officials and their structures, but at the same time, we want our words and deeds to blow up the social relationships that make acceptable and sometimes procreate the authorities in our everyday lives. Thirdly, we support the International of Anarchists Federation. We desire that our hostilities in the interior of the states we are living in to be connected as moments of an overall anarchist war internationally. We are exchanging ideas, we are sharing experiences, we are creating relationships of solidarity and we pursue the constitution of an international anarchist federation where the fragments of an explosion in Santiago, Chile, will reach to Athens and then multiply ... Fourthly, we do not give up on our imprisoned comrades ... Finally, we promote the diversity in anarchist actions ... The authentic diversity of the struggle essentially has to support and promote the armed clash with the system ... It is the rite of passage from theory to action, from the serendipitous to the organized, from the fortuitous to the planned. (CCF: Urban Guerilla Cell/FAI 2016)

This lengthy communiqué establishes five points of affinity for identification with the "anarchist urban guerrillas" (i.e. insurrectionary anarchists) and, in doing so, further clarifies the borderlands of an insurrectionary tendency, and a politics of identification. Similar attempts, such as Sasha K's (2001) "Some Notes on Insurrectionary Anarchism," focus on identifying insurrectionary commonalities. Despite noting that "these notes are in no way a closed or finished product" (K 2001), the author offers eight unifying points of identification based around notions of attack, self-management, illegality, informality, individualism, and other recurring insurrectionary themes. Other thinkers have spoken in similar terms, such as imprisoned militant Nikos Romanos (2016) who noted "three principles that shape this informal anarchist platform ... autonomy, diversity of means of struggle, and coordination, always in the content of informal organization." These ideological signposts, as well as numerous others, are explored at length in Chapter 6.

In the Introduction to his book, *Anarchy Alive!*, Uri Gordon (2008, 3) offers a model for understanding anarchism "not in terms of its content, but in terms of what *kind of thing* anarchism is." Gordon suggests that anarchism should be thought of as a social movement, political culture, and a collection of ideas. He goes on to explain that as a social movement it is characterized by "dense networks of individuals, affinity groups and collectives which communicate and coordinate intensively, sometimes across the globe, and generate innumerable direct actions and sustained projects" (Gordon 2008, 3–4). Certainly the insurrectionary networks fit this definition in spirit, yet, as a global milieu, it refuses the collective imposition of a stable definition. This malleable delineation of collective identity facilitates attackers' use of new forms of praxis, which are subsequently evaluated via digital networks and either found to be *within* the insurrectionary logic or outside of it. Insurrectionary anarchism may be most anarchistic through what Gordon calls "culture." As a political culture, Gordon (2008, 4) notes that anarchism is based around, among other things, "a shared repertoire of political action based on direct action ... shared forms of organizing – decentralized, horizontal and consensus-seeking" as well as shared (sub)cultural expressions in the arts, diet and dress.

Insurrectionary anarchists do in fact share and co-constitute such a "shared repertoire" including through their use of specific websites, their deployment of recurring imagery and slogans, their remixing of moniker brands, and their memorialization of famed individuals – typically captured comrades and those killed in battle. Gordon also notes that a major feature among anarchists is a "shared political language that emphasizes resistance to capitalism, the state, patriarchy and more generally to hierarchy and domination" (Gordon 2008, 4). This shared language and discourse is a main premise of this book and its recurrence in the insurrectionary milieu is explored at length. Finally, within Gordon's three manners of anarchism, we come to anarchism as a collection of ideas. In the same way that I argue that insurrectionary action is distinguishable through its shared terminology and discursive deployment, these are reflected in the tendency's collectively penned collection of ideas – those in favor of attack and against mediation, and those offering the temporary, informal, opaque, and clandestine networks while rejecting movements of individuals measured in mass and through public, aboveground collective action.

Perhaps the best evaluative tool for maintaining or abandoning the use of anarchism when describing insurrectionary action is Cindy Milstein's book *Anarchism and Its Aspirations* (2010) published by the Institute for Anarchist Studies, an anarcho-think tank and scholarly hub. Milstein's book constitutes the best contemporary primer on anarchism written by one of the movements' clearest authors and strongest rhetoricians. Because of Milstein's ability to encapsulate this particularly modern decade of anarchism, typified as the time between the WTO protests in 1999 and the book's publication, it is an especially well situated tool for the task of evaluation. Milstein (2010, 1:13) suggests that anarchism can be understood as a "dual project: the abolition of domination and hierarchical forms of social organization, or power-over social relations, and their replacement with horizontal versions ... a free society of free individuals." While the focus of insurrectionary action is *not* the development of these horizontal counter-institutions and services, Milstein goes on to argue that anarchism – as an inherently freedom-seeking framework – will change over time as manifestations of new unfreedoms are unearthed. Therefore, like Sasha K, Milstein discusses anarchism through its eight most prominent, unifying aspirations: "liberty and freedom," "equality of unequals," "from each, to each," "mutual aid," "ecological orientation," "voluntary association and accountability," "joy and spontaneity," and "unity in diversity."

While a point-by-point comparison is unwarranted, examining Milstein's usage of these concepts, insurrectionary action meets nearly all of the definitional checks. Insurrectionary anarchism is most certainly based around classical anarchism's notion of direct action organized horizontally and autonomously in informal, voluntary, free associations. Insurrectionary networks are characteristic of a manner of collective individualism, where individualists assemble in these temporary structureless bodies for the purposes of mutual aid – often aid required to carry out an attack. However, insurrectionary practice diverges from Milstein's ideas by avoiding prefigurative imagining and proscriptive formulations. Milstein (2010, 1:111) notes that prefiguration, a central feature of anarchist praxis, is "the very strength of direct action, where the means themselves are understood to intimately relate to the ends." Now while Milstein's anarchism would feature participatory decision making to prefigure a decentralized, horizontal community, insurrectionary methods do not inherently imagine and prepare for a post-state, post-capitalist society in any meaningful way.

Insurrectionary action is based in the rejection of the present far more than it is a revolutionary visioning for the future which is central to Milstein's democracy-laden anarchism.

Based on the discussions provided by CrimethInc., Gordon, and Milstein it appears as if insurrectionary action, while diverging from classical anarchism at times, is similar enough to warrant a shared discussion. Not only does it resemble the anarchism of Bakunin and his "classical" ilk, but it also resembles the modern infusion of poststructuralism into anarchism, often termed post-anarchism (e.g. Rousselle and Evren 2011). In a nod to this comingling of analyses, insurrectionary anarchism understands power through a language that both Bakunin and Foucault would have likely found familiar. In a lengthy communiqué entitled "Beyond Right and Wrong" (2015) authored by a cell of the CCF-FAI/IRF, the authors define power as "a social relation, a social hierarchical organization model, a way of life management." The authors explain that through this diffuse analysis they seek to challenge both the physical agents of hierarchical power, but also the broader relationships of domination of coercion. The authors write:

> Power, however, has proven to be more like [a] Hydra. This is why, while our armed targeting gathers its firepower on the heads of the managers of power and their uniformed mercenaries, our words seeks to blow up the social relationships that give rise to power ... [we] hit both the heart of the beast (armed attacks against the officials of the power) and the veins of the social machine (criticism and rejection of the submission mindset). (CCF-FAI/IRF 2015)

Such a dualistic framing of power – as both a physicality embodied in police and politicians as well as an ideological social order to organize society – is reflected in anarchism's focus on prefiguration and lived praxis, as well as its varied strategies for building horizontal power and attacking that which is hierarchical.

Therefore, the insurrectionary position, though in tension with some aspects of anarchism (e.g. prefiguration), can be understood as emanating from a shared history of critiquing, challenging, and attacking power at large, and focusing their strikes on the state and capital.

A modern history of insurrectionary attack

> While each of the [armed revolutionary] organizations ... is deserving of in-depth study and analysis, only a scant handful have thus far received it. The matter is by no means of mere academic interest. Only through excavation of their histories in substantial detail can lessons of their

much-varied experiences be extracted, their errors corrected, and a better praxis of armed struggle in the metropoles achieved. (Churchill 2009, 5)

The following historical account will attempt to develop the record of a social movement that is still in a formative stage. Because we are denied the luxury of historical hindsight, this account will inherently be incomplete. Combatants written about in the present tense may be captured or killed before these words reach the reader. Buildings will burn, laws will be passed, and fighters will be jailed. All of these events collectively constitute the history of modern insurrectionary warfare, and while one aims to present the most complete historical account possible, as networks are in constant flux and the conflict is ongoing, one must proceed with an acknowledgement that despite best efforts, much of this history is yet to be written. In order to connect the various configurations of post-millennial, insurrectionary resistance, we will explore three of its most identifiable components, the FAI, CCF, and emergent networks in Mexico. Following these network-specific histories, this chapter will explore a case study of an internationalized call to action. In exploring this single campaign, one can begin to understand the process through which monikers deterritorialize, expand, and diffuse.

The Informal Anarchist Federation

One becomes part of FAI-IRF only at the very moment he/she acts and strikes claiming as FAI, then everyone returns to their own projects, their own individual perspective, within a black international that includes a variety of practices, all aggressive and violent. (Cospito 2014)

An idea that started its journey ten years ago from Italy from the brothers and sisters of the Italian [FAI] and today is stronger than ever. [FAI] definitely is not a theoretic game of harmless words and symbols, but an idea to live dangerously and anarchically with all our senses, without dead time and cowardly excuses ... The Informal Anarchist Federation ([FAI]) consists of an international anarchist formation between individuals and cells that speak different languages, but however pursue to express through their actions, their common desire for the anarchist revolution. This is why the translations of texts and communiques that circulate in the circles of [FAI] are of great value in order for one to meet the ideas of the other. (The Imprisoned Members of the Conspiracy of Cells of Fire 2011)

Though a variety of direct attack networks, monikers, and individual cells have emerged since the post-millennial reinvigoration of the urban guerrilla, the strategy and momentum of direct, anti-state attack was carried forth most notably by the Informal Anarchist Federation [*Federazione Anarchica Informale*]. The FAI has been linked to attacks as early as 1999, but its current, internationalized, adoptable-moniker form, emerged around 2004 in the Italian city of Bologna. In 1999, the network sent mail bombs to the Greek embassy in Italy, a tourism office in Madrid, and a branch of Citibank in Barcelona (Hanrahan 2013). Subsequently, pre-2003 FAI bombs targeted newspapers, churches, courts, police, prisons, and other targets located in Western Europe, largely in Spain and Italy.

In the final days of 2003 (29 December), two letter bombs were mailed to Europol – a Europe-wide police data center – headquartered in The Hague, and the head of the European Central Bank, Jean-Claude Trichet as part of the FAI's "Operation Santa Claus." Technicians defused the Europol bomb, and German police discovered the IED sent to Trichet in the bank's mailroom. Both bombs were postmarked in Bologna. One day prior, a third mail bomb exploded at the Bologna home of Romano Prodi, the head of the European Commission, and former Prime Minister (1996–1998, 2006–2008). According to FAI communiqués, this was the third bomb to target Prodi that week (BBC 2003b). Two previous explosions occurred in trash receptacles, and the third IED, the one delivered with the mail, was assembled inside a book and addressed to Prodi's wife. The book bomb, according to Prodi, "[produced] a big flame but without an explosion" (BBC 2003a).

The next day, a fourth letter bomb was mailed, this time to the headquarters of Eurojust, a European policing agency. The IED did not explode and, according to officials, was the work of the same network (BBC 2003c). Additional IEDs, also originating in Bologna, were sent to the president and vice-president of the European People's Party, as well as Gary Titley, leader of UK Labour and British member of the European Parliament. Titley called the bombings an unjustified "attack on democracy ... [likely] from an Italian anarchist group" (BBC 2004). In response to the six mailed IEDs, the Italian city of Bologna halted the delivery of parcels from the region to European institutions such as European Union administrative bodies (BBC 2003d).

The FAI (2003) explained their motivation in a communiqué entitled "Open Letter to the Anarchist and Anti-Authoritarian Movement." This document serves to announce the FAI to the world, to begin to develop its methodology for attack, and to communicate with sympathetic allies in the producing of future attacks. According to some historical accounts (Cospito 2014), the letter is a signpost marking the real emergence of the FAI global network. In the text, the network claims responsibility for the attacks, calling their targets the "repressive apparatus that plays the democratic farce and that will bring the main characters and institutions to the new European order" (FAI 2003). The attackers quantify their enemy as "the various police departments ... a prison system ... bureaucrats and politicians," proclaiming:

> Attack and destroy the responsible for repression and exploitation!
> Attack and destroy prisons, banks, courts and police stations!
> Revolt is contagious and can be reproduced!
> Social war against capital and the State! (FAI 2003)

The FAI describe their network as "a federation formed either by groups of action or by single individuals, in order to go beyond the limits implied in single projects and to experiment the real potentialities of informal organization" (2003, 3). The communiqué goes on to describe the network's interpretation of "informal," "anarchist," and "federation" and discusses strategy, organization, and other questions of practicality.

Following the Bologna-based bombing campaign, the FAI expanded, forming components such the "Armed Cells for International Solidarity Brigade" which continued to mail explosives (2 April 2004, 10–11 December 2004), the "Metropolitan Cells" which detonated IEDs in Milan (29 October 2004), and numerous joint formations, such as the FAI/"July 20 Brigade" and the FAI /"Crafts and Fire Cooperative," which detonated IEDs targeting police and prisons (3 March 2005). These cells operated in the Italian cities of Bologna, Genoa, Rome, and Milan, and were responsible for at least 16 explosive attacks, with security sources estimating the network's composition to be 50–250 individuals (Marone 2014). According to pro-FAI movement historians, between December 2003 and December 2006, the network carried out "7 revolutionary campaigns ... [and] 30 incendiary and explosive attacks on things and people" (Anonymous 2006). These bombs targeted courts, police buildings, and individual officials such as mayors and corporate directors.

Years later, the FAI would prove to be longlasting, sending additional parcel bombs including:

- 15 December 2009: Director of Center for Identification and Expulsion, an immigration detention center, in Gradisca d'Isonzo, Italy.
- 16 December 2009: Bocconi University in Milan.
- ~28 March 2010: Headquarters of the Northern League, a right-wing political party in Milan. The device injured a postal worker.
- 23 December 2010: Embassy of Greece in Paris.
- 23 December 2010: Embassies of Chile and Switzerland in Rome. These devices injured two.
- 30 March 2011: Nuclear company Swissnuclear in Olten, Switzerland. This device injured two.
- 31 March 2011: Barracks of Italian paratroopers deploying to Afghanistan located in Livorno, Italy. This attack injured one soldier severely.

- 7 December 2011: The Chief Executive of Deutsche Bank. The device was intercepted in Frankfurt.
- ~9 December 2011: Josef Ackermann, director of Equitalia state tax collection agency in Rome. This attack seriously injured Ackerman.
- 9 April 2013: *La Stampa* newspaper in Turin, Italy.
- 10 April 2013: Europol offices in Brescia, Italy.

Of its scores of attacks, the most infamous is likely that which occurred on 7 May 2012. On this date, a cell of the FAI was responsible for the non-fatal shooting (i.e. "kneecapping")[1] of Roberto Adinolfi, the 56-year-old chief executive of Ansaldo Nucleare, an Italian nuclear company affiliated with defense/aerospace firm Finmeccanica. The masked attackers fired three times, shooting Adinolfi in the knees from atop a motorcycle, as the target left his Genoa home. The shooting of Adinolfi was claimed via a four-page communiqué – as the "Olga Nucleus"[2] (2012) cell of the FAI-IRF – received on 11 May 2012 by an Italian newspaper. A year after the shooting, the FAI named the attack as part of "Operation Hunt the Spy" (Hornby and Rossi 2013) linking it to the 2013 bombings of *La Stampa* and Europol. The three attacks were rhetorically linked in the communiqué, noting:

> [Europol] provides the forces of order with equipment such as microchips, micro-cameras and other technological wickedness ... [and] "La Stampa" [is] always ready to corroborate the frame-ups of the carabinieri [Italian military police] and police, especially when they strike those who are at war against the state. (FAI/IRF Damiano Bolano Cell 2013)

In September 2012, two male individuals, 35-year-old Nicola Gai and 46-year-old Alfredo Cospito, were arrested in Turin and linked to the crime via surveillance footage, wiretaps, and textual analysis of the communiqué. The two individuals were convicted and imprisoned for a combined sentence of 20 years. Their sentence was assigned a *"finalità di terrorismo"* [purpose of terrorism] condition due to the anti-state politics of the shooting.

With similar regularity to its IEDs, FAI cells have used timed improvised *incendiary* devices (IIDs) such as the ones that ignited under the cars of Lord Mayor of Bristol, Geoff Gollop, and Tory Councilor, Kevin Quartley (7 November 2011), claimed by the FAI's "Class Terror" (2011) cell. Despite being conservative functionaries within the British state, the two men expressed shock that they were targeted. Lord Gollop stated, "I am at a total loss why anyone would want to do this. I have got absolutely no idea what the motive could possibly be" (*The Bristol Post* 2011). Councilor Quartley expressed similar sentiments stating, "I've got no idea why this has happened" (*The Bristol Post* 2011).

While the FAI was established in Italy, like other moniker-based networks it was quickly exported as an internationalist model. In June 2012, police arrested eight individuals in Italy, one in Switzerland, and one in Germany, all accused of affiliation with the FAI/IRF. In at least one case, an Italian judge, issuing warrants, charged the accused with "subversion, terrorist conspiracy and international terrorism" (Hooper 2012). State officials noted presumed links between the arrested FAI members and the Greek CCF. As the imprisoned members of the Greek network stated in their letter to the Italian FAI, "The Informal Anarchist Federation travels over borders and cities, carrying with it the momentum of a lasting anarchist insurrection" (Ekonomidou et al. 2012). By 2014, cells of the FAI had claimed attacks in a variety of countries beyond Italy including Argentina, Bolivia, Chile, Greece, Indonesia, Mexico, the Netherlands, Peru, Russia, Spain, the UK, and the US. Also, while the FAI name would be combined in endless combinations with the CCF, IRF, and others, it also was regularly used in conjunction with the ALF/ELF monikers, such as an attack in Moscow, Russia (~21 February 2012) where a group ignited two IIDs to burn cellular phone towers in an area popular with hunters.

Around September 2011, two Italian FAI nodes operating since 2004 – the "Artisans Cooperative of Fire and Similar (occasionally spectacular)" cell and the "20th July Brigade" – released a lengthy statement entitled, "Do Not Say That We Are Few" (2011). In this document – termed a "contribution to discussing communication, organization and armed struggle at the dawn of a new era" (2011) – the authors claim responsibility for several mail bombs, express solidarity with the CCF, and discuss an international campaign of insurrectionary direct action. The anonymous authors speak of the deterritorialization of their network, writing:

> Many things have happened since we launched the proposal for an "Informal Anarchist Federation". Today, thanks to the sisters and brothers of the "Conspiracy of Cells of Fire", who have re-launched it, the "FAI/International Revolutionary Front", the "FAI/Global Network", the "International Network of Action and Solidarity", the "Informal Anarchist Federation–Global Network" has become reality with their one thousand names. A reality that needs to grow up especially now through the instrument of informal organization on a worldly level and thanks to a federation of action groups. Dozens and dozens of cells, nuclei, movements, individual comrades, united by a clear and strong horizontal and widespread pact of mutual aid, wage war on the existent in a chaotic and destructive way. (FAI-IRF Artisans Cooperative of Fire and Similar (occasionally spectacular) and FAI-IRF 20th July Brigade 2011)

Following this, the statement details the names and national locations of 36 cells spread across nine countries.[3]

Following the shooting of Adinolfi, and in response to repeated attacks targeting Equitalia – the Italian tax collection agency – the Italian Ministry of the Interior reassigned 18,000 officers to "security detail" (Delaney 2012) and carried out a series of police raids, arresting eight and serving warrants to already imprisoned (and infamous) anarchist militants Gabriel Pombo Da Silva[4] and Marco Camenisch.[5] Since its emergence, there have been at least nine individuals (Loadenthal 2015, 465–467) arrested in connection to FAI attacks, though in general, the network has been resistant to disruption. Because the FAI's attacks have tended to avoid injury, the network's actions have been consistently "underestimated" (Marone 2014) by both police and academics. In a report to the Italian parliament by the Ministry of the Interior, the FAI is described as the "most dangerous form of domestic non-jihadist terrorism in the country" (Marone 2014), yet Muslim non-state actors still receive far more "focused intensity" (Winfield and Gatopoulos 2010) from police. Nonetheless, according to Europol, "attacks by far-left and anarchist militant groups jumped 43 percent in 2009 [compared to 2008]," and have doubled since 2007 (Winfield and Gatopoulos 2010).

The Conspiracy of Cells of Fire

> In 2008, there were very few people in the United States who read the communiqués from the Conspiracy of Cells of Fire. At the time, communiqués for low level vandalism, sabotage and a few arsons had just started being issued from various parts of North America and these were only disseminated through a few sources on the internet. But while the gringos were busy burning some trucks against the Olympics or paint bombing some condos, something else was transpiring across the Atlantic, at the end of the Mediterranean. A group of people, large in number, chaotic in nature and diffuse in scope, began to increase their attacks against capitalism, its police and its military. They had a proclivity for using fire and explosives in their actions. They loved fire so much that they referred to themselves as the singular group called the Conspiracy of Cells of Fire. (CCF 2011, 2)

Rivaling the prominence of the FAI, the Greek network known as the Conspiracy of Cells of Fire[6] [Συνωμοσία των Πυρήνων της Φωτιάς], has paved the way for an era of insurrectionary attack (Schwarz 2011). Though the FAI has older roots, the near celebrity status of the CCF has allowed the insurrectionary-nihilist network to rapidly internationalize. Besides obvious ideological, organizational, tactical, and strategic similarities, the FAI and CCF have also been linked via police investigations. In June 2012, Italian police investigating FAI bombings included at least six Greek members of the CCF, calling the CCF-FAI link a "proven connection" (Marone 2014).

The CCF emerged on 21 January 2008,[7] when cell members carried out near simultaneous arson attacks targeting "4 cars at a Porsche dealership, 3

Eurobanks, 16 cars and a motorcycle at a car exhibition, a Piraeus bank, a Citibank, a PV Motors dealership, and a public power company crane vehicle" (CCF 2011, 4). The IIDs were built from gas canisters, a method that CCF cells would repeat throughout the years. The origins of the CCF align with the more generalized rise in leftist militancy seen in Greece following the shooting death of Alexandros Grigoropoulos (6 December 2008) by police, which led to a wave of "rioting, street violence and small-scale terrorism" (Kassimeris 2013). The police's killing of 15-year-old Grigoropoulos sparked weeks of rioting, occurring in conjunction with increased police repression focused on Athens's Exarchia neighborhood – a semi-autonomous neighborhood in Athens made up of a variety of squats, social centers, and political projects and known to be extremely hostile to police presence. Nationally, the Greek state also experienced a steep economic downturn that led to a more popularized opposition to the state, which was seen as "[serving] the interests only of the rich" (Maltezou and Babington 2013). Moreover, with the rise of explicitly right-wing fascistic parties such as Golden Dawn, renewed violence between such groups and leftist movements has become commonplace. For example, two members of Golden Dawn were shot (1 November 2013) and killed, and a third man injured, while standing outside a party office in Athens (Ekathimerini 2013). They were shot by two assailants who arrived on a motorcycle, dismounted, left their helmets on and then opened fire, releasing at least twelve rounds from a semi-automatic pistol and hitting the three men in the chest and head. The attack is assumed to have been carried out by leftist urban guerrillas including Revolutionary Struggle, the Sect of Revolutionaries, and/or the CCF.

One month after the initial attacks (20 February 2008), an IED detonated at the law firm of former Minister of Justice Anastasios Papaligouras injuring one employee. That evening (21 February 2008), cell members carried out a series of separate attacks throughout the Attica region. These attacks targeted eight banks, four luxury vehicles, and an insurance company. A few weeks later, cell members in Thessaloniki set fire to a government building and three security vehicles (19 March 2008). In April (9 April 2008), in solidarity with prisoners of the Italian FAI, CCF cells in two cities attacked an Italian educational institution and an Italian car exposition, destroying 35 cars. In July 2008, CCF carried out a series of attacks targeting police motorcycles (9 July 2008), diplomatic vehicles of the Moroccan embassy (10 July), three banks (10 July), and an office of New Democracy (15 July).

In mid-September (13 September 2008), at least 15 members of the CCF, in a rare semi-public action, attacked a Thessaloniki police station. The guerrillas threw Molotov cocktails from their motorcycles, igniting two police cars, 20 police motorcycles, and portions of the station's exterior. No CCF members were arrested in the attack. Later that month (25 September 2008), CCF cells used gas canister IIDs to set fire to diplomatic vehicles belonging to the Czech Republic and Italy as well as luxury cars, private businesses, and three banks. Between 2008 and 2010 regular attacks would continue to utilize IIDs and IEDs to target government buildings and other property, banks, the homes of current and former officials, press offices, car dealerships and vehicles, and a variety of private businesses. While many attacks struck functional property of the state (e.g. police vehicles, embassies) and capital (e.g. bank ATMs, car dealerships) other attacks focused on more symbolic targets.

In November 2010, CCF deployed a series of 14 mail bombs targeting state officials. Packages were sent to the Mexican Embassy in Athens and Eurojust in the Netherlands. The embassy package reached its target and injured an employee while the Eurojust IED was located and destroyed by police. Two men – Panagiotis Argyros, 22 years old, and 24-year-old Gerasimos Tsakalos – were arrested in connection with the attacks. When detained, the men were found to be in possession of two additional mail bombs addressed to French President Sarkozy and the Belgian Embassy. The suspects were wearing wigs and carrying 9mm pistols. One of the men was also wearing a bulletproof vest. The day after their arrest, another wave of mail bombs was discovered. Two bombs exploded outside of the Swiss Embassy and the Russian Embassy. A third IED was located and destroyed en route to an office of Europol. Three additional IEDs were also destroyed after being dispatched to the embassies of Chile, Germany, and Bulgaria. Two more IEDs were located and destroyed. One device reached the offices of Italian Prime Minister Berlusconi and another reached the offices of German Chancellor Merkel. The devices caused no injuries. The Greek response to the wave of attacks was to suspend all international airmail for 48 hours (3–4 November 2010).

In late December 2010, a month after the international mail bomb campaign, CCF cells in Athens returned to action and detonated an IED attached to a motorcycle, damaging a courthouse. The device caused no injuries after the bomber made a warning call to police, who evacuated the area. Less than five months after the motorcycle attack, in May 2011, Athenian police attempted to arrest suspected members of the CCF. Upon confrontation, the two suspects opened fire and injured two officers. In mid 2010, the CCF saw its methods and name exported from Greece to the Netherlands in a series of attacks targeting Rabobank, a Dutch, multinational banking and financial service company. According to a communiqué claiming responsibility for three arsons, the authors state that Rabobank was chosen due to its connections to the weapons industry. The authors align themselves with an international campaign of clandestine direct action targeting arms military-linked companies such as Royal Dutch Shell, ING Group, ABN AMRO Bank N.V., and Randstad Holding NV. In the communiqué for the Dutch arsons, the authors dedicate the fires to "our brothers of the prisoner's cell of the members of Conspiracy of Cells of Fire and the oppressed people of the world." In the text, the authors claim responsibility for three arsons (June 2010–February 2011) of Rabobank's high-rise offices in the Netherlands and the hacking of a corporate website. The communiqué is signed, "Conspiracy of Cells of Fire, Dutch Cell" (2011). In the self-assessment zine authored by imprisoned members of the CCF, the collective notes this adopted name stating:

> ... any comrade who agrees ... with the [aforementioned] three key points ... [can] use the name Fire Cells Conspiracy in connection with the autonomous cell she is a part of. Just like the Dutch comrades who, without us knowing one another personally but within the framework of consistency between discourse and practice, attacked the infrastructure of domination (arson and cyber attacks against Rabobank) and claimed responsibility as the Fire Cells Conspiracy (Dutch Cell). (G. Tsakalos et al. 2012, 14)

Back in Greece, on 7 June 2013, a one kilogram, dynamite-based IED exploded from underneath the BMW of Maria Stefi, director of an Athenian prison where CCF comrades were detained. The CCF claimed the bombing the following day. Earlier in 2013, the various Grecian cells of the CCF claimed responsibility for the bombing of a shopping mall, additional bombings targeting homes and offices of government and media officials, as well as the drive-by shooting of an office of Prime Minister Antonis Samaras. According to one police study, there were 527 bombings in 2012, and 254 during the first six months of 2013. The source attributes the majority of these attacks to "anarchist or leftist 'anti-establishment' groups" (Maltezou and Babington 2013). Though not all of these bombings are explicitly linked to the CCF, according to police the network has carried out about 150 "criminal acts" 2009–2013 (Maltezou and Babington 2013), typified by small IEDs built inside pressure cookers. During this time, at least 30 individuals have been arrested in connection to CCF activity. According to one deploring account of the perpetuators, the activists are described as breaking from the traditional utopianism of Marxism, and instead are "educated, disaffected ... 'nihilist[s]' ... [who] care little about ideology" (Maltezou and Babington 2013).

During a brief period (2012–2014), the various formations of the CCF have been involved in at least four trials, linking them to particular crimes. The first case, known as the Halandri Case, was instrumental in altering the method of attack employed by clandestine guerrillas as explained by imprisoned members of the CCF who write:

> [The Halandri Case] represents a decisive point in the trajectory of the new urban guerrilla war ... About two years had passed since the appearance of the Conspiracy of Cells of Fire and – more generally – the new

anarchist urban guerrilla warfare ... anarchist groups engaged in propaganda by the deed were collaborating with one another in some cases, coordinating arson rampages on a national level. In many of the texts/communiqués accompanying those attacks, a new perception was being documented, settling the crosshairs of its critique on social inertia, people's passivity, and the complicit silence that allowed power to define our lives.

In parallel, and for the first time in Greece, words and concepts like anarcho-individualism, nihilism, and antisocial anarchy were escaping the immobility of theoretical texts and seeking their place within the communiqués of practice ... Meanwhile, the Conspiracy of Cells of Fire shifted from arsons to the strategy of placing explosive devices in churches, politicians' homes, and ministries. (Economidou et al. 2012)

Following the Halandri Case, three CCF "members" – Gerasimos Tsakalos, Panagiotis Argyrou, and Harris Hatzimichelakis – were tried for mailing IEDs. Later, other conspirators were connected to "250 attacks" (The imprisoned comrades of the CCF FAI/IRF 2013) and tried. Lastly, in July 2013, Andreas Tsavdaridis was tried for a mail bomb attack targeting Dimitris Horianopoulos, former commander of Greece's anti-terrorist division, as part of the "Phoenix Project" campaign.

From prison, many CCF members have continued to remain active, frequently issuing theoretical, strategic and organizational texts, often as a so-called "imprisoned members cell." In one such communication issued May 2012 and entitled "Bullets of Words for the Bullets of the FAI/IRF," ten imprisoned guerrillas used the text to praise the shooting of Adinolfi, whom they call "a high priest of the new totalitarianism of science and technology imperatives" (Ekonomidou et al. 2012). The authors speak of expanding the practice of armed struggle and state, "The practice of armed attacks was, is and will be an integral part of the new anarchist urban guerrilla warfare" (Ekonomidou et al. 2012).

The CCF has been integral in furthering the conversational, call-and-response nature of the global insurrectionary network. For example, in a CCF communiqué the authors write:

We do not share our choices only by speaking and writing texts against the state and its society but also when we offer each other possible practical ways, to make our theory practice. This is why we propose to the comrades of the FAI-IRF that we proceed to the publication of manuals which describe i.e. the way to construct an explosive mechanism, the wiring of a time bomb, the assembling of a parcel bomb, the use of a home-made system of time-delaying in incendiary attacks, the strengthening of the destructive power of a molotov, the synthesis and mixtures of ingredients for the creation of explosive materials ... [and] the chaotic arts of sabotage ... from the destruction of cameras, the blocking of ATMs and the construction of home-made smoke bombs up to burgling and stealing cars and motorbikes and the conservation and use of weapons. (CCF-FAI/IRF Imprisoned Members Cell 2012, 43)

In response to this call, a group calling itself "CCF-FAI/IRF International sector for spreading heretical arts (occasionally spectacular) of sabotage" (2014) published a seven-page manual detailing the construction of parcel bombs from easily available materials, addressing the manual to "all anarchists of praxis, nihilists, anarchists individualists, anticivilization." Prior to this, another collective, described as "siblings unknown to us who share the mutiny of FAI/IRF comrades" (CCF-FAI/IRF International sector for spreading heretical arts (occasionally spectacular) of sabotage 2014, 1) had published another guide to IIDs/IEDs in response to the CCF call. Though estimating the size and activity of a clandestine, non-membership based network is rather difficult, according to one study, the CCF networks involved at least 60 "militants and sympathizers ... [and] 15 safe houses" responsible for 220 attacks prior to June 2014 (Kassimeris 2016, 4).

The example of the CCF and its internationalization is meant to highlight the network's success in expanding the scope of its struggle. Its ability to successfully produce attacks, avoid mass arrest, and maintain an international discourse of resistance has had a wide impact on all of the cells and networks that followed. Not only are the arrested members of CCF held up as martyrs, but their continued involvement with the international insurrectionary network (largely through letters penned in prison) has furthered the development of an insurrectionary strategy and method that is still ongoing. The announcement of CCF cells in Mexico, the Netherlands, and other locales carried forth the FAI's encouragement for local groupings to join the battle and, through the CCF's sustained propaganda, adherents are able to include even imprisoned members in the development and spreading of the Black International.

The Mexican networks

Beginning around 2010, a sudden surge of insurrectionary-styled, clandestine guerrilla networks emerged in Mexico and launched a series of attacks on the state and capital. While a complete chronology and historical accounting of this movement is beyond the scope of this book, a brief review is warranted. Within Mexico, attacks have been claimed under a variety of the commonly occurring monikers including CCF, ELF, FAI, and so on. To trace a single example of internationalizing monikers, we turn towards the emergence of a Mexican tendency linking CCF and the FAI. According to an inter-movement, self-narrative account authored by the "Mexican Fire Cells Conspiracy/Informal Anarchist Federation" (2011), "[On] September 15 [2011] The Conspiracy of Cells of Fire (CCF) faction of the Mexican Informal Anarchist Federation (FAI-M) is formed by affinity groups and like-minded people in several Mexican states." The following day (16 September 2011), the CCF/FAI-M "carries out three simultaneous arsons ... Liberatory fire destroys merchandise, as flames consume Textiles Suburbia, CV Directo, and TF Victor" (Mexican Fire Cells Conspiracy/FAI 2011). From there the network engaged in frequent arson attacks and, in less than two months, set fire to sites including a warehouse, an airport staff training school, two Walmarts, a shopping mall, a lumber warehouse, and at least four other businesses. From the CCF's Greek roots and those of the FAI found in Italy, it is notable that such a formation occurred so far away, and in such a culturally different venue as Mexico. The development of this new network is reflective of national tendencies, wherein Mexico becomes a site for a renewal of militant actions and the fostering of newly lethal tendencies.

Beyond the rapid expansion of CCF/FAI-M, Mexico also saw the development of nationally-restricted networks, two of which will be examined below. This is not to discount the actions of a variety of other clandestine attackers, but rather to discuss in greater detail two such networks that display interesting rhetoric, strategies, and methods. The following accounting of history will focus on two district networks, that of the Práxedis G. Guerrero[8] Autonomous Cells for Immediate Revolution (CARI-PGG), and Individualists Tending Towards the Wild (ITS). While, ideologically, the former mirrors the more traditional approach of Western European anarcho-guerrillas such as CCF and FAI, the ITS network resembles a newly emergent praxis borrowing from anarchism's primitivist and anti-technology tendencies, exacted through an atypically-violent pattern of attack. ITS and CARI-PGG's predominant deployment of IEDs make them an apt network to study as their tactical and strategic patterns fall well outside of those seen in other insurrectionary networks. In short, these networks' goals are often to kill and maim individuals associated with targeted institutions, while typical insurrectionary attack aims to destroy symbolic property while avoiding individual targeting of persons for injury and death.

Práxedis G. Guerrero Autonomous Cells for Immediate Revolution

While possibly being one of the shorter lived insurrectionary moniker associations, CARI-PGG emerged in late 2010 and would carry out attacks for only three years. In the early months of 2010, a series of communiqués were circulated on the traditional, English-language network hubs claiming responsibility for the machine gunning of police vehicles, the erection of

3.1 CARI-PGG's logo included in communiqués

flaming street barricades, Molotov cocktails thrown at banks, and the bombing of a McDonalds. By October 2010, the first stable, repeated moniker appears – CARI-PGG – though the group reports it was active for years prior. According to CARI-PGG (2013):

> CARI-PGG are coordinated cells who began acting in 2008 without transmitting any claim of responsibility for our actions, and it wasn't until 2009 that a claim appeared for an action against a Renault auto company ... We do not have vanguardist ideas, nor much less militarist ones, we are groups of anarchist action and we base ourselves on informality; we have often questioned ourselves on the use of signatures, but we reached the conclusion that they are only necessary as part of a strategy and nothing more. We do not pretend to bring anybody to insurrection – insurrections are spontaneous and collective, we take up the conflict in the first person.

CARI-PGG are quick to state their willingness and desire to carry out lethal violence, not simply the destruction of property or the intimidation of individuals. The network makes this aim quite clear, writing:

> The Sole-Baleno insurgent cell of the CARI-PGG declare that ... a package bomb was mailed addressed to the general offices of the PGR

[Federal Attorney General], to be explicit the package was addressed to the attorney general Miguel Mancera. Although our objective was to wound the heads or apparent heads of the police system, being that the package apparently "originated" from the general offices of Telmex, specifically from the person in Telmex responsible for the Secure City project ... the package would have been returned to him if it did not reach its destination. The package bomb was composed of a galvanized metal pipe, dynamite, a 2.5 volt source, matches, cable, a 9 volt battery, and shrapnel. (CARI-PGG, FAI 2011)

Here one can observe the network's lethal aims, to "wound" either an individual associated with the PGR or another associated with Telmex.

CARI-PGG follows the generalized insurrectionary rejection of systems of control and governance targeting "the police as an institution, their computers, their surveillance systems, their patrols, their criminologists, their experts" who work for "the interests of those who have power, for the protection of the 'social order'" (CARI-PGG, FAI 2011). Furthermore, CARI-PGG has at times claimed attacks as part of the FAI (e.g. CARI-PGG, FAI 2011; CARI-PGG, Gabriella Segata Antolini cell, and FAI/IRF 2011) and in discussing the shooting of an Italian nuclear executive they write, "we are totally in accordance with the action of the Olga Cell of the FAI in having shot in the legs that bastard of nuclear energy in Italy" (CARI-PGG, Cell of revolutionary action for the destruction of the State 2012). Similar to other networks, CARI-PGG regularly expresses solidarity with CCF and prominent political prisoners involved in the insurrectionary model of attack. The network's targeting selection is not surprising and includes IEDs targeting police vehicles, banks, Starbucks, the homes of politicians' and prison directors, the Chilean and Italian embassies, the Mexican ambassador to Greece, the Attorney General, the Federal Electricity Commission, the Mexican head of Monsanto, and the Mexican Archbishop. Between January 2010 and December 2013, the moniker was used to claim responsibility for 22 bombings (IEDs and mail bombs) and two arsons (Loadenthal 2015, 468–470). Despite their ferocity in their initial strikes, CARI-PGG appears to have disbanded, exemplifying the insurrectionary logic of temporary affiliation. Interestingly, the network embodied a unique relationship with the wider anarchist milieu and, unlike the network discussed below, CARI-PGG did not disparage the non-guerrilla components of the wider insurrectionary milieu (Llud 2015, 10).

Individualists Tending Toward the Wild

In April 2011, another distinct moniker emerged through the international counter-information and translation service of the so-called "black

3.2 Image circulated with "First communiqué of Wild Reaction (RS)"

international" – Individualists Tending Toward the Wild/Savagery [*Individualidades Tendiendo a lo Salvaje*] (ITS). Although this discussion includes ITS within an insurrectionary anarchist genealogy, the network itself rejects these labels entirely. It has explicitly rejected association with anarchism (ITS 2013, sec. IV), and via a subsequent (i.e. second generation) moniker, rejected both the label of "leftist" and "insurrectionary" (Wild Reaction 2015a). Despite this self-(anti)identification, ITS and its various formations will be discussed as the networks' communiqués are circulated and consumed through the same channels, and their tactics have at times resembled the insurrectionary methods of clandestine attack. While they are certainly distinct in their tactics, strategy, rhetoric, and image, discussion of ITS often occurs alongside that of the FAI/CCF (e.g, Llud 2015) and it is for this reason that they have been included in this book.

In a rare interview the group provided in 2014, it describes its purpose, stating:

> [ITS] deemed it necessary to carry out the direct attack against the Technoindustrial System. We think that the struggle against this is not only a stance of wanting to abandon Civilization, regressing to Nature, or in refuting the system's values, without also, attacking it. (contra-info and ITS 2014)

ITS has received international attention after repeatedly targeting scientists and researchers with lethal force. ITS has stood out from other bombers due to its lengthy, academic-styled communiqués and direct attacks on individuals from outside the typical target set: heads of state and corporations, officials in law enforcement, jailing, etc. ITS is unique in at least two matters: its stated objective to *kill*, and its specific, tech-related target set. In the 2014 interview, cell members explain:

> Our immediate objectives are very clear: injure or kill scientists and researchers (by the means of whatever violent act) who ensure the Technoindustrial System continues its course. As we have declared on various occasions, our concrete objective is not the destruction of the Technoindustrial system, it is the attack with all the necessary resources, lashing out at this system which threatens to close off all paths to the reaching of our Individual Freedom, putting into practice our defensive instinct ... ITS has from the beginning proposed the attack against the system as the objective, striving to make these kinds of ideas spread around the globe through extreme acts, in defense of Wild Nature, as we have done. (contra-info and ITS 2014)

According to their own historical account, the group began experimenting in 2011 with "arson attacks on cars and construction machinery, companies and institutions ... until we decided to focus on terrorism and not sabotage" (ITS 2014). From 2011–2014, ITS deployed at least 13 mail bombs, two mailed threats accompanied by bullets, and assassinated Méndez Salinas, a biotechnologist with the Institute of Bio-Technology at the National Autonomous University of Mexico. Salinas was shot in the head, and according to ITS (2014), killed by "the most violent cell of ITS in Morelos, being already familiar with the purchase and use of firearms."

Through their various communiqués and interviews, ITS has claimed responsibility for a series of attacks, many of which were claimed under other monikers and later linked to the ITS network. For example, in August 2014, ITS declared the formation of Wild Reaction (RS):

> After a little more than three years of criminal-terrorist activity, the group ... [ITS] ... begins a new phase in this open war against the Technoindustrial System ... we want to explain that during all of 2012 and 2013, various groups of a terrorist and sabotage stripe were uniting themselves with the group ITS, so that now, after a long silence and for purely strategic reasons, we publicly claim [10 attacks from newly affiliated networks] ... All of these have now fused with the ITS groups in Morelos, Mexico City, Guanajuato, Hidalgo, Coahuila and Veracruz ... Due to this union, the extravagant and little-practical pseudonym of " "Individualists Tending toward the Wild' (ITS) ceases to exist, and from now on the attacks against technology and civilization will be signed with the new name of "Wild Reaction" (RS). (Wild Reaction, "Kill or Die" Group 2014)

Prior to this announcement, in April 2014 a group calling itself Obsidian Point Circle of *Analysis* (OPCAn) activated a new clandestine cell (which would later be absorbed into RS) called Obsidian Point Circle of *Attack* (OPCA). The formation of OPCAn was preceded by three commentaries (2013a; 2013b; 2013c) on ITS and the authors "becoming tired of simply writing." In its opening declaration OPCA (2014) writes:

> It has been some time since we started writing about some situations that had arisen in Mexico concerning the terrorist group ITS; we published a total of three analyses, in which we have publicly demonstrated our support of the group ITS, in their actions as much as their position. Until now we have decided to solely be those who comfortably spread and highlighted the group's communiques and actions, but that is over. The violent advance of the techno-industrial system, the degradation that civilization leaves in its wake and the oblivion they are forcing us toward, ceasing to be natural humans to the point of turning into humanoids: there must be a convincing response.
>
> We abandon words and analyses in order to begin with our war ... We only seek confrontation with the system, the sharpening of the conflict against it. From this day we publicly put aside the word "analysis," in order to become The Obsidian Point Circle of Attack.

Thus, according to its own narrative, ITS inspired public commentary and critique by OPCAn and, in September 2014, when ITS became RS, it was announced that RS included OPCA as well. In the first declaration by RS (Wild Reaction, "Kill or Die" Group 2014), the authors explain: "during this year ... two more terroristic groups have united with us who have put the development of the Technoindustrial System in their sights ... The 'Obsidian Point Circle of Attack' ... [and] ... The 'Atlatl Group.'" Therefore, a complete history of ITS's actions includes both attacks claimed under their name, those claimed under the OPCA and RS, as well as smaller groupings merged under the network's banner. According to a chronology assembled from the networks' communications (Loadenthal 2015, 471–474), the network has claimed at least 27 distinct actions including 22 IED attacks (mostly mail and package/parcel bombs), three written threats, several arsons of property, one animal release, and one fatal shooting.

In early 2016, the ITS moniker saw its first usage outside of the borders of Mexico. In the second ITS communiqué of 2016, the "Uncivilized Southerners" (2016) cell "abandoned a homemade explosive charge" on a bus in Santiago, Chile writing:

> The Eco-Extremist tendency spreads ... We are accomplices to its ideas and acts, forming part of it. We are giving life to an international project against civilization.

> Because we are bullets to the head, mail-bombs, indiscriminate bombings and incinerating fire, we are:
>
> Individualists Tending Toward the Wild – Chile.

A few days later, in the fourth ITS communiqué of 2016, an ITS cell in Argentina claimed responsibility for placing an IED in a Buenos Aires bus station. In the message accompanying the bomb, the attackers wrote: "ITS is in Argentina" (ITS – Argentina: Wild Constellations 2016). The emergence of new ITS cells appears to be an ongoing trend. Five days after the Argentina communiqué was posted to a Spanish-language insurrectionary hub, the same site featured a communiqué signed by five cells of ITS, three from Mexico, and one each from Argentina and Chile. The communiqué traces the origin and expansion of the ITS and RS monikers and announces "a new phase of the war against all that represents and sustains the advance of civilization and progress" (ITS – Mexico, ITS – Chile, and ITS – Argentina 2016).

In Mexico, ITS's bombs have targeted civilian, seemingly 'non-political' scientists, professors, technical experts, researchers, and technocrats and within a politic most closely described as (Green) anarcho-primitivism. Famed "Unabomber" Theodore Kaczynski popularized this framework in the 1980s during a 17-year (1978–1995) bombing campaign involving 16 bombs, which killed three people and injured 23. Following the publication of "Industrial Society and its Future" (quoted in Skrbina 2010) – popularly known as the "Unabomber manifesto" and released five months after his final attack – Kaczynski's spirit has been carried forth by ITS and a few similar networks.

A comparison between the critique, tactics, and rhetoric of ITS and Kaczynski has been made in an overwhelming majority of press accounts of ITS activity (e.g. Corral 2011; Stevenson 2011; Ángel 2013; Ingersoll 2013; Bartlett 2014; Sable 2014). The tendency for scholars and reporters to make such comparisons may have led ITS (2011) to specifically address their relationship to Kaczynski in their fourth communiqué:

> Have *ITS* copied Ted Kaczynski? The million-dollar question.
>
> Without a doubt, we see this person as an individual who with his profound rational analysis contributed greatly to the advance of anti-technological ideas; his simple way of living in a manner strictly away from Civilization and the persecution of his Freedom in an optimal environment make him a worthy individual who due to a family betrayal is serving multiple life sentences in the United States … If we cite Stirner, Rand, Kaczynski, Nietzsche, Orwell, some scientists and other people in our communiques they are only for references, we do not have reason to be in agreement with all their lines and positions … It has been said

that we imitate the Unabomber; perhaps we have seen as strategic the action of [Kaczynski's moniker] the Freedom Club against scientific personalities in the United States in the 70's, 80's and 90's, and we have adopted this, but let it be clear that we have not imitated all his discourse in its totality, since as we said above, there are points that are plainly contrary to the positions of the FC.

In their sixth communiqué, ITS (2012) notes that their early writings (i.e. first and second communiqués) did in fact borrow from Kaczynski, but that after reflecting on their "poor interpretations" the group has "discarded [Kaczynski's ideas] and now for us they have no validity." Despite what many regard as similarities in critique, and despite ITS occasionally quoting Kaczynski directly, ITS subsequently denies ideological connections. In the first communiqué as "Wild Reaction, 'Kill or Die' Group" (2014) the group writes:

> We deny being followers of Ted Kaczynski ... we have indeed learned many things from reading Industrial Society and Its Future, the texts after this and the letters before this text signed by 'Freedom Club' (FC), but that does not mean that we are his followers. In fact our position clashes with Kaczynski's, FC's ... since we do not consider ourselves revolutionaries, we do not want to form an 'anti-technological movement' that encourages the 'total overthrow of the system,' we do not see it as viable, we do not want victory, we do not pretend to win or lose, this is an individual fight against the mega-machine; we don't care about getting something positive from this, since we are simply guided by our instincts of defense and survival.

Here one can witness RS's declared revolutionary intent, to "bring it all crashing down" while avoiding the trapping of movement building and conceiving of the conflict in terms of winners and losers. In this communiqué, after the group changed its name, RS goes on to further declare their ideological independence from the prominent critics of technology (e.g. primitivists) as well as the global anarcho-insurrectional milieu through which their communications are circulated and consumed. In their proclamation of non-affiliation, RS states:

> Thus neither Kaczynski ... or any other with the (supposed) "primitivist" stamp represents RS. Nor do the Informal Anarchist Federation (FAI), the Conspiracy of Cells of Fire (CCF), Feral Faun, or any other with the "ecoanarchist" or "anti-civilization cell of ..." stamp. RS and its groups only represent themselves. (Wild Reaction, "Kill or Die" Group 2014)

Despite ITS/RS's insistence to the contrary, prominent anarcho-primitivist thinker John Zerzen, often spoken of as the "founder" of the movement, notes that "ITS group is real slavish to Ted Kaczynski" (Morin 2014). Zerzen goes on to say that he does not believe ITS's methods will prove successful and that he is "turn[ed] off" by their usage of mailed explosives and their cavalier dismissal of human causalities (Morin 2014).

Case study: internationalizing campaigns of attack

... we make a call for multiplication of direct attack actions. We do it without arrogance, but with the knowledge that anarchist proposal of autonomous attack by groups of related comrades horizontally organized, is possible, real, ever-present and necessary.

We also claim this action as a part of [FAI/IRF] ... sharing the objectives it raises: **ANARCHIST AUTONOMOUS ATTACK**, always on offensive, without hierarchies and without specializations. **INTERNATIONALISM**, as the anti-authoritarian praxis knows no bounds, states or nations, connecting with other insurgent wills around the world. And **SOLIDARITY**, because we do not forget about our comrades inside the enemy's prisons.

Also we claim this action as Phoenix Project, to give new impetus to the anti-authoritarian violent action in this area dominated by the Chilean State, as a way of facing repression and show that the anarchist attack is still alive and it will not surrender. (Arsonist Anarchist Attack-"Fire and Consciousness" Cell FAI/IRF 2015 [emphasis/capitalization in original])

The insurrectionary movement is organized through a decentralized model drawn from the larger anarchist praxis. The roles played by anti-authoritarian, horizontalist politics in the molding of leftist networks has been the subject of much scholarship. Anarchist theorist Uri Gordon (2008, 14) described the generalized anarchist milieu as a "network of informal interactions between a plurality of individuals, groups and/or organizations ... on the basis of a shared collective identity." Gordon goes on to state that this "movement's architecture" is "a decentralized global network of communication, coordination and mutual support among countless autonomous nodes of social struggle, overwhelmingly lacking formal membership or foxed boundaries" (2008, 14). Such a description is applicable to the insurrectionary milieu, which can be understood as a subset or derivative of the larger anarchist tendency. For the insurrectionists, international campaigns of attack are coordinated through a diverse, virtual exchange of ideas played out via the texts of communiqués and claims of responsibility.

To accurately portray this organizational tendency through a modern insurrectionary example, we can examine the 2013–2015 Phoenix Project. The campaign began 7 June 2013, when a cell identifying with the CCF-FAI/IRF moniker claimed responsibility for a bomb attack in Athens. The targeted vehicle belonged to Maria Stefi, the director of the prison where members of the CCF were being held. The attackers were quick to claim the attack "as a display of genuine solidarity with our ten imprisoned brothers and sisters" (CCF-FAI/IRF, Consciousness Gangs-FAI/IRF, and Sole-Baleno Cell 2013). Interestingly, the IED disrupted a period of inactivity for the CCF, as the authors write:

> After almost two years of silence throughout the Greek territory, the CCF returns. Maintaining a common front with the ... FAI cells ("Antifascist Front", "Unscathed Cell of Vengeance", "Lone Wolf Cell", etc.) ... we support and strengthen the international conspiracy of the Informal Anarchist Federation/International Revolutionary Front. (CCF-FAI/IRF, Consciousness Gangs-FAI/IRF, and Sole-Baleno Cell 2013)

The reemergence of the CCF moniker, and the reinvigoration of this network, was portrayed as the rising of the phoenix. The attackers called the bombing part of the Phoenix Project, implying that the incident was not a single occurrence.

Less than two weeks later, the "International Conspiracy for Revenge/FAI," (2013a) claimed responsibility for the second Phoenix Project attack – the bombing of a car belonging to a "hated prison guard in Argos, Greece." A few days later, in what the attackers called "Phoenix Project – Act Two," the third in a series of attacks in Greece occurred, similarly targeting the vehicle of a prison worker. Around 22 June 2013, the "FAI-International Conspiracy for Revenge" (2013b) – the same moniker which claimed the second Phoenix attack – blew up the car of a prison guard whom they accused of abuse, intimidation, and bullying, writing that "the enemies of freedom have names and addresses." The communiqué addresses the issue of prison abuse and uses the text to further expand on the internationalist network, writing:

> The new anarchist urban guerrilla is not a means of struggle, it is our existence itself. All the rest which does not promote the continuous anarchist insurrection is ideological cowardice.

> FAI (Informal Anarchist Federation) in cooperation with the Conspiracy of Cells of Fire aims to create a diffuse network of direct action cells in the Greek territory which will strike where the enemy does not expect it. Small autonomous flexible armed cells watch, collect info, sometimes cooperate sometimes not and choose the moment of sudden attack. Only

in the attack is there life. We are anarchists of action, chaotic, nihilist, egoists, godless, we are the carriers of the black flags of anarcho-nihilism. (International Conspiracy for Revenge/FAI 2013b)

A few days after this communiqué was issued, expanding on and articulating the networked reality of the FAI, the Phoenix Project internationalized.

On 26 June 2013, insurrectionists in Jakarta, Indonesia, carried out an arson attack targeting the Sheraton Hotel. The arsonists labeled their attack "Phoenix Project – Part 3" and noted that they acted as "[their] decision to respond to the call from our Greek comrades" (International Conspiracy for Revenge/FAI-IRF and Anger Unit 2013). In their closing remarks, the authors encouraged further continuation of the campaign, writing "Let's make the Phoenix project as an international project for revenge!" signing the communiqué the "Anger Unit of the International Conspiracy for Revenge/FAI-IRF," (2013) once again utilizing that shared moniker and adding a new service unit. After the attack in Jakarta, at least 13 more attacks would occur, totaling 17 Phoenix Project attacks (in nine countries)[9] as of 3 January 2016 (Loadenthal 2015, 475–477; Anarchist Arson Attack Cell "Fire and Consciousness" FAI-IRF 2016). Following one such attack, the authors summarize the intent of the campaign writing:

[The] Project Phoenix is a punch in the gut. A punch in the gut because the new anarchist urban guerrilla is here and tears down the desires of all these worms to terminate our actions. Old groups are activated and new are created, with the promise to give life to the nightmares of authority and its subjects. (Commando Mauricio Morales/FAI-IRF 2013)

From the brief history of the Phoenix Project, one can see the deployment of adoptable network monikers used to claim cell-level responsibility for attacks while simultaneously demonstrating coordination and ideological affinity within larger movement-level initiatives. We see monikers deterritorialize, adapt, grow, and change. From one initial challenge and call to action, cells around the world attack and, in doing so, develop a decentralized campaign of sorts.

Borrowing from the work of anthropologist Jeff Juris, Gordon (2008, 15) points out that anarchist networks display a uniqueness, seeking not traditional social movement "recruitment" but instead the reproduction of networks through a "horizontal expansion and enhanced 'connectivity.'" In describing the structuring and strategy of the global network of attack, the authors describe these horizontally-connected networks and state:

We coordinate our attacks through the FAI/IRF international network ... FAI/IRF is an international conspiracy of anarchists of praxis ... It gets rid of the smell of mold that has settled in anarchy seen at amphitheaters, and fills the air with the smell of gunpowder, black anarchy, nighttime, explosions, gunshots, sabotages. This explains why the International Revolutionary Front of FAI and Conspiracy is on top of the anarchist dangers list as cited in recent Europol reports.

Diffusion and informal organizing within the new anarchy into autonomous cells of direct action are what really scare the police of the whole world. Therefore, the State and the enemies of anarchy do not easily forget the anarchist militants who are held captive under their prisons' authority. (CCF-FAI/IRF, Consciousness Gangs-FAI/IRF, and Sole-Baleno Cell 2013)

This was the method which originated in Italy and rapidly spread to Greece, Mexico, and scores of other countries. More than two and a half years after the initiation of the Phoenix Project, combatant cells were still carrying the model forward. In a communiqué issued April 2015, the authors state that their IID attack targeting an office of Microsoft was carried out as a "contribution to the comrades of Czech FAI/IRF suggestion, who burned a police car and suggested the creation of an international action project with the name 'modeled on the 'Phoenix' Project'" (Combative Anarchy, FAI-IRF 2015). A few days later, yet another Phoenix Project-linked attack was claimed, this time the arson of a meat company's office in Chile.

Conclusion

Clearly the notion of carrying forth campaigns of attack initiated by one cell and furthered by others will only continue. Other campaigns have included an annual call to action during the month of December – known as Black December – or campaigns in response to specific events, individuals, companies, and institutions. As a Grecian cell of the CCF/FAI stated, reflecting on the Black December of 2015:

> "Black December" was an open call to everyone, but was mainly recorded as a point of reference for the insurrectionary, the anarchist-nihilists, the young comrades, the non-aligned, the "troublemakers" against the state (and partly against the inactivity of the official "anarchist space", against its pacifist transformation) ... Each call for action is an instance of a more comprehensive history that preceded it and perhaps the accelerator of a perspective that follows. (CCF: Urban Guerilla Cell/FAI 2016)

During this one month period, at least 120 attacks, demonstrations, and other actions were reported as part of Black December (Anonymous 2015), including several dozen arsons and other acts of property destruction spread across North America, South America, Europe, and Australia. Imprisoned militant Nikos Romanos (2016), in a reflective piece entitled "I Attack, Therefore I Am," notes that such campaigns amount to:

> [a] gathering point for the strategic direction of informal organization and to restart continuous anarchist uprising[s] … an open framework for action … a dialectical overcoming of theoretical bottlenecks so as to create a reverse dynamic in opposition to the culture of ideological entrenchment … The Black December campaign contributed much content to the discussion of revolutionary tactics and showed this through the polymorphic action that I developed.

The description by Romanos demonstrates the strategic self-awareness the network helps to advance, through the promulgation of structures that avoid ideological infighting and fragmentation in favor of the reproduction of continuous attack. Since the emergence of the FAI, CCF and others in the dawn of the millennium, the expansion of clandestine insurrectionary attack has been swift. The preceding history has traced this history, not only from its nineteenth-century ideological roots, but also from its more modern organizational genesis.

This history of struggle is meant to develop a genealogy of insurrection based around the most often-invoked characters and periods. While there is not a chronologically-direct lineage from Fawkes to Bakunin and onwards to the CCF, these pre-modern actors, movements, and events constitute the foundational precursors to the present. Most, if not all, of the individuals in this history are unearthed in the propaganda and theory offered through insurrectionary communiqués. Ideas are adopted and stolen without attribution, and names of the fallen are summoned from centuries past to inspire and incite. For example, OPCA writes: "We abandon words and analyses in order to begin with our war," a notion reminiscent of Nechayev's recommendation that those conspiring to attack should "prove himself (sic) not by words but by deeds" (1869, sec. 12). In this manner, in the construction of an insurrectionary pre-history, one must examine the actions of attackers as well as their theories as the latter is often presented as ahistorical, operating independent of obvious precursors.

Notes

1 The use of "kneecapping" (*gambizzazioni* in Italian) was common among the RB active in 1970–1980s Italy.
2 The "Olga" namesake is a tribute to Olga Ikonomidou, an imprisoned member of the CCF network in Greece.

3 Italy (twelve cells), Mexico (nine cells), Greece (eight cells), Chile (two cells) and one cell each in Indonesia, Russia, Peru, the Netherlands, and England.
4 Gabriel Pombo Da Silva is an anarchist militant who has been involved in revolutionary bank expropriations since age 15. After being imprisoned in Spain, he escaped in 2004. While trying to flee to Germany, he was discovered at a border crossing and exchanged fire with security forces. No one was injured in the shooting, but Da Silva was arrested and convicted of attempted murder and kidnapping. He is currently serving 13 years.
5 Marco Camenisch is an anarchist militant currently imprisoned for murder. Camenisch was involved in radical environmental movements prior to his arrest and had served time for industrial sabotage and other actions targeting power stations. After being arrested in 1980 for sabotaging a Swiss power station, he was sentenced to ten years in prison. In 1981 he escaped along with five other prisoners. During the escape, a prison guard was shot and killed and a second injured. From 1981–1991, Camenisch went underground, and on 5 November 1991, Italian security forces arrested him. Upon capture, Camenisch opened fire wounding one soldier, and was shot and injured in the process. In 1992, he was sentenced to 12 years for the shooting and the sabotage, serving 9 years in solitary confinement. In 2002 he was extradited to Switzerland, and in 2004, sentenced to 17 years in prison for the alleged killing of a Swiss border guard in 1989.
6 The network's name is occasionaly recorded as Conspiracy of Fire Cells or Conspiracy of Fire Nuclei.
7 This is the same day of the year that the FAI began their campaign and an obvious show of solidarity between the two networks.
8 The group's namesake, Práxedis Guerrero (1882–1910) was a Mexican soldier-turned revolutionary leader who worked as a publisher (*Alba Roja, Revolución, Punto Rojo,* and *Regeneración*) and revolutionary leader before he was killed in a raid on the town of Janos, Mexico.
9 Greece, Italy, Germany, England, Czech Republic, Russia, Chile, Mexico, and Indonesia.

4
Insurrection as warfare, terrorism, and revolutionary design

I believe that the action of these specific incendiary groups contributed to the unstoppable course of anarchist insurrection. Incendiary attacks are an inseparable part of the struggle because they are easy to carry out by new comrades, keep the fire of belligerent hostilities burning and contribute to the spreading of anarchist violence. They add their own pebbles to the continuation of the anarchist urban guerrilla and cause trouble to the smooth running of the system. Of course arsons must occur in relation with all the expressions of anarchist violence (bomb attacks, political executions, violent mass clashes, raiding excursions), in order to create a common uncontrollable and dangerous front for action, which sets the total destruction of the existent as its only limit. (Romanos 2014b)

Most researchers in the late twentieth century feel far more ambivalent about armed struggle than they do about unarmed protestors in the streets. (Seidman 2014, 228)

The structuring of social war

Insurrectionary struggle must be understood as more than the sum of its communiqués. To understand it only in this regard is reductionist and misses important occurrences, such as frequent street-level confrontations, marches, building occupations, riots, blockades, and clandestine attacks. A defender of insurrectionary strategy commented in an anarchist message board, trying to succinctly explain this strategy and framework, writing:

The insurrection purposed by many contemporary anarchists is an informal non-military non-non-violent communization or egoist campaign. An insurrection is the actualization of our desires that go against the ruling order. An insurrection spreads cracks in the spectacle of social peace. The anarchist insurrection is the riot, the social war, the blockade, the strike, the gang, the commune, and so much more. (Anonymous 2014h)

The insurrectionary strategy, or rather the strategy proposed by insurrection*ists* is a multifaceted initiative based around building autonomous spaces (e.g. squats, communes, police-free neighborhoods, zones of opacity (IEF 2013, 50; TIC 2007, 107–108), temporary autonomous zones (Bey 1991)), fostering conflict to expose inequality (i.e. making social war), and directly attacking forms of domination through informal, individualist, illegal action including property destruction, sabotage, propaganda, expropriation, and strikes at individuals.

Unlike Marxism and other revolutionary frameworks, insurrectionary anarchism is not rooted in a specific theory of change (e.g. historical materialism) but is rather a theory of critique and action, not prefiguration. In his discussion of guerrilla warfare and terrorism, conflict theorist Richard Rubenstein (1987, 29–30) points to a two-stage understanding advocated by Vietnamese leader and military strategist General Vo Nguyen Giap who divided the conflict into two stages, beginning with guerrilla war before moving into more conventional forms of warfare. General Giap (1965, 52 [Emphasis in original]) understood the role played by guerrilla violence, stating:

> At the price of their hard-won experiences, our compatriots in the South realized that the fundamental trend of imperialism and its lackeys is violence and war; that is why *the most correct path to be followed by the peoples to liberate themselves is revolutionary violence and revolutionary war*. This path conforms strictly to the ethics and the fundamentals of Marxism-Leninism on class struggle, on the state and the revolution. Only by revolutionary violence can the masses defeat aggressive imperialism and its lackeys and overthrow the reactionary administration to take power.

While the guerrilla warfare resembles the strategies and tactics of the insurrectionists, it is in this second stage, where one moves into a phase of more regular combat, that the comparison breaks down. While the Marxist and nationalist struggles of this era were defined by the desire to foster a "mass-based guerrilla army" in order to "move from large-scale rebellion to revolution" (Rubenstein 1987, 30), the insurrectionary perspective lacks this prescriptive chronology and sees only the moment of the attack, the resulting rupture, and the attacks that follow.

These ruptures do not necessarily culminate – in terms of scale and mass – in a revolution in the traditional Marxist sense, but there is a presumption that attacks lead to more attacks, which in some way lead to structural change, frequently envisioned as a form of anti-authoritarian communism, termed communization. The authors of Tiqqun may be the best example of this:

> Tiqqun does not see communization as taking or changing power, since historically that has meant that the takers and changers of power become the new rulers ... [Tiqqun envisions] a revolution rooted in the transformation of every day life. (José and Corrales 2015, 69)

The insurrectionary milieu maintains a strategic understanding, and while many individuals quite obviously possess a clearly demarcated theory of change, the movement on the whole is not based in this predictive reality. While not advocating a shared theory of social change, the insurrectionary milieu shares a "violence framing" which speaks to a "set of culturally salient violent practices through which [the actor can] ... contextualize a political situation ... or a proposed course of action" (Ramsey and Holbrook 2014, 86–87). This shared frame is prevalent despite the lack of a clearly established, and often repeated, long-term, prescriptive vision. It could be argued that this represents a "global framing" wherein the milieu "[utilizes] international symbols to frame domestic issues for the purpose of mobilizing support" (Drissel 2014, 3), but as these networks actively ignore nation-state boundaries, such transnational distinctions become less relevant and meaningful. Insurrectionary attackers are extremely unlikely to call for the revolutionary overthrow of specific nation-states, but instead advocate a totalized war wherein *all* beings are emancipated from *all* forms of domination.

Instead of predicting the forms of change, the movement is focused on the production of attacks – what social movement theorist Donnatella della Porta calls "the logic of [material] damage" (della Porta and Diani 2006, sec. 7.3.2) – making these attacks larger and more frequent. While these attacks have a variety of aims, one central goal is to "interrupt the flow of commodities" (TIC 2007, 119). This is achieved when a bank is unable to open after having its windows smashed, a fleet of police cars needs to be replaced and is unable to patrol for a period, or a multinational office is forced to lockdown after receiving an explosive package or theat. These strikes against state and capital which seek to "interrupt the flow" are not centrally directed, yet follow a basic guiding logic, as explained by the authors of *The Coming Insurrection* who instruct, "As for methods, let's adopt the following principle from sabotage: a minimum of risk in taking the action, a minimum of time, and maximum damage" (TIC 2007, 111). The strategy is thus simultaneously aimed at tearing down (the state) and building up (the commune). As one anonymous writer states, "The commune is the basic unit of partisan reality. An insurrectional surge may be nothing more than a multiplication of communes, their coming into contact and forming of ties" (TIC 2007, 117). This strategy offered by TIC seeks to replace "the institutions of society: family, school, union, sport club" with counter-formations, based in an anti-authoritarian structure that meets the "material and moral" (2007, 102) needs. To "build the commune" one seeks to create counter-bodies that sap power from the institutions of the society one seeks to destroy. It is the expansion and multiplication of ungovernable zones, and communities of resistance based around mutual aid, solidarity, self-sufficiency, and resistance to domination.

TIC slyly lays out their macro strategy in the chapter headings of *The Coming Insurrection*. While the beginning of the book describes and critiques the society at large (modeled after Dante Alighieri's "nine circles of Hell"), the final four chapters lay out a method that brings one from the moment of the present, constrained by domination, to a future that is more free. The authors (2007, 7) describe these stages as:

Get Going!
Find Each Other
Get Organized
Insurrection

This is the broadly defined insurrectionary proscription for action. The insurrectionary action advocated in *The Coming Insurrection* is one of building up communities of resistance, and fostering conflict and direct confrontation with the state through organized networks.

These forms of insurrectionary action and resistance are integrated into daily existence and reject some aspects of the 1960s-era guerrillaism. While the *ethics* of armed struggle are maintained from these predecessors, forms of daily resistance become markers alongside isolated armed attacks as "the urban guerrilla figure of the previous decades collapses into the average city dweller who doesn't pay for the subway" (IEF 2013, 46). The goal of an insurrectionary strategy is to "widen the breach between politics and the political" (TIC 2007, 25), to bring about radical social change through initiating conflict. Arson, explosives, graffiti, animal release, and various forms of vandalism comprise a wide tactical array that is often patterned nationally or within networks. While Mexico, Greece and Chile, Italy and Spain have frequent bombings, the US, Canada, and Germany rarely see this tactic. Greece has had frequent armed expropriations from banks, while Chile has seen frequent armed clashes with police at universities and in city streets. In Mexico and Italy, mail bombs have been used to target officials, political leaders, technocrats, and scientists. These differing realities are likely the results of interconnected cultural and historical conditions outside the scope of the current discussion. Is it merely a coincidence that the nations experiencing active bombings campaigns, such as

Chile, Greece, Italy, and Spain, all have recent national experiences with fascism?

This book focuses its attention on attacks recorded in the public registry through the issuing of a communiqué through online channels. It is limited in this regard. Though these websites' communiqué repositories are extensive, and utilized frequently to communicate attacks, it is certainly not the entirety of insurrectionary activity. Street actions such as confrontational marches and riots, building and university occupations, demonstrations outside and within prisons, provoked clashes with security forces, spontaneous road blockades, and other insurrectionary-aligned occurrences, while essential, fall outside of the scope of this discussion. The following will explore the macro strategy of insurrectionary action as a strategy and form of warfare. It will explore the means, strategy, and organization of political violence, which are necessary to historically encapsulate modern conflict.

Re-reading urban guerrilla warfare

> I stand here as your declared and unrepentant enemy, I do not beg for your lenience, I do not seek to engage in dialogue with you and your peers. My values are at war with yours, so that every phrase I come out with against you is a razor scoring the masks of your hypocrisy and making clear the position and the role of each of us … The simple laws of physics dictate, that reaction is the consequence of action. Outside this courtroom on free lands, there are rebellious people, comrades for me, terrorists for you, who don't intend to tolerate our extermination, without making you and your political supervisors bleed first. You can take this as a threat if you like. I believe, that this is the cynical reality. Each option has its own cost. I guess, that, as judges and servants of the law, you would agree with me on this. (Romanos 2014a)

The new assemblage of clandestine attackers has borrowed from many previous incarnations of anti-state and counter-hegemonic resistance movements. While the tactics have ranged from the vandalism of property to the outright lethal targeting of individuals, this tactical continuum has been deployed within a framework of asymmetric, protracted combat, with practitioners frequently referring to themselves as "urban guerrillas," "armed guerrillas" or "anarchist urban guerrillas." Though there is no insurrectionary consensus on strategy or organization, there are fluid, constantly reinterpreted guiding principles. In a 2014 interview, a Canadian, self-described insurrectionary anarchist outlines three points of broad-based affinity, explaining:

The part of the anarchist movement I come out of is very influenced by the insurrectionary anarchist practice that was theorized in Italy in the [19]70's, the principal points that are applicable to our struggle are:

A) a break from the traditional worker's movements in favour of more fluid organizing, less tied to our roles in the economy.
B) an emphasis on attacking the enemy in small easily reproducible ways, that allow more possibilities for these tactics to spread across the social terrain, and avoid some of the traps that the urban guerrillas of previous generations fell into.
C) Most important of all, is informal organizing, this means that we do not want to create organizations that waste energy on keeping themselves alive, just for the sake of it, and instead to work on projects on a basis of affinity ... (Anonymous 2014f)

Here we see basic insurrectionary ethics such as the avoidance of populist movements, fluid, temporary, and informal organizations based on networks of affinity, and an emphasis on direct confrontation and attack through simple, "easily reproducible" means. While the target set is vague, this reflects the totalized conflict position of those at war with society at large, and the state-capital nexus more centrally. This modeling is in contrast to the forms of urban guerrillaism, which peaked in the 1970s. The differences and similarities between these two articulations of armed struggle are key and will be explored throughout this chapter.

The fluidly-defined yet ever-present nature of the systems of domination creates a veritable smorgasbord of available targets for attackers; targets they can consider and weigh based on symbolism, feasibility, opportunity, etc. It is in this manner that the asymmetric nature of the state v. non-state relationship benefits the latter. For the attacker, they can strike when the means and opportunity avail themselves, but for the state, they must defend all capital at all times. The insurrectionary vandal can set out to burn a police car, find it well guarded and set fire to an adjacent bank, all within the same logic and rhetoric. This is especially true in urban environments (Wiberg 1974, 14–15). Furthermore, with the technologization, automation, and dispersal of capital, the targets multiply. As one anonymous, insurrectionary theorist writes, "the spreading of production and control that the new technologies allow makes sabotage easier" (Anonymous 2001a, 21). In so-called "city terrorism ... the government must, since it is the government, protect everywhere the interests of property owners; the *guerrilleros* don't have to protect anything anywhere" (Debray 1967, 75 [emphasis in original]). This is part of the revisioning of the *urban* guerrilla embedded within a locale with endless targets all interwoven through a single revolutionary narrative; from a slaughterhouse to a police cruiser, all manifestations of domination, politics, and power are fair game.

Though this strategic and tactical revisioning is unique in some aspects when compared to more traditional instances of political violence, one can observe a patterned regularity. When examining what sorts of *targets* attackers choose to strike, a great deal of similarity exists between the insurrectionary milieu and other non-state attackers. To draw this comparison, one can examine a single national locale, in this case the US. In a 2014 study of "domestic terrorism" occurring in the US (1940–2012), the authors conclude that while 84 attacks caused 134 fatalities, none were the product of attacks by "left-wing extremists" (Becker 2014, 966). Scholarship specifically focused on "white leftist groups" of the late 1960s and early 1970s notes that during this period, while European leftists and anti-colonial movements directed a large portion of their attacks at people, this was not the case in the US (Falciola 2015, 1–2). According to the study, this was an adaptive process through which leftist groups reined one another in through inter-movement critique and criticism, and breaking ties with those that transgressed the questions of violence against people (Falciola 2015, 17). Despite its infrequency in the US, a great number of modern publications seemingly fixate on preparing for armed struggle in Western metropolises through strategic discussions (e.g. Anonymous n.d.; Buck, Gilbert, and Whitehorn 2003; Mead 2007; Aubron, Menigon, and Rouillan 2009; Churchill 2009; Hansen and Belmas 2009; D. Jensen, McBay, and Keith 2011) as well as practical guides in military matters (e.g. North Carolina Piece Corps n.d; Anonymous 2002; N, D, and S 2004) adapted for revolutionary movements.

The context through which anti-state violence is created is context-specific and may require the examination of difficult questions dealing with notions of legitimacy, labeling, power, and structural violence. *Why* a particular site was attacked and what social critique this was meant to highlight draws attention to the underbelly of the social order. An attack targeting a slaughterhouse will likely speak to issues of speciesism and capitalist commodification, while the arson of a police station speaks to a discourse surrounding the legitimacy of law enforcement at large. In her work examining the poststructuralist approach to the study of terrorism, Harmonie Toros (2012, 29) speaks of the need to "resituate terrorist violence within its context" and to ask these questions:

> A bomb exploding in a square does not make sense unless one can situate it. For this, there are more direct questions that all scholars ask: Where is the square? Who did the bomb aim to kill? Who did it aim to impact? Who claimed responsibility and/or to which group was it attributed? ... What are the power structures and balances at play – locally, regionally, nationally and internationally? What preceded the explosion and what succeeded it? What are the aims of those who claim responsibility ... What are the struggles – political, social, economic – that surround the violence?

I would add to the list: *was* the bomb intended to kill. Since most insurrectionary bombings target property (similar to the ALF, ELF, and other contemporaries), and those aimed directly at human targets (e.g. ITS, Kaczynski) have often been small in size, it is essential to question the notion of *intent* in terms of lethality. Nonetheless, Toros encourages us to focus critical attention towards matters of context, especially that which can help to explain why a particular target and method was chosen. Therefore, when an insurrectionary cell sets fire to a cellular tower (as has been done frequently), this must be understood not as an isolated, anti-social act of meaningless rebellion, but a contextually-situated attack emanating from a socio-political critique of alienation, anti-capitalism, and anger finding a target in the infrastructure of corporate interests. A similar, if not more meaningful, self-reflection would follow the intentional targeting of a person with, for example, an IED sent through the mail. In this case, *why* that person was chosen from among a much larger community of contemporaries must be understood in both micro and community-level terms, as well as global discourses critical of, for example, nanotechnology, nuclear science or certain corporate interests.

This tendency to target property and not people mirrors the insurrectionary history where property damage is substantial and human/animal casualties are nonexistent. Furthermore, "terrorists" tended to target "easily accessible, familiar, unhardened targets ... with easily attainable weapons" (Becker 2014, 967), in this case IIDs, rocks, and glue. Attackers often target "nodes, paths and edges" (Brantingham and Brantingham 1993): sites that are already integrated into their daily reality, such as those which occur near their residence or places of frequent activity. Though there is no evidence to assert for the insurrectionary milieu, it may account for the seemingly mundane nature of the networks' targets, such as bank branches (not headquarters or corporate offices), ATMs, phone booths, automobiles, and other civilian (i.e. non-government, non-military) manifestations of their criticism peppered throughout daily life. In general, through both the traditional studies of violent non-state actors and the observation of insurrectionary attack, both groupings seem to choose "targets that were congruent with their stated political ideology, but they mainly confined their target selection to areas with which they, verifiably, had familiarity based on their daily routines" (Becker 2014, 968). Though it may seem presumptuous, it bears mentioning that research supports the assumption that attacks by non-state actors correspond to ideological posturings, thus selecting deserving, "enemy" targets from a functionally unlimited pool of potentials (Becker 2014, 962). This strategy of attack increases the cost of doing business for the movement's opponents, and while isolated attack alone is not sufficient to cause mass social upheaval, it is the wedge driven deeper by insurrectionists that seeks to damage the enemy, inspire the ally, and put into practice forms of resistance that are ends in themselves.

Throughout the insurrectionary literature, there is a consistent warning regarding the dependence or fetishism of the underground, armed guerrilla, the vanguard, and the "mythology of clandestinity and combat organisations" (Anonymous 2001a, 30). From anonymously-penned texts, potential fighters argue that as a *strategy*, the use of guerrilla warfare is devoid of politics and can be adopted by any radical actor from reformist to sectarian communists.

> "Armed struggle" is a strategy that could be put at the service of *any* project. The guerrilla is still used today by organizations whose programmes are substantially social democratic; they simply support their demands with military practice. Politics can also be done with arms.

While such cautionary warnings exist, modern insurrectionary warfare can certainly be classified as a branch rooted in the tree of asymmetric, guerrilla strategy. To historicize this evolution of thought, one can examine earlier proponents of guerrilla warfare strategy, including Ernesto "Che" Guevara, Mao Tse-tung, and Vo Nguyen Giap[1] – the senior military commander of the Vietnamese National Liberation Front. These past warfare theorists contended that such wars of asymmetry must be fought in the countryside (Wolf 1981, 20–21) by militarily-trained units, not dispersed networks of part-time activist-turned-guerrillas, based in cities.

The insurrectionary anarchist strategy descends from an urbanized form of guerrilla warfare. It is an asymmetric war of attrition wherein the dispersed network temporarily assembles to strike the ever-present, near enemy – the state and capital – and then retreats into safety. This approach acknowledges the power imbalance between the clandestine networks and the state's armories, and seeks to avoid protracted, military-styled engagement, as the authors of *The Coming Insurrection* explain in the conclusion to their treatise:

> From a strategic point of view, indirect, asymmetrical action seems the most effective kind, the one best suited to our time: you don't attack an occupying army frontally. That said, the prospect of Iraq-style urban guerrilla warfare, dragging on with no possibility of taking the offensive, is more feared than to be desired. The *militarization* of civil war is the defeat of insurrection. (TIC 2007, 129)

Traditional guerrilla warfare campaigns, whether urban or rural, have relied on fighters immersing themselves in full-time underground living.[2] This follows the advice of theorists who argued that "the armed unit … is organically separate from the civilian population" (Debray 1967, 29). This dependence on full time forces is standard among a variety of armed non-state actors including the FARC, the PIRA, and ongoing anti-occupation insurgencies in locales such as Iraq, Afghanistan, and Palestine.

When speaking of the more famed armed conflicts – such as those occurring in Ireland, Palestine, Colombia, and the Basque region – one must account for the existence of armed cadres in conjunction with broader-based, mass uprisings. Rubenstein argues that a key strategic distinction exists between situations where guerrilla warfare acts to support ongoing mass uprisings, and others where guerrillaism acts as a driving force to *encourage* such uprisings. In relation to these methods, termed "terrorism" in Rubenstein's (1987, 196) discussion, the author states, "Guerrilla fighters may be terrorists, but terrorism, properly defined, is exemplary small-group violence. Its function is to *create* the mass movement." Certainly there are cases where this occurs, such as Ho Chi Minh's experience in Vietnam where the North Vietnamese leader was able to "convert ... a small guerrilla band into a mass-based people's army" (Rubenstein 1987, 197). Rubenstein (1987, 201) also points to the resistance to French colonialism in 1950s Algeria. In this case, as Rubenstein explains, acts of violence by the Algerian paramilitaries did not succeed in expelling the French, but the resistance's use of small-group violence forced the hand of the French occupation authorities, and they were forced to repress the population in the name of counterinsurgency. This forcing of the state's hand towards retaliatory violence aids in the construction of "us v. them" narratives offered by the broader segments of the anti-colonial struggle.

This strategy of striking the enemy, forcing the enemy to respond, and then using that response to further recruit and mobilize supporters is common in asymmetric conflicts, and can certainly be seen in the insurrectionary method as well. In Rubenstein's (1987, 201) understanding of history, acts of small scale violence have never "mobilized the masses" but they have been successful in "disrupt[ing] normal life, incit[ing] the authorities to excesses of indiscriminate violence, and generat[ing] states of political emergency." Such discussions of "small-group" versus mass-based violence are typically reserved for conflicts in rural areas, especially those with large agricultural and other laboring constituencies. In these rural venues, individuals typically termed "militants," "guerrillas," "combatants" or simply "terrorists" engage in a lifestyle of 24-hour activity. When an individual is not engaged in active preparation or commission of an act of violence, they are living a subterranean existence as their activities are known to the security forces and thus normal, day-to-day living is altered in the cat and mouse game of attacker versus defender.

This is, of course, not to claim that guerrilla warfare as a strategy began with Algeria or Vietnam – nor with Guevara or Mao – rather the *strategy* dates back to at least the Maccabean Revolt (167–160 BCE) where the Judean people fought the state through guerrilla warfare after Antiochus IV Epiphanes forbid them to practice their religion. Other early examples include the Numidians' war against Rome (100 BCE) and the Spartacan Slave Revolt against the Roman Republic (70 BCE). The term *guerrilla warfare* also appears during the Spanish fight against Napoleonic occupation occurring around 1810 CE (Wiberg 1974, 12; Teitler 1974, 111). Other historical usages of note include the French Revolution of the 1790s, which saw peasants attack regimented armies with some degree of success, the Second Sino-Japanese War of the 1940s which involved a guerrilla campaign led by Chinese military commander Chaing Kai-skek against Emperor Hirohito's Japan, or the Dutch resistance to Nazi occupation during World War II. Although these examples span centuries, continents, and a range of political ideologies, they share a tactical and strategic framework of guerrillaism that involves asymmetry, mobility, and the exploitation of the enemy's weaknesses.

In a well-known and "classical" revolutionary guerrilla movement, such as Republican Northern Ireland, PIRA fighters struck at British interests wherever present and available for attack. Strikes were targets of opportunity carried out with lengthy planning. In this way, contemporary insurrectionary attacks operate within a similar strategy; striking at the representatives of the near enemy when able, and then retreating into the masses. The aim is to make system maintenance more costly, to provoke the violent actions of the security apparatus, and to promote propaganda of the deed and the dissemination of radical, critical theory through written propaganda. For those operating in an urban setting, the goal is likely not to seize power through controlling large areas of physical territory. Instead, as urban movements tend to be numerically smaller, their war is one of attrition rather than outright victory. In discussing the strategic differences between urban and rural armed movements, John Wolf (1981, 22–23) writes:

> Urban-based terrorists at best can only hope to raise the cost of governing for the incumbent so that he abdicates ... the destruction of an enemy involves breaking either his ability or his will to resist ... force is employed to demoralize the enemy more than defeat him ... Consequently, the use of terror entails more than the impairment of the enemy's will to fight. It seeks to build the morale both of the insurgent forces and of the wider masses, by demonstrating through daring acts that the incumbent is not unassailable.

The goal throughout guerrilla struggle – urban or rural – remains the same: to tire and frustrate the enemy, creates zones of ungovernability, and compete for popular support in the public sphere. Insurrectionary attack seeks to create rupture – temporary "breaks" or spaces within otherwise occupied zones of control – which can demonstrate alternative modes of existence, temporary sites of counter-systemic living. Through the use of revolutionary, anti-statist and anti-capitalist violence, attackers hope to demonstrate that not only is actualized, visible opposition possible, but that the creation of such tension with one's opponent is a victory in itself. For the insurrectionists, when a bank is set ablaze and painted with revolutionary messages, that bank's function within the socio-political arena of structural control is disrupted and its function temporarily changes from that of structural maintainer to symbol of resistance (ACME Collective 1999). Such a transformation of property from a manifestation of capital to one of utility and resistance is a continuation of the anarchist social movements that spiked in prominence just before the emergence of the post-millennial insurrectionists.

The questions of "terrorism" and "violence"

> I still remain proud of my choices and for joining the Conspiracy of Cells of Fire and its overall action, which undergoes your trials again and again constantly repeating the same and the same charges: Terrorist, terrorist, terrorist ... I will always be a terrorist ... I will always be guilty ... Not a single millimeter back. 9mm to the heads of the judges. (Argirou 2016)

> Terrorists are simply the members of their societies who are the most optimistic about the usefulness of violence for achieving goals that many, and often most, support. (Pape 2005, 8)

How various armed formations have responded to the post-9/11 rhetoric of terrorism is telling when seeking to understand their internal logic. Before examining the specific networks' interaction with this term, one can examine the insurrectionary milieu through foundational readings of social movement taxonomies, such as the work of theorist Roberta Garner. The structuring of a movement will have great ramifications for its strategic functioning. In her widely cited social movement theory, Garner examines these structural realities, applying them to past movements. For the insurrectionary movement, several of Garner's (1996, 28–30) typologies apply. The broad insurrectionary milieu utilizes "clandestine organizations," "armed insurgencies," and employs strategies akin to "destabilization" and "terrorism." Garner explains that the development of clandestine organization is the product of a political system that fails to allow for an open space for movement participation, thus forcing activists underground into cell structures. While the result (e.g. underground cells) can be seen in the insurrectionary networks, the cause identified – lack of political opportunity – fails to adequately describe the contemporary actors. Similarly, Garner's "armed insurgency" (1996, 29–30) typology is the result of a state that is too repressive. While insurrectionary networks certainly do attempt to foment insurgency against the state through the use of armed action, this is not the result of political repression, as insurrectionary networks thrive in liberal democracies of Western nations. Once again, while the organizational tendency is present, the cause is not.

More applicable than her organizational models are the strategies outlined. Garner explains the strategy of destabilization in a manner far closer to the insurrectionary model. "The movement takes action that polarizes the society, weakens support for the incumbent government, and suggests to the public that the state is no longer in control" (Garner 1996, 30). While Garner links this to paramilitaries who then attempt to fill the power vacuum (something completely counter to an anti-authoritarian objective), the strategy of polarizing, weakening, and creating zones of ungovernability is certainly present. It would be difficult to argue that modern insurrectionary methods have accomplished this (e.g. polarizing society, weaken state support and image of control) though the movement maintains these markers as a goal.

Terrorism, according to traditional understandings, is essentially an act that aids in the "creation of ideological politics" (Gillespie 1986, 5), something key to the insurrectional project and its deployment of violence. The insurrectionary strategy is firmly committed to widening and exasperating the polarization of class antagonisms – damaging the population's image of the state – though their efforts thus far have only made slight inroads in this regard. In another, more abstracted sense, insurrectionary attack has succeeded in damaging the population's image of the market, showing its vulnerability to crisis and attack and the state's wedded nature through corporate bailouts and other acts of protectionism. Perhaps the best example was the decentralized Stop Huntingdon Animal Cruelty campaign (1999–2014) against Huntingdon Life Sciences, an animal testing and breeding company. This campaign, which included the use of insurrectionary-styled tactics, successfully isolated Huntingdon, forcing the British state to support the besieged company economically when other potential financial backers broke ranks in light of protests.

Garner states that "terrorism" is used as a means towards destabilization, adding that it serves the cause of polarization and demonstrating weak state control. Building upon this understanding, scholars have argued that *terrorism* can be separated from other forms of anti-social violence by its political orientation focused on influencing the public, state or the social structures at large (Quinton 1990, 35–36). Though *typically*, practitioners of political violence do *not* self-identify with the terrorist label – instead posturing as "highly symbolic and moral" (Heath and O'Hair 2008, 18) – some insurrectionary networks have embraced it. Modern insurrectionary groups self-identifying with "terror" include the "Terrorist Cells for Direct Action – Anti-Civilization Faction" (2011), a Mexican, anti-civilization, primitivist network responsible for several bombings. The word *terror* is also seen in the monikers of several contemporary cell-level formations identifying as elements of the FAI-IRF and CCF, such as:

- **IRF**: "Terrorist Complicity Warriors of the Abyss Severino Di Giovanni Commando," "Deviant Behaviors for the Spreading of Revolutionary Terrorism, Cell of Anarchist Action," "Anarchist Revolutionary Front: Deviant Behaviors for the Spreading of Revolutionary Terrorism, Cell of Reflective Attack"
- **CCF**: "Breath of Terror Commando," "Terrorist Guerrilla Unit"
- **IRF/CCF**: "Revolutionary Groups for the Spreading of Terror – Nucleus of vandals," "Revolutionary Groups for the Spreading of Terror, Cell Abnormal – Heretics"
- **FAI-IRF/CCF**: "Revolutionary Groups of Terror Dispersion."

In examining the embrace or rejection of the value-laden term *terrorism*, Alfredo Cospito, imprisoned for the FAI-IRF shooting of an Italian nuclear executive, wrote an essay bemoaning the wider anarchist movement and offering a defense of militancy. Cospito argues that while the broader anarchist movement praises sabotage of property, when such force is directed towards people, anarchists' rejection of such means aids the state in its defamation of aggressive resistance. He argues the property destruction common among more civil milieus amounts to a "spectacle ... a complete and utter recuperation of sabotage." Cospito (2015 [emphasis in original]) writes:

> [The anarchist movement] has used its superior "*ethical code*" to blacklist all violent direct action that goes beyond striking a compressor with a Molotov ... [thus] transforming the act of burning the compressor into a spectacle, into mediation, into politics ... According to the superior "*ethical code*" of a large part of the "*movement*", those who strike people, weapon in hand, are terrorists. To the calculative and well-meaning ethics of "*sabotage*", I prefer terrorism, with its clear, wicked and distinctly linear logic.

Cospito is keen to remind the reader that anarchism's history is intertwined with that of "terrorism" and as such, for insurrectionists, "terrorism is part of our history the history of anarchism." As a single, yet prominent, proponent of an insurrectionary methodology, Cospito's comments not only embrace the spirit of terrorism, but also reject the wider movement's tactical policing on the ground of morality and ethics.

Beyond the FAI/IRF/CCF networks and individuals – such as Cospito or CCF member Panagiotis Argiro – there are clandestine animal liberation cells who have chosen to not identify with the ALF moniker (which prioritizes Cospito's "spectacle of sabotage") and instead adopt terrorist-themed names such as "Columna Terrorista de lxs[3] Revolucionarios de Negro" [Terrorist Column of the Black Revolutionaries] operating in Mexico. This trend is far from new as early proponents of property destruction in favor of the environment self-labeled as "Evan Mecham Eco-Terrorist International Conspiracy" (EMETIC),[4] naming themselves after the then-Governor of Arizona where the attacks were carried out. EMETIC can be seen as a precursor to the ELF as both utilized spectacularly dynamic forms of property destruction to economically damage targets seen to be damaging the Earth, afterwards announcing their acts and intent via a communiqué. According to the National Consortium for the Study of Terrorism and Responses to Terrorism (2015), the EMETIC group carried out five attacks in Arizona (1987–1989), using acetylene torches to down several ski lifts, in addition to energy infrastructure used to power a uranium mine and an electrical substation.

While numerous groups have incorporated the value-laden term into their names, others have consciously utilized such means, even commenting on such tactical considerations. The Mexican eco-insurrectionary network ITS (2014), which has focused its attacks on nanotechnologists and other researchers, wrote:

> ... in 2011 the (newly formed) ITS was testing various modus operandi (from known and attempted arson attacks on cars and construction machinery, companies and ... until we decided to focus on terrorism and not sabotage), some were successful and some not, the most violent cell of ITS in Morelos, being already familiar with the purchase and use of firearms, decided to implement the act by then.

ITS acknowledged several times in a single communiqué that they were consciously employing *terrorism* as a strategic model. In their eighth communiqué, which claims responsibility for several parcel bombs sent to researchers, the cell states: "With this statement we do not intend, in the least, that technologists give us their academic acceptance ... because obviously that will never happen, as they will never accept terrorism against them" (ITS 2014). Less than one month after ITS issued their communiqué self-identifying their strategy to include *terrorism*, a newly emerged group (OPCA) claimed a parcel bomb. In OPCA's communiqué (2014), they speak in support of ITS, yet identify them as "the terrorist group ITS." The new faction/cell writes, "we published a total of three analyses ... in which we have publicly demonstrated our support of the group ITS, in their actions as much as their position" (Obsidian Point Circle of Attack 2014), providing footnoted references to the documents.

Member of the CCF's Imprisoned Members Cell have reflected in a similar fashion, embracing the identification with *terrorism*. In a 2014 communiqué written from within Greece's Korydallos Prison, the authors write:

The authority says "those that I cannot befool, at least I will intimidate ..." So fear rules. The Conspiracy of Cells of Fire have made our intentions clear. **To terror you respond with terror.** The only way to dissipate fear and its tyranny is to transfer it in the enemy's yard. The **anarchist armed guerrilla** through autonomous affinity cells that sometimes meet inside the **FAI** informal network and sometimes they don't is our response to the authority. (CCF-FAI/IRF Imprisoned Members Cell 2014 [emphasis in original])

Of course this is not a completely new phenomenon. Possibly one of the first groups to embrace the term, to proudly self-label, was also a group formed around a nihilist-infused form of anarchism. In the mid 1800s, Nechayev, the Russian anarcho-nihilist, labeled his actions, and that of his group, People's Retribution,[5] as *terrorism* (M. Crenshaw 1995, 77). One hundred years later, counterculture Yippie hero Jerry Rubin – described as "the fighting man's version of Abbie Hoffman" (Acton, LeMond, and Hodges 1972, 187) – stated to a House Committee on Un-American Activities committee, "Here we were, terrorists, anarchists and freaks" (Rubin 1970, 204). In other self-referential pearls from Rubin, he terms himself a "hippie guerrilla" and a "one-man international revolution, a walking conspiracy" (1970, 202).

A great deal of political violence is labeled terrorism; typically dependent on who is deploying the violence and who is the recipient. If the perpetrator is a non-state actor, and the recipient the state, this act will be declared terrorism with near universal regularity. Activists are aware of this discursive and rhetorical shift, and some have explicitly addressed it when discussing their tactical decision-making. In one example, ALF militant Walter Bond, convicted of three arsons, notes that since the state is in control of this rhetorical process, he may as well aim for tactical effectiveness since any action will likely be labeled as "terrorism." Bond (2010) writes:

The first thing I knew was that I would work alone ... The next thing I knew was that I wanted to go big. With the current government crackdown on any kind of effective ... campaign, I might as well go for it. If they're gonna try to catch me and call me a terrorist for breaking a McDonald's window, I might as well think much bigger.

In a sense, Bond embraces the state's rhetoric and uses it to justify his own tactical choices, since to meter one's actions, according to Bond, would not avoid such a labeling anyway. This embracing of the rhetoric of terrorism is also not restricted to the actions of revolutionary anti-statists and has been employed by members of the right, such as anti-abortion militant Clayton Lee Wager. In a series of communications posted online on 2001, Waagner directly threatens clinic workers with assassination, and reflects on his terrorism labeling. In one such letter circulated by the clandestine, anti-abortion network known as The Army of God, Waagner (2001) writes:

> The government of the most powerful country in the world considers me a terrorist. That label set me aback at first. Then it struck me: They're right. I am a terrorist. To be sure, I'm a terrorist to a very narrow group of people, but a terrorist just the same ... I'll drop you [targeted clinic workers] a note and we'll get this terrorism thing started in earnest.

Despite Waagner's embracing of the label, many social movement activists – including those who reject and embrace militant means – have sought to challenge this framing.

A revolutionary reading of political violence

> Perhaps the dominant mainstream perception of anarchism is its equation with violence, disorder "bomb throwing," and – even more odiously, in today's parlance – terrorism ... The negotiation of the "violence versus non-violence" terrain is one of the many dichotomies presented by anarchist praxis, and it further represents something of a political litmus test of movement culture. (Amster 2012, 43)

Certainly such an asymmetric labeling of political violence is deserving of challenge. Anarchist and revolutionary leftist scholarship on theories of violence – both that directed against property as well as direct/physical and structural forms – has been a mainstay of theory since scholars put pen to paper. Furthermore, as Randall Amster (2012, 58) points out, a great deal of anarchist scholarship dealing with an explicit endorsement of pacifism is present, including works by Henry David Thoreau, Leo Tolstoy, Ammon Hennacy, Dorothy Day, Paul Goodman, and Alex Comfort. To that list I would add contemporary anarcho-peace educator Colman McCarthy.

Contemporary anarchist theory has tended to problematize the state's labeling of acts as "violent" or "nonviolent," arguing that *non*violence can insulate the state from effective modes of resistance. Peter Gelderloos (2007; 2013) argues that democratic forms of statecraft are predicated upon the government encouraging its citizenry to express dissent through legalistic means, such as voting, dialogue, and lobbying elected representatives. While some have argued that the violence/nonviolence binary is a limiting frame for the analysis of social movements (Mitcho 2014), others such as Gelderloos have based their work precisely at this point of distinction. Gelderloos (2013) argues that the state's position – that all social conflict can be resolved through legalistic means – is an essential aspect of maintaining social order in democratic societies, serving to insulate the state from revolutionary violence. On the other hand, the insurrectionary critique argues that the fostering of social tensions acts to demonstrate the state's oppositional relationship to the citizenry, showing that the former is in constant conflict with the latter. Therefore, for the insurrectionists, an atmosphere of sustained social warfare is counter to more traditionally leftist calls to maintain nonviolence.

Both Gelderloos and the insurrectionists represent a rejection of pacifism, arguing that its deployment to dissuade revolutionary violence is a strategic maneuver by the state as a means for control. Other anarchist scholars have similarly argued that not only is violent resistance permissible, but that it has been a mainstay in all social struggles. This argument is made by modern (i.e. twenty-first century) authors as well as "classical" (i.e. twentieth century) anarchists, such as Alexander Berkman. For Berkman (1929, 5), he argues in his foundational work *The ABC of Anarchism* that not only do anarchists not dominate the deployment of political violence, but that such methods are an inherent part of social movements.

> You see, then, that anarchists have no monopoly on political violence. The number of such acts by anarchists is infinitesimal as compared with those committed by persons of other political persuasions. The truth is that in every country, in every social movement violence has been a part of the struggle from time immemorial.

In the modern era, many activists focusing on political violence agree with such an assertion. One such scholar, Craig Rosebraugh (2004), who has served as a spokesmen for the ALF/ELF, argues that to isolate so-called nonviolence from more militant forms of resistance is a historical impossibility, and that the portrayal of social movements (e.g. US Civil Rights) as nonviolent is a form of historical erasure of more militant strands of protest. Rosebraugh argues that a great many social struggles historically understood as nonviolent were in actuality a symbiosis between those avoiding violence on ethical and moral grounds and those embracing it for tactical and strategic ends. Now while some who choose to adopt more militant methods do so while embracing a discourse that separates themselves from "terrorists," other evolutionary actors have worn this disparaging title as a mark of distinction.

While some insurrectionary actors have toyed with self-identifying as *terrorists*, typically awareness of such trappings have led post-9/11 movements to markedly dis-identify with those that hijack planes and bomb buses. Though often militant, violent, and clandestine, the nature of insurrectionary warfare is that it is not directed outwards at the masses, to terrorize and coerce; it is directed upwards at power. Not only does this allow for a more sincere, non-delegated articulation of strife, but it does not create a combatant/civilian, revolutionary/non-revolutionary duality. To de-fetishize the insurrectionary cell is to blend it seamlessly into a more distributed dissent. As one anonymous (2001a, 32) author states:

> For its part, the State has every interest in reducing the revolutionary threat to a few combat organizations in order to transform subversion into a clash between two armies: the institutions on the one hand, the armed party on the other. What power fears most is anonymous, generalized rebellion. The media image of the "terrorist" works hand in hand with the police in defense of social peace.

Part of this awareness of powerful state labeling is a product of the post-9/11 state reliance on a newly invigorated boogey man to follow that of fascism and Soviet communism. Following the attacks of 2001, *terrorism* could be mobilized to rally patriotism, nationalism, and jingoism.

The early Marxist Leon Trotsky cautioned against the dependency on terrorist-styled methods of attack. In his aptly named essay, "Why Marxists Oppose Individual Terrorism," Trotsky (1911, para. 10) argues that such a strategy "belittles the role of the masses in their own consciousness" falsely offering a "great avenger" to lead a revolutionary path. Trotsky (1911, para. 10) argues that while these individualist methods of attack are thought to raise a revolutionary consciousness, their effectiveness disincentives the masses and those targeted are easily replaced.

> The anarchist prophets of the "propaganda of the deed" can argue all they want about the elevating and stimulating influence of terrorist acts on the masses. Theoretical considerations and political experience prove otherwise. The more "effective" the terrorist acts, the greater their impact, the more they reduce the interest of the masses in self-organization and self-education. But the smoke from the confusion clears away, the panic disappears, the successor of the murdered minister makes his appearance, life again settles into the old rut, the wheel of capitalist exploitation turns as before; only the police repression grows more savage and brazen. And as a result, in place of the kindled hopes and artificially aroused excitement comes disillusionment and apathy.

For Trotsky, it is not a moral objection to political violence but a strategic argument about its effect on the revolutionary program. Trotsky asserts that terrorist acts do not aid in organizing the masses for collective revolt but rather resigns them to "spectators" of the act, and that their outsider observation will eventually lead to a desire for enforcement of order (Rubenstein 1987, 108–109).

Others on the anti-capitalist left have made similar arguments against individualistic modes of direct attack (e.g. terrorism), such as the 1979 essay, "You Can't Blow Up A Social Relationship" (Libertarian Socialist

Organisation 1979), written in response to the Sydney Hilton Bombing (13 February 1978), which killed two garbage collectors and a police officer. In a similarly reactionary manner, following the assassination of Italian King Umberto I in 1900, James F. Morton, Jr. (1900), an American, individualist anarchist, once again engaged the question of direct attack, writing:

> Do I therefore applaud the act of the assassin? By no means. The shedding of human blood, though at times to be justified or excused, is never a fit cause for exultation. Nor is the spirit of revenge an element of the Anarchist philosophy. Our mission is not to incite to violent acts, but to wage an eternal warfare against the crime-producing and misery-breeding conditions of the day. When the down-trod proletarian, filled with a deep sense of the myriad wrongs inflicted on himself, his dear ones and his kind, strikes a blow of vengeance against the representatives of the system which has transformed men into beasts, we do not rejoice – nor condemn. We simply explain. Would you put an end to the assassination of rulers? Then end the conditions which make men miserable; end the wrongs which provoke men to resistance; cease to outrage flesh and blood as human and as sensitive as that of kings.

The author proposes a solution of sorts to stemming the tide of anarcho-political violence: If one hopes to quell resistance, one must seek to change the material conditions that oppress the masses and create the conditions for such a critique to develop.

The novel and relevant question is not whether placing an IED in the lobby of a bank or police garage is *strategic*, or amounts to an act of *terrorism*, but rather, "What does one's hatred of police tell us about how law enforcement is critically understood in the society?" Is terrorism a "response to a certain kind of social crisis" as Rubenstein (1987, xx) suggests, or perhaps sometime more akin to a strategy adoptable by anyone? Can terrorism be a tactic utilized within other strategies? Can a tactic be intimidating, effective, and targeted yet not be *terrorism*? Does labeling something terrorism have any effect other than to pejoratively describe and defame? Rubenstein (1987, 17) suggests that "to call an act of political violence terrorist is not merely to describe it but to judge it ... imply[ing] illegitimacy." This declarative statement clearly identifies the strict discursive reality of the rhetoric of terrorism. If a state-backed paramilitary can kill union leaders to un-incentivize union activity and be labeled "paramilitary guerrillas," why should an anarchist burning banks to strike at capitalism be inextricably likened to *terrorism* – often regarded as the intentional targeting of civilians and other secondary target audience for socio-political or religious purposes? Furthermore, the ability to extricate oneself from such a rhetorical gaze is not often possible. For example, after being imprisoned for an alleged conspiracy to disrupt the May 2012 North Atlantic

Treaty Organization meetings in Chicago, Mark "Migs" Neiweem was classified within the prison system as having "Gang or Unauthorized Organization Activity." This disciplinary violation alleges that Migs's tattoos – which include the anarchist "circle A" and the pro-equality "circle E" – constitute gang affiliation (Potter 2013), and that such markings, in conjunction with the inmate's friends and possession of related reading materials, mark him as a security threat. This example shows the powerlessness often bemoaned by activists unable to control their rhetorical portrayal within a discourse of securitization by state forces. Furthermore, such association between labeling (e.g. a tattoo) and affiliation (e.g. with a moniker-based network) provides a disincentive for clandestine activists to claim attacks via monikers, as to associate with the FAI, CCF, ALF, etc. could constitute similar "gang"' affiliations and be used to further criminalize dissent through the anti-gang discourse.

While one can (and should) challenge the rhetoric of *terrorism* to describe a strategic deployment of illegal violence, it is certainly true that insurrectionary methods such as bombings leave a state with two options, both of which benefit radical politics: (1) Fail to stop "terrorism" and appear weak and ineffectual, or (2) stop "terrorism" through repression and fulfill your typecast role as a violent apparatus furthering polarization (Garner 1996, 30). Certainly there are examples from the revolutionary past where option two was chosen by the state yet the polarization produced served counterrevolutionary purposes. In response to a campaign of violence waged by Italy's RB, the polarization of the left led to the Communist Party moving towards the political right, creating an unfilled vacuum (for a time) for mass-based, leftist mobilization (Rubenstein 1987, 109). While aged social movement typologies and strategic models are inadequate for describing the contemporary milieu, they are instructive in developing broad categorical reference points for positing new tendencies within existing patterns of sociological behavior.

Affinity groups, monikers, and guidelines

FAI, the Black International, the CCF, the affinity groups of anarcho-individualists and nihilists is the community we want to live in. This has nothing to do with the cumulative perception of power. FAI is not the model of a centralized organization. On the contrary, it promotes informal organization, affinity between cells and the uniqueness of each individual. We are against the dictatorship of numbers and central committees. Neither do we follow the logic of two fighting armies but instead we promote the diffusion of hundreds of points of rapture and action, which sometimes cooperate in an international coordination and sometimes express themselves as unique cells or individuals. FAI is simply the invisible community where the desires of attack against our era, meet. In this way, we promote New Anarchy and the Black International. (CCF-FAI/IRF Imprisoned Members Cell 2013)

The new guerrillas of insurrectionary attack should be understood as an international network of disconnected and sometimes loosely federated affinity groups, ad hoc collectives, and individuals. The *affinity group model* has its roots in a variety of social movements often linked to the so-called anti-globalization, global justice movements that crescendoed around the millennium, embodied in mass demonstrations opposing multinational trade bodies. However, their roots in anti-state, anarchist resistance are a bit older. The use of the affinity group model dates back to at least the anarchist resistance to Francoist Spain and fascism in the 1930s. As the CrimethInc. Ex-Workers' Collective (2013) recounts in their discussion of the history of insurrectionary anarchism, the speaker describes these structures as "small, nimble groups that wage attacks, assassinated political figureheads and police, and freed prisoners, while robbing banks to support themselves and living illegally and clandestinely." The affinity groups would be constituted or disbanded depending on the changing nature of the conflict and preferred direct combat with the state rather than mediated representations through politics. According to one social movement scholar, "affinity groups" can be defined as "small, semi-independent units, pledged to coalition goals, tactics, and principals ... but [are] free to make their own plans" (Finnegan 2003, 213–214). They are "small units of activists, effectively mirroring, in organizational terms, a group of friends ... based on organic horizontality" (Feigenbaum, Frenzel, and McCurdy 2013, 168).

This analogy to networks of friends is shared in the aforementioned comments from the CCF activists. Typically affinity groups are between three and ten people and are organized for the specific needs of the action (G-MAC and People Within The ARA 2002, 208) on hand and may possess varied skillsets based on the individuals involved. This tendency to organize towards the small is interwoven into the leftist tradition or organizational struggle. In a 1905 "Warning to the Insurgents" of Moscow it is written:

> Main rule: do not act en masse. Carry out actions in three or four at the most. There should be as many small groups as possible and each of them must learn to attack and disappear quickly ... It is easier to defeat a hundred men than one alone, especially if they strike suddenly and disappear mysteriously. (Quoted in Anonymous 2001a, 19)

While the aforementioned descriptions are meant to describe alternative formations (e.g. affinity groups participating in mass demonstrations, or Russian "insurgents") the framework can be utilized to trace the borders of the insurrectionary tendency as well. For networks such as CCF/FAI/ALF (described as *clusters* when applied to affinity groups) small groupings of activists ally toward the broadly defined goals of the coalition as identified by their moniker. For traditional affinity groups the same rules apply. "Rather than agreeing an overall strategy for political action, the plurality of affinity groups, at times combined with a broad 'action consensus' (e.g. non-violence), leaves the decision over which action to take and how far to go with the individual groups" (Feigenbaum, Frenzel, and McCurdy 2013, 23). While an affinity group may agree to an "action consensus" (e.g. Points of Unity), a cell network will agree to a set of guidelines. Within this guided frame, individual cells can decide how best to pursue the "broad consensus" tactically within a shared strategy.

The friendship/affinity group model, whether used to coordinate civil disobedience through snarling traffic or mailing IEDs to political officials, both rely on a basic, self-contained (David et al. 2002, 237), small scale, temporarily assembled tactical model. Groupings may merge, split, and transition from organizing public disturbances to clandestine guerrilla warfare. This is the case with the Students for a Democratic Society's factionalization around the 1969 Days of Rage. Around this time, the movement's wing known as the Revolutionary Youth Movement – including Bernardine Dohrn, David Gilbert, and Mark Rudd who would later constitute the WUO's first generation – split from the larger network during the movement's National Council meetings in Texas (David 2002, 13–14). The tendency for social movements to factionalize is largely avoided in the insurrectionary model as the movement's "leaderless resistance" structure and focus on temporality allows collectivities to form, act, and then disband only to be remixed and reconstituted at a later date. The formation of temporary cells for the purpose of striking a target is exemplary of the insurrectionary approach which privileges informality, spontaneity, and replication and direct attacks against sites of power. This lack of requisite coordination or mobilizing mechanisms makes insurrectionary networks both increasingly subterranean, and difficult to identify, isolate, expose, and repress. In this manner, both the *manner* of insurrectionary attack, as well as the networks' organizational methods, are a form of insurrectionism – a fluid yet identifiable style of acting which seeks to communicate through violence. There are no spokespeople but everyone can speak. There are no centralized coordinators allowing all cells equal opportunity to set the pace of internationalized campaigns of attack.

Insurrectionary praxis is key to its identity. Notions of informality and temporality inform the cells' understandings of self, as well as their integration into international networks. In the model of affinity groups and clandestine, networked cells – "the horizontal linking of affinity groups" (Anonymous 2001a, 32) – only remain assembled for the length of time required to complete their specific actions. Individuals do not hold onto group membership in perpetuity or as long as dues are paid, but only as long as the co-conspirators find that it provides organizational, tactical or strategic utility. Before and after the action, the collective does not exist. This affinity group-styled mode of resistance functions in tandem with the deployment of communiqués to determine attack authorship, and further demarcate group membership and inter-community inclusion and exclusion. This phenomenon can be seen in an examination of the communiqués and network guideline as markers of identity within a fluid social movement.

Following the 1999 WTO demonstrations, where window-smashing anarchists caused approximately $20 million in property damage and lost revenues (CBC News 2000), many correspondents were searching for a "group" to associate with the violence, though the vandalism and property destruction was carried out by a variety of individuals, both "affiliated" and independent. Following such an attack, whether by the 1999 black bloc or the 2014 arsonist, the goal is to generate another strike in a long series of attacks. In this sense, the strategy of protracted combat is open-ended as the attackers do not imagine that any single incident will lead to the collapse of capital or the state. The attackers do not expect the branch to fail or the parent company to capitulate to some reformist demands, rather the strike against the enemy is in itself the end goal. It exists within a chronological ordering of similar attacks that occurred before and will occur after. These attacks collectively represent a social force that seeks to create structural change.

In this manner, insurrectionary strategy is simultaneously pessimistic and optimistic. It is pessimistic because it does not believe that a campaign of attack will lead to the sudden yielding of power by the state, but maintains an optimism that such a series of attacks does serve a revolutionary goal of radicalizing the population, exposing the violence of state and capital, and temporarily focusing the attention of the population on issues of structural violence through forcing people to ask the question: "Why did those people blow up that bank?" The goal is thus to localize the struggle, to allow one's anti-state actions to serve as a negation of the systems domination and a transcendence of mediation of capitalist relations (Wood 2013, 15). Since the nature of the insurrectionary understanding of control is one where the forces of domination are transnational, ever-present, and boundless, the goal is not to defeat this amorphous body but rather to create ruptures – however temporary – which allow one to imagine another world of greater freedom and autonomy.

Most importantly, the carrying out of attacks can be seen as an end in itself as they serve to confront the enemy, in the "urgent immediacy" (Wood 2013, 39), through an unmediated method of struggle. To produce an attack is to rhetorically link it to thousands of attacks from the past, and to provide yet another example of praxis for those acting in the future. This is the precise functional use of the adoptable moniker. By uniting disparate incidents through a shared brand, these seemingly disconnected acts of resistance are linked together into a collective history – what one could term "collective behavior" (Dolata and Schrape 2016, 1) from globally-dispersed (i.e. non-collective) actors. This collectivity then shares a narrative, it shares intellectual resources, and creates a "digital community"[6] which serves to "produce and provide ideological frameworks, knowledge concerning tactics, equipment and targets, but of greatest importance, inspiration and the idea that one is part of a vivid, supporting community and *not* alone" (van Buuren and de Graaf 2013, 176–177). In this manner, between 1972 and 2010, the ALF/ELF monikers have been used to claim responsibility for over 7,200 attacks in at least 36 countries (Loadenthal 2010, 81–89, 94–95). The power of such a unifying marker should not be understated. Using the ALF/ELF as a model, the shared identity creates a social movement from seemingly unconnected broken windows, slashed tires, and burned out slaughterhouses. In other words, the moniker functions as a rallying point, a centrally-located means of movement identification, wherein a window breaker in Berlin and an arsonist in Tel Aviv can feel as though they are part of the same movement, united in a shared guideline for action, and moving towards the same goal (e.g. ending speciesism, opposing capitalism).

The groups that share a moniker or brand in order to claim responsibility for attacks often adopt a "guideline" approach to drawing in-group/out-group distinctions. In 1973, the German group RZ began encouraging cells and individuals to act, stating that "anybody could carry out and action within the context of the RZ's politics ... and claim it as an RZ action" (Moncourt and Smith 2009b, 2:69). While RZ did not appear to maintain a static, numbered list of rules, it created thematic borders for its actors, defining their areas of operation into three categories:

> 1.) anti-imperialist actions, 2.) actions against the branches, establishments, and accomplices of Zionism in the FRG [Federal Republic of Germany], and 3.) actions supporting the struggles of workers, wimmin[7] and youth, and attacking and punishing their enemies. (Autonome Forum n.d.)

RZ urged its adherents to carry out cell-level attacks against targeting fitting the above criteria and *encouraged* the destruction of property, not the targeting of individuals, similar to the strategy of the ALF/ELF.

According to the BBC (2007), RZ carried out 186 actions in approximately 20 years. Around the same time RZ was forming in Germany, the ALF was emerging as a newly militant direct action tendency in England, separating itself from the Band of Mercy (Molland 2006) which had used similar tactics of vandalism, sabotage, and arson in defense of animals. The

ALF in its formative years developed a set of five "guidelines" that an individual must adhere to in order to claim that action as that of the ALF.

1. To inflict economic damage on those who profit from the misery and exploitation of animals.
2. To liberate animals from places of abuse, i.e. laboratories, factory farms, fur farms etc., and place them in good homes where they may live out their natural lives, free from suffering.
3. To reveal the horror and atrocities committed against animals behind locked doors, by performing nonviolent direct actions and liberations.
4. To take all necessary precautions against harming any animal, human and non-human.
5. Any group of people who are vegetarians or vegans and who carry out actions according to ALF guidelines have the right to regard themselves as part of the ALF.

The ELF, modeled after the ALF, developed a similar set of guidelines and, through its aboveground press offices and publications, is careful to disseminate such texts widely. According to a document circulated from the North American ELF Press Office (2001), the guidelines are:

1. To cause as much economic damage as possible to a given entity that is profiting off the destruction of the natural environment and life for selfish greed and profit.
2. To educate the public on the atrocities committed against the environment and life.
3. To take all necessary precautions against harming life.

The Press Office makes it clear that based on these guidelines, "ELF" is simply a political framework that anyone can adopt.

> The ELF does not have any sort of physical membership list or meetings you can attend to become involved. Remember, the ELF revolves around not a physical base or classically designed structure, but instead an ideology. If you believe in the ELF ideology and you follow a certain set of widely published guidelines, you can conduct actions and become part of the ELF. (2001, 14–15)

Such a model has continued to expand as new formulations of resistance networks emerge.

In 2003, a series of bombings targeting affiliate companies involved in funding animal research were targeted. In August, two pipe bombs packed with nails exploded at the offices of Chiron Corporation in Emeryville, CA.

One month later, a second bombing occurred, this time targeting the offices of Shaklee Inc., in Pleasanton, CA. Both Chiron and Shaklee were economically linked to Huntingdon Life Sciences, the target of a multi-year, international protest campaign led by SHAC because of its breeding of animals for experimentation. The Revolutionary Cells – Animal Liberation Brigade (RC-ALB) claimed both bombings through emailed communiqués sent to media and *Bite Back Magazine*, a website and print periodical established to publicize ALF and ideologically aligned actions. In the second such text, which claimed responsibility for the September IED, the author outlined the guidelines for future RC-ALB (2003) actions.

> The revolutionary cells exist as a front group for militants across the liberationary movement spectrum. We are anarchists, communists, anti-racists, animal liberationists, earth liberationists, luddites, feminists, queer liberationists, and many more things across various other fronts ... Anyone who takes part in the war against the oppressive hierarchies [sic] in this world can consider themselves a member of the Revolutionary Cells.

Revolutionary Cells Guidelines:

1. To take strategic direct action (be it non-violent or not) against the oppressive institutions that permeate the world
2. Make every effort to minimize non-target casualties, be they human or non-human.
3. Respect a diversity of tactics, whether they be non-violent or not.
4. Any underground activist fighting for the liberation of the humyn,[8] earth or animal nations may consider themselves a Revolutionary Cells volunteer.

Clearly one can see the influence of earlier incarnations on that of the RC-ALB. Not only did they directly borrow the namesake of RZ, a group inactive for nearly a decade, but also three of the four guidelines can be easily likened to those of the ALF/ELF. It is only guideline three – which allows for the RC-ALB to target people not property – that separates it from the ALF/ELF. In this understanding, the RC-ALB is similar to animal liberation networks such as the Justice Department and Animal Rights Militia in that it largely resembles the ALF except for its tactical allowance or outright endorsement for attacks against human targets.

It is important to note that the first two RC-ALB bombings, both carried out in California, are said to be the work of Daniel Andreas San Diego, the first American animal rights activist added to the FBI's Most Wanted Terrorist list. After noticing surveillance of his vehicle in 2003, San Diego disappeared, and despite his addition to the Most Wanted list has remained at large. While FBI and Department of Justice materials link San Diego to both 2003 IEDs, the RC-ALB moniker has been used to claim responsibility for six additional attacks, four in California, one in Maryland, and one in Switzerland. The attacks have included the arson or attempted arson of six targets, two bomb threats, and two mailed IEDs. While it is *conceivable* that San Diego created the RC-ALB and carried out all of the above mentioned attacks, it is more likely – according to Congressional testimony (109th Congress 2005a; 2005b) and court papers (Special Agent Christine Loscalzo 2003) – that San Diego was successful in creating an appealing, adoptable moniker, and that others chose to act as self-appointed members of the RC-ALB and carry his message forward.

While taking a slightly different approach, the CCF *proposed* guidelines in their self-assessment zine, *The Sun Still Rises*, and suggested three points of affinity for cells seeking to expand the social war, writing:

> We are ... making a proposal for a new Conspiracy comprising a diffuse, invisible, network of cells that have no reason to meet in person, yet through their actions and discourse recognize one another as comrades in the same political crime: the subversion of Law and Order. This Conspiracy would consist of individuals and cells that take action, whether autonomous or coordinated (through call-outs and communiqués), without needing to agree on every single position and specific reference point ... instead they would connect on the basis of mutual aid focused on three key points ... [1.] the choice of direct action using any means capable of damaging enemy infrastructure. Without hierarchization of methods of violence, comrades can choose from rocks to Kalashnikovs ... accompanied by a corresponding communiqué ... claiming responsibility and explaining the reason behind the attack, thus spreading revolutionary discourse ... [2.] wage war against the state while simultaneously engaging in a pointed critique of society ... [3.] international revolutionary solidarity ... a solidarity that cries out through texts, armed actions, attacks, and sabotage to reach the ears of persecuted and imprisoned comrades, no matter how far away they may be ... Any comrade who agrees (obviously without having to identify herself) with these three key points of the informal agreement we are proposing can – if she wants – use the name Fire Cells Conspiracy in connection with the autonomous cell she is a part of ... [and] be able to organize arson and bombing campaigns ... communicating through their claims of responsibility. (G. Tsakalos et al. 2012, 11–15)

The CCF model is far more open than that of previous networks. It encourages points of generalized affinity, not specific rules, with the hopes that cell-level decision-making remains autonomous while some form of international coordination can occur thorough the communiqués accompanying actions. The CCF even note how this idea has already been actualized by a cell of Dutch attackers who chose to attack Rabobank and claim the strikes as the CCF Dutch cell.

To claim or not to claim?

> I must say that the debate on using or not acronyms and claims is still very strong. Even in this case, I wouldn't make an "ideological" approach of the subject, I have nothing against actions not claimed, from my point of view they simply tend to disappear, they do not stimulate debate, they have a minimum potential of reproducibility … That's why I made the FAI-IRF methodology my own … Whoever claims responsibility with an acronym is an enemy worthy of denigration. (Cospito 2014)

Insurrectionary anarchism is often an identity of self-description, even in its more "civil" forms. In the media's reporting of anarchist activity (e.g. protests, arrests), it is exceedingly common for news outlets to describe activists as "self-proclaimed anarchists" (e.g. Kathimerini 2014; M. Morris 2014; Rosoff 2014), "self-described anarchists" (e.g. Associated Press 2013; Palmer 2013; Hensley 2014), and other such labels that imply the ambiguity of authoritatively assigning such a label. This sort of linguistic practice speaks to the self-adoptability of the anarchist "identity" with or without a clandestine moniker. While the label is just as often undeservingly applied to those seen as acting "violently" or "chaotically," in a great deal of coverage of actual anarchists, their self-labeling becomes a constant reference. Does this self-labeling function differently when individuals and groups choose to self-label within a specific factional moniker, be it the FAI, CCF, ELF, or others? Are there important considerations in determining how and if to claim responsibility for an attack?

Certainly discussions as to the pros and cons of *claiming* an attack, and the role played by stable monikers, have occurred.[9] Some have argued that by announcing an attack, issuing a communiqué, and labeling it with a group name, one is aiding state authorities in collecting evidence and eventually stopping the resistance activities. These activists argue that the action speaks for itself, and to further expose oneself with a written claim of responsibility – especially one that uses a moniker to link it to past and future attacks – is glamor-seeking, vain, self-indulgent, and ultimately without purpose. Others, such as those who regularly pen, translate, post, and circulate such claims, obviously feel otherwise. In one of the most direct and plainly stated discussion of this question, the Indonesian anarchist guerrilla known as Eat (2014) writes:

... I've realized from some of my correspondences with individuals from the so-called "general activist and anarchist milieu from local to international", that the idea of naming one cell as FAI is a big issue ... [I've been asked] ... why I "labeled" the cell of attack. I answered ... with a very simple logic: it was labeled as Informal Anarchist Federation because we shared the same ideas of sporadic attack and the critique of organization that came from anarchist-insurrectionalism.

It was a conscious choice to identify the revolt, whether by an individual or by groups, against the machinery of control. It was a gesture of solidarity to every anarchist prisoner around the world ... FAI is also a manifestation of the idea of sporadic attack and the general critique on the specialization of attack – such as professional terrorist organization and the past Marxist-Leninist hierarchical and vanguardist form of armed struggle. It is also not necessarily an armed struggle, but more of a means of arming ourselves against the machine.

The question that was raised ... originated from the critique of organization itself: the naming of the attack by a sort of invisible organization and in this case, it was the FAI/ IRF ... I think it is a very simple logic for every conscious individual who has a passion for waging war against the capitalist system. I have never met nor even corresponded with the FAI before I conducted the action, but I understood very well the ideas that lay behind it. And for me, our action was also a form of communication between individuals, anarchists especially, in the global sense. And it did, so I was very happy when I read and heard that so many solidarity actions were done for my case and it didn't occur to me that it was just a FAI/IRF inclusive project, but it was a firestarter, a test for our theory and formula of action and organization. FAI/IRF for me was a global meeting point ... FAI/IRF is maybe only just a name for some individuals who share some ideas, but it is also an experience in action and organization and not a form of fetishism. There are no individuals nor groups monopolizing the ideas, because the dialogue and debate is still ongoing. The action never stopped.

Eat's thoughts externalize this debate well. He chooses to claim attacks from within the FAI moniker precisely because of the power of an internationalized namesake. Eat explains the deterritorialized, disembodied insurrectionary milieu as an "experience," a "form of communication," a "global meeting point." Eat was able to consume the communiqués of the FAI produced in Italy, Greece, and elsewhere, incorporate their ideas into his own framework, carry out a local attack, and immediately vault from onlooker to participant in an international network of anarchists guerrillas.

In the times of urban guerrilla warfare that preceded the FAI and its allies, similar debates occurred. During the 1960s and 1970s, when more frequent armed guerrilla actions were occurring from the revolutionary left, the Angry Brigade which was active in the UK proposed the idea of a freely-adoptable moniker. The utility of such an approach was discussed in a 2012 publication chronicling the Angry Brigade. In their discussion of the usefulness of static labels, the author writes:

> Action Directe, the RAF, the CCC, RZ and other armed struggle groups in Europe were in fact the trees hiding the forest of autonomous groups of attack, far more numerous and diffused. On the one hand, one can find interesting the possibility mentioned in the communiques that anyone can appropriate the signature Angry Brigade: "Where two or three revolutionaries use organized violence to attack the class system ... there is the Angry Brigade. Revolutionaries all over England are already using the name to publicise their attacks on the system" and "The AB is the man or woman sitting next to you. They have guns in their pockets and anger in their minds." But on the other hand, one can doubt the usefulness of creating an entity and identity based on a fixed signature. And if "revolutionaries throughout England already use this name to publicize their attacks against the system", the opposite is also true, and this is all the better, because it decentralizes the attack and makes it less legible to the eyes of cops, preventing them from being able to attribute socially diffuse practices to a particular group. (Ravage Editions 2013)

For this author, by advocating the diffuse usage of an adoptable moniker, this functions to obscure identifiable patterns of attack that may be useful to law enforcement, multiplying the "trees that hide the forest of attack." This sort of approach is also briefly mentioned in *The Coming Insurrection* wherein the authors speak of "not claiming your illegal actions, only attaching to them some fictional acronym" (TIC 2007, 113).

Certainly the same can be said about the modern attacks claimed under the FAI, CCF, and other monikers. One author argues that the modern groups "recognizing themselves under the logos FAI or IRF" (Ravage Editions 2013) function to "stifle" revolutionary fervor by claiming attacks under a stable, repeated moniker. Calling it the "spectacle of practices and logos" the author encourages the issuing of explanatory communiqués but cautions against acts of resistance becoming commodified spectacles as to apply a stable label to an attack is to make it "permanent ... claim[ing] belonging to it as in any other formal and permanent organization" (Ravage Editions 2013). This form of self-labeling serves to, "in view of police history ... facilitate one's own repression ... putting the spotlight on the authors of the attacks rather than the attacks themselves" (Ravage Editions 2013). At the level of the cells carrying out attacks, similar debates are ongoing. Besides the reflections of past attackers such as Eat, an Italian cell of the FAI, calling itself "Conspiracy of Black Fire," spoke of similar concerns while claiming responsibility for an arson attack targeting a gasoline pump, and sabotaging ATMs. In their claim of responsibility, offered as the 13th Phoenix Project attack, the authors write:

> We spent a great deal of time pondering on the question of informality [not claiming via a moniker] and the possibility of giving birth to a group of action [through creating a new moniker]. During our discussion, among laughter and seriousness, lively debates, desires and anxiety, projects and strategies, we decided to give birth to the Conspiracy of Black Fire and wage war to the mega-machine of dominion. (Conspiracy of Black Fire – FAI-FRI 2014)

This choice to use the acronym was likely done for several reasons, one of which being to more completely integrate into the Phoenix Project. Similarly, since the FAI name was coined, cells have popped up around the world quite rapidly. In May 2014, a new cell was announced in Hong Kong, the second such country in Asia following Indonesia. In their communiqué, the new cell states:

> We, the Autonomous Cell for Revolutionary Class Struggle/Informal Anarchist Federation/International Revolutionary Front, would like to announce our formation ... Through autonomous action and in conjunction with other revolutionary cells around the world and an FAI cyber cell here in Hong Kong we aim to strike a blow to the spectacle, to the enslaving system. (Autonomous Cell for Revolutionary Class Struggle – FAI/IRF 2014)

In other cases, the decision of adopting attacks through monikers has been enough to splinter networks and foster divergent assemblages. For example, in August 2015, the RS network – speaking in the name of 12 "groupuscules" (sic) – announced that its "affinity groups" would divide into four groupings, described as:

> A) *Anonymous groups or individuals unwilling to claim their acts of terrorism or sabotage, with no interest in a fixed name or standing by initials.*
> B) *Groups or individuals with no direct claim by Internet of the attacks carried out, but they WILL be leaving small claims of action with the detonating explosives, and graffiti in places where they act, etc.*
> C) *Groups with distinctive names and claims on the internet and/or at the location of the attacks, these may be terrorist or sabotage. We won't mention names now, these groups will be revealed in their own time and guidelines.*

D) *Individualists Tending to the Wild will continue executing acts of terrorism, as it did before RS.* (Wild Reaction 2015b [Italics/ emphasis in original])

The CCF-FAI Imprisoned Members Cell weighed in on the issue of adopting monikers in their essay "Let's Become Dangerous ... for the Diffusion of the Black International." This essay speaks to the utility and danger of adoptable monikers and stable acronyms, reacting to a critic of this approach who argues: "when an action is followed by a communiqué, it is like a joke accompanied by an explanation" (CCF-FAI/IRF Imprisoned Members Cell 2013). The cell refutes that claim made by "exponents of political anonymity [who] often say 'with communiqués and acronyms, the actions get owners'" (CCF-FAI/IRF Imprisoned Members Cell 2013). The imprisoned authors rhetorically ask and answer this challenge, writing, "'but why are you obsessed with acronyms and naming cells?' We answer, that we have no obsession, we just feel the strong desire to define ourselves" (CCF-FAI/ IRF Imprisoned Members Cell 2013). The authors proceed to discuss the power of separating oneself from the larger leftist milieu, stating:

> We believe that by simply stating that we are "anarchists", in order to speak through a communiqué or an action, is inadequate and problematic. We choose to separate our positions from the "anarchists" who cooperate with the leftist grassroot labor unions, use Marxist analyzes, unionize their misery, slander direct actions, fantasize workers' communes, participate in residents' local committees and transform anarchy into a social therapy. Also, actions speak for themselves through communiqués, because they keep their distances from the "anarchist" opposition, which may sometimes burn down a bank in the name of "poor people and against plutocracy's capital", in order to prove it does at least something. No, our burned banks is not a way of protest or a token of friendship and solidarity with the "poor people" who does nothing and sits on his couch ... So, we choose to identify ourselves and not to be lost in the anonymity of an imaginary anarchist movement. (CCF-FAI/ IRF Imprisoned Members Cell 2013)

The Imprisoned Members Cell represent only one contribution to a growing debate on this matter among proponents and detractors of clandestine attack claimed via communiqué, and a continued dialogue concerning utility, function, and risk is warranted.

While, in this manner, a moniker can be a useful disambiguation tool to mark certain political tendencies, the ease in adoptability for such labels can make the discussion and analysis of clandestine political violence tricky at best. Without the means to transparently verify attack claims, the potential for provocateurs producing false flag attacks is ever present. In a well-documented example occurring in 1990, three attacks involving IEDs occurred in England targeting vehicles belonging to hunters. The attacks were blamed on animal rights militants, through a false claim of responsibility by the British Animal Rights Society, a fictional group. Subsequent investigation proved these attacks to be the work of Jim Alan Newbury-Street, the director of the British Hunting Exhibition (Sorenson 2009, 248). Newbury-Street was found to have manufactured the bombs and was arrested with bomb components in his possession (Mann 2009, 157–158). Other notable examples from the animal liberation movement include the case of Fran Trutt (Ravo 1989; Rudacille 2001, 153–155; G. T. Marx 2003; Potter 2009, 20) who was arrested while placing a sophisticated pipe bomb in laboratory supplier US Surgical. It was later revealed that US Surgical had contracted an outside agency to coordinate the attack on its own property in order to discredit anti-animal testing campaigners. Within the insurrectionary tendency, similar accusations have been made. The Coordinating Committee of the *Italian* Anarchist Federation (2003) issued a statement, calling the Bologna-based mail bomb attacks by the *Informal* Anarchist Federation "phantom-like." The statement "denounces the serious and infamous nature of attributing the kind of facts to initials alluding to the monogram of FAI" (Coordinating Committee of the Italian Anarchist Federation 2003). The Committee points out that the FAI acronym has been used by the *aboveground* anarcho-federation since 1945 and, therefore, its usage by a clandestine network of bombers is a violation. The union movement writes that it "asserts once more its condemnation of bombs, exploding parcels and such devices, that may strike without discrimination" (Coordinating Committee of the Italian Anarchist Federation 2003). The ability for any individual to adopt an insurrectionary label post-attack exemplifies both the utility and potential pitfalls of the adoptable moniker model. While it may allow for a decentralized movement of informal allies, it also allows for provocateurs and opponents to misrepresent and confuse through the production of false flag attacks.

While these insurrectionary, moniker-based, internationalist attack networks do not publicize specific guidelines like the ALF, ELF, RZ, and RC-ALB, they still function through a praxis comprised of the strategies and tactics developed through action (e.g. attacks) and theory (e.g. communiqués). If these networks do have exclusionary guidelines to identify self and other, what does it mean to call one's attack an act of the FAI? From their texts, we can deduce that those that carry out the attacks in effect make the theory. They make the theory through action as well as interpretation. In their self-assessment pamphlet, imprisoned members of the CCF state their process for authoring communiqués, writing:

> The writing of a communiqué on a specific topic was usually shared out among those who wanted the responsibility, and after it was written, we

> got together to read it and make corrections, additions, and final touches. If the communiqué was connected to a separate initiative, then the comrades involved in that separate initiative were responsible for writing it.
> (G. Tsakalos et al. 2012, 5)

In other words, those that took initiative and those that showed up made the politics. This seems to be a common pattern among non-centralized clandestine groups of a variety of natures. Even at times when hierarchical coordination is commonplace, the politics of attack seem more driven by those who hold the Molotov than those that hold the pen. To quote an imprisoned member of the RAF interviewed in 1991, "we have always said that it is part of our basic politics that those who carry out the practice also determine the concrete policy" (Moncourt and Smith 2009b, 2:343).

The moniker has other important purposes. It serves to reduce the impact of ideological disagreement among individual cells that could lead to disunity, inter-network bickering, and factionalization. One scholar, writing about the ELF specifically, notes that by its very structure, such actors can, "avoid ideological cleavages by eliminating all ideology extraneous to the very specific cause ... thereby eliminating opportunities for ideological debate" (Joosse 2007, 364). He explains that for the ELF, its open structure "creates an overlapping consensus among those with vastly different ideological orientations, mobilizing a mass of adherents who would have never been able to work together in an organization" (Joosse 2007, 364). In other words, if networked movements were membership-based organizations or otherwise federated movements, disagreements between smaller collectivities could lead to the creation of factions from among the larger group. In the case of an adoptable moniker, if a faction chooses to reject certain aspects of the larger collectivity's framework, they can simply not link their actions to that name, or as commonly occurs, create a new group name. This can be seen when, for example, the Justice Department and Animal Rights Militia emerged from amongst the ALF's constituency; the former two groups rejecting the ALF's demand to not harm humans in their protest actions. In the modern examples, this can be seen in the evolution, factionalization, re-branding, and internationalization of the ITS/RS moniker.

For those acting in the name of modern insurrectionary anarchism, this surface-level ideological harmony serves a mobilizing and unifying purpose. While the individuals responsible for burning a bank in Brazil, and those redecorating a police facility in England, may disagree passionately over the role of technology as a tool for creating social war, this disagreement is masked by both cells claiming their actions under the FAI banner. To the outside observer, the FAI appears decentralized yet united. In their self-assent pamphlet authored by imprisoned members of the CCF, the writers explain this trend within their own network, writing:

Even in cases when there wasn't collective agreement on a particular action ... the minority of comrades who insisted on carrying out the attack took the autonomous initiative to move forward with their choice. That happened in parallel with the rest of the collective, which supported them at specific times if necessary, naturally playing a part in our overall organization. That's why a number of communiqués were signed by groups ... that arose out of each separate initiative. (G. Tsakalos et al. 2012, 4)

Therefore, claims that such open, decentralized structures "avoid ideological cleavages" (Joosse 2007, 364) seem to hold true for a variety of clandestine actors. While some may disagree as to the function – positive or negative – of the communiqué and acronym, it seems undeniable that such measures allow for a diffuse collectivity of attacks to act with a singular momentum, creating theory as they go through a constantly reinvented discourse patterned by attack, communiqué, critique of attack/communiqué, counter–critique, and so on.

Conclusion

This history draws key distinctions in terms of clandestine networks' methodologies of attack. One key difference which separates twentieth-century groups, such as the RAF, from the modern insurrectionary attacks, such as the CCF, is that while the former tended to attack symbolic targets, the latter have attempted to focus on *tactical* targets; those which can most effectively – in a strategic sense – serve to disrupt the flow of state and capital. This desire to cause material damage and disruption is recurrent in social protest (della Porta and Diani 2006, pt. 7.3.2), but perhaps particularly important to the insurrectionary logic. The targeting logic of 1970s guerrillas tended to focus on visible representations of larger social movement struggle – army bases, corporate offices, government offices – to strike against The Military, or The Corporation or The State (O'Goodness 2014b, secs. 11:00–12:38). On the other hand, twenty-first-century insurrectionary cells have tended to attack more localized manifestations of these systems, such as individual bank branches/ATMs, police vehicles, and key technocratic individuals. While this pattern is by no means a consistent description, it does differentiate those who target the symbolic representations of the state can capital from those who strategically strike its "functional logistics" (The Institute for the Study of Insurgent Warfare 2014, 10) aiming at financial damage and interruption. This desire to "hit [them] where it hurts" (Kaczynski 2010a) focuses on the operational abilities of the target rather than the symbolic capital it carries in a larger movement sense. Strategies that seek to diagram the weaknesses, bottlenecks, and soft underbellies of grandiose targets are common in the post-millennial clandestine networks and can be seen in the ALF's mapping and serial attacks on fur farms (e.g. The Blueprint, Final Nail) or Ted Kaczynski's (2010a, 251, 253) calls to "strike at the most sensitive and vital organs of the system ... [the] points at which it cannot afford to give ground."

The preceding analysis and discussion is designed around not only understanding the evolution of the insurrectionary tendency, but also differentiating it from bygone eras of armed struggle. The insurrectionary movement, devoid of strictly enforced movement boundaries, can best be identified through the various debates explored above – rural v. urban warfare, the role of vanguards, the structuring of cells, the usage of anonymity v. known monikers, the embracing or rejection of "terrorism", etc. It is precisely where the actors stand vis-à-vis such debates that indicates their inclusion or rejection from the insurrectionary milieu. This speaks to the fluid and multifaceted nature of social movement (self)-identification. Since insurrectionists do not carry membership cards, fly a specific flag, don uniforms or participate in transparent political processes, one can only judge them on the basis of their actions and their ideas.

Moving forward, one can begin to develop the philosophical and ideological component of modern insurrectionism. This "critical synthesis ... [of] anarchist thought, Italian autonomist-Marxism from the 1970s, French ultra-gauche communism, the squatter's movement in Europe in the 1980s, and the Situationist International" (Wood 2013, 7) is built upon the foundational concepts of poststructural philosophy. This philosophical discourse is woven through the proceeding chapters and will serve as the foundational basis for the evaluation of one of the book's central concerns. The historical record and strategic decision-making described in the preceding chapters cannot be understood without a discussion of the ideas that inform them. This is precisely why history must precede strategy, and strategy must precede ideology. Therefore it is essential that readers remain conscious of the historical precursors, but allow themselves to nuance that understanding as it is explored in light of the wider theory.

Notes

1 It should be noted that such a listing is quite cursory. Other famed proponents of guerrilla warfare include (in chronological birth order): Sun Tzu, Maha Thiha Thura, Teingya Minkhaung, Michael Dwyer, Carl von Clausewitz, Omar Mukhtar, Izz ad-Din al-Qassam, Muhammad Ibn 'Abd al-Karim al-Khattabi, Yousef Borahil al-Msmare, Nestor Makhno, Thomas Edward Lawrence, Michael Collins, Ho Chi Minh, Alberto Bayo y Giroud, Albert Levy, Tom Barry, Georgios Grivas, Orde Wingate, Lin Biao, Abraham Guillén,

Hoàng Văn Thái, Hans von Dach, Jonas Savimbi, Edén Pastora, Hugo Spadafora, and Ahmad Shah Massoud. This diverse list of fighters waged armed guerrilla campaigns for Irish Republicanism, anti-Soviet jihad, Zionist and Palestinian brigades against the British, and a variety of conflicts throughout Asia, Africa, and the Americas.
2   This requirement for total commitment to struggle (i.e. "full time revolutionaries") is repeated in Nechaev's *Catechism of a Revolutionist* where adherents are told that they must be completely committed to creating revolution and that this aim must dictate every manner of life including desires and friendships, the latter of which was meant to be judged by potential allies' commitments to revolution.
3   This is an intentional misspelling, provided by the communiqué author, to de-gender the word.
4   EMETIC is an understudied piece of radical history. Few historical accounts (Pickering 2013) of the group's activity exist.
5   This is sometimes translated as "People's Reprisal."
6   Discussions which focus on the formation of communities through protest-based social movements include: della Porta and Piazza (2008); Graeber (2009); Feigenbaum, Frenzel, and McCurdy (2013).
7   This spelling of "women" is intentional and common among radical feminist writers and other anti-patriarchal leftists. It is intended to remove the root "men" from the female person. Other examples of this phenomenon can be seen in the "misspelling" of the Spanish word "compañerxs," replacing gender-specific indicator letters ("a" or "o") with "x" to de-gender the word. This Spanish language example is borrowed from a communiqué written by Adrián Díaz, entitled "Communiqué from Adrián Díaz on Solidarity and Against the Rumors" published 13 July 2013 by War on Society.
8   This is an intentional "misspelling" of human to remove the "man" and create a gender-neutral, sexless term, similar to "wimmin."
9   These issues are persistent in both communiqués and longer strategic pieces discussing the role of anonymity, monikers and claiming attacks. For further discussion see: Anonymous (2011; 2013c; 2014b; 2014e); CCF of the first phase, Mavropoulos, and FAI/IRF (2014); Wild/terrorist Behaviors (2015).

5
Insurrection as theory, text, and strategy

By a revolution, the [revolutionary] Society does not mean an orderly revolt according to the classic western model – a revolt which always stops short of attacking the rights of property and the traditional social systems of so-called civilization and morality. Until now, such a revolution has always limited itself to the overthrow of one political form in order to replace it by another, thereby attempting to bring about a so-called revolutionary state. The only form of revolution beneficial to the people is one which destroys the entire State to the roots and exterminated all the state traditions, institutions, and classes. (Nechayev 1869)

The force of an insurrection is social, not military. Generalized rebellion is not measured by the armed clash but by the extent to which the economy is paralyzed, the places of production and distribution taken over, the free giving that burns all calculation and the desertion of obligations and social roles. In a word, it is the upsetting of life. No guerrilla group, no matter how effective, can take the place of this grandiose movement of destruction and transformation. Insurrection is the light emergence of a banality coming to the surface: no power can support itself without the voluntary servitude of those it dominates. Revolt reveals better than anything else that it is the exploited themselves who make the murderous machinery of exploitation function. The wild, spreading interruption of social activity suddenly tears away the blanket of ideology, revealing the real balance of strength. (Anonymous 2001a, 25)

The following chapter is meant to be read in conjunction with the preceding historical account of illegalism, propaganda of the deed, revolutionary warfare, and the evolution of post-millennial, insurrectionary networks of attack. In attempting to trace this evolutionary genealogy, we will examine the strategy of Blanquism, the contribution of "classical anarchists," the influence of the largely French, post-millennial theorists such as Tiqqun and TIC, and the contributions of shorter, anonymously authored publications. Following this account, we will focus on the contributions of Queer insurrectionary praxis before examining the question of canonization. The central thesis contends that through a genealogical review of the insurrectionary tendency, one can construct the broad outlines of a canon, which serves to inform contemporary action such as the attack strategies of the CCF or FAI.

In attempting to develop this canon, the following will first explore the key theoretical contributions of select individuals, linking their texts to their modern implementation. As there is no clearly demarcated, linear path from the nineteenth century to the modern era, this journey will inherently be punctuated by the most obvious and unmistakable signposts available, and in doing so will without a doubt exclude a variety of key texts and thinkers. In attempting to develop the markers of insurrectionary theory, the goal is to identify the tendency's values, and how it understands itself as a counterculture vis-à-vis not only mainstream political culture – its "conflict with the values of the dominant culture" (Koehler 2014, 1) – but also from allied trends in anti-state, anti-capitalist revolutionary theory. This modeling develops the insurrectionary milieu as a Radical Social Movement, conceived of as a "synergy" between Social Movement Theory and Counterculture Theory (Koehler 2014, 2).

Blanquism, its detractors, and the "classical" anarchists

Based partially on his experience in the revolution of July 1840 and several armed demonstrations in 1870, Louis Auguste Blanqui was a careful tactician with a keen focus on revolutionary method and strategy. He was an influential figure in the defense of the 1871 Paris Commune and, from these experiences, developed a revolutionary framework based in small unit conspiracies; a radical departure from the mass-based approaches of Marxism. Blanqui's writings are numerous and vary from short, fiery declarations, to more traditional theoretical discussions. Most notable are his frequent discussions of tactics and strategy (known as Blanquism), and his frequent encouragements for the armed masses to confront the state and revolt. The strategic writings were sometimes astoundingly specific and at other times more comprehensive and broad.

Blanquism as a revolutionary framework was complementary to the socialist project, but because of its dependence on a professionalized minority, and its lack of belief in the power of the workers, both Marx and Engels wrote to distinguish themselves from it. In an essay first published by Engels (1874), the foundational Marxist thinker writes:

> Blanqui is essentially a political revolutionist. He is a socialist only through sentiment, through his sympathy with the sufferings of the

people, but he has neither a socialist theory nor any definite practical suggestions for social remedies. In his political activity he was mainly a "man of action", believing that a small and well organized minority, who would attempt a political stroke of force at the opportune moment, could carry the mass of the people with them by a few successes at the start and thus make a victorious revolution.

Marxist revolutionary thinker and author Rosa Luxemburg (1904, chap. 1) similarly wrote about Blanquism, pointing out what differentiates Blanquism from Leninism writing, "in the place of a handful of conspirators [Blanquism] we have a class-conscious proletariat [Leninism]." Luxemburg also reflected negatively on the elitist and detached nature of Blanquist's methods of organization outside of the proletariat class. She points out that the Blanquist framework is top-down, minoritarian, and organized without mass participation from the oppressed class, writing:

> Blanquism did not count on the direct action of the working class. It, therefore, did not need to organize the people for the revolution. The people were expected to play their part only at the moment of revolution. Preparation for the revolution concerned only the little group of revolutionists armed for the coup. Indeed, to assure the success of the revolutionary conspiracy, it was considered wiser to keep the mass at some distance from the conspirators. Such a relationship could be conceived by the Blanquists only because there was no close contact between the conspiratorial activity of their organization and the daily struggle of the popular masses. The tactics and concrete tasks of the Blanquist revolutionists had little connection with the elementary class struggle. (Luxemburg 1904, chap. 1)

In his writing, Lenin (1932, chap. 6) also comments on the Blanquist strategy, noting that despite the efforts of some critics (writing of social democratic thinker Eduard Bernstein), it is inaccurate to link the minoritarian approach to the revolutionary Marxism of the time. Lenin is careful to explain the works of Marx (pointing specifically to Engels and Marx 1848; K. Marx 1871) in light of criticism and accusations of excluding the proletariat. Lenin (1906) speaks of Blanquism as an "intellectually-led conspiracy," writing "Blanquism is a theory which repudiates the class struggle. Blanquism expects that mankind will be emancipated from wage slavery, not by the proletarian class struggle, but through a conspiracy hatched by a small minority of intellectuals."

More important than its detractors, and those who have distanced themselves from such forms of vanguardism, is the influence Blanquism has had on subsequent movements. The approach was influential for the French illegalists who emerged from the Paris Commune, including the Bonnot Gang, and this idea of a minoritarian, professionalized, armed vanguard would reemerge in popularity nearly 100 years later with the 1960s and 1970s urban guerrillas (e.g. WUO, RAF). These groups continued the Blanquist tradition of seeking to "make the revolution" beyond (or without) mass mobilization of the proletariat. The revolution was to be a sort of insurrection where the socialists would seize power before delivering that power back to the people. This approach – which seeks to seize power in the interim – is rejected outright by anti-statists, including all brands of anarchists, but remains a salient tendency among the Leninist left and other non-anarchist revolutionaries. Therefore, while Blanquism served to influence the evolution of insurrectionary combat in terms of means, it differs greatly in terms of a strategic vision for the destruction and reconstruction of the socio-political order.

Following Blanqui and the conflicts of the late nineteenth century, the period of "classical anarchism" – approximately from the beginning of the twentieth century until the end of World War II – continued to advance theories of revolutionary warfare, insurrection, and revolt. As these works have been the subject of a great deal of anarchist scholarship, they only require a brief exploration before proceeding to the less-studied works. Around World War I, the main trend in violent anti-state theory came from the so-called illegalists, largely based in France. This illegalist tendency demonstrated methods such as financial expropriation, common in 1910s France, as well as direct attacks against the state which occurred throughout Western Europe and the US. From the robberies of the Bonnot Gang to the frequent bomb attacks by Galleanists, the illegalist trend has never strayed from the insurrectionary tendency, nor that of a minoritarian, armed revolutionary force.

Works that embody this period include Sergey Nechayev's "The Revolutionary Catechism" (1869), Johann Most's *Attack is the Best form of Defense* (1884) and *Science of Revolutionary Warfare* (1885), Giuseppe Ciancabilla's *Against Organization* (~1900), Luigi Galleani's *The Health is Within You* (1905), and Renzo Novatore's *My Iconoclastic Individualism* (1920). These pieces comingled with shorter essays, pamphlets, and speeches of propagandists of the time including those by Errico Malatesta, Alexander Berkman, Victor Serge,[1] Bruno Filippi, and Severino Di Giovanni. Once settling in the US, Galleani was involved in the publication of *Cronica Sovversiva* [*The Chronicle of Subversion*], an influential Italian-language, anarchist newspaper active 1903–1920, which would carry works by anarchist figureheads such as Peter Kropotkin, Mikhail Bakunin, and Malatesta. The paper infamously included a hit list profiling members of the ruling class, termed "enemies of the people." These classical texts, along with intersecting influences such as those of the nihilists, individualists, egoists, and communists amounted to a large volume of revolutionary works. This period of thought, which ebbed alongside World War II, developed the theoretical foundation for decades of armed struggle that would unfold through the world less than 25 years later. After the start of the Vietnam War, and the resulting protest movement, a new era of insurrectionary theory began to emerge from Italy before quickly expanding to a global audience.

The modern insurrectionary turn

> We must build a rhythm of struggle which resonates in our bodies and builds the links between attack, memory, and the ... terror we experience in daily life. It is simple enough to begin a discussion of insurrectional strategy with the notion of the attack. Yet many confuse this process with merely smashing a random bank and writing a communiqué telling the cops to fuck off. Of course, I'm not interested in condemning such a practice, I'm merely more interested in examining the ways in which various notions and methods of attack are positioned in relation to our memory and all of the emotions that have built up over time due to all of the ... violence we've endured. (Untorelli Press 2012, 23)

While the majority of the twenty-first-century insurrectionary canon is derived from a history of actions as reported via communiqués, a number of more central texts are consistently referenced and make up a sort of pre-history for the tendency. These texts are often anonymously authored and lengthy. They include the publications of Alfredo Bonanno, Tiqqun, TIC, and The Institute for Experimental Freedom (IEF). These texts differ from the historically produced canonical texts of revolutionary theory. While Marx wrote the texts later collected as the *Grundrisse* from the comforts of British Museum Reading Room, the insurrectionary canon is often penned by active revolutionaries, living (semi)clandestine existences, and engaged in acts of anti-state illegality. Furthermore, these texts are inherently products of an international, frequently un-attributing/plagiarizing form of "intertextuality" where authors "habitually cite, allude to and otherwise reference other texts ... [where] readers do not treat each text they read as a discrete item" (Cameron and Panovic 2014, 71). In constructing this *canon*, it is useful to first identify what is meant by the term, as anarchists have an understanding reminiscent to that of the Biblical canon. In his explanation of this term, anarchist philosopher Nathan Jun (2013, 82–83) writes:

> The "Western canon" ... describes a standard set of literary, scientific, historical, philosophical, and religious texts that are considered especially significant in the historical development of Western culture. When anarchists speak of a "canon," we generally have in mind something similar to a Biblical or cultural canon – that is, a standard set of texts (or thinkers,

or theories) regarded as authoritative for anarchist thought and practice or especially significant in the historical development of anarchism.

Therefore, the task becomes identifying these "texts, thinkers and theories regarded as authoritative for [insurrectionary] anarchist thought and practice." In doing so, this chapter will briefly detail these works and unveil a history of the development of modern insurrectionary theory as told through text.

Alfredo Bonanno

Beginning in the mid 1970s, Italian Alfredo M. Bonanno began publishing insurrectionary essays in conjunction with his translator and co-collaborator Jean Weir. Bonanno rose to prominence during the 1960s when Italy saw an increased presence from so-called ultra-left direct action networks. Through publications such as *Anarchismo Editions*, which Bonanno edited, the informal, networked, decentralized direct action model was developed, refined, and expanded. It would be this model that would eventually prefigure the FAI, CCF, and others. In his time, Bonanno lived an insurrectionary praxis involving numerous forms of agitation. In the late 1990s, Bonanno was arrested in connection with the bombing of Milian's Palazzo Marino (25 April 1997), and in 2003 was sentenced to six years in prison for his involvement in an insurrectionary armed robbery. He was arrested again in 2009 along with a Greek anarchist and accused of involvement in an additional bank robbery. He was sentenced to four years in prison and served approximately one year.

A full detailing of Bonanno's writings is beyond the scope of this book as his works span 40 years and include: *Revolution, Violence, Anti-Authoritarianism – A Few notes* (1974), *Class War* (1975), *Armed Joy* (1977), *Why A Vanguard* (1977), *Fictitious Movement and Real Movement* (1977), *And We Will Still Be Ready To Storm The Heavens Another Time: Against Amnesty* (1984), *Let's Destroy Work, Let's Destroy the Economy* (1987), *From Riot to Insurrection: Analysis for an Anarchist Perspective against Post-industrial Capitalism* (1988), *For An Anti-Authoritarian Insurrectionist International* (1993), *The Anarchist Tension* (1996), *A Critique of Syndicalist Methods* (1998), *The Insurrectional Project* (1998), *The Theory of the Individual: Stirner's Savage Thought* (1998), *Insurrectionist Anarchism – Part One* (1999), and *Locked Up* (2008). Other writings are contained in a verity of publications including *Insurrection* magazine (1982–1989), *Willful Disobedience* (2001–2003), and numerous more works written in Italian and not widely circulated in English. Bonanno's writings deal with the theory, strategy, tactics, and communications of armed insurrection. He speaks about prisoner negotiations, cell formations, economic analysis, and theories of symbolism, language, and individualism.

Bonanno's advocacy for the need for immediate attack is perhaps his most significant contribution to the insurrectionary tendency. His promotion of direct confrontation with the state is clearly encapsulated in *Armed Joy*, a text deemed so provocative by the Italian state that Bonanno was jailed for 18 months following its release. In it Bonanno (1977, 19) writes:

> People are tired of meetings, the classics, pointless marches, theoretical discussions that split hairs in four; endless distinctions, the monotony and poverty of certain political analyses. They prefer to make love, smoke, listen to music, go for walks, sleep, laugh, play, kill policemen, lame journalists, kill judges, blow up barracks ...
>
> Hurry comrade, shoot the policeman, the judge, the boss. Now, before a new police prevent you.
>
> Hurry to say No, before the new repression convinces you that saying no is pointless, mad, and that you should accept the hospitality of the mental asylum.
>
> Hurry to attack capital before a new ideology makes it sacred to you. Hurry to refuse work before some new sophist tells you yet again that "work makes you free".
>
> Hurry to play. Hurry to arm yourself ...

Later in the text Bonanno (1977, 22) reassures the reader of the feasibility of armed revolt, writing:

> It's easy. You can do it yourself. Alone or with a few trusted comrades. Complicated means are not necessary. Not even great technical knowledge.
>
> Capital is vulnerable. All you need is to be decided.

In a piece authored decades later, Bonanno (1998b, 14) responds to the rhetorically-posed question "Why are we insurrectionalist anarchists?" with seven reasons, one of which states: "Because we are for the immediate, destructive attack against the structures, individuals and organizations of Capital and the State." He also reasserts the call for immediacy writing:

> Because rather than wait, we have decided to proceed to action, even if the time is not ripe.
>
> Because we want to put an end to this state of affairs right away, rather than wait until conditions make its transformation possible. (Bonanno 1998b, 14)

Bonanno's large, multi-decade body of work offers a central thesis: Attack is possible, effective, and immediately necessary as a means to confront the drudgery, alienation, and abstraction of life under late capitalism and state domination.

Tiqqun and TIC

Following widespread protest in France (December 1997–January 1998), known as the "movement of the unemployed" (Daniel 1998), radical social theory commenting on the events drew influence from the autonomist and poststructuralist tendencies. It was within this spirit that the Tiqqun collective assembled and published two journal editions (1999; 2001b) in French. The journal mixes insurrectionary anarchist theory with that of poststructuralism (especially the work of Giorgio Agamben and Foucault), post-Marxism, and shows heavy stylistic influence from the French Situationists, Lettrists,[2] and Dada-Surrealists. Tiqqun and its publications have been described as post-Situationists, Communizationists, ultra-leftists, or simply insurrectionists. Many of the journals' more popular pieces have been translated into English and published by university presses including *Introduction to Civil War* (2010a), *This is Not A Program* (2011), *Theory of Bloom* (2012a), and *Preliminary Materials for a Theory of the Young-Girl* (2012b). Agamben's influence is central to Tiqqun, especially the author's work on forms-of-life, state of exception, and biopolitics. This phrase "forms-of-life" is frequently seen in writings by Tiqqun (2001a; 2010a; 2011; 2012a; 2012b)[3] and TIC (2007, 67; 2011; 2013, 5, 8). It also appears in insurrectionary texts such as those dealing with the Queer insurrectionary network Bash Back!. In this text, the author defines Agamben's "form-of-life" as "a life that can never be separated from its form" (Eanelli 2011, 6). In a final tribute to Agamben, the title of the foundational insurrectionary work, *The Coming Insurrection*, is in itself a reference to Agamben's (1993) work, *The Coming Community*.

The overlapping nature between European poststructuralism/continental philosophy and the works of Tiqqun and TIC is sometimes difficult to trace. Despite the insurrectionary tendency away from strict attribution and historicizing ideas, there are undeniable links with the works of Agamben (the "whatever singularity"), Gilles Deleuze and Felix Guattari (the "war machine"), Martin Heidegger (a critique of metaphysics), Alain Badiou (the "event"), Georges Bataille (nihilism), Carl Schmitt (sovereignty), and Walter Benjamin ("divine violence") (Wood 2013, 7–8). From these thinkers, the insurrectionary Tiqqunistas and TIC members borrow most heavily from Foucault's (2010) notion of "biopower," Antonio Negri and Michael Hardt's (2001) notion of "Empire," and Debord's (1967) "Spectacle."

Though the exact authors of the Tiqqun journal are unknown, it involved Jean Coupat, a French activist indicted as part of the "Tarnac 9." The Tarnac 9 were accused of sabotaging French TGV train lines in November 2008, an act the French state termed "terrorism." Coupat was jailed for six months and released May 2009; the other eight arrestees having been released previously. The nine individuals were described as "an anarcho-autonomist cell" (Michèle Alliot-Marie, quoted in Anonymous 2013b; Anonymous 2008, 2; Wedell 2014), and in its prosecution, the state claimed that Coupat, along with other Tiqqunists, were members of TIC, responsible for authoring *The Coming Insurrection*. Though the exact make up of Tiqqun and TIC is unknown, it is clear that some overlap in the authors exists, and at the very least TIC is well versed with Tiqqun (Anonymous 2016, 4), building upon its aesthetic and theory. The Invisible Committee moniker appears in *Tiqqun #2*, presenting the Committee as a faction from the larger Tiqqunist milieu for some interpreters. TIC has gone on to produce subsequent texts such as *Spread Anarchy, Live Communism* (2013), presented at the New School for Social Research. In this presentation, the unnamed speakers described as "The Accused of Tarnac" presented their paper in view of the audience, but asked for the talk to not be filmed, allowing only audio to be recorded.

Tiqqun's basic framework – assuming such a philosophically complex set of texts can be described as basic – is for the immediate implementation of *full communism*. Its analysis is predicated on an inherently poststructuralist reading of power, one that understands force and violence to be without a physical base (deterritorialized); it is without "a center to attack ... a castle wall to breach" (Williams and Thomson 2011, 273–274). Therefore, without the grandiose, clearly demarcated enemy of *The State* or *Capitalism*, one engages in a resultantly fluid strategy of combat, one that is "wild, untamed – guerrilla-style, if not entropic – resistance" (Williams and Thomson 2011, 274). The strategy advocated by TIC – here understood as the oldest child of Tiqqun – is to continue to foster confrontation aimed at increasing the frequency and density of so-called "zones of opacity" (TIC 2007, 107–109): milieus and physical areas of anti-state resistance which become unreadable by state authority. This desire for confrontation defines the milieu vis-à-vis its established opponent, what Tiqqun satirically terms "building the Party." The fostering of the "us v. them" framework – the "continuation and intensification of encounters ... [to] further the process of ethical polarization" (Tiqqun 2011, 14) – serves to spatially define those in revolt from those in power, or as Tiqqun writes:

> Building the party no longer means building a total organization within which all ethical differences might be set aside for the sake of a common struggle; today, building the Party means *establishing forms-of-life in their different, intensifying, complicating relations between them, developing*

as subtly as possible civil war between us. (2011, 13 [Emphasis in original])

The practitioners of this strategy of civil war are not seeking to *govern* a separatist territory, but rather to gather from within the confines of the metropolis and, while living within it, make it a site of revolt and full communism. Practically, this can be conducted through the occupation of public space, the construction of communes and squats, and through clandestine sabotage and disruption. Because Tiqqun and TIC understand the powers of state control to be endlessly multifaceted, and because this model is without a *front, rear* or *flank* to attack, the authors advocate "indirect, asymmetrical attack ... [as] the most effective kind [of attack], the one best suited to our time" (TIC 2007, 129). This reading of strategic posturing is carried forth in modernist cell networks that seek to strike manifestations of the enemy where they are most available.

Beyond Tiqqun's notions of strategy and war are its understandings of power that are representative of the larger insurrectionary tendency. The authors borrow from Foucault's "biopower" – the management of the body including issues of life/death through institutions and systems of power – asserting that the "management of maintenance of life-itself" (Wood 2013, 8) is within the purview of institutional domination (e.g. state and capital). This is interrelated to their reading of Empire,[4] as this post-Marxist concept rejects bordered understandings of nationalism, imperialism, and sovereignty in favor of "the liquidation of ... political differences in favor of a totalizing control of society or civilization itself" (Wood 2013, 9). These concepts of biopower's management of the self and Empire's ever-present, non-physically-linked power dictate the insurrectionary critique of "The Totality": a boundless, fluid reading of domination which seeks to emancipate all beings from all forms of control. Power is understood to be a totalizing force of ever-present coercion that extends from the material to the spiritual. In this manner, the insurrectionary position offered by Tiqqun and the TIC extracts the elements of poststructuralism that are most amenable to their argument; any texts where they can find "the seeds of insurrection lay[ing] dormant" (Wood 2013, 12). In other words, one of the key contributions of Tiqqun and the Committee are their abilities to bring poststructuralism into the discourse of insurrection, and to find elements of insurrection throughout the European critical philosophical tradition.

Magazines, zines, and anonymous texts

Throughout the end of the twentieth century and the early years of the twenty-first, a variety of shorter, often anonymous works were written that contributed to the insurrectionary tendency. These include often-cited essays contained in *Insurrection* Magazine, such as "Autonomous Base Nucleus" (O.V. 2011), "The Affinity Group" (O.V. n.d.), "Beyond the Structure of Synthesis" (n.d.), and "Beyond Workerism, Beyond Syndicalism" (2009b). Other publication series of this nature include "Killing King Abacus," "Willful Disobedience," and "A Murder of Crows." Also widely cited are essays and pamphlets such as "The Question of Preservational Violence" (Tatanka 1995), "At Daggers Drawn with the Existent, its Defenders and its False Critics" (2001a), "Rebelling Against our Domestication: Towards a Feral Revolution!" (2001b), "Toward the Queerest Insurrection" (2008), and "Insurrectionary Mutual Aid" (Curious George Brigade 2009). There were also several recurrent publications that emerged from the 2009 student occupations in response to the University of California tuition hikes. These occupations of university properties took a decidedly insurrectionary character and through these collective actions several influential texts were written and circulated including "Communiqué from an Absent Future" (2009), and "20 Theses on the Subversion of the Metropolis" (2009a). In the early years following the millennium, longer works by the IEF including "Politics is Not a Banana" (2009) and "Between Predicates, War: Theses on Contemporary Struggle" (2013) served to keep such ideas current and under development.

During the era of deterritorialized insurrectionary attack, other pieces would be written by clandestine cells and widely circulated, constituting another portion of the insurrectionary library. These include longer essays by cells of the FAI such as "Rain & Fire" (International FAI 2011), "Do Not Say that We are Few" (2011), "Fire and Gunpowder" (2011), and "The Urgency of the Attack", written by Nicola Gai (2013), one of the shooters of Italian nuclear chief Adinolfi. Similarly, cells of the CCF have written widely circulated pieces, which have contributed to the development of insurrectionary theory including "The Sun Still Rises" (G. Tsakalos et al. 2012), "The Direct Urgency of Attack" (C. Tsakalos 2013), "Let's Become Dangerous ... for the Diffusion of the Black International" (CCF-FAI/IRF Imprisoned Members Cell 2013), and "Urban Guerrilla Cell" (CCF: Urban Guerilla Cell/FAI 2016). There have also been a great number of well-circulated publications that re-mix and aim to distribute the writings and analysis of CCF, FAI, etc. These include English-language publications such as "Escalation ..." (2007), "A Conversation Between Anarchists ..." (2012), and "Why We Set Your Nights on Fire" (2014c), as well as foreign language publications such as *UpprorsBladet* (2011) in Swedish, and "La Nueva Guerrilla Urbana Anarquista" (2013a) in Spanish.

There is an inherent difficulty in establishing how these texts have or have not influenced the attackers that strike within the same (anti-)political framework. Rarely do communiqué authors include citations to previous works, and while announcements often make reference or quote prior communiqués or statements from jailed fighters, there is not as vivid an argumentative discourse as Rosa Luxemburg had with Eduard Bernstein in *Reform or Revolution*, or those of Marx and Bakunin around the First International. Therefore, the works identified are those that speak to original approaches – as opposed to publications that largely compile news, and the words of others such as *Fire to the Prisons* (12 issues, 2007–2015) – and those that aim towards the creation, refinement, and critique of *theory*. Other contemporary insurrectionary publications surveyed but not discussed herein include international magazines such as *325 Magazine* (2014b) and *Dark Nights* (2014), national publications such as Mexico's Spanish-language *Conspiración Ácrata* (2012), and regional US publications including *Modesto Anarcho* (2012) (Modesto, CA) and "'Til it Breaks" (2009c) (Denver, CO).

An overview of insurrection

Insurrectionary anarchy is a revolutionary theory, practice, and tendency which emphasizes attack and a refusal to negotiate or compromise with enemies. It is critical of formal organizations such as labor unions and federations and instead advocates informal organizations and small affinity groups. (Anonymous 2014g)

In her comprehensive account of twentieth century European leftist militants, political violence theorist Donatella della Porta (2013, 208) writes, "in the left-wing underground, justifications for violence are sought in the traditional, revolutionary discourse of the Left." But a key motivation for choosing to examine post-millennial insurrectionary networks is precisely that they defy the assertions – by abandoning the stagnant criticism of Marxism, Maoism, Leninism, Trotskyism, anarchism, and other libertarian socialist tendencies – and, instead, demand a new reframing informed by poststructuralism, Queer theory, and centuries of experimental street politics delivered through broken windows, scorched banks, and explosive bravado. The insurrectionary violence, embodied in the FAI, CCF, and others is a newly *revisioned* discourse that does not seek justification, mediation, or assimilated acceptance but rather embraces the fostering of social tension and the furtherance of socio-political ruptures. These newly emergent networks, while informed by the structural Marxism of the nineteenth and twentieth centuries, have sought to embrace a newly disembodied subject, a deterritorialized power that is omnipresent, ever oppressive, and vulnerable to attack.

The nature of the socio-political order that insurrectionary action seeks to attack is based in the notion of governance at large, not in particular institutions, methods or applications. This approach constitutes a totalizing critique of power and domination that is familiar to both insurrectionary proponents and poststructuralists and thus weds the two nicely. While Marxists understand the nature of power to reside in the logic of capitalism and the stability of the state, this is largely due to the proscriptive strategies for social change (e.g. how the proletariat organizes for revolution). For insurrectionary action, the focus is on the present, eschewing contemplation of a future utopia beyond the state, capitalism, and other manifestations of the dominant order. In this sense, insurrectionary visioning resists the construction of a modeled utopia, asserting instead that the present embodies the real, and the future – what will come after the fall of the state – is to be determined only at that point in the future when individuals are provided the autonomy and temporal space to consider new possibilities. Thus it is less important for insurrectionary actors that their "violence" is legible by the population. Unlike traditional social movements, insurrectionary proponents do not seek to interact with traditional legalistic processes and, therefore, their overall strategic vision is not a paramount focus as their attacks do not seek a respectable acceptance in the political discourse.

This is the goal of the insurrectionary network: not to raise the revolutionary consciousness of the proletariat to join a workers' revolution but rather to attack, attack, and attack again in order to show the erroneous nature of the social spectacle and expose the violence inherent in everyday life. For the subjects spoken of by della Porta (2013, 208–209), conflict framing by non-state actors revolved around the "working class" v. "fascist state" (for the Italian RB), and the marginalized yet revolutionary subjects of the Third World and urban metropolis v. the imperialist nation-states (for the German RAF). These outmoded, traditionally Leftist positions have been reconfigured through the contributions of poststructuralism that understand discursive control, knowledge production, ascribed legitimacy, and coercion as various assemblages of a central power. When gay bashing, ecological destruction, economic racism, and police brutality can be understood through a central thesis – as the insurrectionary framework posits – then the era of worker v. boss, student v. teacher, citizen v. leader have long since been left by the conceptual wayside.

Emerging in the latter part of the twentieth century and the early years of the twenty-first, a strong nihilist and postmodern/poststructuralist influence began to surface within anti-authoritarian theory. Insurrectionary conflict mapping encompasses not only a large, grandiose physicality but also a vast temporal space. Therefore, many insurrectionary anarchists assert the constant presence of a war-like atmosphere in the social ordering. Such a timelessness in one's mapping of conflict can also be seen in poststructural theorists such as Derrida (2006, 86) who states:

As soon as war is possible, it is taking place ...Whether the war takes place, whether war is decided upon or declared, it is a mere empirical alternative in the face of an essential reality; war is taking place; it has already begun before it begins, as soon as it is characterized as *eventual* (that is, announced as a non-excluded event in a sort of contingent future). And it is *eventual* as it is *possible*.

This vastness of critique, combined with the urging of immediate attack, an abandonment of the protracted preparatory stage of revolutionary mobilization, and a rejection of mediation, coalesced into what I am terming the insurrectionary framework. It is part collectivist anarchism, part nihilist, individualistic-egoism, and part poststructural, *queered* critique of power. Insurrection refigures social struggle as war-like, with a large set of actors dressed in enemy garb – cops, soldiers, politicians, bankers, developers, loggers, homophobes, etc. The goal of insurrectionary warfare is to expose these "sides" and to damage one's opponent at any site of contact. It is not campaign-driven activism but insurrectionary insurgency. The Institute for the Study of Insurgent Warfare (2014, 10), an anonymous, insurrectionary-aligned think tank, speaks to this strategy of dis-identifying with Leftist forms of activism, writing:

> An activist's enemies then are the particular set of abstract bad things they endeavor to set aright and their opponents are fellows who merely happen to be on the wrong side of the issue. By comparison, an insurgent's enemies are never abstract, but rather discrete entities of flesh, stone, or steel, from bodies to buildings, which at a specific time and place obstruct their interests. These enemies are not party to the insurgent's project and are instead defined by their exteriority to it, making elimination of the opposition the basic mode of conflict.

This critical "us v. them" approach is focused on the boundless, structurelessness nature of intersectional systems and the best way to bring them crashing down. Such a diffuse critique is visible in the language choices of the attackers; for example, imprisoned members of the CCF (CCF-FAI/IRF Imprisoned Members Cell 2013) who describe their efforts as "new sabotages against the authority of the social apparatus."[5] Furthermore, Foucault himself wrote of coercive power in a manner that is often repeated by modern insurrectionary actors. For instance, he explains the concept of "domination," describing it as "power relations [that] are fixed in such a way that they are perpetually asymmetrical and allow an extremely limited margin of freedom" (1998, 441–442).

This manner of insurrectionary, action-oriented analysis borrows a great deal from earlier strands of anti-authoritarian theory, including the "green" elements of anarchism typically associated with primitivism. One such centrally located publication, *Green Anarchy* (published 2000–2009), carried an article that provides a breakdown of green anarchist theory. The four benchmarks identified in this essay mirror those discussed in the subsequent section and are therefore deserving of some attention. In the essay "Play Fiercely! Our Lives are at Stake!," famed anti-civilization, post-left, insurrectionary anarchist Wolfi Landstreicher (aka Feral Faun or Apio Ludd) describes the method of the "anarchist revolutionary outlaw" as being comprised of four tendencies.

> 1) direct action (acting on our own toward what we desire rather than delegating action to a representative); 2) autonomy (refusal to delegate decision-making to any organizational body; organization only as coordination of activists in specific projects and conflicts); 3) permanent conflict (ongoing battle toward our end without any compromise); 4) attack (no mediation, pacification or sacrifice; not limiting ourselves to mere defense or resistance, but aiming for the destruction of the enemy). (2006, 12)

Within this milieu is a host of writers advocating for "social war" against the entirety of the world around them. For the insurrectionists, their target would include and extend beyond merely the state and thus, for these theorists, the old Marxist enemy of the market, or the anarchist enemy of the state, becomes "the totality" encompassing religion, family, politics, markets, patriarchy, capitalism … It is a "war … being waged. A war that can no longer be called simply economic, social, or humanitarian, because it is *total*" (Tiqqun 2012b, sec. A).

Finally, it is important to understand the assumptions about society contained within the insurrectionary logic that are specific to its position. While the milieu's conceptions of power and structure are discussed throughout, they are based in a reading of domination that is fluid, opaque, and ever-present. Though not stated explicitly, there exists the notion that attacks lead to more attacks that lead to more widespread conflict. Though not an insurrectionist in the sense presented in this book, American urban guerrilla Ed Mead[6] (2007, iii) argues in *The Theory and Practice of Armed Struggle in the Northwest*, "revolutionary violence will help build the aboveground movement, in addition to other positive effects." Mead presents an understanding of the strategic role of *terrorism* in revolutionary social change. In 1976, while he was imprisoned he wrote:

> It is true that terrorism as the principal form of political action, as a strategy for revolution, cannot be the means or the liberation of the masses and is therefore incompatible with Marxism … But not all revolutionary violence is terrorist. Terrorism is a tactic, not an entity, and it is a tactic used by people who have a political grievance. Terrorism is eliminated

by addressing the political problems that give it birth ... In addition to communicating a state of mind to the enemy, terror, if correctly applied, can be an important deterrent to some of the most flagrant manifestations of fascism, and a tool for raising the consciousness of the masses. (Mead 2007, 22–23)

Mead's presentation of terrorism as an effective tactic, freely adoptable, in response to a political grievance resembles the insurrectionary presumption concerning the positive influence of armed actions against the state, and their legitimacy despite terrorist trappings. Though the insurrectionary vision concerning the steps between isolated acts of disobedience and insurrection is far from a revolutionary program crafted by a Party, it does carry with it a set of presumptions about human behavior and the way social movements interact with the state.

Despite the frequency with which insurrectionary texts are penned, very little of this writing is focused on a paced prediction for social transformation, despite Bonanno titling his essay, "From Riot to Insurrection." In this essay, despite its misleading name, Bonanno (1988, 22–23) rejects the need for such a plan, an answer to *How is It to be Done?*, writing:

... the only possible strategy for anarchists is an informal one. By this we mean groups of comrades who come together with precise objectives, on the basis of affinity, and contribute to creating mass structures that set themselves immediate aims, while constructing the minimal conditions for transforming situations of simple riot into those of insurrection ... What is dead is the static anarchism of the traditional organisations, based on claiming better conditions, and having quantitative goals. The idea that social revolution is something that must necessarily result from our struggles has proved to be unfounded. It might, but then again it might not. Determinism is dead, and the blind law of cause and effect with it. The revolutionary means we employ, including insurrection, do not necessarily lead to social revolution.

Bonanno asserts that while social revolution may not be the outcome of insurrectionary attack, it contains the possibility of such an outcome. Therefore it is difficult to determine *how* the insurrectionary tendency understands the connection between increasing attacks against the state, and the subsequent stages of revolutionary conflict. However, the approach presumes that by engaging in individual-level acts of illegal, anti-social attacks against power, one can spread an oppositional posture (vis-à-vis the state, capital, etc.) and lead to a more generalized revolt and rupture with systems of power. This largely open, unpredictable, and un-mapped method is a clear differentiation from eras of past armed struggle.

This method of prescriptive, ordered visioning is common in the revolutionary left texts from urban (largely Marxist) guerrillas of the 1960s and 1980s. Book-length texts such as Guevara's *Guerrilla Warfare* (1961), the WUO's *Prairie Fire* (1974), the Black Liberation Army's *Message to the Black Movement* (Coordinating Committee Black Liberation Army 2002), and *The Politics of Bombs* (Anonymous n.d.) all contain discussions of how small-scale armed vanguards transition into more generalized armed revolt and then more direct confrontation with the state. Quoting the RAF, the anonymous authors of *The Politics of Bombs* write, "The mass armed capability which will destroy the state has its beginnings in very small armed actions, and through these guerrilla actions the armed mass capability develops" (Anonymous n.d., 5). The authors, no longer quoting the RAF, continue their prescriptive analyses, writing:

> By engaging in armed struggle, even in its most formative stage, the guerrilla raises the issues of militant armed resistance to the capitalist State from a dim theoretical concept to an immediate practical possibility ... While this preliminary armed resistance will, de facto, receive only limited support, even on the left, this limited support is the potential nucleus for the eventual armed struggle that will be necessary for revolutionary change to occur in any nation-State. (Anonymous n.d., 5–6)

In this text – likely authored by associates or allies of Ann Hansen's so-called Direct Action 5 – the strategic nature of small-scale violence is explained as laying the groundwork for its expansion. The WUO (1974, 33) make similar claims as well, writing, "From the very beginning of guerrilla action, mass armed capability develops. Its spontaneity will be slowly transformed into the energy of a popular armed force." In the words of the WUO, RAF, and DA5, the period between isolated vanguardism and broad revolt appears to be little more than a matter of scale. Therefore, increasing the rate and support for attacks is integral to this strategy. While the Marxist-aligned left makes these sorts of arguments with great frequency, the macro strategy advocated by the insurrectionists must be understood as the sum total of the still-ongoing discourse.

Insurrectionary Queer theory

One of the main overlapping discourses contributing to insurrectionary theory is that of Queer theory, specifically anti-assimilationist, postmodern Queer theory. This strand of thought problematizes identity-based politics and furthers a theory of intersectionality. It reminds us that intersectionality as a political project of feminism (e.g. Truth 1851; K. Crenshaw 1989;

Collins 1991; hooks 2000), is about power and systems, not individualistic identity. It is about the system of racism, not one's race. Prior to exploring its main tenets (i.e. *canon* of insurrectionary thought), a brief exploration of *Queer* insurrectionary politics is warranted as these conceptual components are derived from the same foundational texts and are commonly hosted and distributed through the same online channels. In discussing an application of Queer theory, it is important to note that such a cross-disciplinary pairing is not reserved for revolutionary critique, as a recent issue of *International Studies Review* (C. Weber et al. 2014), a mainstream International Studies journal, featured six short pieces based around the application of Queer theory to the field of International Relations.

Drawn from Queer theory and abstracted from the specificity of sexuality and gender, contemporary insurrectionary theorists have argued for the destabilization of identity-based politics through a refocusing on what constitutes "us" and "them." The ever-popular authors at CrimethInc (2015, 77) made this observation, writing, "some comrades theorized a few years ago that the refusal of fixed identity would be central to the coming insurrections – that rejecting our individual subjectivities was essential to rewriting our culturally held mythologies of power." This observation reflects dominant trends in postmodern Queer theory, which furthers a non-essentialist view of self (Butler 1990) vis-à-vis social hierarchies (e.g. sex, gender, sexuality, race) and a severing of the inherent linkages between embodiment (e.g. sex) and identity (e.g. gender). One way this Queered us/them identity is made clear is through Tiqqun's concept of "community" developed in their work *Introduction to Civil War* (2010b). For Tiqqun, the divergent lines drawn between the LGBT "community" and the Queer experience can clearly be seen. Liberal NGOs rally around a perceived community – for the Human Rights Campaign (HRC) for the LGBT or the National Organization for Women – creating identity-based constituencies, yet Tiqqun argues that the individual becomes a member of a community, a "we," as they experience and understand themselves in relation to power (2010b, 37–46). Tiqqun (2010a, 37–41 [Emphasis in original]) writes:

> When, at a certain time and place, two bodies affected by the same form-of-life meet, they experience an objective pact, which precedes any decision. They experience *community* ... There is no community except in singular relations. *The* community doesn't exist. There is only community, community that circulates ... Community never refers to a collection of bodies conceived independently of their world. It refers to the nature of the relations between these bodies and between bodies and their world.

For Tiqqun, the shared nature of identity is what is experienced as "form of life," and thus two male-bodied persons who have sexual contact with two other male-bodied persons might both be members of different "communities" as both experience these "forms-of-life" (i.e. the homosexual act) divergently in relation to regimentation. One may be a male-bodied, white-skinned, homosexual, member of Congress who *passes*, and another a transgendered, undocumented citizen, financially struggling as a transient sex worker. If both of these male-bodied individuals engage in fellatio with another male, that act will be disciplined differently despite the similarly *homo*sexual nature of the performance. Thus it is not the act that defines identity but how one understands oneself vis-à-vis the disciplining powers of the body. Tiqqun (2010a, 22) even goes as far as to define "form-of-life" as "*how* I am what I am." This disciplining is reflective of not only how one understands self vis-à-vis the disciplining powers of the body but, because identity is a product of social interaction, it is also constituted through notions of how one understands self vis-à-vis others.

Another way to understand insurrectionary theory's Queerly informed rejection of *identity* is to discuss it as an opposing force to *affinity*. In this manner, milieus are formed not from those who self-identify as "anarchists," "revolutionaries," or "militants" but rather a shared sense of ethics. In an anonymously authored insurrectionary critique of the environmental direct action network Earth First!, the author explores this concept, urging action on the basis of shared affinities and not the various ghettoized encampments of the Left.

> If ... one's priority is to perpetuate a general culture (and develop new practices) of revolt, it makes more sense to be antagonistic to the Left but tight with one's neighbors or co-workers or "non-political" friends, whomever one judges might go crazy with you when the shit hits the fan. Affinity rather than political identity becomes the center of gravity of the relationship. What someone "thinks about the environment" is meaningless to me. Do they hate the police? Do they hate work? Do they hate having mercury stored up in their gut? Do they hate some aspect of capitalist life? Do they want to knee-cap nuclear execs? Do we do similar kinds of crime to get by? Could I be friends with them, and do we have meaningful skills or ideas to share ...? (s.t. 2014, 3)

This framework of community on the basis of affinity disrupts identity-based politics and instead offers a demarcation on the basis of the "objective pact ... [of] community" (Tiqqun 2010b, 37), a community of those negating identity. The notion of hegemonic forces as disciplining the physical emanates from Foucault's *biopower*, which according to Foucault (1990, 141), acts as, "an indispensible element in the development of capitalism ... [through] the controlled insertion of bodies into the machinery of production, [leading to] segregation and social hierarchization ... guaranteeing relations of domination and the effects of hegemony." The regimentation of Queer bodies via biopower serves to engender social outliers towards assimilation for the purposes of faux-pluralism within the framework of the tranquil, tolerant nation-state.[7]

While one influential insurrectionary thinker (Tiqqun) attempted to problematize the "us-versus-them" nature of identity politics, another collective of radical actors worked to flatten these distinctions, creating clearer demarcations. The anonymously authored, *Towards the Queerest Insurrection* (2008) problematizes the identity of "Queer" while simultaneously simplifying the division between ally and enemy. The authors of this text *queer* the notion of Queer identity, stating:

> "queer" as synonymous with "gay and lesbian" or "LGBT." This reading falls short ... queer is not a stable area to inhabit. Queer is not merely another identity that can be tacked onto a list of neat social categories, not the quantitative sum of our identities. Rather it is the qualitative position of opposition to presentations of stability – an identity that problematizes the manageable limits of identity. Queer is a territory of tension, defined against the dominant narrative of white-hetero-monogamous-patriarchy, but also by an affinity with all who are marginalized, otherized and oppressed ... Queer is the cohesion of everything in conflict with the heterosexual capitalist world. Queer is the total rejection of the regime of the Normal. (A Gang Of Criminal Queers 2008, I)

This set of distinctions exists at the heart of the insurrectionary critique of identity-based, movement building efforts but is not solely the product of this movement. In his book, *Saint Foucault*, David Halperin (1997, 62) repeats a similar idea, stating, "Queer is by definition *whatever* is at odds with the normal, the legitimate, the dominant."

For conflict transformers seeking to intervene within protracted social conflicts where insurrectionary actors are present, this Queer positioning has important ramifications. If one envisions their battle as attempting to confront domination wholesale and not simply legalistic challenges to LGBT equality, this framing has a wide-reaching impact on the potential intractability of the conflict. Second, insurrectionary tendencies to reject involvement with the political process further complicate propositions for a piecemeal solution where the passage of legislation (e.g. Don't Ask Don't Tell), or similar actionable program could be marked as successful. Insurrectionary Queer theory positions Queers as those contesting normative identities and those oppressed by the forces of "The Totality." In *Towards the Queerest Insurrection*, the authors argue that Queer liberation is predicated on "the annihilation of capitalism and the state," arguing that to inhabit Queerness, to claim this rejectionist self-moniker, is to:

Challenge oppression in its entirety ... total negation of this world ... [to] become bodies in revolt ... to destroy not only what destroys us, but also those who aspire to turn us into a gay mimicry of that which destroys us ... [to] be in conflict with regimes of the normal ... [to] be at war with everything. (A Gang Of Criminal Queers 2008, secs. VII, IX)

Such calls for "total social war" encapsulate the insurrectionary tendency both in terms of critique and the action such criticism demands. Both the problematized notion of "community" and that of a newly contested Queer subject demonstrate how this revolutionary politic not only complicates the gay–straight binary, but also more nuanced delineations that would lead one towards an identity-based conflict. While the construction of an insurrectionary *Queer* canon poses the same problems as that of a generalized (i.e. non-Queer) canon, one can nonetheless identify some central texts and publications that are recurrent throughout this milieu. These include *Towards the Queerest Insurrection* (2008), *Militant Flamboyance* (Schulz and Thomason 2009), *Queers Read This* (Anonymous Queers 2009), "Terror Incognita" (CrimethInc 2012), the writings of Bash Back! compiled through projects such as *Bash Back! An Unofficial Zine* (2009a), and *Queer Ultraviolence* (2012), as well as the multi-issue zine *Pink and Black Attack* (e.g. 2010).

Queer (anti-)assimilation

It is obvious that the Queer insurrectionary politic is inherently revolutionary and thus challenges state authority and other more diffuse forms of power. Because of their direct attacks on state institutions, the insurrectionary tendency has garnered a negative framing, placing it into an oppositional relationship with state forces. This is of course *not* solely the domain of this specific brand of non-state actors. Violent non-state, sub-state, and quasi-state actors are regularly defined as illegitimate within the linguistics of statecraft. Those choosing to disengage from traditional representative politics, or those choosing to violently interact with the system of governance, quickly become targets of the state's defamatory rhetoric (i.e. framing, labeling, legislating), as well as direct, actualized violence (i.e. police, military). Irish Republicans who were disaffected by the assimilationist and reformist incarnations of Sinn Féin formed dissident factions that carried out acts of violence timed to derail political processes. As their rejectionism denied the group an opportunity to engage at a negotiation table, those Republicans instead engaged the political realm through extra-legal acts of violence. This is a similar pattern seen in a series of bomb attacks targeting the Israeli citizenry carried out by Palestinian anti-assimilationist/

rejectionist factions (e.g. Hamas) choosing to engage in disruptive violence to protest bilateral, Palestinian–Israeli negotiations from which it was excluded. In these cases, when reading a state's continuum of legitimacy, the more reformist elements (e.g. PIRA/Sinn Féin, Palestinian Authority/Fatah) are portrayed positively, while the violence-producing rejectionists (e.g. Continuity IRA/Real IRA, Hamas/Islamic Jihad) are presented as purposely disruptive and incorrigible. When a state sets preconditions for negotiations with non-state actors, typically involving a "renouncing of violence," the state is in effect delegitimizing the rejectionist actors' production of violence – a challenge to the state's solitary claim to force and coercion.

It is at this site of the violent reification of rejectionism where one can understand why the state would seek to interrupt the advancement of an insurrectionary *Queer* tendency within LGBT politics – such an *ideology* could threaten citizens' social and civil engagement, further adding to networks that advocate direct attack. State forces would prefer if Queer concerns were handled in the "depoliticized" *private* spheres, and thus not present a challenge to the codified system of social relations (Sullivan 2003, 24–25) or economic structures. The Queer networks producing and transmitting these challenges have sought to create praxis mirroring their politics of negation, anti-assimilation, and social war. To these ends, a number of acts of property destruction have been carried out by cell-based direct action networks appearing to function similarly to the CCF, FAI, ALF, etc. The most prominent of these networks, was Bash Back! (BB!), an insurrectionary Queer network, based in the US, and active 2007–2011.

These insurrectionary Queer networks have frequently targeted reformist, corporate, and state-based institutions purporting to help non-heterosexuals. These attacks amount to an anti-assimilationist, non-rights-based critique of heterosexism, patriarchy, capitalism, transphobia, etc., as developed within an insurrectionary politic of direct confrontation. A variety of these actions have targeted festivals and other public gatherings linked to gaining rights for non-heterosexuals such as:

- 2 July 2008, Chicago, IL: BB! joins Pride parade carrying banners critiquing the event. One such banner reads, "No Pride in Corporate Greed," in reference to Pride's corporate sponsorship. BB! also distributes "barf bags" with the words "Corporate Pride makes me sick" written on them (Nair 2008).
- 28 August 2008: Denver, CO: BB! protests HRC party held in conjunction with the Democratic National Convention. Flyers distributed critique HRC for "dumping transgender people," receiving corporate funding, and "rather than saving the lives of queers here and in Iraq, HRC fights to stockpile the military with queer fodder for Bush's crusade" (Bash Back! 2009b, 19–20).

- 5 October 2008, Washington, DC: BB! pickets outside of an HRC, "$250/plate" fundraiser held to benefit "the force of gay assimilation" (dandee lyon of bb!dc 2008).
- 12 October 2008, Chicago, IL: BB! attends an event commemorating the 10th anniversary of the murder of Matthew Shepard and leads confrontational chants directed at police and endorsing property destruction (Bash Back! 2009b, 25).
- 10 October 2009, Washington, DC: "Queers Against Assimilation" vandalizes HRC's headquarters with graffiti reading "Quit leaving queers behind."
- 26 June 2011, Seattle, WA: "Some Queer Hooligans" disrupts Pride events (for the third year in row), and distributes a flyer titled, "Queers Fucking Queer: NO Homonationalism, NO Homomilitarism, NO Assimilation." During the illegal march, two police cars, a Bank of America, an American Apparel, and a Ferrari dealership were attacked (Pugetsoundanarchists.org 2011).
- 29 June 2011, Washington, DC: "The Right Honorable Wicked Stepmothers' Traveling, Drinking and Debating Society and Men's Auxiliary" (2011) vandalizes the HRC gift shop with pink paint projectiles, and painting "Stonewall" on the sidewalk.

Taken as a collectivity, these actions represent a critique of the LGBT, equal rights lobby, what some rejectionist Queers have termed the "Gay Non-Profit Industrial Complex."

The decision made by insurrectionary Queers to attack an organization like HRC is important in understanding proscribed methods of sociopolitical engagement. While both HRC and BB! oppose contemporary state policy, only HRC acts to change such laws. On the opposing end, BB! seeks to widen the gap between gay proponents of voting and lobbying and Queer advocates of social war. This politically strategic duality is critical in understanding statist efforts to regiment dissent. For the state, the legalistic efforts of HRC fail to challenge the distribution of power within the society *even* if such efforts were able to effect change. In order to maintain the systematizing of protest, the state presents the efforts of HRC as the fruits of tolerant pluralism, as "democracy in action," while the attacks of BB! are framed as "mindless vandalism" by unappeasable extremists. This good citizen/bad citizen, good protestor/bad protestor dichotomy is used to delegitimize strategies of political engagement that challenge the state's monopoly on violence (M. Weber 1919; Thompson 2008) and advocate a cultural reality that is inherently anti-state centric.

A secondary problem for statist efforts to dictate how dissent is to be managed comes in the form of the insurrectionary rejection of identity-based politics. Such a political framework, wherein one sees the fragmented creation of a Civil Rights movement (i.e. African Americas challenging white racism), a Women's Rights movement (i.e. female bodied/gendered persons challenging sexism), etc. allows the state to be challenged in disparate venues by segmented, single issue groups. Judith Butler (2004, 24–25), in her discussion of a groups' struggle for collective rights, repeats this analysis, writing:

> When we argue for protection against discrimination, we argue as a group or a class. And in that language and in that context, we have to present ourselves as bounded beings – distinct, recognizable, delineated, subjects before the law, a community defined by some shared features. Indeed, we must be able to use that language to secure legal protections and entitlements. But perhaps we make a mistake if we take the definitions of who we are, legally, to be adequate descriptions of what we are about.

The Queer analysis supports this line of argumentation as it advocates *against* a "bounded ... delineated" legal subjectivity. Instead, the insurrectionary tendency seeks to blur these lines of boundary, to present an *un*bounded, *non*delineated politic that only separates the oppressed from the oppressor. Whereas HRC seeks to draw lines between the LGBT "community" and the hetero community, Queers deny this simplification and argue that *who* one desires sexually is not the ultimate determination of what community they occupy. The Queer community, as discussed by Butler, is a *non*class, unbounded by the limits of group description. This newly articulated, queered form of *identity*, inherently leads one towards an alternative method of analyzing conflicts. An identity-based, single-issue movement is preferable to the state as it is bounded by the ability to be appeased and recuperated through piecemeal, legalistic concessions. For forms of state control, such *identity-based* conflicts, groups, and movements are smaller, more fragmented, and thus easier to contain when faced with the opposing option of a generalized revolt in the form of insurrectionary social war.

Conclusion: an insurrectionary canon? More like an insurrectionary cannon!

Removed from the specificity of Queer revolt, insurrection can be understood as "the *whole* of social relations opening up to the adventure of freedom" (Anonymous 2001a, 15), and total war with the forces of domination, control, and governance. There is a goal to "interrupt all social activity and paralyze normality" (Anonymous 2001a, 23). In trying to trace the borderlands of the current discussion, one is tempted to speak of an insurrectionary *ideology* or, worse yet, an insurrectionary *canon*. While both of these terms are inadequate to explain the boundaries of poststructural-inspired theory, discussions occur through words and we are limited to the vocabularies we possess. Therefore, while I prefer the use of descriptive nouns such as *tendency* and *framework*, it is instructive to examine a definition of *ideology* – borrowing from social movement theorist Roberta Garner – that most closely resembles the task at hand. In her efforts to define, Garner (1996, 15–16 [Emphasis in original text]) writes:

> Ideology refers to the discourse of the movement, to what people think and say. The ideology is the ideas held by the people who see themselves as connected to the movement ... Usually, an ideology has some degree of coherence; the ideas hang together in some way. The discourses are interconnected. The discourses specify some way of looking at reality. They specify what is *really important*. They are a way of making sense of life experiences and situations. The discourses spell out what the current situation is and why it should be changed. They identify some preferable state of affairs that becomes the goal of the movement ... Movement discourses speak about some elements of reality, not others, and this selection of a sphere of discourse contains the *why* of the movement.

Ideology, at large, can thus be read as a "belief system" with its corresponding discourse and practices. These systems by their very nature are inherently multi-person, community-level groupings "comparable to socio-cultural knowledge ... shared by (epistemic) communities" (Dijk 2011, 382) and can be quantified, in a limited sense, as "the *fundamental, 'axiomatic' beliefs shared by a group,* that is *general* beliefs that control – and are often derived from – more specific beliefs about concrete events, actions and situations with which group members may be confronted" (Dijk 2011, 383 [emphasis in original]). It is through this discourse-centric understanding that ideology will be utilized and discussed.

The following discussion attempts to outline the insurrectionism as best it can be quantified. It examines the recurrent themes found in theory, propaganda, and claims of responsibility (i.e. communiqués) to identify the *discourse* of insurrection and the insurrectionary "way of looking at reality." This exercise in canonization is conducted without the luxury of hindsight. The task at hand is to trace the outlines of a process of canonization that is not yet in the past but rather ongoing, in flux. Philosopher Cornel West (1987, 193) cautions us against such pursuits, writing, "Any attempt to expand old canons or constitute new ones presupposes particular interpretations of the historical moment at which canonization is to take place." Certainly this is true in relation to the insurrectionary project. What is precisely attempted here is the constitution of a new canon, presupposing the understanding of history as a cumulative record of international attack. This reading of history posits that while the People's Will of 1880s Russia is not a *direct* ancestor of the post-millennial, global FAI, in constructing the canon in the present, what remains of the nineteenth century philosophy will inherently be understood through the particular political realities of modern conflict. In other words, in support of West's assertion, this discussion presupposes an interpretation of the historical account of illegalism and insurrection as intertwined and formative for the modern discourse.

In determining where this canon begins and ends, a certain amount of judgment is employed. Since revolutionary actors do not often provide taxonomic labels when writing, it is up to the researcher to determine in-group and out-group distinctions. This task is likely easier with sectarian Communist movements as these organizations are keen to self-identify as Marxist-Leninists, Trotskyists, Stalinists, Council Communists, etc. In anti-authoritarian, clandestine networks, this sort of self-labeling is less common but does occur. In one example, an American anarchist self-identifies as an insurrectionist in a letter distributed announcing his return to the US after living in Canada for a time to resist state efforts to convene a grand jury. The activist, Steven Jablonski (2014), writes of his support for the insurrectionary attack that began the state's grand jury:[8]

> I also want to be clear that I stand in full solidarity with those anonymous vandals who attacked the [courthouse] ... There are few things I desire more than to see institutions of power targeted and attacked. I strongly identify with the insurrectionary anarchist tendency and believe that those acts of crime and rebellion that occurred on that day in Seattle serve as a small example of how people can physically attack institutions of Capital in their never-ending quest for liberation.

Despite Jablonski's clear self-labeling, other texts are more difficult to categorize.

A prime methodological determination of categorization rests in where the document was located (i.e. insurrectionary versus non-insurrectionary website), as well as the presence of certain terms, rallying cries, and group monikers. In another example of self-labeling, the announcement of a new Greek anarchist website described the site's content as "Promoting anarcho-individualism, insurrectionary anarchism, anti-social and anti-political nihilism. For total liberation of humanity! Against capitalism, state and mass-society!" (The Parabellum 2013). Not only does this announcement explicitly self-label as insurrectionary, anti-political, individualist nihilists, it also evokes the "total liberation" position, all key markers of the insurrectionary tendency. In a notably similar announcement for another counter-information website, the anonymous authors write: "What is the purpose of this project? Promoting anti-social and anti-political nihilism, individualism, egotism, insurrectionary anarchism. For total liberation! Against state, capital and society!" (Nihilist Abyss 2013). Often these clear word choice demarcations are absent, as anarchist praxis is meant to exemplify political tendencies to a far greater degree than hollow self-labelings. Therefore, in constructing the "ideological canon" of the insurrectionary tendency, a certain amount of subjectivity is employed, informed by familiarity with the literature,and the wider social movement's language choices.

Notes

1. In the period around 1908, Serge aligned himself as an anarchist, publishing anarchist essays and sympathizing with anarcho-individualism/illegalism. He was arrested for his involvement with the anarcho-illegalist Bonnot Gang in 1913, yet, around 1919, he joined the Bolsheviks after arriving in Russia.
2. A French avant-garde movement of 1940s Paris rooted in Dada and Surrealism.
3. Also lesser known essays and articles including: "Call," "Theses on the Terrible Community," "The Cybernetic Hypothesis," The Problem of the Head," "Theses on the Imaginary Party," and "What is Metaphysical Criticism."
4. Tiqqun builds upon the discourse concerning Empire in numerous works, including (2001b, 286), (2010a), and (2011).
5. The use of the term "apparatus" is seen in numerous critical, anti-capitalist thinkers, including Louis Althusser, Michel Foucault, and Gilles Deleuze/Félix Guattari.
6. Ed Mead is a Marxist-communist in his 70s who served 18 years in prison for armed guerrilla actions with the George Jackson Brigade.
7. This point is argued and expanded upon in, for example Žižek (1997; 2002) and Loadenthal (2014a).
8. On 1 May 2012, anarchists in Seattle assembled for a demonstration to coincide with May Day. During the march, a black bloc engaged in a series of attacks on property, including the targeting of a courthouse.

6
Insurrection as values-driven theory and action

Establishing eight values of the insurrectionary canon

Following the discussion on canonization, this chapter seeks to construct the basis for an insurrectionary framework based around a shared politic. This approach borrows from insurrectionary theory's rejection of strict ideological encampments as understood through self-imposed identities (e.g. anarchist, Green/anti-civilization anarchist, illegalist ...), and instead focuses on the basis of overlapping affinity (s.t. 2014). Therefore, the insurrectionary borderlands can be traced through examining where these affinities begin and end, where political analysis and calls for action overlap and diverge. The values embodied in the insurrectionary canon are constituted from a hodgepodge of lesser texts, none of which carry the suggestion of centrality on their own, but collectively constitute the modern insurrectionary discourse – as told through the words and actions of the rock throwers, fire starters, and bomb builders whose names we never know.

Important taxonomic questions persist such as: "Whose participation constitutes this discourse?" Where this movement begins and ends is even more difficult to determine. Though no strict, easy to identify, in-group/out-group determination exists, one can *choose* to think of such camps in binary terms. Though such a modeling has obvious limitations, it can be useful to understand self and other in this regard. To quote *At Daggers Drawn* ..., "One part of this society has every interest in its continuing to rule, the other in everything collapsing as soon as possible. Deciding which side one is on is the first step" (Anonymous 2001a, 5). In the following sections we will explore these "parts of society" found in the insurrectionary milieu by examining eight recurrent, ideological tendencies.

Attack: continuous, immediate, and spontaneous

> We must take another step further. And what should this step be? Attack. Demonstrative at first, for goodness sake! I do not want to talk about a

definitive attack, as basically only the militarist illusion feeds off this kind of thing to the point of indigestion. I mean an attack on the concrete targets that establish, nurture, guarantee, justify, and finance the management of such a monstrosity ... After all, anarchists, even on their own, have historically been capable of carrying out actions of attack, which in their small dimension and reproducibility have inspired those who suffer exclusion, exploitation, and genocide. (Bonanno 2013, 2–3)

Social revolution cannot be postponed to an indefinite future, nor be limited to an indistinct projectuality. It requires constant revolutionary action in the present time, and involves the organization and formation of a ground-breaking revolutionary movement that will elaborate and define its strategic steps, and clash with the establishment's centralized policies. It involves the political process and willingness to put specific revolutionary proposals into practice. (Commando Lambros Foundas 2014)

The insurrectionary tendency towards *attack* is not based around an attempt to "out flank" and defeat the state in head-to-head warfare, but instead attempts to harm and destabilize the system with a constant string of ideologically-linked attacks that collectively constitute a revolutionary force. While these attacks are certainly carried out to urge system-level rupture and eventual collapse, this is a secondary goal wherein individual acts of resistance are quantifiable victories in themselves. Some insurrectionary actors explain that while they do not envision defeating the state in a classical two-party, winner/loser model, they nevertheless feel motivated to act by a personal ethic that furthers the *political* outside of politics through the deployment of continual attack. The Mexican eco-insurrectionary network ITS (2014) explains this in a communiqué, which claims responsibility for a series of parcel bombs sent to scientists and researchers, writing:

... with these attacks we have executed we are not trying to win or lose (because who thinks they will win, since that time, has already lost). Our attacks address the system and that which sustain it, our acts demonstrate that we have NOT submitted, we have NOT accepted their values, we remain human rather than robots, that we have NOT fully domesticated our behaviour, that we are reluctant to join their lies and their negotiations, covenants that we do not want. We do not want something more beneficial or less harmful. We want confrontation, war to the death against this dirty system.

Here one can see that ITS acts without a false, utopian vision of the system conceding. This pattern is repeated from the 1960s when a variety of armed groups waged campaigns of direct attack against the state "regardless of what the major theories said about the likelihood of success" (Brum 2014, 387).

Some insurrectionary theorists have argued against the revolutionary's dependence on weaponry as not only does it set the non-state actor up for likely defeat, but it also creates clear lines of demarcation between those in revolt and those not. This military-minded perspective is explored in *At Daggers Drawn* ..., wherein the authors write:

> The more extensive and enthusiastic the rebellion, the less it can be measured in the military clash. As the armed self-organization of the exploited extends, revealing the fragility of the social order, one sees that revolt, just like hierarchical and mercantile relations, is *everywhere*. On the contrary, anyone who sees the revolution as a coup d'état has a militaristic view of the clash ... The most useful thing one can do with arms is to render them useless as quickly as possible ... we feel just as far removed from those who would like to desert daily normality and put their faith in the mythology of clandestinity and combat organizations, locking themselves up in other cages. No role, no matter how much it puts one at risk in terms of the law, can take the place of the real changing of relations. There is no short-cut, no immediate leap into the elsewhere. The revolution is not a war. (Anonymous 2001a, 30 [Emphasis in original])

Modern insurrectionary attackers understand that massive interlinked apparatuses of governance will not likely be toppled through sporadic attacks on property and individuals, but they strike regardless. These attacks are aimed at creating a space, however temporary, for insurrection to occur; for anti-systemic ideas to be fostered, and for spontaneous revolt to find a home. In this manner, *spontaneity* as a tendency is also quite important. These spontaneous forces seek to disrupt the system, to demonstrate its fallibility, but not to seize power after its fall. It does not seek to lead, but to fight. This is functionally different from socialist movements that often seek to foment armed insurrections with the goal of eventually taking power though the vehicle of the party, council, trade union, etc.

While discussing Marxist revolutionary warfare, one prominent strategist urges adherents to fight militarily, yet not to seek state power. In this text, the famed French foco/focalism-theorist Régis Debray (1967, 29–30) writes:

> Just as spontaneity does not aspire to political power for the exploited and consequently does not organize itself into a political party, self-defense [i.e. armed vanguards] does not aim at military supremacy for the exploited and consequently does not aspire to organize itself as a popular regular army.

Indeed the spontaneous, ad hoc, self-defense units of the insurrectionary underground do not envision military supremacy nor eventual integration into a post-revolutionary state. Instead they understand the notion of attack, the need to remain on the offensive, and the psychological and propaganda purposes of operation beyond simple reactionism.

Certainly, one of the hopes behind carrying out attacks and publicizing claims of responsibility is to inspire additional actions. This historically-rooted notion of "propaganda of the deed" understands that "only violent action ... would impress the world [of] both the desperate nature of the social situation and the ruthless determination of those who wanted to change it" (Joll 1964, 121). In 1886, Charles Gallo threw a bottle of sulfuric acid into the Paris stock exchange and fired three shots from a pistol into the air. At his trail he shouted "Long live revolution! Long live anarchism! Death to the bourgeois judiciary! Long live dynamite!" (quoted in Joll 1964, 131). When he was sentenced, he "gave the jury an hour and a half lecture on anarchist theory and said specifically that he had intended to carry out 'an act of propaganda by the deed for anarchist doctrine'" (quoted in Joll 1964, 131). This form of propaganda has its roots in the ideas of Bakunin who turned towards insurrectionary tendencies declaring "nowhere are there more favorable conditions for the Social Revolution than in Italy" (quoted in Pernicone 1993, 82). Following the failure of a general insurrection in Italy in 1874, Bakunin argued for such individualistic forms of attack, and advocated contemporarily alongside Malatesta, who witnessed the failure of *organized* armed revolts in Naples in 1876.

Such acts of demonstrative armed propaganda have proved successful from some non-insurrectionary, guerrilla movements such as the Uruguayan Tupamaros who deployed it as a focus during their height (early 1969 to mid 1970). According to scholarship focused on this group, armed propaganda was distinct from "classic guerrilla strikes against the security service" and consisted of the "transmitting [of] political messages through violence of a spectacular and symbolic, yet measured, nature" (Brum 2014, 388). These strikes are designed primarily as message generators and transmitters and, therefore, unlike traditional guerrilla tactics, are not *primarily* aimed at "degrading the capacities" (Brum 2014, 390) of the target. Anarchist sociologist Jeff Shantz (2011, 53) speaks to this tradition, writing:

> ... "propaganda of the deed," a notion popular in the nineteenth century that exemplary acts against representatives of the state and capital might serve as pedagogical tools in the process of de-legitimizing bourgeois morality and encouraging the oppressed to shed such ingrained values as respect for property and the law ... [thus] attacks on corporate property, represent a dramatic, if symbolic, shattering of hegemonic corporate claim on ownership and property rights which are deeply ingrained but which anarchists hold to be illegitimate ... [They are] a rushing wave of

negation crashing against the material manifestations of the most central and vigorously defended beliefs of capitalism and liberal democracy.

Here one can understand propaganda of the deed to embody not only a proof of concept for the attacker, but also a functional attack on state/capital as well as the embodiment of *negation*. This negation rhetorically challenges reformism, bureaucracy, traditional politics and instead offers a radically divergent alternative, that of struggle through armed confrontations with all discernable targets of power, control, and oppression. To attack is to negate other, more mediated forms of politics; to critique their methods while simultaneously offering a revisioned praxis of social change that is both nihilistic and utopian at the same time. This ability for the dominated to act through negation is essential as "the exploited have nothing to self-manage but their own negation" (Anonymous 2001a, 11). The utopianism offered by negation is of a post-conflict world based on the principals of freedom, autonomy, mutual aid, voluntary association, informality, and horizontalism. This new era of conflict is ignited and continued permanently, until the breakdown of the present system and the space is created to envision another that allows for the imagining of new forms of social relations.

Attack to learn to attack ... attack now!

> With this we make a call to all the lone wolves or affinity clans who are indecisive about attacking the system, let's not wait any longer, we don't have the luxury of waiting any longer, it's true that even though we do what we do, everything will turn into a technological pile of garbage, but before that happens, we have decided to attack and resist the system's barrages, without glory or victory, just with our individual dedication to continuing the war, which our fierce huntergatherer nomadic ancestors started centuries ago against the invader, European outsider or native outsider. (Obsidian Point Circle of Attack 2014)

The strategic imperative for insurrectionary attack is also based in a temporal logic that states that to delay acting is to fail to act. The insurrectionary tendency towards *immediate* action is not only strategic, it is also pedagogical; in other words, one learns to attack through attacking and through no other means. In one of the most often quoted pieces of insurrectionary prose, the authors of *At Daggers Drawn* ... write:

> The secret is to really begin. The present social organization is not just delaying ... The only way to learn what freedom is, is to experiment it ... Insurrection does not come up with the answers on its own, that is

true. It only starts asking questions. So the point is not whether to act gradually or adventureistically. The point is whether to act of merely dream of acting ... The method of spreading attacks is a form of struggle that carries a different world within it. To act when everyone advises waiting, when it is not possible to count on great followings, when you do not know beforehand whether you will get results or not, means one is already affirming what one is fighting for: a society *without measure*. (Anonymous 2001a, 15, 18)

These notions are consistent; learning through action, the need to "simply begin," and that the crossing of a threshold to move from theorizing to acting is itself a liberatory act. In the appropriately titled essay "Insurrectionary Anarchy: Organising for Attack!," the anonymous authors clearly make this point, writing, "It is through acting and learning to act, not propaganda, that we will open the path to insurrection, although analysis and discussion have a role in clarifying how to act. Waiting only teaches waiting; in acting one learns to act" (Anonymous 2003). In communiqués, essays, and letters from prisoners the message is repeated: attack, attack, attack! In a September 2014 essay entitles "That Which Stagnates Rots," (2014, 3) wherein Mexican insurrectionist Carlos López, known as Chivo, explains:

> We understand insurrectionary anarchy as an action born from individuality, like the rupture that everyone carries with themselves, transforming the entirety of what surrounds them ... If something identifies with the insurrectionary struggle it is precisely that which carries one farther away from illusion and words, of taking the initiative in the conflict of classes and breaking with the passive attitude of resistance to go into action, without limiting oneself to waiting to be repressed, to therefore have justification to attack; but rather doing it already, here and now. Permanent conflict, we carry it in our daily life, in our heads and hearts, always seeking to generalize it in the neighborhoods, colonies, towns, and beyond; to come to organize ourselves – through base nuclei [i.e. the cell model].

Here we can see not only the emphasis on individualism, self-identification, and preemptive attack, but also the concept of "rupture." The insurrectionary logic and strategy utilizes the concept of *rupture*, an "upsetting [of] the imperatives of time and social space ... to imagine new relations and surroundings" (Anonymous 2001a, 10). This involves not only breaking from commodity fetishism, wage slavery, alienation, and other such named manifestations of social control, but one must also "snatch time and space from social obligation ... breaking social normality by force" (Anonymous 2001a, 13–14).

In one final example, we can see these themes made more explicit in an excerpt from a short-lived Denver-based insurrectionary magazine *'Til It Breaks*. In an article entitled "Strategic Social War," the authors write:

> Our [insurrectionary anarchist] subculture has come to emphasize the attack. We are compelled to act immediately, despite the sheer impoverishment of our revolutionary context. We cannot wait until the "right moment," the progression of capital is too rapid to spare even one more second. To the quiet satisfaction of our most intelligent enemies, the ethos of attack has come to imply a neglect of a developed long-term strategy. We of course understand that every recruiting center, police station, and real-estate development needs to be razed as soon as possible. But we ask: is attempting to do this all right now the most efficient or strategic approach? Here, we ask those not concerned with efficiency to reconsider; we desire an efficient destruction of capitalism. A destruction that is efficient not only in the overthrow of the social order, but also in the production of love, rage, and revolutionary joy. A destruction that is efficient, not in the sense of Taylor's assembly line, but in the sense of his worst nightmare: the disassembly of the assembly line. ('Til it Breaks collective 2009, 17)

This text is interesting not only because it advocates attack, but also for its acknowledged strategic concessions. The authors seek to explore the notion of tactics of attack versus the strategy of insurrection, and conclude that to utilize such a means may not be "efficient," but doing so exemplifies the rejection of such concerns.

"Making the social *war*"

> This is not to be a POLITICAL revolution. Its object will be to overthrow not governments but the economic and technological basis for the present society ... The two main tasks for the present are to promote social stress and instability in industrial society and to develop and propagate an ideology that opposes technology and the industrial system. (Kaczynski 2010b, pts. 4, 181)

The insurrectionary strategy is based in the task of creating social conditions akin to active combat, termed the "social war." Theory posits that if – to borrow from Prussian military theorist Carl von Clausewitz – "war is politics by other means," and using Foucault's (1977, 168) inversion[1] which states "war as strategy is a continuation of politics" then the insurrectionary task is the creation of social tension, putting the state within a defensive state of siege, negating political solutions, and cultivating revolt. This revolt creates a rupture in the social fabric, a temporary space where new forms of power and organization can develop. The theory is based in a form of nihilist anti-politics which engages in the revolutionary discourse through state terms (e.g. war, capital, power) yet envisions a post-state society which is also post-war and post-politics. One of the more theoretically situated, insurrectionary groupings, the IEF (2009, 134–135), write of warfare and strategy, stating:

> To use war as a means for dispute management between nations is the prerogative of the state; to use war as the means to negate society based on classes is the strategy of insurrection. When these two distinct types of war blur in spectacular society, then we have entered into the biopolitical stage of warfare, that is social war … war cannot end until the specific, historical form of total management known as politics ends. To escape war requires a subtraction from politics, an act unregulated by law and indecipherable in discourse. By reversing Napoleon's maxim: that "it is not for an event to govern politics, but for politics to govern events," we find a hint of how to accomplish this. An event that "governs" politics, in essence, destroys it. It is up to us to make such events possible.

The roots of this insurrectionary strategy of conflict may be most directly derived from the theory of "civil war" developed in *Tiqqun #2*, having been adopted from Situationist Guy Debord's (1998) spectacle (e.g. virtual) war, and from Foucault's (2003, 59–60) "social warfare."

This deployment of Foucault is tricky. In its older, outmoded understanding, war (including social war) functioned *outside* and *against* the state, yet subsequent understandings exhibit such power as working *for* the state. In his discussion of Foucault's application to concepts of war, International Relations theorist Julian Reid (2011, 88) writes:

> Originally conceived in terms of their exteriority to the state, certain of these historico-political discourses are reconceived … discourses of war and politics undergo a marked shift. No longer is the politics that war continues a war against the state in which state institutions are the source of domination and subjugation but instead politics becomes a continuation of a war for the state.

Therefore, while war is often understood as something that is carried out against the state's authority, the same posturing is adopted for statist aims; for the continuation of "politics through other means." In his series of lectures collected in *Society Must Be Defended*, Foucault (2003) develops this reading on the connection between war and politics, especially in light of Clausewitz. Clausewitz argued that war occurs when politics fails – continuing forward to accomplish the political goals (Edwards 2012, 22) – thus

Foucault's assertion that the motives of politics resemble those of war seems an obvious conclusion.

Therefore the insurrectionary position can be read as a third stage in this evolutionary idea. If politics *is*, as Clausewitz suggests, "the continuation of war through other means," and therefore both forms of social change are sometimes indistinguishable, it is a fair assumption that with the insurrectionary rejection of *politics* in the Clausewitzian and Foucauldian sense, there is a resulting increase in *war*. This aligns well with the generalizable insurrectionary position, which rejects political representationism and abstracted forms of decision-making in favor of direct confrontation between opposing forces. Therefore it appears entirely possible to chronologically order these positions – from Clausewitz, to Foucault, and onto the insurrectionists – as a continuation of a single discourse concerning war and politics as a solution to tensions created by less-than-egalitarian societies.

For Foucault, social classes are constantly in conflict in an attempt to establish their own power (Danaher 2002, 86). Ruling class ideology is maintained through constant war, and until such control is subverted and challenged, it will continue to reproduce. The modernist interpretation of this civil/social war is most clearly articulated by TIC. In a talk delivered in New York, an anonymous member of the Committee (2013, 1–2) stated:

> There is a war going on – a permanent, global civil war ... the meaning of this war is not understood. Everything said about the asymmetrical shape of the so-called "new wars" only adds to the confusion. The ongoing war we speak of does not have the Napoleonic magnificence of regular wars between two great armies of men, or between two antagonistic classes. Because if there is an asymmetry in the confrontation it is less between the forces present than over the very definition of the war itself. That is why we cannot talk about a social war: for if social war is a war that is led against us, it cannot symmetrically describe the war that we wage from our side and vice versa. We have to rethink the words themselves in order to forge new concepts as weapons.

Here TIC speaks to the ongoing and ever-present nature of structural conflict (i.e. "permanent, global civil war"), noting its shift from traditional forms of violent conflict. And while they take issue with labeling it a *social* war, they do argue that the powers of domination are "leading a social war against us."

The insurrectionary social war *is* a strategy, just like guerrilla warfare is for Leninists. It seeks to initiate conflict with the state and force tension. Insurrectionary attack is not defensive despite often employing justifications based in a position of defensive violence. The strategy of insurrectionary social war is fought through the tactics of the clandestine cell network. The role of the wider propagandist and mobilizing structures are thus to create waves of activity, temporary spaces of insurrectionary revolt. Though globally dispersed and often minimally disruptive, the constant strikes by clandestine attackers create an atmosphere where the social war can thrive. In an advertisement for an anarchist conference focused around the theme of social war, the advertisers write:

> There was Social War last century during the Vietnam War, an era filled with draft-dodgers, soldier riots on US military bases, troops blowing up their commanders (fraggings), and calls for "Bring the War Home." Further back, one could perhaps look to the Scorched Earth strategy. The contemporary theory and application of Social War largely focuses on sabotage, rioting, human strike, and squatting reclaimed space ... Can Social War resist the urge to simply return to guerrilla acts or can it explode across every terrain of present existence, and if so, how would that look? Could manifestations of Social War include something other than a kind of drop-out culture that might include willful participation in the economy with the aim of amassing resources and capital intended to be used as a force of social destruction? (BASTARD 2014)

Here we see a clearly articulated link between the *tactics* of insurrectionary movements and the *strategy* of insurrectionary, anti-social warfare. TIC (2007, 25) covers this tactical praxis as well, arguing that tactics such as vandalism are part of its strategy, writing: "This whole series of nocturnal vandalisms and anonymous attacks, this wordless destruction, has widened the breach between politics and the political." Thus the politics of insurrectionary attack aim to create space and tension between the means of governance (i.e. "politics") and the struggle of liberation (i.e. "the political").

The creation of a political space devoid of politics is a matter of autonomy, albeit a temporary autonomy. Hakim Bey's (1991) concept of a "temporary autonomous zone" (TAZ) reflects this tendency. Bey's TAZs emerge "like an uprising which does not engage directly with the State, a guerrilla operation which liberates an area (of land, of time, of imagination) and then dissolves itself to re-form elsewhere ... before the State can crush it" (1991, 101). For Bey, these TAZs are the creation of spaces of resistance and revolution beyond the various apparatuses of state power; "'areas free of the State' in which to elaborate new ideas and practices" (Anonymous 2001a, 13). These temporary areas are filled by the actions of affinity groups, cells, and networks which dissolve following the action/protest/attack, only to be reconstituted in another locale, at another time, with newly configured participants (Gabay 2010, 129). According to scholars writing about autonomist tendencies in social movements, "autonomy has become ... a central figure in the articulation of social movements" (Feigenbaum, Frenzel, and McCurdy 2013, 23) and, in this manner, insurrectionary anarchism fits squarely within such a tradition. The insurrectionary tendency borrows from autonomism and "seek[s] autonomy from capital, from the state, and from international interstate organizations" (Feigenbaum, Frenzel, and McCurdy 2013, 24). The concept of a TAZ is expanded upon by the insurrectionary theorists into a "zone of opacity," the fostering of communities which, through their "density" and "solidarities" are "opaque to all authority" (TIC 2007, 107–108; IEF 2013, 50). Hence, the creation of zones of opacity does not usurp or succeed lands from the state or seek to possess territory, but rather is seeks to "*be* the territory" (TIC 2007, 108).

These urgings of direct attack recall earlier, Marxist strategies. Guerrilla *foco* theorist Debray wrote of the need for not only *defensive* revolutionary apparatuses but *offensive* ones as well. In prose that is repeated in spirit in the insurrectionary tendency, Debray (1967, 30) writes, "self-defense is partial; revolutionary guerrilla warfare aims at total war by combining under its hegemony all forms of struggle at all points within the territory." Insurrectionary theory would certainly agree; the purpose of war-like struggle is the fostering of "total war" in all physical locales and within all manifestations of power, domination, and violence.

Beyond intersectionality: total liberation and "The Totality"

> The social body is not made up of a pyramid of orders or of a hierarchy, and it does not constitute a coherent and unitary organism. It is composed of two groups, and they are not only quite distinct, but also in conflict. And the conflictual relationship that exists between the two groups that constitute the social body and shapes the State is in fact one of war, of permanent warfare. The State is nothing more than the way that the war between the two groups in question continues to be waged in apparently peaceful forms. (Foucault 2003, 88)

The insurrectionary epistemology rests in a poststructurally-infused articulation of anarchism – often termed post-anarchism (e.g., Rousselle and Evren 2011) – which seeks to locate a form of ultimate intersectionality,[2] a total liberation philosophy that does not rest its critique in institutions or specific hierarchies (e.g. racism, colonialism). Frequently, it is described as an anti-oppressive framework that links human, animal, and eco-concerns, through the typically anthropocentric notion of intersectionality. One self-described "anti-social individualist nihilist anarchist" defined "total liberation" as "liberation of human animals, non-human animals and the earth … the total liberation that I am speaking about could be nothing less than aggressive and in total conflict with the existent" (Archegonos 2015, 22). Such a notion of "aggressive conflict" is often repeated in reference to "total liberation" as it strives towards the "end[ing] of every concession" (Anonymous 2001a, 22). The insurrectionary critique sees its opponents everywhere, in all manners of society, governance, and civilization. In their announcement for an anarchist conference centered on social war, the organizers describe this unbridled critique, writing:

> What if our opponent was the whole of society and our will was the destruction of the complex network of social ties that hold together and reproduce the present? What would that kind of war look like and how might it happen? How would we grapple with the reality that we, too, as anarchists with our own identities and cultures, are part of that complex network that is to be torn asunder? Is Social War, perhaps foremost, also the incessant war waged by Society against all destabilizing forces? (BASTARD 2014)

If this milieu understands a post-binary opposition between themselves and "the whole of society that reproduces the present," what does this mean for defining a liberationist framework?

The total liberation, insurrectionary framework borrows from the anarchist critique of domination as a core principle for its epistemology. In his discussion of anarchist perceptions of power and authority, anarchist and political theorist Uri Gordon (2008, 51–52) writes:

> ... the word domination is more comprehensive than another concept often used by anarchists – hierarchy. While hierarchy is an apt description for the structure of many of the social relations making up domination, it does not express them all. In hierarchical relations inequalities of status are visible, either because they are formalized (say, in the relations between a CEO and a secretary), or because one can identify their presence in a particular behavior or utterance. But the domination of human beings is often an insidious dynamic, reproduced through performative disciplinary acts in which the protagonists may not even be conscious of their roles. Many times, the dominated person can only symbolically point to an embodied source of her or his unfreedom. These insights feed into an anarchist critique of power which goes beyond the structural focus on hierarchy, and points to new avenues for resistance.

The insurrectionary project can be understood as a further excavation of these social relations, behaviors, utterances, "performative disciplinary acts," and "embodied sources of unfreedom." While insurrectionary theory (especially "high" theory such as is offered by Tiqqun) serves to expose these manifestations through a poststructuralist lens, the methodology of attack seeks to locate these sites in the physicality of the lived world, through the targeting of government, state, corporate, religious, scientific, and private properties. Further conflict can be located in the personal – the conflict with the pre/un-liberated self – though such a discourse is noticeably less frequent within communiqué texts.

These "embodied sources of unfreedom" abound in the social, political, economic, and cultural realms. To specifically locate them is an individualistic act and, therefore, cells are left to their own internal processes to identify appropriate targets for attack. This targeting variety is related to the wide, expansive critique offered by the insurrectionary attackers. In a communiqué penned by imprisoned members of the CCF, the authors describe the borders of these areas of domination, writing:

> The war is raging with thousands of faces. With the face of the techno-industrial totalitarianism, of the economic crisis, of the plunder against nature, the repression, the military operations, the tele-propaganda of the spectacle … Economic misery, poverty, arrogant exploitation by the bosses, bank dictatorship, corporatism, electronic policing, digital world, genetic experiments, laboratory diseases, nanotechnology, deforestation, water and air pollution, extermination of animals through vivisection, massive meat-eating, new high-security prisons, concentration camps for immigrants, arrests of anarchists, police everywhere, army against demonstrators, hecatombs of dead in "humanitarian" military operations, nuclear and chemical weapons, propaganda by journalists, uniform aesthetics in advertising, despotism of dead commodities … Authority cannot be found on a single point. That's why we want FAI and affinity groups to meet also on new grounds. To combine blown up banks with the debris of an advertising company. To spread our hostility towards the techno-industrial section, corporate exploitation of nature and animals, pharmaceutical industry, civilization and every compromise, that enslaves us. We promote the anti-civilization anarchist tension and invent a new way of life. Away from the fantasies of an idealized primitivism, we want to attack each structure that exploits and murders nature, animals and humans. Away from the fetishisms of the value of human life, we clarify that our goal is not only the building facilities, but also the individuals who manage them, so we promote and practice the executions of human targets. (CCF-FAI/IRF Imprisoned Members Cell 2013)

This is perhaps the clearest articulation of an insurrectionary anarchist form of boundless intersectionality – one wherein a nanotechnologist, meat eater, boss, and cop are all understood as constituting the same enemy class or potential target set. It is yet another articulation of "The Totality" and, as such, acts in a shared system of oppression and domination. The individualistic development of cell-level policies (e.g. whom to target, whom to *not* target) is integral to leaderless resistance networks and serves to develop, evaluate, and expand notions of an intersectional totality. This "Totality" is aimed at identifying the *causes* of domination, coercion, oppression, and system-level violence at their most base terms. The totality reading of intersectionality speaks beyond the police, banks, and multinational trade bodies, and focuses at the roots of power, seeing the larger enemy as "not simply as an assemblage of machinery, but as a social relation, a *system*" (Anonymous 2001a, 20). This is precisely why the insurrectionary concept of a totality is functionally open and descriptively fluid; it is not meant to be a litmus test for attack but rather an overarching framework to inform analysis and action.

Against management and movements, for temporary informality

> Because this is what anarchist urban guerrilla exactly means: bringing the attack in first person and present tense, without needing the camouflage of social protest ... At the same time, various anarchist politicians and clowns satisfy their conscience by participating in opportunistic street-fights and fantasize the social revolution of the masses. It is them, who using social struggles as an alibi, characterize the anarchist urban guerrilla as an outdated and self-destructive choice ... Through "social struggles", we want to create a bridge, so that rebellious and unsatisfied minorities can cross over to the anarchist urban guerrilla, where the attack is continuous. (CCF-FAI/IRF Imprisoned Members Cell 2013)

In the opening pages of the IEF's (2013, 9) mini-book, *Between Predicates. War* ... the collective of insurrectionary theorists caution, "'Contemporary struggle' is our way to conceptualize what links the events of our epoch – events that cannot be defined as social movements or categorized within leftist conceptions of reform and revolution." The authors write that even the language used to understand social movements is without merit as it is part of a discourse controlled by "the enemy" (IEF 2013, 12). Insurrectionary positions are oppositional to so-called social movements in a number of key ways. First they oppose the reduction of struggle to *issues*, which are then ghettoized into *movements* with specific socio-political aims. This would include the animal rights movement, women's rights movement, global debt relief movement, etc. Not only are these often portrayed as piecemeal, reformist, and myopic, they are burdened with the weights of age-old discourses of liberalism, namely "the grammar of justice, democracy, and equality" (IEF 2013, 12). Therefore, not only is insurrectionism opposed to this form of reductionism, it is also opposed to the emphasis on mass, workerism, and organization. In other words, the insurrection does not require for revolt to be broad-based, situated in the working class or the result of capacity building from movements.

This notion of rejecting "mass" as an undesirable measure or hindrance is repeated by anarcho-primitivist and insurrectionary proponent Kevin Tucker (2009, 10), who writes in, *Revolution And/Or Insurrection: Some Thoughts on Tearing This Muthafucka Down*:

> I'm not for any kind of "mass consciousness" or mass anything, in fact, "mass" is one of the underlying problems that comes with civilization. I'm most interested in autonomous resistance ... Insurrection is the act of people who simply refuse to sit by and wait for revolutions ... Insurrection remains a tactic for those who seek an outlet for their rage against the great domesticating force.

Modern insurrectionary theorists thus critique the failing of the mass-centric movements of the 1960s to 1990s, arguing that they "created the conditions for general self-management [of dissent]" and that in actualizing the freedoms for specific classes (e.g. people of color, non-heterosexuals, women) the systems of governance and state have been able to integrate these new avenues through capitalist commodification and new forms of social control (IEF 2013, 14). Moreover, insurrectionary logic posits that the social movement's tendency to act as a tangible representative of collective dissatisfaction is self-serving and exploits the hardships of the community for the mobilization of the party. It is worth noting that concurrent strands of anti-state, poststructuralist thought similarly maintain a central rejection of representation (May 1994, 47–48), such as poststructural anarchism.

According to insurrectionary theorists, representationism becomes ever more distant as those speaking for the exploited (i.e. social movement participants) grow detached from the actual communities they claim to represent, and the work of representationship becomes akin to a job.

> Too often revolutionaries have claimed to be the exploited's consciousness and to represent their level of subversive maturity. The "social movement" thus becomes the justification for the party (which in the Leninist version becomes an elite of professionals of the revolution). The vicious circle is that the more one separates oneself from the exploited, the more one needs to *represent* an inexistent relationship. Subversion is reduced to one's own practices, and representation becomes the organization of an ideological racket – the bureaucratic version of capitalist appropriation ... We do not want to direct or support social movements, but rather to participate in those that already exist, to the extent to which we recognize common needs in them. (Anonymous 2001a)

This strategic frame often comes in the form of rejection of more traditional forms of leftist action. Insurrectionary proponents who may have partially come of age politically in the realm of anti-globalization protests, anarchist infoshops, and group houses have moved past this, seeing these tired forms of lifestyleism and activism as insular and unwinnable.

In their essay "Taking Communion at the End of History," contained within the IEF's (2009, 63) larger work, *Politics is Not a Banana*, the authors write:

> The rhythm anarchists in the US have grown accustomed to – that of food not bombs, of collective living, of bicycle programs, and of black blocs and summit hoping – are merely improvised practices with a certain force of resonance. Each begins either as an intentionally ritualized practice or as an experiment at opening up new practices.

These "rituals" thus begin to lose meaning as forms of resistance and become ends in themselves, robbing them of their disruptive and hence revolutionary potentials. This ritualization of resistance is abhorrent to the insurrectionary, as they advocate direct confrontation through informal organization, not abstracted advocacy through mass-movement organization building. There is a constant urging to abandon the constraints of the movement, the organization, the party, and the committee and to simply begin the attack. In a Mexican communiqué claiming responsibility for a parcel bomb, the authors write:

> We abandon words and analyses in order to begin with our war, the war against what kills us and consumes us, against the invincible megamachine which only wild nature or its very own technology can collapse. We do not seek victories, triumphs or results from what we do or have done, we are not revolutionaries, platformists or anarchists. (Obsidian Point Circle of Attack 2014)

The authors are careful to note their distance from those advocating the building of movements and organization, who they group into the camps of "revolutionaries, platformists or anarchists," choosing to see themselves as something else, something more direct in its confrontation and contestation with the system at large.

Rejecting the (capital "L") Left

These forms of rejectionism are recurrent in critiques of social movements, representative politics, platformism, and also the concept of an organized Left. Leading the charge against the Left is Theodore Kaczynski – not identified as an insurrectionist – who dedicates a substantial portion of "Industrial Society and Its Future" (also known as the "Unabomber's Manifesto") to condemn their approaches. Kaczynski notes that leftists often rely on personalized identification with oppressed classes (e.g. non-white communities) which hides the former's feelings of inferiority toward the latter. He argues that the Left mobilizes based on a rejection of the "strong, good and successful ... [such as] America ... Western civilization ... white males ... [and] rationality" (2010b, 41). Kaczynski thus rejects the Left's cultural relativism and their claim that its actions are motivated by "compassion or by moral principles" (2010b, 42–43). He argues throughout numerous works that Leftists are "disorganized, irrational types" ruining the anarchist/anarcho-primitivist movement and participating in a form of "escapism" (2010c, 272, 317). The author's analysis shifts between the personal, political, and the psychological as Kaczynski argues that the Left chooses to engage in struggle out of a "need for rebellion and for membership in a movement" (2010b, 106) of like-minded persons. He equates Leftism to a form of religion, rejecting the psychological crutch it serves, and describing the movements as a "totalitarian force" (2010b, 108). Therefore for Kaczynski and insurrectionary networks that draw inspiration from him, the Left as a constituency is a self-serving, non-revolutionary force of mentally weak individuals who capitalize on the oppression of others who feel called upon to act. It is for this reason that critics choose to reject the Left's efforts and distance themselves from their parties, movements, subjectivities, and initiatives.

This perception of Leftism – which is by no means assigned to only Kaczynski – asserts that the channeling of dissent and contestation into rights-based campaigns is a central method of indirect repression (and recuperation) designed to defang modes of radical resistance to the state and capital. In his discussion of the Left's policing of more militant forms of resistance, anarchist author Doug Gilbert terms this a "recuperative element ... within social struggles" (O'Goodness 2014a, secs. 9:40–10:50). For Gilbert, Leftism is a form of mediated social relations between the people and the state where diverse forms of revolt are methodically channeled into rights-based campaigns which can be appeased with piecemeal concessions such as the passage of new laws, the hiring/firing of individuals, or the establishment of new governmental bodies (e.g. a new office to oversee Latino police affairs).

This form of Leftism is routinely exploitative of the population's discontent, as it seeks to collect the general dissatisfactions expressed throughout the society and target this at a campaign – for example a campaign for the rights of women, homosexuals, differently-abled individuals, non-human animals, or campaigns which seek to oppose or support a specific individual, law or initiative. Therefore it should be clear that a rejection of this style of Leftism is not simply offered by Kaczynski, but is common throughout the insurrectionary discourse. Returning to Gilbert, the author states that a dichotomy exists between "self-organized [forms of] struggle," such as riots and building occupations, and forms of mediated struggle that the Left seeks to organize and direct. Gilbert describes these latter groupings as "official organizations which seek to manage people and their struggles ... and people who seek to lead people into politics ... [and] political parties" (O'Goodness 2014a, secs. 11:57–12:50). This is representative of the larger insurrectionary discourse which seeks to critique "managed struggles" and embrace those which are based around spontaneity, immediacy, and confrontation, pronouncements traditional Leftism (in this preparative usage) rejects.

Informal, temporary collectivities of affinity

> For us, the starting point is informal anarchist organization ... Informal, because we dislike the conditions and norms of predefined roles and organizational statutes. The roles of the orator who captivates the audience in assemblies, of the thief, the bomber, the author of communiques and the arsonist, divide and fritter life and our capabilities. Division is the principle of authority. The informal authority of roles, which we often be encountered in anarchist circles, is more insidious than the institutional authority, as it remains well camouflaged and in this way invisible and invulnerable. We say EVERYTHING FOR EVERYONE. Each of us, away from roles and specializations, can develop his/hers skills and test everything through comradely mutuality ... robberies, arsons, bombs, executions, texts, conversations and any other form of expression, which promotes new anarchy. (CCF-FAI/IRF Imprisoned Members Cell 2013)

> It is the horizontal link that concretises the practice of liberation: an informal link, of fact, without representation. (Anonymous 2001a, 17)

The idea of a vanguard, and specifically a vanguard party, is (in)famously developed by Vladimir Lenin who argued that proletariats were unlikely (or incapable) of independently reaching class consciousness and, furthermore, the proletariat as a whole is unable to form a revolutionary organization beyond the reformism of trade unions. Therefore, if the masses were unable to form such a mechanism on their own, this became the task of a vanguard party to organize the workers, teach class consciousness, and foment revolution. In this model, the vanguard party hijacks the agency of the people and uses it to accelerate their radicalization and self-organization. While insurrectionary theory posits that the riotous ruptures of a minority can lead the way for mass withdrawal of consent and revolt, the movement does not see itself as a leadership destined to guide and teach. This of course carries with it a presumption about the nature of struggle and human behavior – for example that the ruptures of the few can lead to the withdrawal of consent by the many. It presumes that, in a general sense, the population is already quite dissatisfied and thus ripe for rebellion. In opposition to the vanguardist model, insurrectionary theory seeks to create the conditions for mass revolt through exposing contradictions and violence within the system itself, and by creating physical and temporal spaces for the articulation of rage, resistance, and new forms of being.

While the organizational, and hence strategic, rejection of vanguardism has been discussed prior, it is useful to further explore the nature of these philosophical rejections. Curiously, if one is against vanguardism, how can a minority help to foment revolt on a large scale? Insurrectionary logic advocates for ad hoc groupings through voluntary association and mutual aid in line with "classical" anarchism. In this manner, collectivities of individuals freely associated through informal temporary networks and, in doing so, act autonomously (as cells, collectives, individuals, affinity groups) and collectively (as federations, informal networks, moniker-based networks). This modeling is repeated in *At Daggers Drawn* ... stating, "Not only does acting in small numbers not constitute a limit, it represents a totally different way of seeing social transformation ... Authentic federalism makes agreements between free unions of individuals possible" (Anonymous 2001a, 17). The temporary, cell-sized, affinity group model is familiar to older networks such as the ALF, as the ALF model has certainly influenced contemporary insurrectionary strategies. Not only have joint ALF/FAI cells carried out attacks, paying homage to their anti-speciesist, saboteur forebearers, but the moniker-based, communiqué-driven method of attack is recurrent. One FAI activist, in an interview from his jail cell, spoke to these connections, writing:

> To comrades like me, formed during the struggles of the 90's in Italy, the contribution of the groups of action ALF and ELF, with their international network, concerning the revolutionary anarchist imaginary and how to organize into affinity groups, was very important. Their environmentalist, animalist perspective has changed the view of many anarchists. In Italy, their propensity to affinity groups was greeted with enthusiasm as a concrete example of informal organization. (Cospito 2014)

The interviewee, jailed for the FAI-claimed kneecap shooting of an Italian nuclear executive, goes on to say that he objects to the ALF/ELF's ban on attacking humans and notes that, because of this position, he feels more closely aligned to ITS who have embraced an "anti-civilizational, wild, anti-ideological" (Cospito 2014) politic.

Though the affinity group model is common within the direct action history, it remains isolated; not commonly part of wider and more commonly known social movements. While affinity groups may interact within a wider social movement, the wider movement context is not necessary for the continuation of its activity. The social movement at large can be thought of as a collectivity of affinity groups ranging in size from the individual to the multinational, all constituted by groupings of people tied together through a shared affinity. This structure allows segments of the population to act from among the generalized milieu while often continuing to maintain "normal" lives the majority of the time. In this form, a minority of the population can be an active force for social change without *leading* or establishing agendas, speaking for the marginalized, or engaging in other forms of representationism. The insurrectionary, minority vanguard can emerge from the population, and help to foment dissident trends as "revolt is always the work of a minority" (Anonymous 2001a, 26). The authors expanded this discussion, writing "Although minoritarian (but in respect to what unit of measure?) in its active forces, the insurrectional phenomenon can take on extremely wide dimensions, and in this respect reveals its social nature" (Anonymous 2001a, 27).

These forms of informal, minoritarian, and sometimes vanguardist collectivities act in an intentional praxis – "the act of will that finds its immediate expression in an act" (IEF 2009, 123) – allowing the means of the attack to mirror the pre-figurative vision of the attackers. Therefore, tactical, strategic, and organizational decisions become not merely a matter of utility or pragmatism, but rather reflective of a political ethic:

> This, then, is how action in small groups of people with affinity contains the most important of qualities – it is not mere tactical contrivance, but already contains the realization of one's goals. Liquidating the lie of the *transitional period* ... means making the revolt itself a different way of conceiving relations. (Anonymous 2001a, 18)

On occasion, communiqués have used the language "anarchists of praxis" to delineate those that participate actively in creating attacks and those that "belong to pseudo-ideologues drowning in words, without ever having been tested in practice" (CCF-FAI/IRF 2014). This self-labeling – "the anarchists of praxis" – distinguishes those in *movements* from those within the insurrectionary war, further widening the gap between the civil and the uncivil.

Against reformism, democracy, and mediation

> We are not looking for a comfortable chair in local administration so we can afford to do what needs be done. We don't accept moanings like: "Violence is bad, we shouldn't be torching vehicles, we should get more signatures under petition, so as to be heard by federal government." This

reminds us of the fears of a person who's afraid to lose the goodwill of powers-that-be ... It is time to stop hiding your inability to act behind phrases like: "we shouldn't act, this is violent tactics" ... or "this is illegal". If you want to ask for permission to protest, you must understand that you're in fact selling yourselves. Only uncontrollable forms of resistance can hope to remain free. Any protest coordinated from under liberal umbrella organization is doomed to a failure. Gather your strengths, stay free and be wild, god damn it! (IRF/ELF – Moscow 2014)

Traditionally, scholarship positioned social movements into one of two camps: reformist or revolutionary. As social movement theorist Roberta Garner (1996, 371) explains, "[Reformist movements] were defined as having limited goals and operating within legitimate political structures ... [revolutionary movements] were defined as having large goals and using nonlegitimate means, like terrorism and armed struggle." Though Garner herself explains that this is often a false dichotomy, within the insurrectionary tendency the movement is decidedly anti-reformist, anti-legitimacy, and pro-armed struggle. Thus while Garner (1996, 371) is correct in asserting that a great variety of movements *are* "challeng[ing] these boundaries," the insurrectionists are firmly planted in the realm of revolutionary, system-level change.

The lack of interest in reformist measures has its roots in core ideological concepts, but also in movement histories and their exposure to violence, specifically violence from state repression. Social movement theorists argue that violent repression by the state constitutes a prime point of consideration for potential participants (Tilly 1978, 3:5–3:10, 3:54–3:55, 4:3–4:18). Therefore, revolutionary-minded activists who engage in street-level protests can be further radicalized through exposures to state repression. This logic posits that the more repressive the experience of the activist, the higher one perceives the potential collective benefit to mobilized action to amend such ills (della Porta and Fillieule 2004, 233–234). Furthermore, activists' exposure to severe violence – epitomized by the death of an ally by police – may demonstrate for reform-minded activists that the political sphere is the realm of an "unfair state" (della Porta 1995) which serves to discourage political engagement as institutions are seen as unresponsive, undemocratic, and illegitimate. As the wider insurrectionary milieu has witnessed numerous comrades' deaths and many more imprisoned, it is logical to assume these occurrences have served to harden those that remain and to reinforce their anti-reformist tendencies. This is especially true of those who formerly participated in mass convergence/summit protests, which were often the site of police violence directed at demonstrators.

The anti-reformist tendency, which understands reformist "revolutionaries" as comparable with the enemy (e.g. police, army, capitalists), is prevalent throughout a broader militant discourse. In his lengthy analysis of the

Italian RB, author Alessandro Orsini (2011) notes that the Brigade's "hatred of reformists is even greater than their hatred of capitalists." For the RB, those proposing sub-system level change were penned as "ultrareactionary and counterrevolutionary" (Orsini 2011, 43). This criticism included not only those who sought less-than-militant action, but also those proposing solutions through democratic parliamentarianism. According to Orsini (2011, 44), in a 1977 communiqué, the RB writes:

> What you [Communists] call "democracy" is only and always a form of politics that conceals the dictatorship of big capital ... there is no continuity between our democracy and yours, as false as a lead coin, but an absolute historic antagonism that has its roots in the class structure of the capitalistic way of production, this is, in the unshakable antagonism that sets the exploited classes against the exploiting ones.

The insurrectionary attack networks opposed to democratic reformism act in furtherance of this goal through both direct attacks against the systems of abstraction and those involved with representationism. In one example, an Indonesian FAI/IRF cell carried out a series of arsons throughout the island nation to not only critique so-called "civil anarchists," but also to demonstrate opposition to the political system at large that speaks of liberalism, participation, and democracy. The attackers used their communiqué to not only claim responsibility, but to state plainly that they are organized to attack, not recruit, convince, or mobilize the masses. In a 2014 communiqué offered as the 12th attack in the international Phoenix Project, the attackers write:

> We performed our disagreement with [politicians and civil anarchists] ... by burning down two offices of the general election committee ... We won't stay away and let our enemy play around with their party of democracy. We directly sent our anger and transformed it into fire. We are not abstaining in this war. We attack ... We are not those anarchists who went to voting spots and painted slogans and chants on the ballot boxes. We won't smear our values by letting our finger be painted with purple ink, a sign used by the authorities to identify who voted and those who did not. We won't let one single inch in our body be polluted by our enemy. On the contrary, we attacked them without compromise ... Abstaining [from voting/electioneering] by not giving our voices is not enough for us. We want to bring this confrontation to be more wild than mere words or posters. We want to speak through fire ... But we don't invite anyone to join us. We are not interested to have new members. We are not a party nor an anarchist collective. We are an armed group of the tendency of violence. To attack, and not to open a dialogue with our enemies. (International Conspiracy for Revenge/FAI-IRF 2014)

Embedded in the rejectionist logic targeting democratic reformism is the notion that aged Athenian forms of governance centered around participation and civic engagement are no more; that "democracy has successfully conquered the terrain of political utterances" (IEF 2013, 41). Therefore, if one is to accept that "the sphere of political representation has come to a close" (TIC 2007, 23) then the only strategy of social change exists outside of representationalism and *politics* as one understands it.

This rejection of mediation and compromised politics is at its base a rejection of representation, as this is seen as a measure of abstraction, separating individuals from actual forms of power. As the authors of *Politics is not a Banana* ... write, "[social] war cannot end until the specific, historical form of total management known as politics ends" (IEF 2009, 135). Thus, to insurrectionary analysis, the nature of this mediation is inconsequential, as the indirect manner of decision-making and management is in itself the problem.

> "Nothing resembles a representative of the bourgeoisie more than a representative of the proletariat," Sorel wrote in 1907. What made them identical was the fact that they were, precisely, *representatives*. To say the same of a right or left wing candidate would be banal ... The point is that power does not allow for any other kind of management [beyond representative politics]. (Anonymous 2001a, 7)

> ... Any demand that is addressed to a precise interlocutor carries its own defeat within it, if for no other reason than that no authority would be capable of resolving a problem of general significance even if it wanted to. (Anonymous 2001a, 22)

The authors clearly argue that the nature of the representation is nearly insignificant as its form dictates its function. As a result of this logic, the authors reject voting, arguing: "Even if they were to vote against it nothing would change as, to be authentic, such a question would *exclude* the existence of voters. A whole society cannot be changed by decree" (Anonymous 2001a, 8).

The insurrectionists are against mediated politics, advocating for directly confronting the systems of domination. They are against the "sacralization of democracy" as they are against the "management" of society's decision-making (Ilya Romanov Cell 2013). Partly this is because of the abstracted and self-serving nature of electoral and representative-based politics, but also because the milieu understands that to increase one's interaction with liberalism and democracy means the "deepening [of] a social system that hides the conflict emerging within it, the very conflict on which it is founded" (Ilya Romanov Cell 2013). Instead of these methods, the authors advocate direct action, writing: "Uncontrollable anarchy is not subjected to democracy and its values. It does not speak of majorities, consensus, or fundamental rights" (Ilya Romanov Cell 2013). Reformism is opposed precisely because it serves to hinder the population's ascent towards insurrection through neutralizing their anger. There is the implied belief that the enemies of insurrection – such as reformism, recuperation, pacification, normalization, assimilation – already exist in the heads of the oppressed. Therefore, reformism in this regard is simply the outward expression of something already present in the minds of the population, namely a tendency towards resigning oneself to a life of drudgery, alienation, oppression, and unfreedom.

Finally, it deserves noting that this rejection of democratic forms of liberal change offered by insurrectionists aid in their enemies' (e.g. the state, media) negative portrayals. As the sacred nature of democracy is upheld in the venue of the state, a rejection of this form of representationalism serves to embolden the anti-insurrectionary dismissal and its resulting repression. As one author explains while discussing contemporary anti-authoritarian movements, "just as liberal narratives of progress erase radical critiques from legitimate forms of dissent, liberal discourses of threat criminalize activism that is militant or illegitimate" (Luchies 2015, 4). In the case at hand, this is certainly true. As long as the state and media can continue to portray insurrectionary attack as an incorrigibly misguided rejection of the entire democratic political sphere, those acting as narrative architects are more able to justify militarized policing, aggressive surveillance, infiltration, and a generalized atmosphere of a criminalized dissent.

For illegalism, against "civil" anarchists

> Two of our Russian comrades attacked the accountant of a factory and, pursued by the crowd and the police, held out in a desperate struggle, the mere recounting of which is enough to make one shiver ... After almost two hours of resistance, having exhausted their munitions, and wounded 22 people, three of them mortally, they reserved for themselves their final bullets ... Words seem powerless to express admiration or condemnation before their ferocious heroism. Lips are still; the pen isn't strong enough, sonorous enough. Nevertheless, in our ranks there will be the timorous and the fearful who will disavow their act. But we, for our part, insist on loudly affirming our solidarity ... We today insist on saying loudly and clearly: The London "bandits" were at one with us! (Serge 1909)

The (false) dichotomy typically presented for the purpose of categorization is one wherein anarchism has two approaches, one of organization and another of explosive spontaneity (Graeber 2009, 254). More accurately, one could summarize them as a fluid debate – one that pits direct confrontation *with* authority against organizing to undermine that same authority (Amster 2012, 50). An integral component of the abovementioned rejection of democratic reformism is a further critique of the broader tendencies within the anarchist movements towards "civil" (i.e. legal or rather non-illegal) forms of protest. This tendency goes two ways: one motion, which insists that insurrectionary anarchists support those on the aggressive fringes of the social war, and another, that supporters do not condemn militant actions. While reviewing the quote above from illegalist anarchist bomber Victor Serge (1909), one sees this tendency as the militant writes, "in our ranks there will be the timorous and the fearful who will disavow their act. But we, for our part, insist on loudly affirming our solidarity." Here Serge clearly demarcates a line between those on the left (i.e. "in our ranks") who claim "solidarity," and those that choose to "disavow." Often, modern insurrectionary attackers have expressed sentiments of betrayal and disappointment with supposed allies within the anarchist left. The famed CCF Imprisoned Members' Cell writes of a similar tension between "anarcho-individualists of praxis … [the] unrepentant anarchist urban guerrillas" and what they term "anarcho bosses." In a 2014 statement, imprisoned insurrectionary fighters make this point, writing: "Today, urban guerrilla in Greece has to face not only the iron state repression but also the anarcho-bosses of the anti-guerrilla tension of the anti-authoritarian milieu" (Polidoros et al. 2014).

Similar expressions of betrayal have been levied at institutions such as the Indymedia network that developed to provide news coverage of the millennial anti-globalization movement. In one such statement, authors identifying as "Anarchist-nihilists against the activist establishment" (2013) contend that the Indymedia structure has been complicit with state efforts and has been co-opted to "smear and denigrate the insurrectional project, that of the FAI/CCF/IRF, 325 and the anarchists of praxis." The anonymous authors accuse Indymedia of "spreading lies and falsities" and failing to protect the anonymity of demonstrators through posting pictures *without* first blurring the faces of participants. Furthermore, they argue that the civil anarchists, including Indymedia, are attempting to rein in and police the more militant (i.e. insurrectionary) elements dedicated to the creation of social war through direct attack.

> They [Indymedia and civil anarchists] sought to impose their discrimination on the [insurrectionary] attacks and upon the action groups, aiming at having a dominating influence on their behavior, like the civil anarchists who also believed through their hysterical denunciations they could impose their own servility on the uncontrollables. (Anarchist-nihilists against the activist establishment 2013)

This narrative is akin to the anti-reformist positioning of the RB and many other manifestations of inter-movement rivalry and criticism. The document proposes that the insurrectionary movement abandons these outmoded structures for counter-information and points to the newly established "informal international translation and counter-information network" (e.g. 325). In their critique of "Indymedia and the Anarcho-Left," the "Anarchist-nihilists against the activist establishment" (2013) write:

> The new anarchist international war also does not need or require such useless people, because it has created its own information structures and helped co-create and form many more, that have solidified struggles in the "social" and "anti-social." The informal international translation and counter-information network has a specific reality that comprises much more than any of its individual parts, one that has eclipsed many Indymedia sites that have been based on a very weak set of political and social values, largely based on the phony social contract of civil rights, negotiation and legal defiance of democracy that characterized the "anti-summit"/"anti-globalisation" period from where it sprang 13 years ago. The informal internet anarchist network overcomes many of these previous sites of information activism, and an ongoing development is taking place internationally. Many of the prior spaces of the "movement", physical and virtual, are now in the hands of the enemy, or might as well be.

This statement makes clear the chronological narrative. Whereas the anti-globalization movement embodied in the 1999 WTO protests in Seattle may have created Indymedia – and, in their time, may have been championed by those who today self-identify as anti-social, illegalist, insurrectionaries, despite these genealogies – the time has come for the outmoded to be replaced by a newly revolutionary, anti-civil network.

While the outside observer may see little difference between the webpages of Indymedia and those of 365, War on Society, and others, a great deal of difference exists. Akin to their informal, ad hoc praxis, the insurrectionary sites are often blog-based, abandoning the Indymedia model of formal websites with stable web presences. In the insurrectionary network, a series of often-redundant blogs are created, operate for a few months or years, and then go silent, only to be replaced by new ones. The blogs interlink to one another, borrow and repost content, mirroring translated documents, and publicizing similar if not identical prisoner pleas, events, and convergences. The nature of the new sites is to announce, not organize. In this sense they are uniquely different from their Indymedia predecessors. They are meant as one-way bulletin boards to disseminate announcements, not internet-based forums for activists to plan around. While Indymedia was used to *plan*, 325 is used to *proclaim*. In this manner, the Indymedia

v. 325 debate embodies the civil v. insurrectionary split, marking the former as counter-revolutionary and capitulating, and the latter as uncompromising and militant.

Against domestication and technology, for re-wilding

> ... an ideology, in order to gain enthusiastic support, must have a positive ideal as well as a negative one; it must be FOR something as well as AGAINST something. The positive ideal that we promote is Nature. That is, WILD nature; those aspects of the functioning of the Earth and its living things that are independent of human management and free of human interference and control. And with wild nature we include human nature, by which we mean those aspects of the functioning of the human individual that are not subject to regulation by organized society but are products of chance or free will. (Kaczynski 2010b, sec. 183)

While, classically, anarchism has located misery and domination in the forms of the state and capital, for some portions of the anarchist milieu – often termed Green, Luddite, anti-civilization, or primitivist – the roots of modern human oppression originate at an earlier locale, namely the formation of civilizations marked by non-nomadic living, tool usage, and, of course, technology. While a host of contemporary thinkers write from these positions, a growing number of clandestine cells have used these theories in the development of their attack methodologies, adopting a critical reception of scientific experimentation in their selection of targets for attack. These groups of attackers – sometimes bluntly referred to as "anti-science anarchists" (Coghlan 2012), "eco-anarchists" (Phillips 2012), "extremist anarchists" (Corral 2011), or simply "terrorists" (Corral 2011) – advocate vanguardist violence to bring forth insurrection leading to the destruction of industrial civilization. This rejection of scientific experimentation, technology, and the like is developed from more familiar Marxist and anarchist critiques having to do with alienation, abstraction, subordination, and centralization. Though a complete review of these anti-tech, eco-tendencies is a project of its own merit, this manner of critique can broadly be generalized in the following text, written by Kaczynski.[3] In this lengthy essay, common referred to as the "Unabomber Manifesto," Kaczynski (2010b, secs. 46, 47) writes:

> We attribute the social and psychological problems of modern society to the fact that society requires people to live under conditions radically different from those under which the human race evolved and to behave in ways that conflict with the patterns of behavior that the human race

developed while living under earlier conditions ... Among the abnormal conditions present in modern industrial society are excessive density of population, isolation of man from nature, excessive rapidity of social change and the breakdown of natural small-scale communities such as the extended family, the village or the tribe.

The preceding text points to the generalizable anarcho-primitivist critique of civilization and technology, a consistent critique found amongst insurrectionary theory. Sometimes this is due to the specifics of the advancement itself (e.g. nanotechnology, genetically-modified organisms, hydraulic fracturing, robotics) and sometimes it is more comprehensive, relating to a biopolitical reality. The authors of *At Daggers Drawn* ... call this the "technological administration of the existent" (Anonymous 2001a, 5) referring to means of technology designed to manage life, death, and social control.

ITS, the network responsible for a long series of attacks in Mexico, has focused its attacks on the techno-industrial system at a specific form of science, namely nanotechnology. The network explains their targeting logic, writing:

We employed direct attacks to damage both physically and psychologically, NOT ONLY experts in nanotechnology, but also scholars in biotechnology, physics, neuroscience, genetic engineering, communication science, computing, robotics, etc ... because we reject technology and civilization, we reject the reality that they are imposing with ALL their advanced science. We deny a life imposed on us by the system that dictates that we must walk mindlessly, obligatorily obeying orders from large organizations (industrial giants that tell you what to eat, what not to do, to say, to wear, where to go, etc.) and people outside our inner circle. We negate the artificiality and we cling to our past as Warriors of the Earth who cling to our darkest instincts of survival, and although we know we are civilized humans, we are awake and we claim ourselves as fierce individualists in TOTAL WAR against all that threatens our nature and Wild Nature that is left. (ITS 2014)

Prior to the emergence of insurrectionary networks, the radical forebearers held critiques of technological society that would closely mirror those developed years later. As one scholar explained in describing the congruence of (post)modern resistance movements:

The critical discourse in ELF and EZLN communiques reflect the same basic critical interpretation of technology – namely, that technology is a historical and ontological formation, rooted in western metaphysics and centering on synthesizing entities including, ultimately, people into cybernetic systems. Technology is not simply a neutral set of tools and methods but a cultural imperative that everything yield to efficient systematization. (Becker 2006, 10)

There is a marked sense of immediacy within the action sensibility of direct action advocates. When viewed in terms of the ecological and animal liberationist tendencies, these relate to quantifiable lives spared or, conversely, quantifiable lives lost due to hesitation, inactivity, and the morbidly slow pace of democratic reformism.

For the eco-minded liberationist there is a very real sense that civilization may exist on the brink of system collapse perpetuated through human action related to resource extraction, energy production, and industrial farming. Certainly mainstream science backs up the claim that the current era of modernity presents real risks for catastrophic and violent ecological crisis. A 2014 NASA-sponsored study concluded "global industrial civilisation could collapse in coming decades due to unsustainable resource exploitation and increasingly unequal wealth distribution" (Ahmed 2014). Furthermore, the report stated that not only is such crisis predictable, it is expected as "the process of rise-and-collapse is actually a recurrent cycle found throughout history" (Ahmed 2014). Interestingly, the fault lines of this cyclical collapse demonstrated in the NASA study closely resemble the rallying cries entombed by the so-called radical eco-left.

The study echoes the recurrent predictions of the insurrectionary eco-tendency, concluding that "the most salient interrelated factors which explain civilizational decline, and which may help determine the risk of collapse today ... [are] ... Population, Climate, Water, Agriculture, and Energy" (Ahmed 2014). The study similarly speaks to the ill effects of a widening economic gap, stating "accumulated surplus is not evenly distributed throughout society, but rather has been controlled by an elite. The mass of the population, while producing the wealth, is only allocated a small portion of it by elites, usually at or just above subsistence levels" (Ahmed 2014). Finally, it even warns of the predictable reaction from upper echelons of society who are likely to downplay the structural nature of the problem

> While some members of society might raise the alarm that the system is moving towards an impending collapse and therefore advocate structural changes to society in order to avoid it, Elites and their supporters, who opposed making these changes, could point to the long sustainable trajectory "so far" in support of doing nothing. (Ahmed 2014)

If state-funded, mainstream science, presented through mainstream media, can reach conclusions reconcilable with the insurrectionary tendency for immediate action, certainly a nuanced and academic reading of social movement ephemera is warranted. Scientists report "unprecedented" heat waves

(Samenow 2012), glacial melting (BBC 2012) described by NASA (2014) as "irreversible," seven million people killed annually from air pollution (World Health Organization 2014) and have concluded that ongoing climate change is "substantially correlated" to rises in violent crime and group conflict (Hsiang, Burke, and Miguel 2013). With such predictable patterns in mind, it is no matter that eco-crisis is a highly motivating factor for a variety of actors across the revolutionary spectrum – especially as these apocalyptic findings are consistently said to be "human-driven" (Gillis and Chang 2014). Even the US President Barack Obama seemed to foster a sense of urgency, when he stated in May 2014:

> We want to emphasize to the public, this is not some distant problem of the future. This is a problem that is affecting Americans right now ... Whether it means increased flooding, greater vulnerability to drought, more severe wildfires – all these things are having an impact on Americans as we speak. (Barack Obama, quoted in Al Jazeera News 2014)

Given authoritative reports of such a nature, is it surprising that a variety of individuals feel the urgency to attack?

Despite these scientific findings and motivating factors, certain sectors of the eco-motivated insurrectionary tendency have articulated a strong rejection of technology and even a broader rejection towards the methods of modern scientific interventionism. While this is best demonstrated in the attacks of certain Mexican direct attack networks, it can be seen in multiple venues. In a Brazilian communiqué claiming responsibility for anti-state attacks – including the use of fire and explosives – the authors write:

> Modern civilization has reached a huge level of devastation of the earth, waters, and all life that inhabits this planet. It's the result of this sick logic of understanding that everything exists to serve some human being and be transformed into money ... Technology is developed to better serve the interests of this logic. To believe in the neutrality of technology is like believing in the neutrality of a police officer or a judge. Technologies blatantly favor domination, control, profit-making. Hydroelectric plants, industries, agribusinesses, microchips, surveillance cameras, transgenics, biometrics, virtual world of social networks. Will the new generations be even more obedient and manipulable? (Savage Vandal Anti-authoritarians 2014)

This anti-technological/industrial system discourse is especially active in Mexico and in the writings of Kaczynski. Several contemporary Mexican networks adopt a Kaczynskian-type analysis and identify most closely with this tendency, such as ITS, RS, and OPCA. In an attack communiqué claiming responsibility for a "package bomb with a considerable quantity of

Shrapnel" (Obsidian Point Circle of Attack 2014) sent to a university rector, the communiqué's author articulates their anti-technological stance in reference to the individual targeted, writing:

> We bitterly oppose the progress of the technological or industrial system, its cultural values and its slave society, since progress is the enormous bunch of attacks against wild nature. It is for progress that rivers, seas and oceans are contaminated, that forests and jungles are deforested, that the species are exterminated from the various environments where they exist on this earth, that other worlds inside and outside of the Milky Way are examined in order to corrupt them like this one, the physique, character and mentality of the human being is manipulated and dominated now by machines, our deepest and darkest natural instincts are domesticated with their propaganda on television, radio, internet, newspapers, schools, jobs and universities. Progress kills, sickens and makes everything artificial and mechanical. (Obsidian Point Circle of Attack 2014)

Clearly, ecological and anti-technological motivations are strong currents within many communities of insurrectionary thought. They are a natural partner to the milieu's embedded sense of urgency, and combined with rhetorical support from the mainstream scientific community may remain the most salient component of an often-silenced political and social critique.

Wild egoist individualism

> A real demonstration has to be "wild," not declared in advance to the police. (TIC 2007, 127)

> We can choose not to live. That is the most beautiful reason for opening oneself up to life with joy ... We can choose not to act, and this is the most beautiful reason for acting. (Anonymous 2001a, 35)

> I should admit, though, that I personally am strongly inclined to individualism. Ideally, I shouldn't allow my individualistic predilections to influence my thinking on revolutionary strategy but should arrive at my conclusions objectively. The fact that you have spotted my individualistic leanings may mean that I have not been as objective as I should have been. (Kaczynski 2010c, 261)

Evoking the notion of a pre-anthropocene period of "the wild" is common throughout insurrectionary rhetoric, especially that which is critical of science, technology, pacification, and civilization. The concept of *wild* harkens to an untamed, free, egalitarian, and plentiful state of non-anthropocentric nature seen in stark comparison to "the realm of human greed and ecological despoliation" (Amster 2012, 70). Therefore, as Randall Amster (2012, 70) states, green infused eco-anarchism centers around *wildness* not the physical wilderness. The wild ethics of pre-modern (i.e. primitive) societies and "natural" "biospheric egalitarianism" assumed to be outside of the techno-industrial civilization of modernity are models for not only personal lifestyleism, but a revolutionary utopianism to be found in the construction of a post-state community.

The individualist framework dovetails with insurrectionary anarchism's rejection of "organized anarchist movements" (D. Miller 1984, 30) and typically endorses the use of individual acts of violence to achieve one's aims. This is true in explicitly insurrectionary acts of political violence (e.g. CCF, FAI) as well as older models (e.g. ELF, ALF). The ELF/ALF – employing tactics of "monkeywrenching" – use such means because "monkeywrenching is specifically constructed as: individual, not organized, dispersed, diverse, deliberate and ethical" (Amster 2012, 77). In its most general terms, the individualist tendency borrows from the classically liberal notion of individual sovereignty, "extend[ing] it until it [becomes] incompatible with the idea of a state" (D. Miller 1984, 30). Individualism is often spoken of – within the anarchist tradition[4] – as closely linked to illegalism, as many illegalist anarchists closely aligned with the individualist logic. In his description of the illegalist mentality, an anarchist scholar writes that they "expressed their desperation and their personal, violent rejection of an intolerable society ... [acts of illegality] were clearly meant to be exemplary, invitations to revolt" (Imrie 1994).

There is an aesthetic of wildness that is pervasive in the self-descriptions of insurrectionary actors. Prominently, you have eco-insurrectionary networks such as Individualists Tending Towards the *Wild* employing such images as a namesake. The authors of *At Daggers Drawn* ... write that insurrectionary warriors who are honest will understand themselves to be "wild," stating:

> If they do not wish to deceive themselves and others, those struggling for the demolition of the present social edifice must face the fact that subversion is a game of wild, barbarous forces. Someone referred to them as Cossacks, someone else hooligans; in fact they are individuals whose anger has not be quelled by social peace. (Anonymous 2001a, 11)

Here one can see that not only are the authors speaking of a wildness, but also of a more generalized uncontrollable nature; an association with those that are "wild, barbarous, hooligans." Cells carrying out attacks have even self-labeled as such, naming themselves "Commando of Free, Dangerous, Wild and Incendiary Individuals for the Black Plague – FAI" and "Luddites Against the Domestication of Wild Nature – FAI."

Similar sentiments are conjured with the egoist influence and an embracing of an anti-political, anti-social analysis. This is clearly articulated in a communiqué composed by OPCA (2014) wherein they write:

> We care little what they call us, such as "barbarian," "foolish," "mediocre," etc, we do not want to give any "good impression" to their eyes, we do not want to be, nor are we, nor will we be, the traditional "social fighters" of Mexico, we are egoist radicals, politically incorrect, irreverently individualist at war against the progress of the technoindustrial system.

The image of a barbarian horde that cares little for social convention and political correctness was also invoked by Victor Serge (1909), the famed Bonnot Gang rebel, who wrote:

> Let this be known. Let it be finally understood that in the current society we are the vanguard of a barbarous army. That we have no respect for what constitutes virtue, morality, honesty, that we are outside or laws and regulations ... We prefer combat. Against us, all arms are good; we are in an enemy camp, surrounded, harassed. The bosses, judges, soldiers, cops unite to bring us down. We defend ourselves – not by all means, for the most peremptory response we can give them is to be better than them – but with a profound contempt for their codes, their morals, their prejudices ... Your codes, your laws, your "honesty": you can't imagine how we laugh at them!

It is not just the fighting barbarian army image that is deployed, but other pre-modern fighting forces, often romanticized and reinterpreted to match contemporary political tendencies. In the text below, the author urges anarchists to avoid attending May Day demonstrations and other manifestations of the left, and instead to let the destructive forces of insurrectionary violence speak for themselves:

> So on May Day, let us say fuck all to the funeral dance of the left. Do *not* attend the protests of the left ... Street demonstrations are both tired and predictable. The terrain is rigged and the audience is small. We rely on the media to tell our story rather than people reading our story by the devastation we leave throughout a city.
>
> The Vandals were a tribe before they were associated with any individual that engages in some level of property destruction ... they set a precedent and all property destroyers wear the name of their tribe as a crime.
>
> I say we remake the Vandals. We remake the tribe and commit its crime. We don't walk in one mass in a city, but as small vandal units, striking

where we can, damaging the most public of things that we can get away with ... Let the battle of the Vandals be May Day! May the tribe of destruction be reborn! (Anonymous 2014d)

Here you can see an embracing of the sort of individualistic, yet collectively experienced, violence typically associated with a riot or insurrection.

The author invokes criticisms of social movement methods and urges activists to not engage in self-sacrifice but to strike, escape, and strike again. Insurrectionary logic privileges the individual; their desires, their abilities. The force of a spreading of insurrection, from small acts of rupture to a more generalized revolt and disruption, is a process of individuals acting outside of central coordination or control. This point is made clearly wherein anonymous (2001a, 26) authors write:

> Insurrection is the process that unleashes this strength [of the exploited], and along with it autonomy and the pleasure of living; it is the moment when we think reciprocally that the best thing we can do for others is to free ourselves. In this sense it is "a collective movement of individual realization."

Furthering this individualist motivational logic, one's ability to *not* revolt makes the act of revolting an actualized freedom. The desire to seek joy and freedom serves to anchor the individualist in their pursuit of fulfillment through autonomous action. Max Stirner, the name most often associated with the egoist tendency, authored *The Ego and His Own* in 1843, arguing the complete denial of absolutes and institutions in favor of the human individual (Woodcock 1962, 94).

Stirner's philosophy approaches the nihilist position – borrowing a great deal from Friedrich Nietzsche. Stirner's ideas are informed by a rejection of a base law for human kind and instead offer another model. According to anarchist historian George Woodcock (1962, 95), Stirner's writing serves to:

> ... sets forth as his ideal egoist, the man who realizes himself in conflict with the collectivity and with other individuals, who does not shirk from the use of any means in "the war of each against all," who judges everything ruthlessly from the viewpoint of his own well-being and who, having proclaimed his "ownness", may then enter with like-minded individuals into a "union of egoists," without rules or regulations, for the arrangement of matters of common convenience.

Stirner's suggestions of achieving such a reality speak to "vaguely insurrectionary means" through which a conflict is created of a "perpetual and amoral conflict of wills" (Woodcock 1962, 95). This sentiment helped to inform the illegalist tradition popular around the turn of the twentieth century and as exemplified by the Bonnot Gang (R. Parry 1987, 5, 19). Part of this insurrectionary logic is the creation of the revolution within the site of the individual, not the entire socio-political sphere. This premise carries with it the rejection of a revolutionary class of proletarian masses and instead understands the world as a collectivity of individuals, each of which must personally achieve revolutionary liberation. This framework has led to some criticism of so-called lifestyleism (Berry 2002, 104), yet lifestyleist sentiments can be seen throughout radical discourse – including those over and beyond the insurrectionary tendency – and are frequent in communiqués. Following a car bomb targeting the Athens office of Microsoft, a cell of the IRF calling itself "Deviant Behaviours for the Spread of Revolutionary Terrorism" (2012) wrote, "Our struggle is, first and foremost, the fight against OUR OWN contracts, OUR fears, OUR imperfections."

Stirner's exclusion of collective efforts for revolution led some prominent anarchists, such as Emma Goldman, to consider him outside of their philosophical camp (Shone 2013, 222). Within the egoist, individualist logic the state must be destroyed as it stands in conflict with human will or, according to Woodcock (1962, 101), the state is the "negation of individual will." Thus the ideal utopianism of these thinkers is an existence devoid of slaves and masters and inhabited only by the egoist striving towards their own "ownness." Stirner shared a base insurrectional contention, namely the assertion that engagement with "politics" in the traditional sense is utterly futile.

Conclusion

The insurrectionary position, as cobbled together from its most visible and widely circulated texts, is a constellation of tendencies and ideas informed by poststructuralism and Queer theory and borrowing from a number of anti-state, anti-capitalist, eco, illegalist, egoist, and nihilist positions. While an insurrectionary "points of unity" is yet to be written – and would likely be seen as counter to the spirit of unrestrained insurrectionary assembly – points of affinity, overlap, repetition, and rearticulation can allow one to assemble this framework. Based on a reading of thousands of communiqués, proclamations, letters, and more traditional texts, one can describe the insurrectionary position as being comprised of the following eight points.

First, the forces of domination must be confronted through direct attack that is immediate, continuous, and spontaneous. An individual only learns how to act through experimentation, and thus anyone is capable of acting in furtherance of greater freedom through the deployment of easily reproducible tactics targeting whatever localized manifestation of the enemy is available. Second, the wider conflict with the state and capital takes the form of a social war, which seeks to create points of rupture in the sociopolitical order through exacerbating existing tensions, dissatisfactions, and sites of alienation present in the society and produced by the nexuses of power and control. Third, in locating the enemy one must move beyond identity-based politics and seek a more all-encompassing idea of intersectionality wherein the goal is confrontation with "The Totality" and total liberation. This understanding is based around a rejection of domination, not specific systems of oppression such as sexism, racism, or homophobia. Therefore the battles of the non-heterosexual and those of the non-white are inextricably interlinked as they both emanate from a single source of power.

Fourth, forms of protest and contestation must be unmanaged, temporary, and outside of the Left's traditional conceptions of social movements. This rejection of representation, mediation, and ritual must be recognized in all aspects of praxis. The prized model for insurrection is thus the fostering of informal, temporary collectives of individuals aligned through friendship and ties of affinity. Fifth, the insurrectionary vision for social change rejects reformist measures and Western notions of democratic participation typically regarded in the liberal tradition as sacrosanct. Reformists are seen as the enemies of radical social transformation, yet are commonly portrayed as allies in resistance. Sixth, insurrection is inherently illegal, and embraces a historical notion of illegalism including the expropriation and a rejection of civil engagement. Seventh, the influence of the ecological crisis, domestication, and technology is counter to the insurrectionary agenda as it further alienates individuals from the world around them that is moving rapidly along the path towards a global collapse. In the final, eighth, point, the insurrectionary milieu seeks to be constituted by individualists, acting in their own right, informed by a sense of wild egoism. The notion of "the wild" runs throughout this understanding, and evokes an untamed, pre-capitalist worldview.

Taken as a collection of values, these components constitute a basis for insurrectionary affinity. This inquiry informs a central question of this exploration of discourse, namely: What constitutes the insurrectionary canon? While there are certainly some texts which appear to recur more often and with more wide endorsement throughout the networks, the major body of work is made up of thousands of smaller texts, authored at the level of the cell, typically following some transgressive act of anti-social, anti-state, and/or anti-capitalist attack. The insurrectionary actor speaks via the mechanism of the communiqué, and utilizes the space created by a temporary disruption to the status quo. In doing so, the actor further develops the political analysis of the wider milieu, and creates another page in the fluid, amorphous canon. The *community* of insurrectionary networks meets at these points of ideological, rhetorical, and strategic affinity, and it is on this basis of affiliation that the movement is constituted and reproduced.

Notes

1 For an extended discussion, see Hanssen (2000, 97–158).
2 This notion of an expanded intersectionality is more fully developed in the concluding chapter of this book, within a larger discussion of poststructuralism.
3 It is important to note that Kaczynski is not considered part of the insurrectionary milieu of thinkers, but rather in the primitivist/anti-technology camp. Despite this, his unmediated, pro-attack message is recurrent throughout insurrectionary communiqués, and his theories have routinely been a part of the eco-insurrectionary discourse.
4 The individualist tradition has long roots in Europe and North America. While a complete history is beyond the scope of this book, famed anarcho-individualist include: In France – Anselme Bellegarrigue, Émile Gravelle, Émile Armand, Jacques Élie Henri Ambroise Ner (aka Han Ryner), Alphonse Gallaud de la Pérouse (aka Zo d'Axa), Henri Zisly, Joseph Albert (aka Albery Libertad), and Charles-Auguste Bontemps. In Italy – Vittorio Pini, Abele Rizieri Ferrari (aka Renzo Novatore), Dante Carnesesecchi, Enrico Arrigoni, and Bruno Fillippi. In Germany – Max Stirner, Adolf Brand, and Horst Fantazzini. In Spain – Joan "Juan" Montseny Carret (aka Federico Urales), and Miguel Giménez Igualada (aka Miguel Ramos Giménez/Juan de Iniesta). In Britain – Wordsworth Donisthorpe, Henry Seymour, John Henry Mackay (aka Sagitta), and Henry Meulen. In Russia – Lev Chernyi and Alexei Alexeyevich Borovoi. In the US – William Godwin, Josiah Warren, Lysander Spooner, Stephen Pearl Andrews, Henry David Thoreau, William Batchelder Greene, Charles Joseph Antoine "Jo" Labadie, James L. Walker, John Veverley Robinson, Benjamin Tucker, Victor Yarros, Steven T. Byington, and Peter Lamborn Wilson (aka Hakim Bey). In the South American continent – Colombian Vicente Rojas Lizcano (aka Biófilo Panclasta) and Brazilian Maria Lacerda de Moura.

7
Insurrection as anti-securitization communication

> People often think that insurrectionalism is a whole, made of concepts and theories frozen in time, in their "ideological" rigidity … Nothing is permanent over time. Women and men through their actions forge ideas. It's not up to those three or four well-known comrades, with their books and articles, to show us the way, not even a matter of the long and inconclusive assemblies. It's those unknown comrades with their practice of attack that push us forward, leading us to life. (RaiNews 24 2013)

On canonization

The original aim of this book, when it was conceptualized as a doctoral thesis, was to trace the borders of an insurrectionary canon through anarchism and poststructuralism, concluding at modern insurrectionary theory. I hypothesized that the High Theory forebears, such as Tiqqun and Bonanno, inform the ideological framework of attackers. After spending several years surveying the literature produced by the anarchists of praxis, the contemporary urban guerrillas, I have observed that, in fact, the communiqué corpus does *not* demonstrate any strongly central, recurrent, theoretical points of reference. This finding mirrors accounts of anarcho-nihilism – a prominent forebear to modern insurrection – described as lacking "a singular, or even a particularly disciplined, body of thought" (Aragorn! 2009, 7). Instead of being comprised of a canon, nihilism/anarcho-nihilism is understood as an "approximation to a body of ideas rather than a body of ideas" (Aragorn! 2009, 7). Murray Bookchin's (1995, para. 15) famous polemic repeats this assertion arguing that "lifestyle" and "individualist" anarchism "bears a disdain for theory" instead preferring "muddy theoretical premises." It is not apparent that all insurrectionary attackers have read or are responding to central, High Theory thinkers (e.g. Bonanno, Tiqqun, TIC, IEF), but instead the networks' members seem to be well informed about previous *attacks* far more than about previous *texts*. This may be similar to understandings of non-insurrectionary guerrillas. For example, though Abraham Guillén's influential text *Strategy of the Urban Guerrilla* served to inform his mentorship of the leftist, Uruguayan, guerrilla warfare-advocating Tupamaros, the militants remarked, "action, practice, came first, and then theory" (quoted in: Gillespie 1986, 155), implying the supremacy of experienced combat over canonical fluency.

The lack of stable, centrally-located, canonical texts in insurrectionary anarchism is mirrored in other more traditional accounts of political violence. In her discussion of European leftist networks operating clandestinely, Martha Crenshaw notes that militants "selected fragments of doctrine from other contexts" (2010, 73), building up ideology, beliefs, and justifications from a "selection of fragments of compatible theories" (2010, 99). This is precisely why, for the insurrectionists, some are explicit in their reference to anarchist, poststructural, nihilist, Situationist, and primitivist thinkers while others are keen to present their ideas without attribution, reference or a clear intellectual tradition. Though rarely quoting Tiqqun or Bonanno, insurrectionary attack communiqués uniformly make reference to previous attacks, previous attackers, and current prisoners. The internationalization of rally cries, coordinated targeting, and a call-and-response upping the ante can be seen clearly in campaigns such as the Phoenix Project and others responding to international calls to action.

In this manner, the issuing of texts (e.g. communiqués, statements, prison letters) acts to facilitate a method of coordination for an internationally decentralized network. This coordination role appears far more impactful then the development of traditional theory. The interplay between texts (and the cells that write them) is necessary for the continuation of an internationalized campaign of attack as well as the continuation of a decentralized discourse. This phenomenon has been noted before, for example in the Palestinian–Israeli conflict, where anonymous leaflets resembling insurrectionary communiqués in form were authored, circulated, and debated, forming a "substitute leadership" (Mishal and Aharoni 1994, 25) for the Palestinian uprising. Through this "pamphlet leadership" (Mishal and Aharoni 1994, 29), nationalist and religious movements debated policy, developed strategy, and distributed criticism from behind the relative safety of anonymous statements read widely in the occupied Palestinian territories. This method of coordination was adopted by all manner of militant factions regardless of *ideology* – from secular nationalists (e.g. Fatah, United National Command), to Islamists (e.g. Hamas), and Marxists (e.g. Popular Front for the Liberation of Palestine). In both the Palestinian and insurrectionary pamphlet-communiqué "leaderships" there is little consistent reference to canonical texts, such as Abdullah Azzam's *Defense of the Muslim Lands* or Tiqqun's *This is not a Program*. Therefore, the construction of an insurrectionary canon is, from its origins, an unnecessary task. If one is to locate a source of commonality and a shared politic, this must be understood as emanating from the events (i.e. attacks) themselves. To put it simply, the events themselves are the canon, and through their methodology of attack, social critics demonstrate their fluency with this contemporary insurrectionary history and its actors through constant recall and reference to prior combatants.

Certainly this assertion is not a simple one. There exists a dynamic relationship between theory, analysis, and practice that cannot be easily observed or measured. Though some may have only heard it discussed, what role can we say *The Coming Insurrection* had on the students who occupied California university buildings in 2009 and penned poststructuralist-infused, insurrectionary-themed texts (e.g., Anonymous 2009a; Research and Destroy 2009; Three Non-Matriculating Proletarians 2009)? Without interviewing the participants in the occupations and the authors of the texts, such discussion is merely speculative. Without a doubt key texts have had a direct or indirect impact on subsequent authors, but precisely how and to what degree is unknown. In thinking through such a calculation, one can revisit past eras of rebellion, such as the riots witnessed throughout African-American urban communities in the 1960s. In the period between 1964 and 1969, racially-motivated riots occurred in the US cities of Rochester, Harlem, Philadelphia, Watts, Cleveland, Omaha, Newark, Plainfield, Detroit, Minneapolis-Saint Paul, Chicago, Washington DC, and Baltimore. While these riots and other displays were spontaneous, often provoked by community-level incidents rather than theoretical critiques or social denouncements, subsequent Black Power theorists such as Malcolm X, Stokely Carmichael, and Bobby Seale engaged in the production of analysis and interpretation which had an undeniable (yet unmeasureable) influence on subsequent assembles. While the structural violence (e.g. racism, economic inequality, police violence) set the stage for the riots, the actions of the citizens created the events that were necessary for the production of subsequent theorizing. Theory did not *produce* action in a Marxist sense, but rather served a role of interpreting the events after the fact and, as a result, informing future incidents of a similar nature. Therefore a relationship certainly exists between a canon, the events that come before, and those that emanate after. This relationship is difficult if not impossible to map, and invisibly borrows ideas from a fluid collection of texts as well as events.

Rather than borrowing and challenging points of argumentation from centrally-positioned texts – in the manner that a Leninist could critique a Maoist – insurrectionary theory borrows from emotive phraseologies commonly invoked in radical, anti-authoritarian politics. Through a combination of elements of illegalism, autonomism, primitivism, Situationism, post-left anarchism, and others, authors are able to develop political perspectives that "align their discursive frames with various transnational ideologies" (Drissel 2014, 1). This hodge-podge approach to insurrectionary theory is related to that of poststructuralism's constitution, as "a fragmentary assemblage of diverse social, political, and philosophical thought" (Vaughan-Williams and Peoples 2010, 63). The intentionality of this insurrectionary openness is reflected in the structure of networks and cells that allow for great diversity among their ranks in terms of ideology, strategy, and tactics. This model allows for individuals, cells, and networks to adapt to changing environments in real time as future attacks and texts reflect back on that which came before. This non-rigid theorizing within a fluid milieu prevents movement factionalization, reduces ideological infighting, and allows the movement to develop, grow, and refine as events unfold.

Just as illegalism and propaganda of the deed attacks built momentum for anarchists of the nineteenth and twentieth centuries, in the twenty-first century, global attacks linked through a network of names and digital dissemination points unite disparate attacks into a movement. While attackers often share a critical framework with obvious Marxist, anarchist, poststructuralist, Tiqqunist, Kaczynskian or FAI/CCFian thought, the events build from one another and not a shared text-centric critique. This interaction can be understood as a form of pan-national, constructive, performative, play – through which disparate actors build off one another through understandings that the original author may not share. The theory seems more to inform the discursive *possibilities* rather than the act that creates them (i.e. the attack), thus the political maneuvering (i.e. the post-attack text) becomes a task of fitting critique to target, and method to strategy. In the end, the communicative *goal* is to make a convincing, impassioned, and logical explanation via the communiqué that ties one strike to many and hopes for more to follow. This is the *intent* of the action–communiqué pairing; though one cannot claim that it is a constant occurrence, ample evidence has been presented demonstrating that such a reflexive relationship is common.

On poststructuralism

At first reading, one could conclude: "Though the insurrectionary critique borrows from poststructuralism, it tells us little about the nature of structural violence. It tells us how a broad-based milieu is critical of the present order but it provides few if any solutions to a better way." Despite its lack of a platform, insurrectionary theory *does* answer the question of "What is to be done?" It expands upon the concept of social war, intersectionality, and a radical condemnation of power and politics as key targets for attack. It also introduces an emboldened critique of domination and social pacification through the boundless enemy embodied in "The Totality." To explore this notion we will first examine the notion of deterritorialized power as conceived of by non-insurrectionary theorists – and included within contemporary insurrectionary analysis – before examining the modern concept of "The Totality" as a new reading of structural violence.

For a new (poststructural) intersectionality

The poststructural reading of power – one wherein control is disembodied from a physical site and is instead transnational, omnipresent, and yet operating invisibly – is a highly influential aspect of modern insurrectionary critique. Where the clandestine authors of Tiqqun and TIC may have popularized this idea of a totalizing yet obscured regimentation of violence, neo-Marxist continental philosophers such as Michael Hardt, Antonio Negri, Gilles Deleuze, and Félix Guattari preceded them by offering further nuanced conceptions of operationalized state power and its inherent violence. Hardt and Negri discuss "social machines in their various apparatuses and assemblages" (2001, 28) while Deleuze and Guattari speak of "relations of domination and subordination" (1983, 221) and the inherent nature of the state as hierarchical (1987, 443); both sets of authors constructing a logic of power that is deterritorialized and disembodied in its powerful service towards the state. These authors, as well as others, are adopted (largely without attribution) by the insurrectionary theorists; taking what provides utility and rejecting that which does not. In this manner, the insurrectionary theorists pillage other traditions – harkening back to Hobsbawm's wild bandit image – and only borrow that which aids in the furtherance of their analysis. In his discussion of the contributions of Tiqqun and TIC, anarcho-theorist Alden Wood (2013, 12) speaks of this form of ideological banditry, writing:

> [Tiqqun and TIC] mark a definitive break from previous radical political theory, their thought depends on the critical evaluation, synthesis, and appropriation of earlier theorizations of existence within capitalism. As this is necessarily the case for all theory, it also allows for a reading of earlier theory in which the seeds of insurrection lay dormant.

Here Wood rightly points out that the insurrectionary method of analysis, while heavily indebted to the poststructural tradition, is conducted through an exploration of text aimed at synthesizing conceptions of power found in continental philosophy with those found in more contemporary anti-state theories. This position is supported by other anarcho-scholars who have argued that "Foucault has been tamed by many academics" and that, in reading such texts through the lens of insurrectionary theory, one is able to "provide a productive challenge to the all-too-safe reading of Foucault found in the American academy" (Culp 2009, 1).

This poststructural analysis moves beyond and advances traditionalist Marxism by not focusing on the singular subjectivity of class, and instead looking at the totalizing effects of power and how Empire inscribes itself over all relations (i.e. social, political, economic) through Foucauldian biopolitics. Through Foucault's understandings of disciplinary power, one can then interpret the micro politics of control and subsequently adopt a biopolitical approach to examine power's more macro control sites. Thus Hardt and Negri complement earlier Marxist and anarchist positions arguing that the target is a deterritorialized, super-national capitalist apparatus, *not* European-era imperialism. These understandings of biopower's relations to Empire and totalized control have not escaped the insurrectionary theorists who, borrowing from both Foucault and the Marxists, speak to a similar social ordering. The authors of Tiqqun (2012b, sec. A, Z), in their paper "Preliminary Materials for a Theory of the Young Girl," write:

> Under the hypnotic grimaces of official pacification, a war is being waged. A war that can no longer be called simply economic, social or humanitarian because it is *total* ... Paradoxically, it's because of the total character of this war – total in its means no less than in its ends – that it could be invisible in the first place ... What's at stake in the ongoing war are "forms of life," which for the Empire, means the selection, management, and attenuation of those forms of life.

The authors later call these Empire-controlled forms-of-life the "bio-political monopoly," speaking to the power/knowledge dominance Foucault wrote of in his work. What we see in the work of Tiqqun is the constant and intentional shift between micro and macro forms of power – from the (micro) biopower of individual psychologies, to the macro ordering of the totality of the social, political, economic, and related spheres of activity. In sum, the newly deterritorialized reading of power as developed by the European continental and post-Marxist philosophers paves the way for the post-millennial insurrectionary turn which begins from this fluid subject and attempts to explain power in its ever-present manifestations through the concept of "The Totality."

The "Totality" and system-level violence

In one well-circulated insurrectionary anarchist publication, the anonymous authors define their critiqued subject – "The Totality" – as:

> Normalcy ... the tyranny of our condition; reproduced in all of our relationships [and] ... violently reiterated every minute of every day. The

> Totality being the interconnection an overlapping of all oppression and misery. The Totality is the state. It is capitalism. It is civilization and empire ... It is the brutal lessons taught to those who can't achieve Normal. It is every way we've limited ourselves or learned to hate our bodies. (A Gang Of Criminal Queers 2008, sec. II)

Reminding one of a more classical leftist position, the authors of the text argue that liberation is predicated on "the annihilation of capitalism and the state" via "social war" (A Gang Of Criminal Queers 2008, sec. VII). Numerous other examples of this framing can be found in a host of post-millennial insurrectionary publications such as the zine, *Dangerous Spaces*:

> There is a violence that dominates. It is gay bashing. It is rape. It is the clear-cut and the vivisection lab. It is the bank and the local coffee shop. It is the patrol car and the prison. It is your job, your late rent, your rotting teeth, your wounds that won't heal. It is the silence that maintains all of the above. There is a violence that liberates. It is the murdered homophobe. It is the knee-capped rapist. It is the arson and the mink liberation. It is the smashed window and the expropriated food. It is the cop on fire and the riot behind bars. It is work avoidance, squatting, criminal friendship, and the total refusal of compromise. It is the chaos that can never be stopped. The maintenance [sic] of this world depends on the internalization [sic] of the former, and the total suppression of the latter. (Untorelli Press 2012, 3)

Once again we see the flattening of violence; speaking of the violence of (human) rape and (non-human) vivisection in the same breath. This "violence that dominates" can find its basis in the actions of typical target sets (e.g. police, politicians, corporate heads) but also more unacknowledged areas one could be tempted to term "counter-revolutionary" milieus. In their self-assessment zine, imprisoned members of the CCF write:

> The enemy can be found in every mouth that speaks the language of domination ... It doesn't just consist of rulers and the whole potbellied suit-and-tie dictatorship. It is also the proletarian who aspires to be a boss, the oppressed whose mouth spits nationalist poison, the immigrant who glorifies life in western civilization but behaves like a little dictator among his own people, the prisoner who rats out others to the guards, every mentality that welcomes power, and every conscience that tolerates it. (G. Tsakalos et al. 2012, 13)

Here one can see that the focus is on the actions (i.e. class aspirations, nationalist jingoism, snitching) not on the identity of typically subjugated classes (i.e. proletariat, immigrant, prisoner).

In a more generalized viewpoint, other insurrectionary thinkers have theorized on "The Totality" of oppression drawing more from Foucault's reading of *power* than *politics*. Such themes are recurrent throughout Tiqqun as well as *The Coming Insurrection*. TIC give more texture to this idea of fluid power and domination, stating:

> When we talk of "apparatuses", we don't only invoke the New York Police Department and the Federal Bureau of Investigation, surveillance cameras and body scanners, guns and denunciation, antitheft locks and cell phones. Rather, in the layout of a town like New York ... we mean whatever captures intensities and vitalities in order to chew them up, digest them, and shit out value ... We call hostility that which governs almost completely the relationships between beings, relationships of pure estrangement, pure incompatibility between bodies. (TIC 2013, 1–2)

In these insurrectionary texts, structural Marxism is replaced with a more affective, subjective fluidity that likens the hierarchal violence of heterosexism with, for example, the construction of "normal" in terms of mental illness. This authoritarian establishment of norms, truths, and knowledge should remind one of Foucault's work, especially that within *Discipline and Punish* (1977), wherein the author historicizes how the institutions of the school, clinic, and prison regiment power/ knowledge through the development of numerical record keeping and the evaluation of such figures based on a scale of normal–abnormal. These insurrectionary texts epitomize the power-centric, amorphous description of the state/Empire as a delocalized form of biopower, a "rhythm that imposes itself, a way of dispensing and dispersing reality" (TIC 2007, 13).

An exemplary display of this intellectual tendency can be found in an anonymously authored text which describes socio-political contestation as boundless, not constrained by the issue-specific politics of social movements, and thus a new form of a more totalized revolt. The authors of the IEF (2013, 9–10) write:

> *Events* are the common form that struggles take after the collapse of the historical subject and the zone of the social. We define contemporary struggle as a vast set of heterogeneous practices of revolt that appear to have *everything* as their object; that is to say, events whose antagonisms are not directed against the state or capitalism per se but against techniques of government, against the productive power of government ... Government no longer sits in a closed chamber of educated men; it acts through each of us and through every apparatus that orients us and amplifies our senses in a particular direction. Government doesn't just repress, it *produces* a distributed multiplication of governable subjectivities.

Here you can see not only the description of an amorphous and fluid state apparatus, but also an implicit nod to political reproduction via biopower or, as the 2013 authors write, "government produced subjectivities." Globally, the insurrectionary tendency is situated within the larger anarchist, communist, and anti-authoritarian movements but has served to redefine the subject vis-à-vis systemic violence. By pointing their critical finger at an even more deterritorialized and ambiguous set of institutional manifestations, the insurrectionists destabilize the traditionalist leftist critique that focuses on the largess of the state and capitalism.

For the insurrectionary anarchists, the violence is much more interwoven in the fabric of the society, and includes everything hierarchical and exhibiting dominance: racism, poverty, monogamy, heterosexism, etc. This is precisely why the insurrectionary, poststructuralist-informed method of analysis is relevant for interpreting the changing nature of structural violence. The clandestine attackers clearly understand violence in structural forms, not as local manifestations that can be reformed away. In one example, after claiming responsibility for the arson of a UK courthouse, the attackers write:

> The system is not interested in changing the root causes of much "crime" (poverty, alienation, boredom, etc) at more than a tokenistic level, but simply manages its distribution while keeping the exploited at each other's throats. This is especially true as the market now makes a booming business out of prisoners' low-cost labor and from the private detention industry. Everything stays in line so long as the personal neighborhoods of bosses and judges remain sanctuaries free from the discontents of the class society they maintain: a sanctuary we fully intend on breaking. (FAI-Conscience & Fury 2014)

Here one can see how power and social change are diagramed. The system is understood to be violent and, moreover, that violence serves dominant class interests and thus will not be changed via reform. Therefore, the object of attack becomes destabilized, moved beyond the simplicity of the state, and thought of in system-level terms. If "the system" is the problem then "the system" can never provide the solution beyond "tokenism" and reform. This reading of structure understands "the system" as a closed, often impenetrable set of networks, where outsiders may be allowed to interact but are incapable of effecting change.

It is precisely at this point of a critique of power that insurrectionary anarchism joins with poststructuralism. The insurrectionary theorists share not only the anti-state praxis of anarchism but also the de-localized poststructuralism. Foucault specifically bears noting as his work "visualized a resistance to power that is completely decentralized, ongoing, and not in direct confrontation with the state as a coercive apparatus" (Garner 1996,

391). Therefore it is not a surprise when insurrectionary theorists such as the IEF (2009, 136–137) describe their opponents in the social war in interconnected forms, stating:

> [our] enemies are constellations of hostile forces which manage our potential, structure our needs, code our territory and determine our time ... the cop, the bureaucrat, the politician, the activist, the boss, the leader, the economist, the owner, the fascist, the racist, the sexist – these are all points of conflict ... which reveal the public enemies of a social war.

For the insurrectionary milieu, its confrontation praxis directly confronts state *power* through localized manifestations (e.g. police property, corporate property) but avoids direct, face-to-face battles like those fought by traditionally militarized non-state armed movements (e.g. FARC). For this intellectual tradition, the root to explaining state-facilitated structural violence thus begins with Marx's expose of the socio-political and economic, explained as an enduring concept through ideology and hegemony, and operationalized in the state as described by the anarchists. The anarchist inquiry paves the way for poststructuralism's searches into power and knowledge construction, just as the critical theorists allow for subsequent examinations identifying and explaining structural manifestation of violence. The final melding of poststructuralism and insurrection is thus found in not only the understanding of power (e.g. biopower, Empire) but also in a newly understood spirit of total rejection and revolt.

Critically reading security and insurrection

Insurrectionary theory builds upon the so-called *critical turn* in Security Studies (i.e. CSS) through challenging the state's relationship to the administration of the physical and biopolitical through a preconception of what constitutes security. Foucauldian biopolitics posits that "[power] emanates from a belief in a particular way of organizing society for a particular outcome, and this power is not solely centralized but is instead disseminated throughout multiple sites which enforce a government's rationale" (Roberts 2012, 72). Therefore, by not only rejecting the state's vision for a social peace (Tadjbakhsh and Chenoy 2007, 72) but also proposing alternative manners of organization (e.g. the commune, the council, the squat, the TAZ, zones of opacity), insurrectionary theory rejects a conception of security based in the interests of the state and its desired outcomes. Insurrectionary actors precisely seek to "break the lie of social peace," (Roberts 2012, 72) and, in doing so, redefine what constitutes biopolitical security as more than simply the absence of direct forms of violence – what Peace Studies terms "negative peace."

This limited concept of *peace* as solely the absence of violence is often said to be a product of Peace Studies (e.g. including the world of John Paul Lederach or Johan Galtung), but was actually used as a term by Martin Luther King Jr. In King's famous "Letter from a Birmingham Jail," the Civil Rights leader defines "negative peace" as "the absence of tension" comparing it to "positive peace" which he defines as the "presence of justice" (1963). Thus, for the insurrectionary actor, the desire is to disrupt the negative peace for the promotion of a positive one – the production of revolutionary violence as a response and remedy for state violence. This is especially difficult within a poststructural framework as biopolitical power seeks the subjugation and control of the collectivity at the "capillary or micro-political level ... target[ing] the individual from the vantage point of the mass of the population" (M. G. Doucet and de Larrinaga 2012, 130); insurrectionary praxis is primed to offer a new understanding, as it is precisely these "micro-political levels" that motivate insurrectionary methods of attack and its rejections of broader, more existential social conditions – complacency, alienation, "imposing the dominant order" (Live Wires FAI/ELF 2014) and "manifest[ing] ... blind discipline" (Random Anarchists 2014). In other words, a biopolitical perspective is valuable for consideration precisely because of its focus on the minutia of the human experience as defined through a reading of security beyond that of the nation-state.

Finally, the insurrectionary position further challenges orthodox notions of security by encouraging the *insecurity* for the state – the central unit of analysis in Security Studies – while reimagining *human* security beyond survival. Insurrectionists posit that the nature of the state places human society (as well as the non-human) in an ever-present condition of insecurity, where one not only is victim to "direct threats" but also "the more indirect but no less real threats that come from structural oppression such as poverty" (Booth 2008, 101). In this manner, insurrectionary theory aligns with the critical critique of securitization (i.e. CSS), labeling the statist determinations as "narrow, inadequate and immoral in the context of 'real' security threats to the individual" (McCormack 2009, 120). The state-centric security rejected by anti-state theorists "prioritized order over justice and human emancipation" (McCormack 2009, 121), something the insurrectionary position seeks to reconfigure, placing the emancipation of all life as central. Security theorist Ken Booth (2008, 106), a key figure in CSS, explains a disjuncture between "survival" and "security," describing the latter as "survival-plus." In this manner, "plus" equates to the sum total of the human experience of self-actualization beyond mere survival, something the insurrectionists attempt to move more centrally to critiques of the social order.

Therefore, in evaluating the original hypotheses, one can conclude that a boundless and inherently ever-expanding understanding of the manifestations and causes of oppression (The Totality) is akin to a diagraming of structural, system-level violence as articled by peace scholars, anthropologists, and others. Though insurrectionary theory provides few centrally located texts, it does constitute a discursive interpretation of violence as structural and security as human-centric, while maintaining a poststructuralist focus on *power*. The explicit influence of European "continental" and critical theorists is common, as the works of Foucault, Hardt and Negri, Agamben, Deleuze and Guattari, and others comingle with theorists involved in armed expropriations, mail bombs, and regicide. The theory of structural violence is told through fractured texts, collectively authored by unknown numbers of individuals and small groups. Communiqués, essays, calls to action, news reporting, letters to and from prisoners, court statements, anonymous rage, and insight all function to constitute an (anti-) canon which simultaneously rejects the abstracted class-privileged, insular navel-gazing of academics, but assumes its readers and critics to understand references to "biopolitical order" and "forms-of-life." In its function, insurrectionary theory adds teeth to critique, and anti-social violence to praxis.

On performativity and spectacle

It appears clear from the aforementioned history that the *performative, spectacular* nature of insurrectionary attack is more prized then substantive changes to the totalizing structures of governance and control. The symbolic, propaganda, and message-orientated results of a scorched bank or an explosive package sent to a politician's office are more meaningful, more impactful, than the lost capital or the scared official. By stringing together thousands of acts into movements, one creates the specter of change, which opens the possibility of change actually occurring. Terrorism scholar Mark Juergensmeyer (2014) builds off this point as a central basis for his work, writing:

> ... most acts of terror are instances of performance violence. They are dramatic events meant to shock, and to lure the viewer into the perpetrators' worldviews. These are performances intended for very specific audiences, including the worldwide audience on television and the Internet ...

Certainly, when cells are deciding which target to strike, through what means, and how to explain it to a globally-situated, internet-accessing audience, the performative value is not lost. *Propaganda of the deed* relies on this calculation, as does the insurrectionary strategy of creating social conflict leading to rupture, and then culminating in direct conflict with the forces of domination; this process too requires demonstrative violence to intimidate the enemy, inspire the ally, and communicate to the populace.

Therefore, the communiqué – as the main medium for communicative talk between actor and audience – must be seen not as a *byproduct* of violence, but as an integral component. It is the sign below the abstract expressionist painting ensuring that the broad strokes of erratic color are read as more than simply splatter. But, once again, one must consider the symbiotic, dependent relationship between the act and the text. Does the desire to write a specific message dictate the attack? Does the attack *require* the text in order to be understood? Does the text *require* an act in order to be written?

Political violence as performative spectacle

After consuming troves of communiqués, anonymous proclamations, and other claims of responsibility, one must wonder: What is the function of all this violence? If a masked anarchist does not believe that breaking the window of a bank will serve to create a rupture with the iron grasp of capitalism, why would they risk their freedom to do it? What is the effect of a single broken window? The answer may be hidden in the performative nature of the attack far more than the substantive impediment it creates for the accumulation and centralization of capital. Postmodern Queer theorist Judith Butler (1990, xv) discusses the performative nature of gender, stating that its production is "manufactured through a sustained set of acts." The hundreds of broken windows, burned banks, and explosives dispatched through the mail collectively constitute these "set of acts," and in producing these events, one is performatively constructing a counter-reality – a break from the normative violence of society toward a non-normative display of society's clandestine inequities. Butler (2015, pt. 4:40) explains that language – in this case that of the communiqué describing an attack and its logic – brings (i.e. performs) the social reality into being through the *performance* of discourse.

These performances (i.e. acts) serve symbolic functions, and thus some have argued that terrorism itself is a semiotic act – one that serves as "a signal, a message, a symbol, and/or media image" (C. H. Miller et al. 2008, 50) – namely the production of spectacularly violent live sights and preserved images, as well as *signs* of that violence. In this regard not only does terrorism seek to *produce* spectacle, but also to reconfigure the reading of its associated signs – the ways through which individuals understand the representations maintained in these images. Political violence serves to "alter the functions of established cultural symbols of power and legitimacy" (C. H. Miller et al. 2008, 51), disrupting the reading of these symbols of state power with revolutionary, anti-social critique. This production of spectacle as a motivation for acting moves the actor away from the purely ideological motivations and towards a more audience-centric, strategic framework.

This embracing of *performative* violence –and the resultant distancing from other articulations of violence, such as those that are purely ideological – may be a result of possibilities offered by emergent communications technologies, most obviously the internet (van Buuren and de Graaf 2013, 157). With this in mind, it is likely that with further increases in accessible forms of global communication, these attacks will increase, as the communiqué as a globally-circulated vehicle of propaganda becomes even easier to produce[1] and circulate. This presumption for increased attack may be influenced by a growing discourse offered by anti-technology attackers. While some, such as Kaczynski, have argued that technology serves an instrumental role in the battle against technology, others have urged for the battle to be taken entirely offline. Though the explicitly anti-technology strand of insurrectionary theory is likely a minority, its critique of the means towards a shared end may have influence on the future of digitally-mediated forms of organization and attack.

The production of attacks allows the actor to circulate their critique via the communiqué. The communiqué is thus the product of the attack on par with the actual financial damage to the target. In his discussion of the 9/11 attacks, sociologist and cultural theorist Jean Baudrillard (2001) writes:

> One tries after the event to assign ... meaning, to find any possible interpretation. But there is none possible, and it is only the radicality of the spectacle, the brutality of the spectacle that is original and irreducible. The spectacle of terrorism imposes the terrorism of the spectacle ... It is both the sublime micro-model of a nucleus of real violence with maximal resonance – thus the purest form of the spectacular, and the sacrificial model that opposes to historical and political order the purest symbolic form of challenge.

The creation of meaning through the radical brutality of spectacular violence is meant as a living, breathing critique against power, coercion, and domination as located in the monotony and drudgery of human existence within the confines of the state and capitalism. To disseminate voluminous descriptions of "real violence" (i.e. communiqués) which serve to identify, critique, and condemn structural violence (Galtung 1969; 1985; Galtung and Höivik 1971; Farmer 1996; 2004; Ladicola and Shupe 1998; Bourgois 2003) and cultural violence (Galtung 1990) is a primary aim of insurrectionary attack.

A performance requires an audience

The enacting of direct violence (e.g. a bomb targeting a government building), is understood as both a substantive strike against one's enemies and a method of performative communication. This premise is applicable to varying diverse incidents often lumped together descriptively as terroristic. Therefore, diagraming the communicative intent simultaneous to the intended audience for those communications is key. To provide a non-insurrectionary example, one can look to individualized acts of anti-social, political violence such as the 5 November 2009 killing of 13 people (and the wounding of 29 others) at Fort Hood in Texas by US Army Major Nidal Hasan. Hasan's attack, which generated the highest rate of casualty on an American military base in history, was primarily directed at those he fired upon – US military personnel. In the shooting, Hasan, an army psychiatrist, killed 12 members of the military and one civilian medical personnel at the Soldier Readiness Processing Center, a medical facility where he worked. The intended recipient for such a generated spectacle is multifaceted, and represented in Figure 7.1 Despite the very direct nature of Hasan's attack, there was a secondary target audience for the attack (TA2), namely the American military that was exposed to this sort of attack and made to feel unsafe or beseiged. If one expands outward, a tertiary target of the attack (TA3) was the citizenry and socio-political order that insulates American militarism, Empire, and one's feeling of safety and security. This communicative relationship is displayed in Figure 7.1.

This conceptual map is meant to demonstrate the communicative relationship between the act of violence, its direct audience, and its associated audiences. In this example, while Hasan may have focused his performance outwardly towards the soldiers and military personnel on site, numerous secondary audiences would look to the target's experience, and be *spoken*

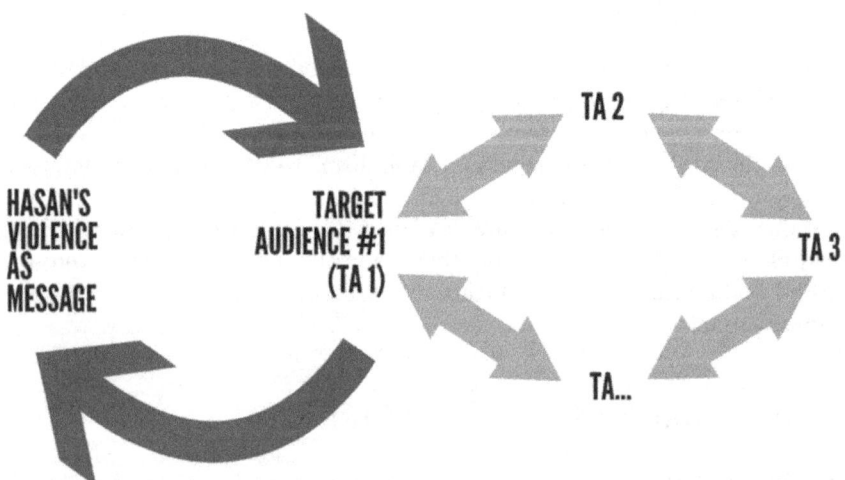

7.1 Secondary–tertiary target audience concept map

to through those acts. A soldier deployed at a Forward Operating Base in Afghanistan can view a news account of a crying widow in Texas and, in doing so, constitute a secondary audience for the traumatic violence. The rapid, semi-synchronous consumption of information regardless of national border, time zone, and language makes the tracing of these non-primary communicative audiences nearly impossible.

The terroristic nature of Hasan's attack sought to sever a sense of stability enshrined in "peace time." This interpretation is supported by Juergensmeyer, arguing that violent attacks are "dramas designed to have an impact on the several audiences that they affect. Those who witness the violence – even at a distance, via the news media – are therefore a part of what occurs" (Juergensmeyer 2003, 126). This assertion has been recurrent throughout decades of terrorism scholarship, such as a 1974 essay published by RAND, which states:

> [Terrorist] violence must be all the more dramatic ... Terrorist attacks are often carefully choreographed to attract the attention of the electronic media and the international press ... Terrorism is aimed at the people watching, not at the actual victims. Terrorism is theater. (Jenkins 1975, 4)

Not only does this author employ the use of intentional descriptive language (e.g. dramatic, choreographed, theater), but he drives home the point of the violence's aim towards secondary and tertiary audiences. Similarly, writing of the nature of terrorism's communicative potential, early Terrorism Studies scholars Alex P. Schmid and Janny de Graaf (1982, 14) write:

> Terrorism, by using violence against one victim, seeks to persuade others. The immediate victim is merely instrumental, the skin on a drum beaten to achieve a calculated impact on a wider audience. As such, an act of terrorism is in reality, an act of communication.

Though Hasan would argue in his legal proceedings that his attack was carried out to defend Taliban leaders in Afghanistan from the US military (Carter and Rubin 2013), his attack against the state was largely performative and symbolic. It is unlikely that he believed that the loss of these soldiers would harm the US war effort, just as an insurrectionary actor does not likely believe that a destroyed police car will bring down the security state. These strikes serve as harbingers of resistance, movements against "the existent." If we can assume Hasan is capable of calculated decision-making (i.e. a rational actor), then we can assume he attacked his colleagues not to defend Taliban fighters abroad, but to raise awareness of the political impacts of the war at home. Hasan knew what scholars have long argued, that often times awareness and resolution of a particular political issue is brought about though "the success of ... terrorists in bringing their cause violently and dramatically before the eyes of the world" (Jenkins 1975, 6).

In creating these spectacular events, the form and function of the attack and its communication strategy are of prime concern. Commentators reporting on insurrectionary attack have often likened its violence to the methods of more traditional non-state actors (e.g. nationalist separatists, such as PIRA, FARC, Hamas). The rhetorical function of these generalized accounts – those which portray the FAI as on par with al-Qaeda – muddy the waters between paramilitary, militia, insurgents, guerrillas, and those best portrayed as a militant tactical tendency within a largely law-abiding social protest movement. One historian, in describing the Islamic State (i.e. ISIL, ISIS), likened them to "19th and 20th century anarchist and nihilist rebel movements who fought against the centralization of state power" (O'Neil 2014). In an article for mainstream press, historian John Merriman (quoted in O'Neil 2014), speaks of this comparison, writing:

> Anarchists believed that dynamite would level the playing field, and for terrorists now, it's roadside bombs that level the playing field ... Both anarchists and terrorists now believe that they can bring down the superstructure, of capitalist states in the case of the anarchists, or the United States and their allies in the case of terrorists now.

If networks like the FAI and CCF really are the descendents of anarchist king slayers, it is fitting that the post-9/11 era of insurrectionary attack came of age within this active image – that of the masked Islamist fighter carrying a Kalashnikov and planting an IED. While the CCF is a polar opposite of the Islamic State in nearly every way, they perform within a tactical, strategic, and communicative mode that is interpreted by many as showing little difference.

Despite such a negative framing of insurrectionary violence in light of a globally invigorated abhorrence of "terrorism" post-9/11, clandestine attack networks continue to posture as more traditional "terrorists" through methods such as detonating explosives, issuing communiqués, condemning the state, and wearing masks. These individuals are plainly conscious of the discourse on terrorism as they interact and react to it routinely in writing. When understood in light of the assertion that the War on Terrorism is a "battle over representation ... [a] 'war of images'" (Creekmur 2010, 83), this is especially intriguing. When insurrectionary and other clandestine actors do not outright reject a frame that is universally rejected, it begs the question: Can the adoption of such methods by anti-state revolutionaries constitute a sort of "culture jamming" (Klein 2000) of the Global War on Terror? Are clandestine attackers responding and "appropriating" (Susan Buck-Morss, quoted in Creekmur 2010, 83) the cultural capital of intimidation created in the wake of 9/11 by embracing the image of the masked villain for maximum spectacle value? Are the clandestine networks of insurrectionary attack selecting to make use of the state's investment in fear mongering (to mobilize public policy) for their own performative benefit?

Defying spectacle

Clearly there is a performative function of this method of self-representation and aggressive action. However, beyond the creation of spectacle, one's involvement in transgressive acts is in itself a powerful step. In his discussion of the "society of the spectacle," the influential Situationist (anarchist) Guy Debord (1967) argued that reality had become something that individuals *looked at* and *thought about* but did not directly experience. It had become an abstraction, a representation of a representation, viewed from behind screens – television screens, computers, car windshields – which all served to act as filters, mediating the interaction between individual and society. As a result of these mediated interactions with reality, individuals grew accustomed to accepting *representations* as reality and, as such, became increasingly alienated (to borrow from Marx) from *real* experience. These conditions served to further encourage spontaneous, informal, anti-social attacks against systems of power, as these outbursts equate to *"the real"*: unmediated, directly targeted, non-representative actions which serve to rupture the abstracted, normative reality of everyday life.

Insurrectionary logic encourages the fostering and replication of these moments when individuals carry forth the Situationist call to "create situations – moments of life directly lived – that undermine the dominant logic of passive consumption and alienated representation" (quoted in Williams and Thomson 2011, 273). The targets of attack are therefore routinely those institutions and physical manifestations of this spectacle. In November 2014, a clandestine cell bombed a Mexican telethon office aiding disabled children – not as part of "demands for social justice" but rather because the charity and the wider mass media it summons serve to "implement alienation through the technoindustrial system's values" (Wild Reaction, Nocturnal Hunter Faction 2014). Debord's abstracted "society of the spectacle" is seen in the function of the larger state apparatus, as according to Giorgio Agamben, "spectacle is the logical extension of the commodity form under late capitalism" (Passavant 2007, 149). Therefore, attacks on this arena of commodity can serve to disrupt and materially damage the spectacle's disengagement with "the real," tying the attacker back into a moment of resistance, actualized in experiential violence.

The spectacle of the attack is thus a co-constituted performance – a "theater of terror" (Weimann 2006, 38) – wherein the attacker is responding to the abstraction of reality by inserting radical critique as a dramatized play for the benefit of the audience. Here the spectacle creates the desire to act – to disrupt the mediated role played by society on the individual – and, in doing so, simultaneously creates a newly revolutionary event for a new audience to view and interpret. These efforts to display ruptures to the society (of the spectacle) contest the media's explanatory model of events that seek to act as an "insertion between man and his (sic) environment … [creating] a pseudo-environment" (Lippmann 1922, 8). The strategic violence of asymmetric warfare thus attempts to carry through a largely symbolic salvo in a war against domination. The attack demands the gaze of the audience in the hopes of drawing them *away* from the spectacle, and towards an actualized, lived experience. One scholar, speaking of the spectacle and alienated action writes: "Insurrectionary actions are ultimately expressions of truth in a postmodern age that stridently disavows any such affirmation" (Wood 2013, 40).

Thus, for the attacker, not only is the strike a demonstration of *their truth* but it also allows a break from the mediated interactions of spectacle; a real, gritty, texture-rich experience wherein one is able to place politics outside the realm of theory and into the venue of action. This action thus requires a discursive explanation (i.e. a communiqué) to ensure that the experience is understood through its intended frame. This is precisely why insurrectionary actors follow up their strikes with a communiqué, as to strike without explanation is akin to telling a joke without the punch line. Sociologist Erving Goffmann's (1959) theory of dramaturgical analysis, expanded upon by Kenneth Burke (1972), posits that one's engagement with public performance is directed at an audience in order to influence the recipient's perception of not only the targets of the attack, but the attacker as well. This notion of performative violence can be examined from a variety of literatures from Gender Studies (Butler 1990) to Philosophy dealing with language (Austin 1975), yet what remains a central focus is the relationship between the producer of spectacle and the audience; a co-dependent, intertwined relationship which unites the audience/victim and the actor/perpetrator. By displaying their critique through actualized violence, the insurrectionary actor is attempting to influence the audience, to engage in a dialogue that leads the passive social actor towards an emancipatory understanding of reality. This is a multi-pronged discourse that attempts to speak to the citizenry, the forces of authority, and its own inter-network community.

Form and (discursive) function

The communiqué as an object, delivered via the internet, is beholden to the constraints of that medium. Certainly it is a banal assertion to write that radical social movements, armed nationalist insurgents of all types, and violent non-state actors use the internet for a variety of purposes. This is obvious. In his descriptions of the post-9/11 rise of al-Qaeda, terrorism scholar Bruce Hoffman (2014, 5) succinctly summarizes these tech trends, writing:

> The growth and communicative power of social networking platforms ... has transformed terrorism: Facilitating both ubiquitous and real-time communication between like-minded radicals with would-be recruits and potential benefactors – thus fueling and sustaining these struggles to a hitherto unprecedented extent ... The advantage of the new social media to terrorists are manifold. Ease, interactivity and networking, reach, frequency, usability, stability, immediacy, publicity, and permanence are benefits reaped by those terrorist groups exploiting and harnessing these technologies. A new generation of celebrity fighters is also being created, heralded and extolled in a familiar vernacular to Facebook friends and Twitter followers alike.

This assertion is repeated throughout the literature, often truncated to reflect the idea that "this [propaganda] war, which was previously fought in written text, audio messaging, or small groups in free spaces is now unfolding across the Internet in unprecedented volume" (T. Morris 2014, 164). This symbiosis between the creators of violence (i.e. terrorists) and the recipients of its reporting (i.e. the news-consuming population) is not a new phenomenon (e.g. Alexander 1979, 160; Wardlaw 1989, 38; C. H. Miller et al. 2008, 53–60) emanating from the transnational powers of the internet. In a survey-based study conducted in the early 1980s, scholars associated with The Centre for the Study of Social Conflicts report quite simply that "the media play ... an important role in the diffusion of terrorism" (Schmid and Graaf 1982, 126). Within the modern age, both media (J. Burke 2016) and the academy (Dolata and Schrape 2016) frequently conclude that the internet and digital communities allow for new forms of deterritorialized, yet collective, action.

While such assertions are commonplace, what is less obvious is *how* these technologies are used for revolutionary aims. Often times, the atypicality of radical media is presumed but may prove to distract from the more mundane and common uses of communications technology. In her discussion of jihadists' use of Twitter and other social media, political theorist Jytte Klausen (2014, 3) writes, "The focus in the terrorism literature ... overshadows the reality that terrorists also use the internet for the same reasons everybody else does; for organization and planning, proselytizing and entertainment, and to educate the believers." Surveys of computer materials seized during post-terrorist attack investigations have shown that while fighters utilized these digital mediums to self-train in *tactics*, their computer contained three times more material aimed at radicalization and propagandizing (Klausen 2014, 3). Therefore, it is not most centrally the digital *form* that is novel but rather the *function* it supports, namely the collection, translation, and redistribution of claims of responsibility.

After reviewing thousands of communiqués and their associated acts of political protest, what can we say is the nature of the connection between form and function; between the text and the discourse? The preceding examination of communiqués is chiefly concerned with "discursive practices as constitutive of knowledge" (Fairclough 1993, 38), in this case the constructed knowledge of a particular political theory enacted by a diverse, transnational social milieu. The production of communiqués and other texts through a particular linguistic reality is exemplary of discursive limiting. Speaking of Foucault's *archeology of knowledge*, Fairclough (1993, 41–42) explains:

> ... the objects of discourse are constituted and transformed in discourse according to the rules of some particular discursive formation, rather than existing independently and simply being referred to or talked about in a particular discourse ... discourse as constitutive – as contributing to the production, transformation, and reproduction of the objects ... language signifies reality in the sense of constructing meanings for it, rather than that discourse is in a passive relation to reality, with language merely referring to objects which are taken to be given in reality.

Thus the linguistic and lexical choices made by communiqué authors are constituted through the movement's macro discourse, as established through the forum of the "informal international translation and counter-information network." This network is therefore not simply discussing and presenting the discourse of the communiqués' struggle against the state, but rather they function to *constitute* the discursive matter, including its goals, methods, identities, lexical choices, and rhetorics. While this may appear as a one-way dialogue – the clandestine speaking to the public – it is in fact a conversation occurring in the openness of the internet, spanning the world. In this relationship, the texts influence the attacks that in turn produce more texts, which influence subsequent attacks. This dynamic relationship is modeled in Figure 7.2.

Sometimes, individual communiqué authors even acknowledge this interrelatedness, thanking those unnamed persons who translated their material. In one such example, a Mexican insurrectionary network concluded their communiqué with, "PS: We give our appreciation to the effort of the translators (of our communiques and claims), through whose effort of diffusion, our words have reached countries that we never thought they would reach" (Wild Reaction, Coyote-Skin Cloak group, Wild Reaction, Kill or Die group, and Wild Reaction, Infamous Aboriginals group 2015).

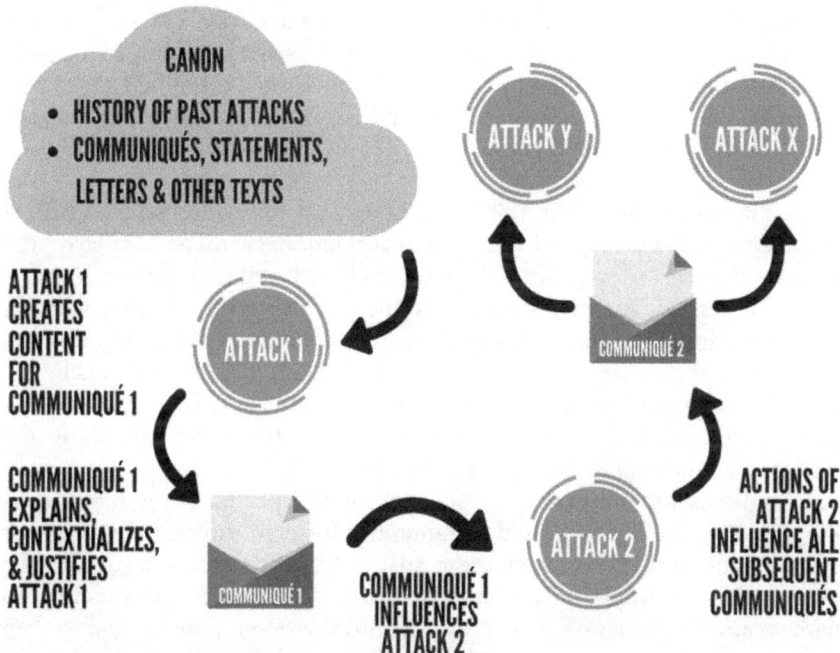

7.2 Communiqué/attack–form/function concept map

The global network thus constitutes discourse through what Foucault describes as establishing and forcing discursive discipline – establishing power/knowledge – as to speak outside of these rules is to exclude oneself from the network altogether. Such a public disciplinary action can be seen in the case of the now ostracized and excommunicated Bristol Indymedia, which is now seen by insurrectionary actors to be complicit in state-led repression and violence. Following a police raid on the website's servers, insurrectionary anarchists voiced their condemnation for the social movement news outlet, stating:

> [Bristol] Indymedia was previously part of the anti-capitalist movement from the alter-globalist era, but has been recuperated by the liberal democratic system. 325 has long regarded the Bristol IMC project to largely be passed any relevancy and considered it as in the hands of the enemy for some time ... It doesn't surprise us at all that their server is now to become part of the regime's hand to be used against the new anarchist urban guerrilla operating in the UK ... 325 was correct to position ourselves in antagonism towards them. Their persistent attempts to denigrate the new urban guerrillas and their lack of any kind of respect when we attempted to communicate to them means they will find no

solidarity from us ... Bristol IMC's recent cowardly and civil society orientated "statement" announcing that they were not going to be publishing any more communiqués for destructive attacks on their pages also confirmed that they were the worst kind of pacifist-judiciary and cowards of the tendency of civil democracy. (325.nostate.net 2014)

This statement reveals the public shaming and denouncement of Bristol Indymedia for refusing to circulate insurrectionary texts. Similarly, the construction of an oppositional group such as "civil anarchists" (Anonymous 2013d) facilitates an inter-movement, discursive *othering*, wherein segments who contest bounds of illegality, violence, and associated rhetoric can constitute an enemy, not an ally, and, as a result, be summarily excluded. This disciplining of discourse can be observed inter-textually (i.e. within a single text's word choices) and among various texts that constitute the movement's messaging at large (Fairclough 1993, 46).

This discussion must take into account the role played by interconnectivity, specially digitally-mediated communities fostered through a global web of exchange, and the impact these spaces have for future struggle. The internet has allowed for a global audience of insurrectionary actors to witness attacks, integrate these critiques into their own politics, and to then strike in new, responsive ways. Without the availability of sites such as 325 and War on Society, the internationalization of moniker-based networks of attack would likely occur in a slower and more localized manner. This digital reconstruction of what constitutes a "community or network" reframes the actions of the individual, linking them in action and meaning to an increasingly lengthy history of attack, and highlighting the moniker-based "branding" of particular networks (e.g. the FAI "brand") (van Buuren and de Graaf 2013, 176–177).

This conundrum – one that problematizes the value added to revolutionary organizing with the advent of online communities – is especially tricky when discussing the networks that seek to abolish industrial civilization and technology as their basis, such as ITS. Discussions of this nature are certainly ongoing among the theorists of struggle, such as recent texts authored by the CrimethInc. Ex-Workers' Collective (2014a; 2014b). The loss of physical community is certainly an acknowledged risk with increased digitalization (Grubbs and Loadenthal 2014), yet the possibility for greater connectivity has been discussed as a strength of modern protest culture. It is important to note here that the use of online networks for communiqué distribution appears to be a function of emergent technology's integration into a wider social scheme, and *not* a necessary component for the continuation of insurrectionary attack. In this regard, one notes the comments made by foundational social movement thinker Charles Tilly, who remarked, "Yes, activists adopt new technologies when those technologies serve their purposes ... but purposes override techniques" (quoted in Polletta et al.

2013 p. 17). Thus, without the online networks, other *offline* networks would likely arise in their place, and while these divergent forms may dictate some manners of action, they will not dictate its complete form.

The communiqué functions as a "transactional and bidirectional" (Tuman 2009, 33) message, rhetorically engaging both the attacker and the public in a discourse. The communiqué itself becomes a site of resistance, as it is a reaction to structural violence and an urging for additional reactionary violence. This sort of dialogue between globally dispersed actors is only made possible by nearly synchronous communications and translations as offered by the internet. The acts of violence function to allow the communiqué to be authored, and to temporarily focus attention towards the politics of structural violence as manifested in the individual or institution that is targeted. Therefore, though communiqués may report acts akin to traditional terrorism, the strategy of attack–communiqué is not terrorism, but something else entirely. It is a form of asymmetric, decentralized war carried out through networked and ideologically-linked attacks at a non-centralized, fluid target. It is not terrorism because it does not seek to terrorize, but rather to exhibit dissent and offer critique. In a dialogical sense, the violence of the attack creates the space for the critic to "be heard" (Toros 2012, 46), and in doing so temporarily disrupts the discourse it is critiquing, for example, the infallibility of market capitalism.

This relationship that exists between the producer of texts (e.g. the attacker), their distributors (e.g. website administrators), and the consumer of texts (e.g. the supporter) is similarly dynamic and fluid. In one sense, active sympathizers maintain the translation and distribution hubs that serve as liaison between the producer and consumer. Therefore, information flows from the attacker to the consumer via the sympathizer – engaging each level of actor in a process of discursive production and information transmission. This relationship between the three parties is diagramed conceptually in Figure 7.3.

This model shows that all actors remain in an active (i.e. non-passive) position, as all individuals are creators, facilitators or recipients of analysis, critique, and incitement. The politics, critical analysis, and praxis of the insurrectionary "ideology" or method can only be developed, refined, and enacted through action, and reinforced through an inter-movement form of "ideological hegemony" (Gramsci 1971b) – the means of social conditioning that informs and enforces the movement's culture of operation.

Thus, only those who light fires are allowed to pontificate, only those constructing fuses and timing devices are welcomed to the debate. Those that construct the insurrectionary canon are globally dispersed actors, reacting to one another's actions and texts in a never-ending dialogue, carried out with relative transparency for a global audience. What connects a vandal in Jakarta, a graffiti artist in Berlin, and an arsonist in Bristol is only their epistemological framework and their critique in the broadest sense.

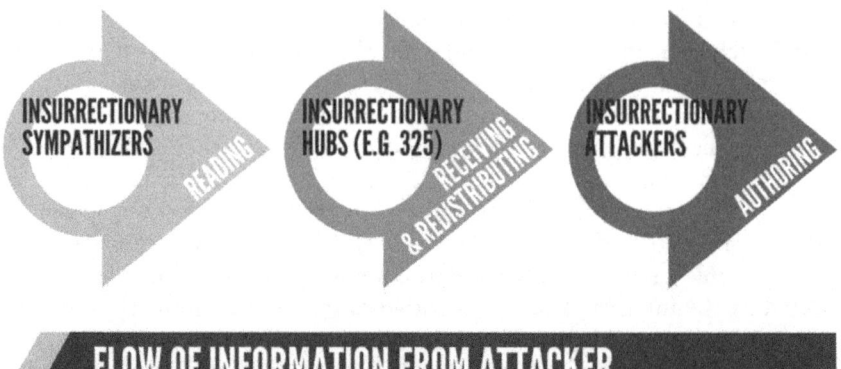

7.3 Knowledge transmission concept map

They will likely possess different positions on "policies" and "alternatives," but their diagraming of society's ills will inevitably center around the same components and in their own manner demonstrate inter-movement hegemony. Therefore, the point of convergence for these disparate actors is precisely the site of systemic violence; what is similar among the thousands of pages of radical speech is a shared understanding of an ever-changing, challenging foe, that of violence, coercion, domination, exploitation, alienation, and control.

Looking towards the future

The preceding chapters have argued for a nuanced, engaged, theoretically-informed, and context-embedded understanding of political violence crafted from primary source documents, not security-focused secondary analysis. This broad approach has been an attempt to propose and operationalize an action-oriented, analytical perspective that asserts itself as against the logic of securitization (i.e. anti-securitization), and de-exceptionalizes *political* violence from other forms of disruptive occurrence. While critical theorists such as Slavoj Žižek (2008) have argued that *any* attempt to change structural inequality that leads to a disruption in the normal way of living is read as *violence*, all violence is not read with the same lens. Violence that is often labeled as terroristic – that emanating from social movements and other non-state actors and targeting sites associated with the state and economy – is typically treated within a realm of exceptionality; marking it as substantively different from violence carried out for criminal or other idiosyncratic reasons. Non-state violence is routinely regarded as illogical, un-strategic, immoral, unethical, needless, illegal, chaotic, and the result of a psychological pathology. At the same time, state violence (including state terrorism) is enshrined in the protective veneer of legitimacy, morality, legality, and assumed to be the result of a measured cost–benefit calculation. Why is this the case? Sociologist Robert White (2000, 96) suggests that media and academic studies of political violence tend to ignore the mundane, and instead focus on the "series of spectacular and often gruesome events." While this can help to explain the myopic nature of broad discussions of how violence is discursively labeled, it fails to account for the wholesale defamation of violence not sanctioned by the state. In practice, non-state violence is displayed in an un-embedded, context-less approach, ignoring the violent conditions that may have preceded, resulted from, and helped to constitute the politics of the attack.

It is essential for future scholarship to foster an understanding of political violence that incorporates "the social, political and economic ills that often surround terrorism and render it possible" (Toros 2012, 35). Therefore, if we can interpret insurrectionary modes of attack through a context-embedded, de-exceptionalized, anti-security framework, the conversation will inevitably arrive at issues of inequality, hierarchy, domestication, alienation, and coercion. This approach is more familiar in sociological discussions of criminal violence, as scholars assert a correlated and often causal linkage between, for example, revenue-generating criminal activity (e.g. distribution of drugs) and poverty. Therefore, while it is commonplace to assert that to reduce crime one must reduce economic inequality and level the field of competition, the same cannot be said of *political* violence. If we were to treat *political* violence in a manner akin to that of *criminal* violence, the "solution" to insurrectionary attack is systemic, revolutionary change that reduces domination and marginalization. These solutions would likely be discounted summarily by policymakers who would prefer a list of targets than a list of arguments for better access to education, housing, healthcare, transportation, etc. In other words, to "solve" the insurrectionary critique would require system-level change aimed at a deconstruction of that very system and, as such, is unlikely to be embraced by power elites. Because the critique is aimed at power itself, to embrace its proscription of change would deny the brokers of that power a great deal of influence and control.

In this sense, to *de*-exceptionalize terrorism and other forms of political violence is to disrupt the discourse that constructs it. By shifting the conversation away from broken windows (or burned offices) and towards gentrification (or prisons, animal slaughter …), a discursive shift occurs which steals power from the state's efforts to mobilize, conceal, and enact its violence. To discuss the alienation produced by capitalism instead of the lost profits produced by arson, one reconfigures the discourse from system maintenance to system transformation. To focus on methods of conflict *transformation* – such as the work of Galtung (2000) and J. P. Lederach (1995; 2003) – refocuses attention away from the direct violence of *attacks*, and towards the "structures of domination and exclusion that generate and perpetuate conflict" (Ramsbotham, Miall, and Woodhouse 2005, 296). Through incorporating approaches from Peace Studies, Conflict Analysis, CSS, CTS, feminist research, and other interrelated disciplines, we can shift the analytical focus from the *manifestations* to the *structures* that "generate and perpetuate" and, in doing so, de-center the state's security as the unit of analysis and focus of attention.

Such predictive patterns should be of primary concern to those seeking a more peaceful society as *counter*terrorism efforts typically serve to "reinforce and reify existing structures of power in society" (Jackson 2009, 67) – the very structures insurrectionary action seeks to eliminate. This creates a feedback loop wherein the structural violence causes insurrectionary attack, which causes increased securitization, which emboldens further violence at the level of the community, adding fuel to the fire of insurrectionary anger. In this case, the newly reified inequality can lead attackers to redouble their efforts to urgently and radically change the socio-political system. With this loop in mind, poststructuralism appears again be an appropriate intervention as it seeks to destabilize *power* – the hub through which all oppression can be said to derive from.

Without the luxury of hindsight, we are forced to interpret these events as they unfold. While the modern articulation of the "insurrectionary *turn*" in anti-state attack began around the millennium, some have argued that this wave has already crested and begun to decline (Nomad 2013); if this is true, the movement's embers continue to burn quite brightly. While the movement has not succeeded in "totalizing the social war," or "bringing it all crashing down," it has served to raise its critique to prominence through the production of spectacular violence. In doing so, the movement has been able to build a revolutionary consciousness, and while it has not yet fundamentally changed the political landscape, it has had an undeniable impact. In all likelihood, the attacks of the FAI, CCF, and others will endure despite combatants' capture and imprisonment. Attacks will likely continue to draw strength and inspiration from the words and deeds of these movement forebearers, and the discourse and logic of anti-state attack will continue to develop.

Social movements do not typically have clearly demarcated starting and ending points. The actions of individuals, cells, and networks rise and fall as the result of a combination of any number of factors. While larger political realities serve to inform and influence patterns of attack, it is incorrect to predict that the passage of new anti-terrorism laws or the authority of newly elected officials will serve to deter future violent contestation. The nature of insurrectionary attacks contends that at its base, the problem is not found in politicians, their institutions, nor their initiatives, but instead in the articulation of a system-level critique which rejects political representationalism, abhors domination, and seeks nothing short of total liberation. With such frameworks serving to inform the movement's understanding of success and failure, the arena of battle will extend far into the future. As wealth gaps widen, forms of state control coalesce, and ecological crises creep closer, it can be expected that those who choose the bomb over the ballot will continue to strike with greater ferocity and with the aim of ever-expanding spheres of freedom and liberation.

Notes

1 In discussing the "ease" of writing such texts, I am reminded of the "Automatic Insurrectionary Manifesto Generator" (http://objectivechance.com/automatic_insurrection), a self-critical and satirical website which cobbles together common insurrectionary rhetoric into a veritable Mad Lib of propaganda. In a single click the user is delivered a hodgepodge of keywords strung together through faux-insurrectionary language. An explanation for *why* this was created is offered at: https://github.com/johm/automatic_insurrection.

REFERENCES

109th Congress. 2005a. "Oversight on Eco-Terrorism Specifically Examining the Earth Liberation Front ('ELF') and the Animal Liberation Front ('ALF')." United States Senate Committee on Environmental and Public Works. http://epw.senate.gov/hearing_statements.cfm?id=237836.

———. 2005b. "Eco-Terrorism Specifically Examining Stop Huntingdon Animal Cruelty ('SHAC')." United States Senate Committee on Environmental and Public Works. www.gpo.gov/fdsys/pkg/CHRG-109shrg39521/html/CHRG-109shrg39521.htm.

325.nostate.net. 2014. "Police Investigating the Incendiary Anarchist Minority Raid Bristol IMC, Who Shut down Their Project (UK)." 325.nostate.net. http://325.nostate.net/?p=11746.

Abrahms, Max, and Justin Conrad. 2016. "The strategic logic of credit claiming: a new theory for anonymous terrorist attacks." *Security Studies* Forthcoming: 1–27.

ACME Collective. 1999. "N30 Black Bloc Communiqué." *No Compromise Magazine*. www.nocompromise.org/news/991204a.html.

Acton, Jay, Alan LeMond, and Parker Hodges. 1972. *Mug Shots; Who's Who in the New Earth*. New York, NY: World Publishing.

Adams, Josh, and Vincent J. Roscigno. 2005. "White supremacists, oppositional culture and the world wide web." *Social Forces* 84 (2): 759–78.

Agamben, Giorgio. 1993. *The Coming Community*. Translated by Michael Hardt. Minneapolis, MN: University Of Minnesota Press.

A Gang Of Criminal Queers. 2008. *Towards the Queerest Insurrection*. Zine. Milwaukee, WI: Mary Nardini gang. http://zinelibrary.info/files/QueerestImposed.pdf.

Agirre, Julen. 1975. *Operation Ogro: The Execution of Admiral Luis Carrero Blanco*. Translated by Barbara Probst Solomon. New York, NY: Quadrangle/New York Times Book Co.

Ahmed, Nafeez. 2014. "Nasa-Funded Study: Industrial Civilisation Headed for 'Irreversible Collapse'?" *The Guardian*, 14 March, sec. Environment. www.theguardian.com/environment/earth-insight/2014/mar/14/nasa-civilisation-irreversible-collapse-study-scientists.

Alexander, Yonah. 1979. "Terrorism and the Media: Some Considerations." In *Terrorism: Theory and Practice*, edited by Yonah Alexander, David Carlton, and Paul Wilkinson, 159–74. Westview Special Studies in National and International Terrorism. Boulder, CO: Westview Press.

Alexander, Yonah, and Dennis A. Pluchinsky. 1992. *Europe's Red Terrorists: The Fighting Communist Organizations*. London, UK: Routledge.

Al Jazeera News. 2014. "US Calls for Urgent Action on Climate Change." *Al Jazeera News*, 7 May. Online edition, sec. Americas. www.aljazeera.com/news/americas/2014/05/us-calls-urgent-action-climate-change-2014570136529322.html.

Alker, Hayward. 2005. "Emancipation in the Critical Security Studies Project." In *Critical Security Studies And World Politics*, edited by Ken Booth, 189–213. Boulder, CO: Lynne Rienner Pub.

al-Zawahiri, Ayman. Letter to Abu Musab al-Zarqawi. 2005. "Zawahiri's Letter to Zarqawi [English Translation]," 9 July. www.ctc.usma.edu/v2/wp-content/uploads/2013/10/Zawahiris-Letter-to-Zarqawi-Translation.pdf.

Amster, Randall. 2012. *Anarchism Today*. Santa Barbara, CA: Praeger.

Anarchist Arson Attack Cell "Fire and Consciousness" FAI-IRF. 2016. "Phoenix Project – Incendiary Attack against a Security Company by FAI-IRF." Insurrection News. https://insurrectionnewsworldwide.com/2016/01/10/chile-phoenix-project-incendiary-attack-against-isp-security-by-fai-irf/.

Anarchist-nihilists against the activist establishment. 2013. "Fuck Indymedia and the Anarcho-Left." In *Anarchy–Civil or Subversive?: A Collection of Texts Against Civil Anarchism*, 52–53. Online: Dark Matter Publications (republished by 325.nostate.net). http://325.nostate.net/wp-content/uploads/2013/11/civil-anarchism-book.pdf.

Ángel, Arturo. 2013. "Van por 'ala terrorista' de anarquistas." Translated by Liberación Total. Liberación Total (republished by War on Society). www.24-horas.mx/van-por-ala-terrorista-de-anarquistas/, waronsociety.noblogs.org/?p=7444.

Anonymous. n.d. *The Politics of Bombs, Armed Struggle in Canada: Direct Action Wimmin's Fire Brigade Vancouver Five*. Print zine. Self published.

———. 2001a. *At Daggers Drawn with the Existent, its Defenders and its False Critics*. Translated by Jean Weir, John Moore, and Leigh Straccross. Zine. London, UK: Elephant Editions.

———. 2001b. "Rebelling Against Our Domestication: Towards a Feral Revolution." *Do or Die*. Zine. http://theanarchistlibrary.org/library/anonymous-rebelling-against-our-domestication-towards-a-feral-revolution.

———. 2002. *Revolutionary Armed Struggle*. Montréal, QC: Abraham Guillen Press & Arm the Spirit.

———. 2003. "Insurrectionary Anarchy: Organising for Attack!" *Do or Die*. Zine.

———. 2006. "Four Years ... Dec. 2006." In *Escalation: Some Texts Concerning the Informal Anarchist Federation (FAI) and the Insurrectionist Project*, Zine. Online, 4–9. 325.nostate.net. http://325.nostate.net/library/escalation1.pdf.

———. 2007. *Escalation: Some Texts Concerning the Informal Anarchist Federation (FAI) and the Insurrectionist Project*. Zine. 325.nostate.net. http://325.nostate.net/library/escalation1.pdf.

———. 2008. "Solidarity & Revolt Across Borders." Self published (republished by Zine Library). http://zinelibrary.info/files/solidarity_revolt.pdf.

———. 2009a. "20 Theses on the Subversion of the Metropolis." Translated by Institute for Experimental Freedom. Institute for Experimental Freedom. www.zinelibrary.info/files/20theses.pdf.

———. 2009b. "Beyond Workerism – Beyond Syndicalism." *Insurrection*. Zine. http://theanarchistlibrary.org/library/various-authors-articles-from-insurrection.pdf.

———. 2009c. "'Til It Breaks #1." *'Til it Breaks.* http://itbreaks.files.wordpress.com/2010/02/itbreaks1.pdf.

———. 2011. "Letter to the Anarchist Galaxy [Lettre à la galaxie anarchiste]." Translated by Act for Freedom Now! Act for Freedom Now! http://actforfree.nostate.net/?p=6610.

———. 2012. "A Conversation Between Anarchists: A Discussion About Tactics, Theory and Practice Between the Imprisoned Members of the Conspiracy of the Cells of Fire and a Few Anarchists in Mexico." Translated by Act for Freedom Now! Black International editions. http://actforfree.nostate.net/wp-content/uploads/2013/05/Conversation-book.pdf.

———. 2013a. "La Nueva Guerrilla Urbana Anarquista: Conspiración De Células Del Fuego." Translated by Individualidades anárquicas atenienses and Conspiración Ácrata. Internacional negra. http://325.nostate.net/wp-content/uploads/2013/03/la-nueva-grl-anrqst.pdf.

———. 2013b. "Neoliberal Public Health and the Rhetoric of War." *A Disorder of Things.* Zine. 4 August. https://adisorderofthings.wordpress.com/2013/08/04/neoliberal-public-health-and-the-rhetoric-of-war/.

———. 2013c. "Anonymity [Anonimato]." Translated by Indymedia Athens. Indymedia Athens. https://athens.indymedia.org/post/1489590/.

———. 2013d. *Anarchy – Civil or Subversive?: A Collection of Texts Against Civil Anarchism.* Online: Dark Matter Publications (republished by 325.nostate.net). http://325.nostate.net/wp-content/uploads/2013/11/civil-anarchism-book.pdf.

———. 2014a. *Since the Bristol Riots: Communiques from the FAI, ELF & Other Attacks (2011–2014).* 2nd edn. Online: Person(s) Unknown & Dark Matter Publications. https://interarma.info/wp-content/uploads/2014/12/Since-the-Bristol-riots-v2.compressed.pdf.

———. 2014b. "Appendix to an Aborted Debate on Anonymity and Attack." *Contra-Info.* http://en.contrainfo.espiv.net/2014/03/26/appendix-to-an-aborted-debate-on-anonymity-and-attack/.

———. 2014c. "Why We Set Your Nights on Fire: Communiques of Greek Nihilist (Conspiracy of the Cells of Fire)." Indymedia.org. https://linksunten.indymedia.org/de/system/files/data/2014/07/8011999085.pdf.

———. 2014d. "Vandal Demonstration May Day 2014." AnokChan. http://anokchan.com/anok/res/1411.html.

———. 2014e. "Notes on an Ongoing Debate on Anonymity." In *Avalanche: Anarchist Correspondence*, Online, Issue 3: 27–29. Avalanche. http://actforfree.nostate.net/wp-content/uploads/2014/11/Avalanche-EN-3.pdf.

———. 2014f. "Insurrectionary Anarchists, Indigenous People, and Pipelines." *Anarchistnews.org.* September 10. http://anarchistnews.org/content/insurrectionary-anarchists-indigenous-people-and-pipelines.

———. 2014g. "Terms and Definitions Which Reflect the Content of This Zine." *Riotous Incognitx.* October.

———. 2014h. "'I Guess I'll Give It a Shot', in Response to 'Anarchist Logistics: Sustaining Resistance Beyond Activism and Insurrection (by Jeff Shantz).'" Comment. *Anarchistnews.org.* http://anarchistnews.org/comment/53648#comment-53648.

———. 2015. "Black December Everywhere." *Contra-Info.* 30 November. https://en-contrainfo.espiv.net/2015/11/30/black-december-everywhere/#more-24799.

———. 2016. *To the Customers: Insurrection and Doublethink*. Berkeley, CA: Pistols Drawn.

Anonymous Queers. 2009. "Queers Read This." Self published. http://zinelibrary.info/files/militantflamboyance_FINALprint.pdf.

Anti-Capitalist Convergence DC. 2001. "Anti-Capitalist Convergence Issues New Call to Action." Urbana-Champaign Independent Media Center Site Archive. http://archive.ucimc.org/127.0.0.1/newswire/display/2126/index.html.

Aragorn! 2009. "Nihilism Anarchy and the 21st Century." Self published (republished by The Anarchist Library). http://theanarchistlibrary.org/library/aragorn-nihilism-anarchy-and-the-21st-century.

Archegonos. 2015. "A Few Words About Total Liberation from an Anti-Social Individualist Nihilist Anarchist Point of View." In *Actualising Collapse #1*, 22–23. UK: Actualising Collapse. http://325.nostate.net/wp-content/uploads/2015/01/Actualising-Collapse1.pdf.

Argirou, Panagiotis. 2016. "Forever Guilty: On the Trial of the 250 Attacks of the CCF/FAI-IRF." 325.nostate.net. http://325.nostate.net/?p=18876.

Ariel, Leona, Jason McQuinn, Lew, Casper, Graeme, Xander, Paul Simon, Tom Nomad, Aragon!, and William Gillis. 2014. *BASTARD Chronicles: Social War Etc. 2014*. Berkeley, CA: Ardent Press. http://sfbay-anarchists.org/wp-content/uploads/2014/08/bastardchronicles1.pdf.

Arsonist Anarchist Attack – "Fire and Consciousness" Cell FAI/IRF. 2015. "Phoenix Project 2015: Attack against Animal Exploitation Company by 'Arsonist Anarchist Attack – Fire and Consciousness Cell – FAI/IRF.'" Translated by Idioma Negro. 325.nostate.net. http://325.nostate.net/?p=15926.

Ashley, Karin, Bill Ayers, Bernardine Dohrn, John Jacobs, Jeff Jones, Gerry Long, Howie Machtinger, Jim Melles, Terry Robbins, Mark Rudd, and Steve Tappis. 1970. "You Don't Need A Weatherman to Know Which Way the Wind Blows." In *Weatherman*, edited by Harold Jacobs, 51–90. San Francisco, CA: Ramparts Press, Inc. (originally in *New Left Notes*).

Associated Press. 2013. "'Hacktivist' Gets Prison in N.Y. Cyberattacks Case." *USA Today/Associated Press*, 15 November. Online edition. www.usatoday.com/story/news/nation/2013/11/15/us-man-gets-prison-in-cyberattacks-case/3582249/.

Aubron, Joelle, Nathalie Menigon, and Jean-Marc Rouillan. 2009. *Resistance Is a Duty!: And Other Essays by Comrades from Action Directe*. Translated by J. Smith. Montréal, QC: Kersplebedeb Publishing.

Austin, J. L. 1975. *How to Do Things with Words*. Edited by J. O. Urmson and Marina Sbisà. 2nd edn. Harvard University Press.

Autonome Forum. n.d. "A Herstory of the Revolutionary Cells and Rote Zora – Armed Resistance in West Germany." Spunk Library. www.spunk.org/texts/groups/anm/sp000268.txt.

Autonomous Cell for Revolutionary Class Struggle – FAI/IRF. 2014. "Formation of New FAI/IRF Cell." 325.nostate.net. http://325.nostate.net/?p=10363.

Avrich, Paul. 1996. *Sacco and Vanzetti*. Princeton, NJ: Princeton University Press.

Ayers, Bill. 2009. *Fugitive Days: Memoirs of an Antiwar Activist*. Boston, MA: Beacon Press.

Bailey, Bill. 1993. *The Kid from Hoboken: An Autobiography of Bill Bailey*. Edited by Lynn Damme. Online: Larkspring Productions/Self published.

Balagoon, Kuwasi. 2003. *Kuwasi Balagoon: A Soldier's Story: Writings by a Revolutionary New Afrikan Anarchist*. 3rd edn. Montréal, QC: Kersplebedeb Publishing.

Bartlett, Jamie. 2014. "As Technology Swamps Our Lives, the Next Unabombers Are Waiting for Their Moment." *UK Telegraph Blog*. 13 May. http://blogs.telegraph.co.uk/technology/jamiebartlett/100013504/as-technology-swamps-our-lives-the-next-unabombers-are-waiting-for-their-moment/.

Bash Back! 2009a. *Bash Back!: An Unofficial Zine (Communiqués and Other Decadent Delights)*. BAMF! Productionz. zinelibrary.info/files/bashback-zine4.pdf.

———. 2009b. *Bash Back!: An Unofficial Zine (Communiqués and Other Decadent Delights)*. BAMF! Productionz. zinelibrary.info/files/bashback-zine4.pdf.

BASTARD. 2014. "Request for Workshops – BASTARD 2014: Social War." Anarchistnews.org. http://anarchistnews.org/content/request-workshops-bastard-2014-social-war.

Baudrillard, Jean. 2001. "The Spirit of Terrorism." *Le Monde*, 2 November. www.egs.edu/faculty/jean-baudrillard/articles/the-spirit-of-terrorism/.

Baumann, Bommi. 2002. *How It All Began: The Personal Account of a West German Urban Guerrilla*. Translated by Helen Ellenbogen. Vancouver, BC: Arsenal Pulp Press.

BBC. 2003a. "Prodi Survives Parcel Bomb Attack." BBC, 28 December. Online edition, sec. Europe. http://news.bbc.co.uk/2/hi/europe/3351697.stm.

———. 2003b. "Letter Bombs Sent to EU Figures." BBC, 29 December. Online edition, sec. Europe. http://news.bbc.co.uk/2/hi/europe/3355521.stm.

———. 2003c. "New Letter Bomb Reaches EU Target." BBC, 30 December. Online edition, sec. Europe. http://news.bbc.co.uk/2/hi/europe/3357063.stm.

———. 2003d. "Bologna Mail Blocked after Bombs." BBC, 31 December. Online edition, sec. Europe. http://news.bbc.co.uk/2/hi/europe/3359281.stm.

———. 2004. "Letter Bomb Explodes at MEP's Office." BBC, 5 January. Online edition, sec. Manchester. http://news.bbc.co.uk/2/hi/uk_news/england/manchester/3370213.stm.

———. 2007. "German 1970s 'Radicals' Surrender." BBC, 4 February. Online edition, sec. Europe. http://news.bbc.co.uk/2/hi/europe/6330213.stm.

———. 2009. "Sudan Convoy Bombing 'Killed 119.'" BBC, 26 May. Online edition, sec. Africa. http://news.bbc.co.uk/2/hi/africa/8067881.stm.

———. 2012. "Satellites Reveal Sudden Ice Melt." BBC, 25 July. Online edition. www.bbc.co.uk/news/world-europe-18978483.

Becker, Michael. 2006. "Rhizomatic resistance: The Zapatistas and the Earth Liberation Front." *Green Theory and Praxis Journal* 2 (2): 22–63.

———. 2014. "Explaining lone wolf target selection in the United States." *Studies in Conflict & Terrorism* 37 (11): 959–978.

Beezley, William H. 2011. *Mexico in World History*. Oxford, UK: Oxford University Press.

Berkman, Alexander. 1929. *The ABC of Anarchism*. London, UK: Freedom Press. https://libcom.org/files/AlexanderBerkman-ABCofAnarchism.pdf.

Berry, David. 2002. *A History of the French Anarchist Movement, 1917–1945*. Contributions to the Study of World History 97. Westport, CT: Greenwood Press.

Bevan, DCI Andy. 2014. "Who Are Bristol's Anarchist Arsonists?" Interview by Paraic O'Brien. News 2 online (UK). www.channel4.com/news/bristol-fire-arson-police-informal-anarchist-fedederation.

Bey, Hakim. 1991. *T.A.Z. the Temporary Autonomous Zone, Ontological Anarchy, Poetic Terrorism*. Brooklyn, NY: Autonomedia.
Biglan, Anthony. 2015. "Where Terrorism Research Goes Wrong." *The New York Times*, 6 March. Online edition, sec. Opinion: Sunday Review, Gray matter. www.nytimes.com/2015/03/08/opinion/sunday/where-terrorism-research-went-wrong.html.
Blakely, Kristin. 2007. "Reflections on the role of emotion in feminist research." *International Journal of Qualitative Methods* 6 (2): 1–7.
Bonanno, Alfredo M. 1977. *Armed Joy [La gioia armata]*. Translated by Jean Weir. London, UK: Elephant Editions. http://theanarchistlibrary.org/library/alfredo-m-bonanno-armed-joy.pdf.
———. 1988. *From Riot to Insurrection: Analysis for an Anarchist Perspective against Post-industrial Capitalism*. Translated by Jean Weir. London, UK: Elephant Editions (republished by The Anarchist Library). http://theanarchistlibrary.org/library/alfredo-m-bonanno-from-riot-to-insurrection-analysis-for-an-anarchist-perspective-against-post.
———. 1998a. *A Critique of Syndicalist Methods*. Translated by Jean Weir. London, UK: Elephant Editions (republished by The Anarchist Library). http://theanarchistlibrary.org/library/alfredo-m-bonanno-a-critique-of-syndicalist-methods.
———. 1998b. *The Insurrectional Project*. Translated by Jean Weir, John Moore, and Leigh Straccross. London, UK: Elephant Editions (republished by The Anarchist Library). http://theanarchistlibrary.org/library/alfredo-m-bonanno-the-insurrectional-project.
———. 2013. "Foreword." In *Anarchists Against the Wall: Direct Action and Solidarity with the Palestinian Popular Struggle*, edited by Uri Gordon and Ohal Grietzer, translated by Jean Weir, 1–4. Anarchist Interventions 5. Edinburgh, UK: AK Press.
Bond, Walter. 2010. "I Am the ALF 'Lone Wolf.'" North American Animal Liberation Front Press Office. https://animalliberationpressoffice.org/NAALPO/2010/12/10/i-am-the-alf-lone-wolf-by-walter-bond/.
———. 2011. *Always Looking Forward*. Los Angeles, CA: NAALPO.
Bookchin, Murray. 1995. *Social Anarchism or Lifestyle Anarchism: An Unbridgeable Chasm*. San Francisco, CA: AK Press.
———. 2001. *The Spanish Anarchists: The Heroic Years 1868–1936*. San Francisco, CA: AK Press.
Booth, Ken. 2008. *Theory of World Security*. Cambridge, UK: Cambridge University Press.
Bourgois, Philippe. 2003. "US Inner-City Apartheid: The Contours of Structural and Interpersonal Violence." In *Violence in War and Peace: An Anthology*, edited by Nancy Scheper-Hughes and Philippe Bourgois, 301–307. Oxford, UK: Blackwell Publishing.
Brantingham, Patricia L., and Paul J. Brantingham. 1993. "Nodes, paths and edges: considerations on the complexity of crime and the physical environment." *Journal of Environmental Psychology* 13 (1): 3–28.
Brum, Pablo. 2014. "Revisiting urban guerrillas: armed propaganda and the insurgency of Uruguay's MLN-Tupamaros, 1969–70." *Studies in Conflict & Terrorism* 37 (5): 387–404.
Buck, Marilyn, David Gilbert, and Laura Whitehorn. 2003. *Enemies of the State*. New York, NY: Resistance in Brooklyn/Kersplebedeb.

Burke, Jason. 2016. "How the Changing Media Is Changing Terrorism." *The Guardian*, 25 February. Online edition. www.theguardian.com/world/2016/feb/25/how-changing-media-changing-terrorism.

Burke, Kenneth. 1972. *Dramatism and Development*. Barre, MA: Clark University Press.

Burton-Rose, Daniel, ed. 2010. *Creating a Movement with Teeth a Documentary History of the George Jackson Brigade*. Oakland, CA: PM Press.

Butler, Judith. 1990. *Gender Trouble: Feminism and the Subversion of Identity*. New York, NY: Routledge.

———. 2004. *Precarious Life: The Power of Mourning and Violence*. New York, NY: Verso.

———. 2015. On Demonstrating Precarity Interview by Arne De Boever. *LA Review of Books*. www.youtube.com/watch?v=3OmCnyXbgwI.

Buttermorth, Alex. 2010. *The World That Never Was: A True Story of Dreamers, Schemers, Anarchists, and Secret Agents*. New York, NY: Pantheon.

Cameron, Deborah, and Ivan Panovic. 2014. *Working with Written Discourse*. Thousand Oaks, CA: SAGE Publications Ltd.

CARI-PGG. 2013. "Communique for Direct Actions in Solidarity with Mario González." Translated by War on Society. contra-info (republished by War on Society). http://waronsociety.noblogs.org/?p=8630.

CARI-PGG, Cell of revolutionary action for the destruction of the State. 2012. "Cell of Revolutionary Action for the Destruction of the State – Autonomous Cells for Immediate Revolution – Praxedis G. Guerrero claim responsibility for sending 2 Explosive Packages to the Greek Embassy." Translated by War on Society. Liberación Total (republished by 325.nostate). 325.nostate.net/?p=5601.

CARI-PGG, FAI. 2011. "The Sole-Baleno Insurgent Cell of the CARI-PGG Claims the Package Bomb sent to the Attorney General." Translated by War on Society. Culmine (republished by War On Society). http://waronsociety.noblogs.org/?p=2010.

CARI-PGG, Gabriella Segata Antolini cell, and FAI/IRF. 2011. "Gabriella Segata Antolini Cell of CARI-PGG Claims Package Bomb to the Archbishop of Mexico." Translated by War on Society. Culmine (republished by War On Society). http://waronsociety.noblogs.org/?p=2051.

Carter, Chelsea J, and Josh Rubin. 2013. "Is Maj. Nidal Hasan's Defense Strategy Martyrdom?" CNN, 19 August. Online edition, sec. Justice. www.cnn.com/2013/08/19/justice/nidal-hasan-court-martial/index.html.

Casper/CrimethInc., and Graeme/IEF. 2014. "What Was the Insurrection?" In *BASTARD Chronicles: Social War Etc. 2014*, 48–55. Berkeley, CA: Ardent Press. http://sfbay-anarchists.org/wp-content/uploads/2014/08/bastardchronicles1.pdf.

CBC News. 2000. "WTO Protests Hit Seattle in the Pocketbook." CBC News Online, 6 January. Online edition, sec. World. www.cbc.ca/1.245428.

CCF. 2011. "We Do Not Forget Any Imprisoned Comrade: CCF 2008." Anarchistinternational.org. http://anarchistinternational.org/wordpress/wp-content/uploads/2011/09/CCF.pdf.

CCF, Dutch Cell. 2011. "Attacks against Rabobank in Utrecht, by Conspiracy of Cells of Fire: Dutch Cell." 325.nostate.net. http://325.nostate.net/?p=1790.

CCF-FAI/IRF. 2014. "Parcel Bomb Sent to the Police Precinct of Itea." Translated by Inter Arma. Inter Arma (republished by 325.nostate.net). http://325.nostate.net/?p=10250.

———. 2015. "Beyond Right and Wrong." 325.nostate.net. http://325.nostate.net/?p=17278.
CCF-FAI/IRF, Consciousness Gangs-FAI/IRF, and Sole-Baleno Cell. 2013. "Responsibility Claim for Explosive Attack on Vehicle of the Koridallos Prisons Director, in the District of Dafni." Translated by contra-info. Athens Indymedia (republished by 325.nostate.net). http://325.nostate.net/?p=8080.
CCF-FAI/IRF Imprisoned Members Cell. 2012. "Lone Wolves Are Not Alone ..." *325*, no. 10 (November): 41–43.
———. 2013. "Let's Become Dangerous ... for the Diffusion of the Black International." Translated by Inter Arma. Informal Days: International Anarchist Symposium, Mexico (republished by 325.nostate). http://325.nostate.net/?p=9490.
———. 2014. "'Fear First Nests in our Souls and then Raises the Walls of its Prisons' – A Communique by CCF about Prisons." Translated by Inter Arma. Inter Arma. https://interarma.info/en/2014/04/12/o-fovos-fwliazei-stis-psyxes-mas-spf/.
CCF-FAI/IRF International sector for spreading heretical arts (occasionally spectacular) of sabotage. 2014. "Chaotic Manuals of Sabotage." 325.nostate.net. http://325.nostate.net/wp-content/uploads/2014/09/pb.pdf.
CCF of the first phase, Theofilos Mavropoulos, and FAI/IRF. 2014. "Do Not Say that we are Few; Just Say that we are Determined." Translated by contra-info. contra-info. http://en.contrainfo.espiv.net/2012/11/29/greece-do-not-say-that-we-are-few-just-say-that-we-are-determined-by-the-r-o-ccf-and-theofilos-mavropoulos/.
CCF: Urban Guerrilla Cell/FAI. 2016. "Urban Guerrilla Cell." 325.nostate.net. http://325.nostate.net/?p=18929.
Channel 4 News. 2013. "Bristol Arson Attack Linked to Anarchist Terror Network." Channel 4 News, 28 August. Online edition. www.channel4.com/news/informal-anarchist-federation-bristol-arson-attack-anarchist.
Churchill, Ward. 2009. "On the Necessity of Armed Struggle: Reflections on the RAF and the Question of Moving Forward." In *The Red Army Faction A Documentary History, Volume 2: Dancing With Imperialism*, by André Moncourt and J Smith, 2:1–13. Montréal, QC; Oakland, CA: Kersplebedeb Pub.; PM Press.
Ciancabilla, Giuseppe. 1890. "Against Organisation." The Anarchist Library. http://theanarchistlibrary.org/library/giuseppe-ciancabilla-against-organisation.pdf.
Class Terror/FAI. 2011. "Attacks against Vehicles of Lord Mayor & Tory Councillor in Bristol." UK Indymedia (republished by 325.nostate.net). http://325.nostate.net/?p=3517.
Coghlan, Andy. 2012. "Violent Anti-Science Anarchists Vow to Strike Again." *New Scientist*, 29 May. www.newscientist.com/article/dn21860-violent-antiscience-anarchists-vow-to-strike-again.html#.VGeOO5RdWcd.
Cohen, Katie, Fredrik Johansson, Lisa Kaati, and Jonas Clausen Mork. 2014. "Detecting linguistic markers for radical violence in social media." *Terrorism and Political Violence* 26 (1): 246–256.
Cohen, Shuki J. 2016. "Mapping the minds of suicide bombers using linguistic methods: The Corpus of Palestinian Suicide Bombers' Farewell Letters (CoPSBFL)." *Studies in Conflict & Terrorism* 39 (7–8): 749–780.
Cole, Robert E. 1990. "Participant Observer Research: An Activist Role." In *Participatory Action Research*, edited by William Foote Whyte, 159–166. New York, NY: SAGE Publications, Inc.

Collins, Patricia Hill. 1991. *Black Feminist Thought: Knowledge, Consciousness, and the Politics of Empowerment*. New York, NY: Routledge.

Combative Anarchy, FAI-IRF. 2015. "Incendiary Attack against the Central Offices of Microsoft by 'Combative Anarchy – FAI/IRF.'" Translated by Inter Arma. Inter Arma (republished by 325.nostate.net). http://325.nostate.net/?p=15815.

Commando Lambros Foundas. 2014. "Responsibility Claim by the Organization Revolutionary Struggle." Translated by contra-info. Athens Indymedia (republished by contra-info). http://en.contrainfo.espiv.net/2014/04/25/greece-revolutionary-struggle-claims-responsibility-for-car-bomb-explosion-in-athens-city-centre/.

Commando Mauricio Morales/FAI-IRF. 2013. "'Commando Mauricio Morales / FAI-IRF' Takes Responsibility for the Sending of a Parcelbomb to Dimitris Horianopoulos, Scumbag Former Commander of the Anti-Terrorist Division." Translated by boubourAs. Act for Freedom Now! (republished by 325.nostate.net). http://325.nostate.net/?p=8334.

Conspiración Ácrata. 2012. "Conspiración Ácrata #18." Conspiración Ácrata. http://325.nostate.net/wp-content/uploads/2012/12/CA18.pdf.

Conspiracy of Black Fire – FAI-FRI. 2014. "Phoenix Project #13." Translated by Act for Freedom Now! Croce Nera Anarchica (republished by Act for Freedom Now!). http://actforfree.nostate.net/?p=16868.

contra-info, and ITS. 2014. "Interview with Individualists Tending toward the Wild." Translated by War on Society. contra-info (republished by War on Society). http://waronsociety.noblogs.org/?p=8802.

Cook, Judith A., and Mary Margaret Fonow. 1986. "Knowledge and women's interests: issues of epistemology and methodology in feminist sociological research." *Sociological Inquiry* 56 (1): 2–29.

———. eds. 1991. *Beyond Methodology: Feminist Scholarship as Lived Research*. Bloomington, IN: Indiana University Press.

Coordinating Committee Black Liberation Army. 2002. *Message to the Black Movement: A Political Statement from the Black Underground (CC-BLA)*. Montréal, QC: Abraham Guillen Press & Arm the Spirit.

Coordinating Committee of the Italian Anarchist Federation. 2003. "La Commissione Di Corrispondenza Della Federazione Anarchica Italiana Italian Anarchist Federation – Press Release." Italian Anarchist Federation. www.federazioneanarchica.org/archivio/20031228cdc.html#eng.

Coronado, Rod. 2011. *Flaming Arrows: Collected Writings of Animal Liberation Front Activist Rod Coronado*. Portland, OR: Warcry Communications.

Corral, Gerardo Herrera. 2011. "Stand up against the anti-technology terrorists." *Nature News* 476 (7361): 373–373. doi:10.1038/476373a.

Cospito, Alfredo. 2014. Interview by CCF – Imprisoned Members Cell with Alfredo Cospito (Greece, Italy) Interview by CCF – Imprisoned Members Cell. Online. Translated by Nihil Admirari. http://325.nostate.net/?p=13394.

———. 2015. "On 'Ethics', 'Sabotage' and 'Terrorism.'" 325.nostate.net. http://325.nostate.net/?p=17959.

Creekmur, Corey K. 2010. "The Sound of the 'War on Terror.'" In *Reframing 9/11: Film, Popular Culture and the "War on Terror,"* edited by Anna Froula, Karen Randell, and Jeff Birkenstein, 83–93. New York, NY: Bloomsbury Academic.

Crenshaw, Kimberlé. 1989. "Demarginalizing the intersection of race and sex: a black feminist critique of antidiscrimination doctrine, feminist theory, and antiracist politics." *University of Chicago Legal Forum* 1989 (1, Article 8): 139–167.

Crenshaw, Martha. 1990. "The Logic of Terrorism: Terrorist Behavior as a Product of Strategic Choice." In *Origins of Terrorism: Psychologies, Ideologies, Theologies, States of Mind*, edited by Walter Reich 7–24. Washington, DC: Woodrow Wilson International Center for Scholars, Cambridge University Press.

———. ed. 1995. *Terrorism in Context*. University Park, PA: Pennsylvania State University Press.

———. 2010. *Explaining Terrorism: Causes, Processes and Consequences*. London, UK: Routledge.

CrimethInc. 2015. "Ferguson and beyond: fighting the police & white supremacy." *Rolling Thunder*, no. 12 (Spring): 20–83.

CrimethInc. Ex-Workers' Collective. 2001. *Days of War, Nights of Love: CrimethInc For Beginners*. CrimethInc. Workers Collective.

———. 2009. "Say you want an insurrection: putting the 'social' in social war." *Rolling Thunder*, no. 8 (Fall): 12–35.

———. 2012. "Terror Incognita." CrimethInc. Ex-Workers' Collective. http://cloudfront.crimethinc.com/pdfs/terror_incognita_reading.pdf.

———. 2013. "The Ex-Worker." Podcast. *No Time to Wait*. Online: CrimethInc. Ex-Workers' Collective. www.crimethinc.com/podcast/9/.

———. 2014a. "Deserting the digital utopia: computers against computing." *Rolling Thunder*, no. 11 (Spring).

———. 2014b. "The Ukrainian Revolution & the Future of Social Movements." CrimethInc. Ex-Workers' Collective. www.crimethinc.com/texts/ux/ukraine.html.

Culp, Andrew. 2009. "Insurrectionary Foucault: Tiqqun, The Coming Insurrection, and Beyond." Conference paper given at "Rethinking Marxism", University of Massachusetts, Amherst: Academia.edu. www.academia.edu/371340/Insurrectionary_Foucault_Tiqqun_The_Coming_Insurrection_and_Beyond.

Curious George Brigade. 2009. "Insurrectional Mutual Aid." Curious George Brigade (republished by The Anarchist Library). http://theanarchistlibrary.org/library/curious-george-brigade-insurrectionary-mutual-aid.

Curry, Marshall. 2011. *If A Tree Falls: A Story of the Earth Liberation Front*. DVD. Oscilloscope Laboratories.

Dalgaard-Nielsen, Anja. 2008. "Studying Violent Radicalization in Europe I: The Potential Contribution of Social Movement Theory." *Danish Institute for International Studies Working Papers*, DIIS Working Papers, 2008 (2). http://mercury.ethz.ch/serviceengine/Files/ISN/48325/ipublicationdocument_singledocument/bd6fe76b-d1ab-49e2-ab2b-8c27ee37c40b/en/WP082.pdf.

Danaher, Geoff. 2002. *Understanding Foucault*. New Delhi, IN: Motilal Banarsidass Publ.

dandee lyon of bb!dc. 2008. "Bash Back! DC Confronts HRC Assimilationism." *DC Indymedia*, October 5. http://dc.indymedia.org/newswire/display/144360/index.php.

Daniel, Christine. 1998. "Widespread Protests by Unemployed People: Towards a New Form of Social Movement?" Eironline. www.eurofound.europa.eu/eiro/1998/01/feature/fr9801189f.htm.

Dark Nights editors. 2014. "Dark Nights #39: 'Long Live the New Anarchy!'" 325. nostate.net. http://325.nostate.net/wp-content/uploads/2014/01/dark-nights-39.pdf.

David. 2002. "Get Busy Living, Or Get Busy Dying." In *The Black Bloc Papers*, edited by David and X, 12–42. Baltimore, MD: Black Clover Press.

David, X, J. M., and Natasha. 2002. "A Communique On Tactics And Organization To The Black Bloc, From Within The Black Bloc (Some Reflections, Proposals and Suggestions, December 2000)." In *The Black Bloc Papers*, edited by David and X, 229–50. Baltimore, MD: Black Clover Press.

Debord, Guy. 1967. *Society of the Spectacle*. Detroit, MI: Black & Red.

———. 1998. *Comments on the Society of the Spectacle*. Brooklyn, NY: Verso.

Debray, Régis. 1967. *Revolution in the Revolution? Armed Struggle and Political Struggle in Latin America*. Translated by Bobbye Ortiz. English translation. Westport, CT: Greenwood Press.

Delaney, Sarah. 2012. "Fearing Anarchist Attacks, Italy Tightens Security." *LA Times Blogs*. 17 May. http://latimesblogs.latimes.com/world_now/2012/05/fearing-anarchist-attacks-italy-tightens-security.html.

Deleuze, Gilles, and Félix Guattari. 1983. *Anti-Oedipus: Capitalism and Schizophrenia*. Translated by Robert Hurley, Mark Seem, and Helen Lane. Minneapolis, MN: University of Minnesota Press.

———. 1987. *A Thousand Plateaus: Capitalism and Schizophrenia*. Translated by Brian Massumi. Minneapolis, MN: University of Minnesota Press.

della Porta, Donatella. 1995. *Social Movements, Political Violence, and the State: A Comparative Analysis of Italy and Germany*. Cambridge, UK: Cambridge University Press.

———. 2013. *Clandestine Political Violence*. Cambridge Studies in Contentious Politics. Cambridge, UK: Cambridge University Press.

della Porta, Donatella, and Mario Diani. 2006. *Social Movements: An Introduction*. Malden, MA: Blackwell Pub.

della Porta, Donatella, and Olivier Fillieule. 2004. "Policing Social Protest." In *The Blackwell Companion to Social Movements*, edited by David A. Snow, Sarah Anne Soule, and Hanspeter Kriesi, 217–241. Malden, MA: Blackwell Pub.

della Porta, Donatella, and Gianni Piazza. 2008. *Voices of the Valley, Voices of the Straits: How Protest Creates Community*. New York, NY: Berghahn Books.

Derrida, Jacques. 2006. *The Politics of Friendship*. Translated by George Collins. Fourth Impression edition. Radical Thinkers. New York, NY: Verso.

Deviant Behaviours for the Spread of Revolutionary Terrorism – IRF. 2012. "Full Communiqué for the High-profile Vehicle-bomb against Microsoft by Deviant Behaviours for the Spread of Revolutionary Terrorism – International Revolutionary Front (Greece)." 325.nostate.net. http://325.nostate.net/?p=6793.

Diani, Mario. 1992. "The concept of social movement." *The Sociological Review* 40 (1): 1–25.

van Dijk, Teun A. 2011. "Discourse and Ideology." In *Discourse Studies: A Multidisciplinary Introduction*, edited by Teun A. van Dijk, 2nd edn, 379–407. Thousand Oaks, CA: SAGE Publications Ltd.

Dohrn, Bernardine, Bill Ayers, and Jeff Jones, eds. 2006. *Sing a Battle Song: The Revolutionary Poetry, Statements, and Communiques of the Weather Underground 1970–1974*. New York, NY: Seven Stories Press.

Dolata, Ulrich, and Jan-Felix Schrape. 2016. "Masses, crowds, communities, movements: collective action in the internet age." *Social Movement Studies* 15 (1): 1–18.

Doucet, Andrea, and Natasha S. Mauthner. 2006. "Feminist Methodologies and Epistemologies." In *Handbook of 21st Century Sociology*, edited by Clifton D. Bryant and Dennis L. Peck, 26–32. Thousand Oaks, CA: SAGE Publications.

Doucet, Marc G., and Miguel de Larrinaga. 2012. "Human Security and the Securing of Human Life: Tracing Global Sovereign and Biopolitical Rule." In *Critical Perspectives on Human Security: Rethinking Emancipation and Power in International Relations*, edited by David Chandler and Nik Hynek, 129–143. New York, NY: Routledge.

Drissel, David. 2014. "Reframing the Taliban insurgency in Afghanistan: new communication and mobilization strategies for the Twitter generation." *Behavioral Sciences of Terrorism and Political Aggression* 7 (2): 1–32.

Duncombe, Stephen. 1997. *Notes from Underground: Zines and the Politics of Alternative Culture.* Brooklyn, NY: Verso.

Dupuis-Déri, Francis. 2014. *Who's Afraid of the Black Blocs?: Anarchy in Action around the World.* Translated by Lazer Lederhendler. Oakland, CA: PM Press.

Eanelli, Tegan. 2011. "Bash Back! Is Dead; Bash Back Forever!: Concluding Notes." The Anarchist Library. http://theanarchistlibrary.org/library/tegan-eanelli-bash-back-is-dead-bash-back-forever.

Eanelli, Tegan, and Fray Baroque, eds. 2012. *Queer Ultraviolence: A Bash Back! Anthology.* San Francisco, CA: Ardent Press.

Eat. 2014. "Some Thoughts on FAI/IRF." *325*, June.

Economidou, Olga, Michalis Nikolopoulos, Giorgos Nikolopoulos, Christos Tsakalos, Gerasimos Tsakalos, Panayiotis Argyrou, Damiano Bolano, Giorgos Polydoras, and Haris Hatzimichelakis. 2012. "Imprisoned Fire Cells Conspiracy Members: Political Statement Regarding Second Halandri Case Trial." Athens Indymedia (republished by 325.nostate). http://325.nostate.net/?p=3978.

Economidou, Olga, Giorgos Polydoras, Christos Tsakalos, and Gerasimos Tsakalos. 2016. "Our Trials Will Turn into a Conviction of the State." Translated by A-politko. 325.nostate.net. http://325.nostate.net/?p=19655.

Edwards, Jason. 2012. "Foucault and the Continuation of War." In *The Metamorphosis of War*, edited by Avery Plaw, 21–40. New York, NY: Rodopi.

Ekathimerini. 2013. "Police Suspect Urban Guerrillas behind Murder of Golden Dawn Members." *Kathimerini/International New York Times*, 2 November. English online edition. www.ekathimerini.com/4dcgi/_w_articles_wsite1_1_02/11/2013_525979.

Ekonomidou, Olga, Giorgos Polidoros, Gerasimos Tsakalos, Panagiotis Argyrou, Christos Tsakalos, Damiano Bolano, Michalis Nikolopoulos, Giorgos Nikolopoulos, Haris Hadjimihelakis, and Theofilos Mavropoulos. 2012. "CCF – Bullets of Words for the Bullets of the FAI/FRI." Translated by contra-info. Athens Indymedia (republished by contra-info). http://en.contrainfo.espiv.net/2012/05/14/greece-ccf-bullets-of-words-for-the-bullets-of-faifri/.

Engels, Friedrich. 1874. "The Program of the Blanquist Fugitives from the Paris Commune." Translated by Ernest Untermann. *Der Volksstaat (trans. for International Socialist Review, Vol. IX, No. 2, August 1908)* 73 (June). www.marxists.org/archive/marx/works/1874/06/26.htm.

Engels, Friedrich, and Karl Marx. 1848. "Manifesto of the Communist Party." republished by Marxist Internet Archives. www.marxists.org/archive/marx/works/1848/communist-manifesto/index.htm.

Esenwein, George Richard. 1989. *Anarchist Ideology and the Working-Class Movement in Spain, 1868–1898*. Oakland, CA: University of California Press.

Ezekiel, Raphael S. 2002. "An ethnographer looks at neo-Nazi and Klan groups the racist mind revisited." *American Behavioral Scientist* 46 (1): 51–71.

FAI. 2003. "Open Letter to the Anarchist and Anti-Authoritarian Movement." In *Escalation: Some Texts Concerning the Informal Anarchist Federation (FAI) and the Insurrectionist Project*, 3–4. Bologna, IT: 325.nostate.net. http://325.nostate.net/library/escalation1.pdf.

FAI-Conscience & Fury. 2014. "Incendiary Attack at Yate Magistrates Court on 22nd May in Memory of Maurico Morales by FAI – Conscience & Fury (UK)." 325.nostate.net. http://325.nostate.net/?p=10367.

FAI/ELF – Rogue Fire Brigade. 2014. "FAI/ELF Claim Four Vehicle Fires in Bristol." 325.nostate.net. http://325.nostate.net/?p=10668.

FAI-IRF Artisans Cooperative of Fire and Similar (occasionally spectacular), and FAI-IRF 20th July Brigade. 2011. "Do Not Say That We Are Few – Statement from the Italian FAI." 325.nostate.net. http://325.nostate.net/?p=3015.

FAI/IRF Damiano Bolano Cell. 2013. "'Damiano Bolano' FAI/FRI Cell Claim the Parcel Bombs Sent to the Daily La Stampa of Turin and the Private Investigation Agency Europol of Brescia." Translated by 325.nostate.net. 325.nostate.net. http://325.nostate.net/?p=7697.

FAI/IRF Nicola and Alfredo Cell. 2013. "Greece: 'Green Nemesis' Project, Sabotage against Coca-Cola and Nestle Products by FAI/IRF (24/12/2013)." *Inter Arma*. December 24. https://interarma.info/en/2013/12/25/sabotage_coca_cola_nestle/

Fairclough, Norman. 1993. *Discourse and Social Change*. Cambridge, UK: Polity Press.

Falciola, Luca. 2015. "A bloodless guerrilla warfare: why U.S. white leftists renounced violence against people during the 1970s." *Terrorism and Political Violence* 27 (2): 1–22.

Faraj, Gaidi. 2007. *Unearthing the Underground: A Study of Radical Activism in the Black Panther Party and the Black Liberation Army*. Online: ProQuest.

Farmer, Paul. 1996. "On suffering and structural violence: a view from below." *Daedalus* 125 (1): 261–283.

———. 2004. "An anthropology of structural violence." *Current Anthropology* 45 (3): 305–325.

Federal Bureau of Investigation Philadelphia Division. n.d. "1919 Bombings." *FBI*. www.fbi.gov/philadelphia/about-us/history/famous-cases/famous-cases-1919-bombings.

Feigenbaum, Anna, Fabian Frenzel, and Patrick McCurdy. 2013. *Protest Camps*. London, UK: Zed Books.

Finnegan, William. 2003. "Affinity Groups and the Movements Against Corporate Globalization." In *The Social Movements Reader: Cases and Concepts*, edited by Jeff Goodwin and James M. Jasper, 2010–2218. Malden, MA: Blackwell Publishing.

Foucault, Michel. 1971. "Nietzsche, Genealogy, History." In *Language, Counter-Memory, Practice: Selected Essays and Interviews*, edited by Donald F. Bouchard, translated by Donald F. Bouchard and Sherry Simon, 139–64. Ithaca, NY: Cornell University Press.

———. 1977. *Discipline and Punish*. New York, NY: Vintage Books.

———. 1980. *Power/Knowledge: Selected Interviews and Other Writings 1972–1977 by Michel Foucault*. Edited by Colin Gordon. Translated by Colin Gor, Leo Marshall, John Mempham, and Kate Soper. New York, NY: Pantheon Books.

———. 1990. *The History of Sexuality, Vol. 1: An Introduction*. New York, NY: Vintage.

———. 1998. "The Ethics of the Concern of the Self as a Practice of Freedom." In *Ethics: Subjectivity and Truth – The Essential Works of Foucault 1954–1984*, edited by Paul Rabinow, 1:253–80. New York, NY: The New Press.

———. 2003. *"Society Must Be Defended": Lectures at the Collège de France, 1975–1976*. Translated by David Macey. Reprint. New York, NY: Picador.

———. 2010. *The Birth of Biopolitics: Lectures at the Collège de France, 1978–1979*. New York, NY: Palgrave Macmillan.

Gabay, Clive. 2010. "What Did the Anarchists Ever Do For Us? Anarchy, Decentralization, and Autonomy at the Seattle Anti-WTO Protests." In *New Perspectives on Anarchism*, edited by Nathan J. Jun and Shane Wahl, 121–132. Lanham, MD: Lexington Books.

Gai, Nicola. 2013. "The Urgency of the Attack." Translated by B.Pd. Terra Selvaggie (republished by 325.nostate). http://325.nostate.net/?p=8762.

Galleani, Luigi. 1925. "The End of Anarchism?" Translated by Max Sartin and Robert D'Attillo. Cienfuego Press (republished by The Anarchist Library). http://theanarchistlibrary.org/library/luigi-galleani-the-end-of-anarchism.

Galtung, Johan. 1969. "Violence, peace, and peace research." *Journal of Peace Research* 6 (3): 167–91.

———. 1985. "Twenty-five years of peace research: ten challenges and some responses." *Journal of Peace Research* 22 (2): 141–158. doi:10.2307/424240.

———. 1990. "Cultural violence." *Journal of Peace Research* 27 (3): 291–305.

———. 2000. "Conflict Transformation by Peaceful Means (the Transcend Method): Participants' Manual/Trainers' Manual." United Nations Disaster Management Training Programme. www.transcend.org/pctrcluj2004/TRANSCEND_manual.pdf.

Galtung, Johan, and Tord Höivik. 1971. "Structural and direct violence: a note on operationalization." *Journal of Peace Research* 8 (1): 73–76.

Garner, Roberta. 1996. *Contemporary Movements and Ideologies*. New York, NY: McGraw-Hill.

g.c. n.d. "Beyond the Structure of Synthesis." In *Articles from Insurrection*, The Anarchist Library, 8–10. Online: The Anarchist Library. http://theanarchistlibrary.org/library/various-authors-articles-from-insurrection.pdf.

Gelderloos, Peter. 2007. *How Nonviolence Protects the State*. Cambridge, MA: South End Press.

———. 2013. *The Failure of Nonviolence: From the Arab Spring to Occupy*. St. Louis, MO: Left Bank Books.

Giap, Vo Nguyen. 1965. *The South Vietnam People Will Win*. Honolulu, HI: University Press of the Pacific.

Gilbert, David. 2011. *Love and Struggle: My Life in SDS, the Weather Underground, and Beyond*. Oakland, CA: PM Press.

Gillespie, Richard. 1986. "The Urban Guerrilla in Latin America." In *Terrorism, Ideology, and Revolution*, edited by Noel O'Sullivan, 150–77. Brighton, UK: Wheatsheaf Books Ltd.

Gillis, Justin, and Kenneth Chang. 2014. "Scientists Warn of Rising Oceans From Polar Melt." *The New York Times*, 12 May. Online edition, sec. Science. www.nytimes.com/2014/05/13/science/earth/collapse-of-parts-of-west-antarctica-ice-sheet-has-begun-scientists-say.html.

Giorgio. 2003. *Memoirs of an Italian Terrorist*. Translated by Antony Shugaar. Paperback, 2nd edn. New York, NY: Basic Books.

G-MAC, and People Within The ARA. 2002. "A Communique On Tactics And Organization To The Black Bloc (Second Amended Edition, July 2001)." In *The Black Bloc Papers*, edited by David and X, 198–225. Baltimore, MD: Black Clover Press.

Goffman, Erving. 1959. *The Presentation of Self in Everyday Life*. New York, NY: Anchor.

Gordon, Uri. 2008. *Anarchy Alive! Anti-Authoritarian Politics from Practice to Theory*. Ann Arbor, MI: Pluto Press.

Graeber, David. 2009. *Direct Action: An Ethnography*. Oakland, CA: AK Press.

Gramsci, Antonio. 1971a. "History of the Subaltern Classes: Methodological Criteria." In *Selections from the Prison Notebooks of Antonio Gramsci*, edited by Quentin Hoare and Geoffrey Nowell Smith, 202–207. London, UK: Lawrence & Wishart/ElecBook.

———. 1971b. *Selections from the Prison Notebooks*. New York, NY: International Publishers Co.

Grubbs, Jennifer, and Michael Loadenthal. 2014. "The Politics of Planning: Conference Organizing as an Act of Resistance." In *Educating for Action: Strategies to Ignite Social Justice*, edited by Jason Del Gandio and Anthony J. Nocella, 137–53. Gabriola Island, BC: New Society Publishers.

Guevara, Che. 1961. *Guerrilla Warfare*. New York, NY: Monthly Review Press.

———. 1997. *Che Guevara Reader*. Edited by David Deutschmann. New York, NY: Ocean Press.

Halperin, David M. 1997. *Saint Foucault: Towards a Gay Hagiography*. New York, NY: Oxford University Press, USA.

Hammami, Omar. 2012. *The Story of an American Jihaadi, Part One*. Somalia: Self published. www.scribd.com/doc/93732117/The-Story-of-an-American-Jihaadi.

Hanrahan, Jake. 2013. "Meet the Nihilist-Anarchist Network Bringing Chaos to a Town Near You." *VICE*. February 13. www.vice.com/read/the-fai-are-the-worlds-true-anarchists.

Hansen, Ann. 2002. *Direct Action: Memoirs of an Urban Guerrilla*. Toronto, ON: AK Press.

Hansen, Ann, and Julie Belmas. 2009. "This Is Not A Love Story: Armed Struggle Against The Institutions of Patriarchy." *Disorderly Conduct #5* (republished by The Anarchist Library). http://theanarchistlibrary.org/library/ann-hansen-julie-belmas-this-is-not-a-love-story-armed-struggle-against-the-institutions-of-pat.

Hanssen, Beatrice. 2000. *Critique of Violence: Between Poststructuralism and Critical Theory*. London, UK: Routledge.

Harding, Sandra, ed. 1988. *Feminism and Methodology: Social Science Issues*. Readers Notes. Bloomington, IN: Indiana University Press.

Hardt, Michael, and Antonio Negri. 2001. *Empire*. Cambridge, MA: Harvard University Press.
———. 2005. *Multitude: War and Democracy in the Age of Empire*. New York, NY: Penguin Books.
Harel, Amos, Yossi Melman, and Barak Ravid. 2009. "IAF Airstrike in Sudan Hit Convoy of Weapons Destined for Gaza." *Haaretz*, 26 March. Online edition, sec. Print edition/news. www.haaretz.com/print-edition/news/iaf-airstrike-in-sudan-hit-convoy-of-weapons-destined-for-gaza-1.272952.
Harrison, Sarah. 2013. "Decoding Manifestos and Other Political Texts." In *Political Science Research Methods in Action*, edited by Michael Bruter and Martin Lodge, 47–63. Hampshire, UK: Palgrave Macmillan.
Hart, John Mason. 1987. *Revolutionary Mexico: The Coming and Process of the Mexican Revolution*. Oakland, CA: University of California Press.
Heath, Robert L., and H. Dan O'Hair. 2008. "Terrorism from the Eyes of the Beholder." In *Terrorism: Communication and Rhetorical Perspectives*, edited by H. Dan O'Hair, Robert L. Heath, Kevin J. Ayotte, and Gerald R. Ledlow, 17–41. Cresskill, NJ: Hampton Press.
Hemmingsen, Ann-Sophie. 2014. "Viewing Jihadism as a counterculture: potential and limitations." *Behavioral Sciences of Terrorism and Political Aggression* 7 (1): 3–17.
Hensley, Nicole. 2014. "Portland Anarchist Calls 911 on Heroin Overdose, Tells Dispatcher to Not Send Police." *New York Daily News*, 17 May. Online edition. www.nydailynews.com/news/national/portland-anarchist-bans-cops-assisting-911-call-heroin-overdose-article-1.1796455.
Hersh, Seymour M. 2016. *The Killing of Osama Bin Laden*. London; New York, NY: Verso.
Hesse-Biber, Sharlene Nagy. 2011. "Feminist Research: Exploring, Interrogating, and Transforming the Interconnections of Epistemology, Methodology, and Method." In *Handbook of Feminist Research: Theory and Praxis*. 2nd edn, 2–26. Thousand Oaks, CA: SAGE Publications, Inc.
Hobsbawm, Eric. 1971. *Primitive Rebels: Studies in Archaic Forms of Social Movement in the 19th and 20th Centuries*. 3rd edn. Manchester, UK: University of Manchester.
Hodges, Adam. 2011. *The "War on Terror" Narrative: Discourse and Intertextuality in the Construction and Contestation of Sociopolitical Reality*. New York, NY: Oxford University Press, USA.
Hoffman, Aaron M. 2010. "Voice and silence: why groups take credit for acts of terror." *Journal of Peace Research* 47 (5): 615–626.
Hoffman, Bruce. 2014. "A first draft of the history of america's ongoing wars on terrorism." *Studies in Conflict & Terrorism* 38 (1): 1–9.
Hoffman, Mark. 1987. "Critical theory and the inter-paradigm debate." *Millennium – Journal of International Studies* 16 (2): 231–250.
hooks, bell. 2000. *Feminist Theory: From Margin to Center*. 2nd edn. Boston, MA: South End Press.
Hooper, John. 2012. "Italian Police Arrest Leftwing Terror Suspects." *The Guardian*, 13 June. Online edition, sec. World news. www.theguardian.com/world/2012/jun/13/italian-police-arrest-terror-suspects.

Hornby, Catherine, and Sara Rossi. 2013. "Anarchists Claim Parcel Bombs Sent to Italy Newspaper and Agency." *Reuters*, 12 April. Online edition, sec. World News. http://mobile.reuters.com/article/worldNews/idUSBRE93B0M120130412?feedType=RSS&feedName=worldNews.

Hsiang, Solomon M., Marshall Burke, and Edward Miguel. 2013. "Quantifying the influence of climate on human conflict." *Science* 341 (6151): 1235367.

Hudson, John. 2014. "FBI Drops Law Enforcement as 'Primary' Mission." *Foreign Policy*. 5 January. https://foreignpolicy.com/2014/01/05/fbi-drops-law-enforcement-as-primary-mission/.

IEF. 2009. *Politics Is Not a Banana: What Are You Doing after the Orgy or the Insurrection or Whatever?* The Institute for Experimental Freedom.

———. 2013. *Between Predicates, War: Theses On Contemporary Struggle*. EPub. The Institute for Experimental Freedom.

Ilya Romanov Cell. 2013. "Phoenix Project #8 – Action with Incendiary/explosive Device against a Board of Elections Office and in Solidarity with Mónica Caballero and Francisco Solar." 325.nostate.net. http://325.nostate.net/?p=9256#more-9256.

Immergut, Karin J., Kirk A. Engdall, Stephen F. Peifer, and John C. Ray. 2007. "Government's Sentencing Memorandum in the United States District Court for the District of Oregon [case Numbers CR 06–60069-AA, CR 06–60070-AA, CR 06–60071-AA, CR 06–60078-AA, CR 06–60079-AA, CR 06–60080-AA, CR 06–60120-AA, 06–60122-AA, 06–60123-AA, 06–60124-AA, 06–60125-AA, 06–60126-AA]." United States District Court for the District of Oregon.

Imrie, Doug. 1994. "The 'Illegalists.'" *Anarchy: A Journal of Desire Armed* (Fall-Winter, 1994–1995). http://recollectionbooks.com/siml/library/illegalistsDougImrie.htm.

Ingersoll, Geoffrey. 2013. "Mexican Anarchists Are Blowing Up Scientists And The Government Is Freaked." *Business Insider*, 8 March. www.businessinsider.com/anarchists-bomb-scientists-like-ted-2013-3.

Ingram, Haroro J. 2015. "An analysis of the Taliban in Khurasan's Azan (Issues 1–5)." *Studies in Conflict & Terrorism* TBD (TBD): 1–20. doi:10.1080/1057610X.2015.1022093.

International Conspiracy for Revenge/FAI. 2013a. "Explosion Destroys the Personal Car of a Prison Guard – ICR / FAI Take Responsibility as Part of Phoenix Project." Athens Indymedia (republished by 325.nostate.net). http://325.nostate.net/?p=8149.

———. 2013b. "International Conspiracy for Revenge / FAI Take Responsibility for Blowing up the Vehicle of Argiris Gelbouras, Navplio Prison Screw." Translated by boubourAs. Act for Freedom Now! (republished by 325.nostate.net). http://325.nostate.net/?p=8174.

International Conspiracy for Revenge/FAI-IRF. 2014. "Phoenix Project #12 : ICR – FAI/IRF Take Responsibility for Arson Barrage in Solidarity with Adriano Antonacci, Gianluca Iocavacci, Other Worldwide Anarchist Prisoners and the Combative Memory of Sebastian O. Seguel." 325.nostate.net. http://325.nostate.net/?p=10306.

International Conspiracy for Revenge/FAI-IRF, and Anger Unit. 2013. "Anger Unit/ICR-FAI-IRF Burn down the Third Floor of Former Sheraton Hotel, 'The Media Hotel and Tower.'" 325.nostate.net. http://325.nostate.net/?p=8227.

International FAI. 2011. "'Rain & Fire' – Statement from a UK FAI Sector." 325. nostate.net. 325.nostate.net/?p=3032.
IRF/ELF – Moscow. 2014. "News 11 January 2014." From Russia With Love. Blog. (republished by *Bite Back Magazine*). www.directaction.info/news_jan11_14.htm.
ITS. 2011. "Fourth Communique from Individualists Tending toward the Wild." War on Society. http://waronsociety.noblogs.org/?p=2913.
———. 2012. "Sixth Communique from Individualists Tending toward the Wild." War on Society. http://waronsociety.noblogs.org/?p=3162.
———. 2013. "Seventh Communique from Individualists Tending toward the Wild." Translated by War on Society. 325.nostate.net. http://325.nostate.net/?p=7218.
———. 2014. "Eighth Communique of Individualists Tending Toward the Wild." Dark Nights #40 (republished by War on Society). http://waronsociety.noblogs.org/?p=8913.
ITS–Argentina: Wild Constellations. 2016. "Fourth Communique of the Individualists Tending Toward the Wild-2016." MALDICIÓN ECO-EXTREMISTA. https://maldicionecoextremista.noblogs.org/post/2016/02/26/argentina-fourth-communique-of-the-individualists-tending-toward-the-wild-2016/.
ITS–Mexico, ITS–Chile, and ITS–Argentina. 2016. "Fifth Communiqué of the Individualists Tending Toward the Wild – 2016." Translated by Act for Freedom Now! MALDICIÓN ECO-EXTREMISTA. http://actforfree.nostate.net/?p=22942.
ITS–Uncivilized Southerners. 2016. "Incendiary Attack on a Bus by Individualists Tending toward the Wild." War on Society. https://waronsociety.noblogs.org/?p=9665.
Jablonski, Steve. 2014. "Grand Jury Resister Steve Returns Home!" Anarchistnews.org. http://anarchistnews.org/content/grand-jury-resister-steve-returns-home.
Jackson, Richard. 2009. "Knowledge, Power and Politics in the Study of Political Terrorism." In *Critical Terrorism Studies: A New Research Agenda*, edited by Richard Jackson, Marie Breen Smyth, and Jeroen Gunning, 66–83. London, UK: Routledge.
Jackson, Richard, Marie Breen Smyth, Jeroen Gunning, and Lee Jarvis. 2011. *Terrorism: A Critical Introduction*. New York, NY: Palgrave Macmillan.
Jacobs, Tom. 2014. "Study: Half of Americans Believe at Least 1 Conspiracy Theory." *Pacific Standard Magazine*. 9 April. www.psmag.com/navigation/books-and-culture/half-americans-believe-least-one-conspiracy-theory-78613/.
Jenkins, Brian M. 1975. "International Terrorism: A New Model of Conflict." In *International Terrorism and World Security*, edited by David Carlton and Carlo Schaerf, 15–16. London, UK: Croom Helm/RAND Corporation. www.rand.org/content/dam/rand/pubs/papers/2008/P5261.pdf.
Jensen, Derrick, Aric McBay, and Lierre Keith. 2011. *Deep Green Resistance: Strategy to Save the Planet*. New York, NY: Seven Stories Press.
Jensen, Richard Bach. 2013. "The pre-1914 anarchist 'lone wolf' terrorist and governmental responses." *Terrorism and Political Violence* 26 (1): 86–94.
Jeppesen, Sandra. 2010. "Creating Guerrilla Texts in Rhizomatic Value-Practices on the Sliding Scale of Autonomy: Toward an Anti-Authoritarian Cultural Logic." In *New Perspectives on Anarchism*, edited by Nathan J. Jun and Shane Wahl, 473–496. Lanham, MD: Lexington Books.

———. 2011. "Things to Do with Post-Structuralism in a Life of Anarchy: Relocating the Outpost of Post-Anarchism." In *Post-Anarchism: A Reader*, edited by Duane Rousselle and Süreyya Evren, 151–159. New York, NY: Pluto Press.

Joll, James. 1964. *The Anarchists*. London, UK: Eyre & Spottiswoode.

Joosse, Paul. 2007. "Leaderless resistance and ideological inclusion: the case of the Earth Liberation Front." *Terrorism and Political Violence* 19 (3): 351–368.

José, Pedro, and Mariblanca Corrales. 2015. *Tiqqun and the Matter of Bloom in Contemporary Political Philosophy*. Berkeley, CA: Repartee/Little Black Cart.

Juergensmeyer, Mark. 2003. *Terror in the Mind of God: The Global Rise of Religious Violence*. Berkeley, CA: University of California Press.

———. 2014. "Why Extreme Terror Works." *Mark Juergensmeyer*. 16 September. http://juergensmeyer.org/why-extreme-terrorism-works/.

Jun, Nathan J. 2013. "Rethinking the Anarchist Canon: History, Philosophy, and Interpretation." *Anarchist Developments in Cultural Studies* 3 (1: Blasting the Canon): 82–116.

Juris, Jeffrey Scott. 2004. "Digital Age Activism: Anti-Corporate Globalization and the Cultural Politics of Transnational Networking." PhD thesis, Berkeley, CA: University of California, Berkeley.

Kaczynski, Theodore J. 2010a. "Hit Where It Hurts." In *Technological Slavery: The Collected Writings of Theodore J. Kaczynski, A.k.a. "The Unabomber,"* edited by David Skrbina, 248–253. Los Angeles, CA: Feral House.

———. 2010b. "Industrial Society and Its Future." In *Technological Slavery: The Collected Writings of Theodore J. Kaczynski, A.k.a. "The Unabomber,"* 38–120. Port Townsend, WA: Feral House.

———. 2010c. "Letters to David Skrbina." In *Technological Slavery: The Collected Writings of Theodore J. Kaczynski, A.k.a. "The Unabomber,"* 256–348. Port Townsend, WA: Feral House.

———. 2010d. *Technological Slavery: The Collected Writings of Theodore J. Kaczynski, A.k.a. "The Unabomber."* Port Townsend, WA: Feral House.

Kaldor, Mary. 2001. *New & Old Wars: Organized Violence in a Global Era*. 2nd edn. Stanford, CA: Stanford University Press.

Karpantschof, Renéy. 2014. "Violence that matters! Radicalization and de-radicalization of leftist, urban movements – Denmark 1981–2011." *Behavioral Sciences of Terrorism and Political Aggression* 7 (1): 35–52.

Kassimeris, George. 2013. "Explaining the Persistence of Political Terrorism in Greece." *Political Studies Association UK: Political Insight*. 25 October. www.psa.ac.uk/insight-plus/blog/explaining-persistence-political-terrorism-greece.

———. 2016. "Greece's terrorism problem: a reassessment." *Studies in Conflict & Terrorism* 39 (5): 1–9.

Kathimerini. 2014. "Police Clear Suspects of Attack on German Ambassador's Home but Not of Terror Plot." *Kathimerini/International New York Times*, 14 October. English online edition. www.ekathimerini.com/4dcgi/_w_articles_wsite1_1_14/10/2014_543712.

Khaled, Leila. 1973. *My People Shall Live: The Autobiography of a Revolutionary*. London, UK: Hodder & Stoughton Ltd.

Khasnabish, Alex. 2008. *Zapatismo Beyond Borders: New Imaginations of Political Possibility*. Toronto, ON: University of Toronto Press, Scholarly Publishing Division.

King Jr., Dr. Martin Luther. 1963. "Letter from Birmingham Jail." *The Atlantic Monthly* vol 212, no. 2.
Kirby, Sandra Louise, and McKenna Kate. 1989. *Experience Research Social Change: Methods from the Margins*. Toronto, ON: Garamond Press.
Klausen, Jytte. 2014. "Tweeting the Jihad: social media networks of Western foreign fighters in Syria and Iraq." *Studies in Conflict & Terrorism* 38 (1): 1–22.
Klein, Naomi. 2000. *No Logo*. New York, NY: Macmillan.
Koehler, Daniel. 2014. "Contrast societies. Radical social movements and their relationships with their target societies. A theoretical model." *Behavioral Sciences of Terrorism and Political Aggression* 7 (1): 1–17.
K, Sasha. 2001. "Some Notes on Insurrectionary Anarchism." *Killing King Abacus*. Zine. https://theanarchistlibrary.org/library/sasha-k-some-notes-on-insurrectionary-anarchism.
Laden, Osama bin. 2005. *Messages to the World: The Statements of Osama bin Laden*. Edited by Bruce Lawrence. Translated by James Howarth. London, UK: Verso.
Ladicola, Peter, and Anson D. Shupe. 1998. *Violence, Inequality, and Human Freedom*. Dix Hills, NY: General Hall, Inc.
Landstreicher, Wolfi. 2006. "Play Fiercely! Our Lives Are at Stake!: Anarchist Practice as a Game of Subversion." *Green Anarchy*. Magazine.
Laqueur, Walter, ed. 2004. *Voices of Terror: Manifestos, Writings and Manuals of Al Qaeda, Hamas, and Other Terrorists from around the World and Throughout the Ages*. New York, NY: Sourcebooks, Inc.
Lather, Patti. 1988. "Feminist perspectives on empowering research methodologies." *Women's Studies International Forum* 11 (6): 569–581.
Lederach, John. 2003. *Little Book of Conflict Transformation: Clear Articulation Of The Guiding Principles By A Pioneer In The Field*. Intercourse, PA: Good Books.
Lederach, John Paul. 1995. *Preparing for Peace: Conflict Transformation Across Cultures*. Syracuse, NY: Syracuse University Press.
———. 2003. "Conflict Transformation." Beyond Intractability. www.beyondintractability.org/essay/transformation.
Lenin, V. I. 1906. "The Congress Summed Up." *Volna* [No. 11, 1906] (Republished by Marxist Internet Archive). www.marxists.org/archive/lenin/works/1906/may/07.htm.
———. 1932. "The State and Revolution." In *Collected Works*, edited by Stepan Apresyan and Jim Riordan, 25: 381–492. London, UK: Lawrence & Wishart.
Letherby, Gayle. 2003. *Feminist Research in Theory and Practice*. Philadelphia, PA: Open University Press.
Lewis, John. 2004. "Animal Rights Extremism and Ecoterrorism." FBI/Senate Judiciary Committee. www.fbi.gov/news/testimony/animal-rights-extremism-and-ecoterrorism.
Libertarian Socialist Organisation. 1979. *You Can't Blow up a Social Relationship*. Queensland, Australia: Libertarian Socialist Organisation (republished by The Anarchist Library). http://theanarchistlibrary.org/library/libertarian-socialist-organisation-you-can-t-blow-up-a-social-relationship.
Lippmann, Walter. 1922. *Public Opinion*. New York, NY: Harcourt, Brace and Co.
Live Wires FAI/ELF. 2014. "Phoenix Project #14: 'Live Wires FAI/ELF' Take Responsibility for 4 Arsons against Bristol's Cellular Transmission Infrastructure over 24 Hours." 325.nostate.net. http://325.nostate.net/?p=10487.

Llud. 2015. "Resignation Is Death: Responding to the Negation of Anarchy." Black Banner Distro (Vancouver, Occupied Coast Salish Territories). https://blackbannerdistro.files.wordpress.com/2016/04/resignation-is-death.pdf.

Loadenthal, Michael. 2010. "Nor Hostages, Assassinations, or Hijackings, but Sabotage, Vandalism & Fire: 'Eco-Terrorism' as Political Violence Challenging the State and Capital." MLitt Dissertation, St Andrews, Scotland, UK: Centre for the Study of Terrorism and Political Violence, University of St Andrews.

———. 2013. "The framing of (counter) state violence: challenging the rhetoric of non-state actors, political violence & 'terrorism.'" *Affinities: A Journal of Radical Theory, Culture, Action* (Simon Frasser University), 6 (1): 1–15.

———. 2014a. "Professor Xavier is a gay traitor! An anti-assimilationist queer framework for interpreting ideology, power & statecraft." *Journal of Feminist Scholarship*, Department of Women's and Gender Studies, University of Massachusetts Dartmouth, 6 (1): 13–46.

———. 2014b. "Eco-terrorism? Countering dominant narratives of securitisation: a critical, quantitative history of the Earth Liberation Front (1996–2009)." *Perspectives on Terrorism* (Center for Terrorism and Security Studies, Terrorism Research Initiative), 8 (3): 16–50.

———. 2015. "The Politics of the Attack: A Discourse of Insurrectionary Communiqués." PhD dissertation, Fairfax, VA: School for Conflict Analysis and Resolution, George Mason University.

———. 2016a. "'Eco-terrorism': an incident-driven history of attack (1973–2010)." *Journal for the Study of Radicalism* 10 (Forthcoming).

———. 2016b. "interpreting insurrectionary corpora: qualitative-quantitative analysis of clandestine communiqués." *Journal for the Study of Radicalism*, Michigan State University Press, 10 (2): 79–100.

López, Carlos. 2014. "That Which Stagnates, Rots ..." *Dark Nights* #41 (republished by 325.nostate). http://325.nostate.net/wp-content/uploads/2014/09/darknights-41.pdf.

Luchies, Timothy. 2015. "Towards an insurrectionary power/ knowledge: movement-relevance, anti-oppression, prefiguration." *Social Movement Studies* 14 (3): 1–16.

Lum, Cynthia, Leslie W. Kennedy, and Alison Sherley. 2008. "Is counter-terrorism policy evidence-based? What works, what harms, and what is unknown." *Psicothema* 20 (1): 35–42.

Luxemburg, Rosa. 1904. *Organizational Questions of the Russian Social Democracy [Leninism or Marxism?]*. Marxists.org online. Integer Press. www.marxists.org/archive/luxemburg/1904/questions-rsd/.

MacLachlan, Colin M., and William H. Beezley. 2010. *Mexico's Crucial Century, 1810–1910: An Introduction*. Lincoln, NE: University of Nebraska Press.

Maguire, Patricia. 1987. *Doing Participatory Research: A Feminist Approach*. UMass Center for International Education/School of Education.

Malik, Shiv. 2012. "Anarchists Claim Responsibility for Railway Signaling Sabotage in Bristol." *The Guardian*, 25 May. Online edition, sec. World: UK: Crime. www.theguardian.com/uk/2012/may/25/anarchists-claim-railway-signalling-bristol.

———. 2013. "Anarchist Group Claims It Started Blaze at Police Firearms Training Centre." *The Guardian*, 28 August. Online edition, sec. World: UK: Crime. www.theguardian.com/uk-news/2013/aug/28/anarchist-fire-police-firearms-training.

Maltezou, Renee, and Deepa Babington. 2013. "Special Report: Inside Greece's Violent New Anarchist Groups." *Reuters*, 14 August. Online edition. www.reuters.com/article/2013/08/14/us-greece-anarchists-specialreport-idUSBRE97D0AK20130814.

Manifesto Research Group/Comparative Manifestos Project. 2014. "Manifesto Project Database: Information." *Manifesto Project Database*. https://manifesto-project.wzb.eu/information/information.

Mann, Keith. 2009. *From Dusk "Til Dawn: An Insider"s View of the Growth of the Animal Liberation Movement*. London, UK: Warcry Communications.

Marcos, Subcomandante. 1996. "Fourth Declaration of the Lacandon Jungle." Indigenous Clandestine Revolutionary Committee General Command of the Zapatista Army of National Liberation Mexico. www.struggle.ws/mexico/ezln/jung4.html.

———. 2002. *Our Word Is Our Weapon: Selected Writings*. Edited by Juana Ponce De Leon. New York, NY: Seven Stories Press.

Marlin, Robert, ed. 2004. *What Does Al Qaeda Want?: Unedited Communiques*. Berkeley, CA: North Atlantic Books.

Marone, Francesco. 2014. "A Profile of the Informal Anarchist Federation in Italy." Combating Terrorism Center at West Point. www.ctc.usma.edu/posts/a-profile-of-the-informal-anarchist-federation-in-italy.

Marshall, Peter. 2010. *Demanding the Impossible: A History of Anarchism*. Oakland, CA: PM Press.

Marx, G.T. 2003. "Recent Developments in Undercover Policing." In *Punishment and Social Control: Essays in Honor of Sheldon L. Messinger*, edited by Stanley Cohen and Thomas G. Blomberg. Berlin, Germany: Aldine de Gruyter.

Marx, Karl. 1871. *The Civil War in France*. Translated by Friedrich Engels. Pamphlet published by the German Council of the International.

May, Todd. 1994. *The Political Philosophy of Poststructuralist Anarchism*. University Park, PA: Pennsylvania State University Press.

Maziotis, Nikos. 2014. "Armed Struggle, Revolutionary Movement, and Social Revolution." Public presentation. Athens Polytechnic, Greece, November. https://server.nostate.net/325-new/html/2016/04/27/presentation-of-nikos-maziotis-armed-struggle-revolutionary-movement-and-social-revolution-athens-polytechnic-2014-greece/.

McCormack, Tara. 2009. *Critique, Security and Power: The Political Limits to Emancipatory Approaches*. London, UK: Routledge.

Mead, Ed. 2007. *The Theory and Practice of Armed Struggle in the Northwest*. Montréal, QC: Kersplebedeb Publishing.

Meinhof, Ulrike. 2008. *Everybody Talks About the Weather ... We Don't: The Writings of Ulrike Meinhof*. Edited by Karin Bauer. Translated by Luise Von Flotow. New York, NY: Seven Stories Press.

Meltzer, Albert. 1969. "The Truth about the Bonnot Gang." Coptic Press (republished by libcom.org, 2007). http://libcom.org/library/truth-about-bonnot-gang-ezra-brett-mell.

Merriman, John. 2009. *The Dynamite Club: How a Bombing in Fin-de-Siècle Paris Ignited the Age of Modern Terror*. Boston, MA: Houghton Mifflin Harcourt.

Mexican Fire Cells Conspiracy/FAI. 2011. "Chronology of Mexican Fire Cells Conspiracy/Informal Anarchist Federation actions." Translated by This Is Our

Job. Culmine (republished by This Is Our Job). http://thisisourjob.noblogs.org/post/2011/10/27/chronology-of-mexican-fire-cells-conspiracyinformal-anarchist-federation-actions/.

Mies, Maria. 1983. "Towards a Methodology for Feminist Research." In *Theories of Women's Studies*, edited by Gloria Bowles and Renate Duelli Klein, 117–139. London, UK: Routledge & Kegan Paul, Limited.

Miller, Claude H., Jonathan Matusitz, H. Dan O'Hair, and Jacqueline Eckstein. 2008. "The Complexity of Terrorism: Groups, Semiotics, and the Media." In *Terrorism: Communication and Rhetorical Perspectives*, edited by H. Dan O'Hair, Robert L. Heath, Kevin J. Ayotte, and Gerald R. Ledlow, 43–66. Cresskill, NJ: Hampton Press.

Miller, David. 1984. *Anarchism*. Modern Ideologies. London, UK: J M Dent & Sons Ltd.

Milstein, Cindy. 2010. *Anarchism and Its Aspirations*. 1st edn. Vol. 1. Anarchist Interventions. Oakland, CA: AK Press & The Institute for Anarchist Studies.

Mishal, Shaul, and Reuben Aharoni. 1994. *Speaking Stones: Communiques from the Intifada Underground*. Syracuse, NY: Syracuse University Press.

Mitcho, Sara Regina. 2014. "The Problem of Nonviolence: Women's Protest in the United States, Post-Civil War to Post-9/11." PhD dissertation. Fairfax, VA: George Mason University. http://mars.gmu.edu/handle/1920/8847.

Modesto Anarcho. 2012. "Modesto Anarchy #18." Modesto Anarcho. www.indybay.org/uploads/2012/04/28/ma18.pdf.

Molland, Noel. 2006. "A Spark That Ignited a Flame: The Evolution of the Earth Liberation Front." In *Igniting a Revolution: Voices in Defense of the Earth*, edited by Steven Best and Anthony Nocella, 47–58. Oakland, CA: AK Press.

Moncourt, André, and J. Smith. 2009a. *The Red Army Faction A Documentary History, Volume 1: Projectiles for the People*. Vol. 1. Montréal, QC; Oakland, CA: Kersplebedeb Pub.; PM Press.

———. 2009b. *The Red Army Faction A Documentary History, Volume 2: Dancing With Imperialism*. Vol. 2. Montréal, QC; Oakland, CA: Kersplebedeb Pub.; PM Press.

Morin, Roc. 2014. "The Anarcho-Primitivist Who Wants Us All to Give Up Technology." *VICE Magazine*, 25 June, sec. VICE Stuff. www.vice.com/print/john-zerzan-wants-us-to-give-up-all-of-our-technology.

Morris, Mark. 2014. "New Charges for Kansas City Anarchist Accused of Attacking Cleaver's Office." *The Kansas City Star*, 7 October, Online edition, sec. News-Local-Crime. www.kansascity.com/news/local/crime/article2563152.html.

Morris, Travis. 2014. "Networking vehement frames: Neo-Nazi and violent Jihadi demagoguery." *Behavioral Sciences of Terrorism and Political Aggression* 6 (3): 163–182.

Morton, Jr., James F. 1900. "Another Blow to Royalty." Free Society Library, no. 6 (republished by Kate Sharpley Library). www.katesharpleylibrary.net/fn3063.

Muntaqim, Jalil. 2002. *We Are Our Own Liberators: Selected Prison Writings*. Toronto, ON: Abraham Guillen Press.

Nair, Yasmin. 2008. "Bash Back! Makes Point at Parade." *Windy City Times*, 2 July. www.windycitymediagroup.com/gay/lesbian/news/ARTICLE.php?AID=18827.

NASA Jet Propulsion Laboratory. 2014. "West Antarctic Glacier Loss Appears Unstoppable." 12 May. www.jpl.nasa.gov/news/news.php?release=2014-148.

Nasrallah, Sayyed Hassan. 2007. *Voice of Hezbollah: The Statements of Sayyed Hassan Nasrallah*. Edited by Nicholas Noe, Ellen Khouri, and Nicholas Blanford. London, UK: Verso.
National Consortium for the Study of Terrorism and Responses to Terrorism. 2015. "Evan Mecham Eco-Terrorist International Conspiracy (EMETIC)." Incidents over time. University of Maryland, College Park, MD: Global Terrorism Database. www.start.umd.edu/gtd/search/Results.aspx?perpetrator=10060.
National Coordinator for Counterterrorism. 2007. "Jihadis and the Internet." Translated by Amstelveen Amstelveens Vertaalburo B.V. Government report. The Hague, Netherlands: National Coordinator for Counterterrorism.
N, D, and S. 2004. *Desire Armed!: A Basic Guide to Armed Resistance and Revolution*. Print. Lawrence, KS: Kansas Mutual Aid.
Nechayev, Sergey. 1869. "The Revolutionary Catechism." Marxist Internet Archive. www.marxists.org/subject/anarchism/nechayev/catechism.htm.
New York Times. 1897. "Angiolillo Died Bravely; Mail Advices Say He Was Collected and Spoke on the Scaffold at Vergara." *The New York Times*, 22 August. http://query.nytimes.com/gst/abstract.html?res=9506E3DE153DE633A25751C2A96E9C94669ED7CF.
Nihilist Abyss. 2013. "Nihilist Abyss – New Anarchist Website." Anarchistnews.org. http://anarchistnews.org/content/nihilist-abyss-new-anarchist-website.
Nomad, Tom. 2013. *The Master's Tools: Warfare and Insurgent Possibility*. Berkeley, CA: Repartee.
North American Earth Liberation Front Press Office. 2001. "Frequently Asked Questions About the Earth Liberation Front." North American Earth Liberation Front Press Office. www.elfpressoffice.org/elffaqs.html.
North Carolina Piece Corps. n.d. *Piece Now Peace Later: An Anarchist Introduction to Firearms*. Online. Carrboro, NC: NC Piece Corps. https://tucsonabc.files.wordpress.com/2013/10/piece-now-peace-later.pdf.
Novatore, Renzo. 1916. "In The Circle of Life: In Memory of Bruno Filippi." In *The Rebel's Dark Laughter: The Writings of Bruno Filippi*, by Bruno Filippi, translated by Wolfi Landstreicher, Online, 5–8. Online: www.omnipresence.mahost.org (republished by The Anarchist Library, 2012). http://theanarchistlibrary.org/library/bruno-filippi-the-rebel-s-dark-laughter-the-writings-of-bruno-filippi.pdf.
———. 1920. "My Iconoclastic Individualism." The Anarchist Library. http://theanarchistlibrary.org/library/Renzo_Novatore__My_Iconoclastic_Individualism.html.
———. 2000. "Toward the Creative Nothing." Pamphlet. Oakland, CA: Venomous Butterfly.
———. 2012. *Novatore: The Collected Writings of Renzo Novatore*. Translated by Wolfi Landstreicher. San Francisco, CA: Ardent Press.
Novenario, Caline Marie I. 2016. "Differentiating Al Qaeda and the Islamic State through strategies publicized in Jihadist magazines." *Studies in Conflict & Terrorism* 39 (1): 953–967.
Noys, Benjamin. 2011. *Communization and Its Discontents: Contestation, Critique, and Contemporary Struggles*. ePub. Minor Compositions.
Oakley, Ann. 1981. "Interviewing Women: A Contradiction in Terms." In *Doing Feminist Research*, edited by Helen Roberts, 30–61. New York, NY: Routledge.

"Obsidian Point" Circle of Analysis. 2013a. "On the Latest Communique from ITS." Translated by War on Society. Material Anarquista (republished by War on Society). http://waronsociety.noblogs.org/?p=7353.

———. 2013b. "El fisgón, la prensa y los terroristas. México." Liberación Total. http://liberaciontotal.lahaine.org/?p=5015.

———. 2013c. "Bomb Threat: An Immediate Response to all the Infamy." Liberación Total (republished by War on Society). https://waronsociety.noblogs.org/?p=7702.

Obsidian Point Circle of Attack. 2014. "Communique for Package Bomb Sent to the Rector of UNAM." War on Society. http://waronsociety.noblogs.org/?p=8967.

O'Goodness, Bursts. 2013. "Nihilist Anarchism." Radio4all.net Podcast. "The Final Straw." Ashville, NC: Ashville FM. www.ashevillefm.org/the-final-straw/07/2013/nihilist-anarchism.

———. 2014a. "Doug Gilbert Saw Fire: A Conversation Riots, Revolts & The Black Bloc." Radio4all.net Podcast. "The Final Straw." Ashville, NC: Ashville FM. www.radio4all.net/index.php/program/76479.

———. 2014b. "Tom Nomad on Insurgent Theory." Radio4all.net Podcast. "The Final Straw." Ashville, NC: Ashville FM. www.ashevillefm.org/the-final-straw/12/2014/tom-nomad-on-insurgent-theory.

Olga Cell: FAI/IRF. 2012. "Italy: Claim of Responsibility for the Armed Attack against Roberto Adinolfi of Ansaldo Nuclear (corrected)." culmine.noblogs.org via waronsociety.noblogs.org/. http://waronsociety.noblogs.org/?p=4610.

Oliver, Anne Marie, and Paul F. Steinberg. 2006. *The Road to Martyrs' Square: A Journey into the World of the Suicide Bomber*. New York, NY: Oxford University Press, USA.

O'Neil, Matt. 2014. "Islamic State Similar to 19th Century Anarchists, Says Expert." Text. Radio National/ABC. 25 September. www.abc.net.au/radionational/programs/saturdayextra/islamic-state-similar-to-19th-century-anarchists-says-expert/5768178.

Orsini, Alessandro. 2011. *Anatomy of the Red Brigades: The Religious Mind-Set of Modern Terrorists*. Ithaca, NY: Cornell University Press.

Orwell, George. 1980. *Homage to Catalonia*. San Diego, CA: Mariner Books.

O.V. n.d. "The Affinity Group." In *Articles from Insurrection*, The Anarchist Library, 6–8. Online: The Anarchist Library. http://theanarchistlibrary.org/library/various-authors-articles-from-insurrection.pdf.

———. 2011. "Autonomous Base Nucleus." www.indymedia.org.uk/en/2011/11/488887.html.

Palmer, Kim. 2013. "Self-Described Anarchist Gets 10 Years in Ohio Bridge Bombing Plot." Reuters, 7 October. Online edition. www.reuters.com/article/2013/10/07/us-usa-security-cleveland-idUSBRE9960WC20131007.

Papadopoulos, Dimitris, Niamh Stephenson, and Vassillis Tsianos. 2008. *Escape Routes: Control and Subversion in the Twenty-First Century*. Ann Arbor, MI: Pluto Press.

Pape, Robert Anthony. 2005. *Dying to Win: The Strategic Logic of Suicide Terrorism*. New York, NY: Random House.

Parry, Albert. 2013. *Terrorism: From Robespierre to the Weather Underground*. Chelmsford, MA: Courier Corporation.

Parry, Richard. 1987. *The Bonnot Gang: The Story of the French Illegalists*. London, UK: Rebel Press.

Passavant, Paul A. 2007. "The contradictory state of Giorgio Agamben." *Political Theory* 35 (2): 147–174.
Peirats, Jose. 2011. *The CNT in the Spanish Revolution: Volume 1*. Edited by Chris Ealham. Oakland, CA: PM Press.
Peltier, Leonard. 2000. *Prison Writings: My Life Is My Sun Dance*. Edited by Harvey Arden. New York, NY: St. Martin's Griffin.
Perdomo, Maria Eugenia Vasquez. 2005. *My Life as a Colombian Revolutionary: Reflections of a Former Guerrillera*. Translated by Lorena Terando. Philadelphia, PA: Temple University Press.
Pernicone, Nunzio. 1993. *Italian Anarchism, 1864–1892*. Princeton, NJ: Princeton University Press.
Phillips, Leigh. 2012. "Anarchists attack science." *Nature* 485 (7400): 561.
Pickering, Leslie James. 2007. *The Earth Liberation Front 1997–2002*. 2nd edn. Portland, OR: Arissa Media Group, LLC.
———. 2013. *The Evan Mecham Eco Terrorist International Conspiracy*. Buffalo, NY: Burning Books.
Pink and Black Attack. 2010. "Pink and Black Attack #6." Pink and Black Attack. http://zinelibrary.info/files/PABA6.pdf.
Polidoros, Giorgos, Haris Hatzimichelakis, Christos Tsakalos, Gerasimos Tsakalos, Panagiotis Argirou, Michalis Nikolopoulos, Giorgos Nikolopoulos, Olga Ekonomidou, Damiano Bolano, and Theofilos Mavropoulos. 2014. "Arming Negation." Translated by Inter Arma. 325.nostate.net. http://325.nostate.net/?p=11742.
Polletta, Francesca, Pang Ching Bobby Chen, Beth Gharrity Gardner, and Alice Motes. 2013. "Is the Internet Creating New Reasons to Protest?" In *The Future of Social Movement Research: Dynamics, Mechanisms, and Processes*, edited by Jacqueline van Stekelenburg, Conny Roggeband, and Bert Klandermans, 39:17–36. Minneapolis, MN: University of Minnesota Press.
Poole, David, ed. 1977. *Land and Liberty: Anarchist Influences in the Mexican Revolution – Ricardo Flores Magón*. Montréal, QC: Black Rose Books Ltd.
Potter, Will. 2009. "Making an Animal Rights 'Terrorist.'" *Bite Back Magazine*, February.
———. 2013. "Prisoner Sent to Solitary for Having 'Copious Amounts of Anarchist Publications.'" *VICE*, 18 October. Online edition. www.vice.com/read/prisoner-sent-to-solitary-for-copious-amounts-of-anarchist-publications.
Pugetsoundanarchists.org. 2011. "Queers Vs. Cops," 26 June. http://pugetsoundanarchists.org/node/730.
Quinton, Anthony. 1990. "Reflections on Terrorism and Violence." In *Terrorism, Protest and Power*, edited by Martin Warner and Roger Crisp, 35–43. Brookfield, VT: Edward Elgar Publishing Company.
RaiNews 24. 2013. "Alfredo Cospito and Nicola Gai sentenced for nuclear boss shooting." RaiNews 24 (republished by Anarchistnews.org). anarchistnews.org/content/alfredo-cospito-and-nicola-gai-sentenced-for-nuclear-boss-shooting.
Ramsbotham, Oliver, Hugh Miall, and Tom Woodhouse. 2005. *Contemporary Conflict Resolution: The Prevention, Management and Transformation of Deadly Conflicts*. Cambridge, UK: Polity Press.
Ramsey, Gilbert, and Donald Holbrook. 2014. "The representation of violence by insurgent political actors: the 'violent' part of 'violent extremism'?" *Behavioral Sciences of Terrorism and Political Aggression* 7 (1): 84–96.

Random Anarchists. 2014. "Attack on Army Cadet Base in Bristol." 325.nostate.net. http://325.nostate.net/?p=11771.

Ranstorp, M. 2007. "Introduction: Mapping Terrorism Research." In *Mapping Terrorism Research: State of the Art, Gaps, and Future Directions*, edited by M Ranstorp, 1–28. London, UK: Routledge.

Rapoport, David C. 2002. "The four waves of rebel terror and September 11." *Anthropoetics* 8 (1). www.anthropoetics.ucla.edu/ap0801/terror.htm.

Ravage Editions. 2013. "Kick It Til It Breaks – An Introduction to Angry Brigade [introduction of Angry Brigade: Elements de La Critique Anarchiste Armée En Angleterre]." Translated by Jean Weir. Ravage Editions. www.non-fides.fr/?Kick-It-Till-It-Breaks-An.

Ravo, Nick. 1989. "U.S. Surgical Admits Spying on Animal-Rights Groups." *The New York Times*, 26 January. Online edition, sec. N.Y./Region. www.nytimes.com/1989/01/26/nyregion/us-surgical-admits-spying-on-animal-rights-groups.html.

Reid, Julian. 2011. "Life Struggles: War, Discipline and Biopolitics in the Thought of Michel Foucault." In *Foucault on Politics, Security and War*, edited by Michael Dillon and Andrew W. Neal, 65–92. Basingstoke, UK: Palgrave Macmillan.

Reinharz, Shulamit. 1992. *Feminist Methods in Social Research*. New York, NY: Oxford University Press, USA.

Research and Destroy. 2009. "Communique From an Absent Future: On the Terminus of Student Life." Self published. https://archive.org/details/CommuniqueFromAnAbsentFuture.

Reuters. 2009. "State Media: Israeli Air Strike on Sudan Convoy Killed 119." Reuters, 26 May. Online edition, sec. Israel News. www.ynetnews.com/articles/0%2c7340%2cL-3721574%2c00.html.

Revolutionary Cells – animal liberation brigade. 2003. "Revolutionary Cells – Animal Liberation Brigades." Animalliberationfront.com. www.animalliberationfront.com/ALFront/Premise_History/RevolutionaryCells.htm.

Roberts, David. 2012. "Human Security, Biopoverty and the Possibility for Emancipation." In *Critical Perspectives on Human Security: Rethinking Emancipation and Power in International Relations*, edited by David Chandler and Nik Hynek, 69–82. New York, NY: Routledge.

Rodríguez, Gustavo. 2011a. "Illegal Anarchism: The False Dichotomy." Zinelibrary.info (republished by The Anarchist Library). http://theanarchistlibrary.org/library/gustavo-rodriguez-illegal-anarchism.

———. 2011b. "The Insurrectionist Current." Conference paper presented at La Case Naranja, Tlalnepantla, Mexico. Published by We Are Not Afraid of Ruins. https://unafraidruins.wordpress.com/illegalism-theory-and-history/the-insurrectionist-current/.

Romanos, Nikos. 2014a. "Statement by Nikos Romanos at the Trial which Started on 03/02/2014." Inter Arma. https://interarma.info/2014/02/05/dilwsi-rwmanou-sto-dikastirio/?lang=en.

———. 2014b. "Letter from Nikos Romanos – 'The Question of Dignity.'" Translated by Act for Freedom Now! 325.nostate.net. http://325.nostate.net/?p=10496.

———. 2016. "I Attack, Therefore I Am." 325.nostate.net. https://server.nostate.net/325-new/html/2016/04/27/i-attack-therefore-i-am-by-imprisoned-anarchist-comrade-nikos-romanos-greece/.

Rosebraugh, Craig. 2004. *The Logic of Political Violence: Lessons in Reform and Revolution*. Portland, OR: Arissa Media Group. http://public.eblib.com/EBLPublic/PublicView.do?ptiID=655683.

Rosoff, Henry. 2014. "KIRO 7 Confronts Self-Proclaimed Anarchist Accused of Smashing Bank ATMs." *KIRO 7*, 23 January. Online edition. www.kirotv.com/news/news/kiro-7-confronts-self-proclaimed-anarchist-accused/nczb9/.

Rousselle, Duane, and Süreyya Evren, eds. 2011. *Post-Anarchism: A Reader*. New York, NY: Pluto Press.

Rubenstein, Richard E. 1987. *Alchemists of Revolution: Terrorism In The Modern World*. London, UK: St Martins Press.

Rubin, Jerry. 1970. *Do It! Scenarios of the Revolution*. New York, NY: Simon and Schuster.

Rudacille, Deborah. 2001. *The Scalpel and the Butterfly: The Conflict between Animal Research and Animal Protection*. Berkeley, CA: University of California Press.

Rudd, Mark. 2010. *Underground: My Life with SDS and the Weathermen*. New York, NY: William Morrow Paperbacks.

Rudolph, Eric. 2015. *Between the Lines of Drift: The Memoirs of a Militant*. 3rd edn. Online: Self published. www.armyofgod.com/EricLinesOfDrift1_18_15.pdf.

Sable, Scarlet. 2014. "Fear Under a Microscope: ITS & the Conflict With Nanotechnology." *The Peak Magazine* 53 (3): 9.

Said, Edward W. 1979. *Orientalism*. New York, NY: Vintage Books.

Salter, Mark B. 2012a. "Introduction." In *Research Methods in Critical Security Studies: An Introduction*, edited by Mark B. Salter and Can E. Mutlu, 1–14. New York, NY: Routledge.

———. 2012b. "The Ethnographic Turn." In *Research Methods in Critical Security Studies: An Introduction*, edited by Mark B. Salter and Can E. Mutlu, 51–57. New York, NY: Routledge.

Salter, Mark B., and Can E. Mutlu. 2012. "The Discursive Turn." In *Research Methods in Critical Security Studies: An Introduction*, edited by Mark B. Salter and Can E. Mutlu, 113–119. New York, NY: Routledge.

Samenow, Jason. 2012. "U.S. Has Hottest Month on Record in July 2012 NOAA Says." *The Washington Post – Blogs*. 8 August. www.washingtonpost.com/blogs/capital-weather-gang/post/us-has-hottest-month-on-record-in-july-2012-noaa-says/2012/08/08/0fae675c-e169-11e1-98e7-89d659f9c106_blog.html.

Savage Vandal Anti-authoritarians. 2014. "Responsibility Claim for Explosion in the Military Tribunal of the Union, and Arson on Vehicles of the Military Police." contra-info. http://en.contrainfo.espiv.net/2014/05/27/porto-alegre-brazil-responsibility-claim-for-explosion-in-the-military-tribunal-of-the-union/.

Schaack, Michael J. 1889. *Anarchy and Anarchists: A History of the Red Terror and the Social Revolution in America and Europe. Communism, Socialism, and Nihilism in Doctrine and in Deed. The Chicago Haymarket Conspiracy, and the Detection and Trial of the Conspirators*. Chicago, IL: F.J. Schulte.

Scheper-Hughes, Nancy. 1995. "The primacy of the ethical: propositions for a militant anthropology." *Current Anthropology* 36 (3): 409–440.

Schiavina, Raffaele. 1974. "A Fragment Of Luigi Galleani's Life." In *Man! An Anthology of Anarchist Ideas*, edited by Marcus Graham. Orkney, UK: Cienfuegos

Press Ltd (republished by Kate Sharpley Library). www.katesharpleylibrary.net/d51cvp.

Schmid, Alex P. 1988. "Goals and Objectives of International Terrorism." In *Current Perspectives on International Terrorism*, edited by Robert O. Slater and Michael Stohl, 47–87. London, UK: The Macmillan Press Ltd.

Schmid, Alex P., and Janny de Graaf. 1982. *Violence as Communication: Insurgent Terrorism and the Western News Media*. London, UK: SAGE Publications Ltd.

Schultz, Heath, and Brad Thomson. 2009. "Militant Flamboyance: A Brief History of the Stonewall Riots and Other Queer Happenings." Self published. http://zinelibrary.info/files/militantflamboyance_FINALprint.pdf.

Schuster, Henry. 2005. "Domestic Terror: Who's Most Dangerous?" CNN, 24 August. www.cnn.com/2005/US/08/24/schuster.column/index.html.

Schwarz, A.G. 2011. "A Contextualization of Conspiracy Cells of Fire." Anarchistnews.org. http://anarchistnews.org/node/19500.

Seidman, Gary. 2014. "Armed Struggle in the South African Anti-Apartheid Movement." In *The Social Movements Reader: Cases and Concepts*, edited by Jeff Goodwin and James M. Jasper, 3rd edn, 224–238. West Sussex, UK: Wiley-Blackwell.

Serge, Victor. 1909. "Anarchists – Bandits." Translated by Mitchell Abidor. *Le Révolté (republished by the Marxists Internet Archive)* No. 36 (February). www.marxists.org/archive/serge/1909/02/anarchist-bandits.htm.

Shakur, Assata. 2001. *Assata: An Autobiography*. Chicago, IL: Lawrence Hill Books.

Shantz, Jeff. 2011. *Active Anarchy: Political Practice in Contemporary Movements*. Lanham, MD: Lexington Books.

Shoatz, Russell Maroon. 2013. *Maroon the Implacable: The Collected Writings of Russell Maroon Shoatz*. Edited by Quincy Saul and Fred Ho. Oakland, CA: PM Press.

Shone, Steve J. 2013. *American Anarchism*. Leiden, Netherlands: Brill.

Silke, Andrew. 2009. "Contemporary Terrorism Studies Issues in Research." In *Critical Terrorism Studies: A New Research Agenda*, edited by Richard Jackson, Marie Breen Smyth, and Jeroen Gunning, 34–48. New York, NY: Routledge.

Skrbina, David. 2010. "Introduction." In *Technological Slavery: The Collected Writings of Theodore J. Kaczynski, A.k.a. "The Unabomber,"* edited by David Skrbina, 17–34. Los Angeles, CA: Feral House.

Smith, Steve. 2005. "The Contested Concept of Security." In *Critical Security Studies And World Politics*, edited by Ken Booth, 27–62. Boulder, CO: Lynne Rienner Pub.

Sorenson, John. 2009. "Constructing terrorists: propaganda about animal rights." *Critical Studies on Terrorism* 2 (2): 237–256.

Special Agent Christine Loscalzo. 2003. "In the Matter of the Application of the United States of America for an Order Authorizing the Installation and Use of an Electronic Tracking Devices on or in Honda Civic, California License Plate 3EKT50 [NO. CR 03–3133 MISC EMC]." United States District Court Northern District of California San Francisco Division.

Spivak, Gayatri Chakravorty. 1988. "Can the Subaltern Speak?" In *Marxism and the Interpretation of Culture*, edited by Cary Nelson and Lawrence Grossberg, 271–311. London, UK: Macmillan.

Sprague, Joey. 2005. *Feminist Methodologies for Critical Researchers: Bridging Differences*. AltaMira Press.

s.t. 2014. "The Issues Are Not the Issue: A Letter to Earth First! From a Too-Distant Friend." Self published (republished by Zine Library). http://zinelibrary.info/files/issues-not-issues.pdf.

Stevenson, Mark. 2011. "'Individuals Tending To Savagery' Anti-Technology Group Sent Bomb To Monterrey Technological Institute Professors." *Huffington Post*. 10 August. www.huffingtonpost.com/2011/08/10/individuals-tending-to-sa_n_923030.html.

Stirner, Max, and Jason McQuinn. 2012. *Stirner's Critics*. Translated by Wolfi Landstreicher. Berkeley, CA: Little Black Cart Books.

Stump, Jacob L., and Priya Dixit. 2013. *Critical Terrorism Studies: An Introduction to Research Methods*. New York, NY: Routledge.

Sullivan, Nikki. 2003. *A Critical Introduction to Queer Theory*. New York, NY: New York University Press.

Tadjbakhsh, Shahrbanou, and Anuradha Chenoy. 2007. *Human Security: Concepts and Implications*. New York, NY: Routledge.

Tatanka. 1995. "The Question of Preservational Violence." Coalition Against Civilization. http://theanarchistlibrary.org/library/tatanka-the-question-of-preservational-violence.

Teitler, G. 1974. "The Urban Guerrilla, as a Revolutionary Phenomenon and as a Recruiting Problem." In *Urban Guerrilla: Studies on the Theory, Strategy and Practice of Political Violence in Modern Societies*, edited by Johan Niezing, Proceedings of the 1st international working conference on violence and non-violent action in industrialized societies, 4:111–127. Brussels, Belgium: Rotterdam University Press/Polemological Centre of the Free University of Brussels.

Tejada, Susan. 2012. *In Search of Sacco & Vanzetti: Double Lives, Troubled Times, & the Massachusetts Murder Case That Shook the World*. Boston, MA: Northeastern University Press.

Terrorist Cells for the Direct Attack – Anticivilization Faction. 2011. "Claim of Responsibility for Two Bombing Attacks and Contributions to the Development of Praxis against the Industrial-Technological System and Civilization." Translated by War on Society. Liberación Total (republished by War on Society). http://waronsociety.noblogs.org/?p=1869.

The Bristol Post. 2011. "Bristol Councillors' Cars Torched in Late-Night Arson Attacks." *The Bristol Post*, 8 November. Online edition, sec. News. www.bristolpost.co.uk/Bristol-councillors-cars-torched-late-night-arson/story-13787504-detail/story.html.

———. 2014a. "Anarchist Group Claims It Carried out Court Arson on North Avon Magistrates' Court." *The Bristol Post*, 3 June. Online edition, sec. News. www.bristolpost.co.uk/Anarchist-group-claims-carried-court-arson/story-21179058-detail/story.html.

———. 2014b. "Anarchists Claim Responsibility for 60 Incidents and Attacks in the Bristol Area." *The Bristol Post*, 16 November. Online edition, sec. News. www.bristolpost.co.uk/Anarchists-claim-responsibility-60-incidents/story-24541906-detail/story.html.

The imprisoned comrades of the CCF FAI/IRF. 2013. "Statement by Conspiracy of Cells of Fire about Being Charged with 250 Attacks." 325.nostate.net. http://325.nostate.net/?p=8428.

The Imprisoned Members of the Conspiracy of Cells of Fire. 2011. "FIRE AND GUNPOWDER: From Indonesia to Chile… A Proposition for FAI/IRF." Translated by Act for Freedom Now!/boubourAs! 325.nostate.net. http://325.nostate.net/?p=3624.
The Institute for the Study of Insurgent Warfare. 2014. *Insurgencies: A Journal of Insurgent Strategy*. Berkeley, CA: Little Black Cart.
The Parabellum. 2013. "The Parabellum – New Greek Anarchist Website." Anarchistnews.org. http://anarchistnews.org/content/parabellum-new-greek-anarchist-website.
The Right Honorable Wicked Stepmothers' Traveling, Drinking and Debating Society and Men's Auxiliary. 2011. "Rowdy Queers Trash and Glamdalize Human Rights Campaign Gift Shop." Anarchistnews.org. http://anarchistnews.org/?q=node/14923.
Thompson, A. K. 2008. "Representation's Limit: The Epistemology of Spectacular Violence." Conference paper delivered at the 15th Annual Conference of the York Centre for International and Security Studies at York University, in Toronto, ON. Published in *Violent Interventions*. York University, Toronto, Ontario: York Centre for International and Security Studies.
Three Non-Matriculating Proletarians. 2009. "The Bricks We Throw at Police Today Will Build the Liberation Schools of Tomorrow." Libcom. http://libcom.org/news/bricks-we-throw-police-today-will-build-liberation-schools-tomorrow-02122009.
TIC. 2007. *The Coming Insurrection*. Intervention series 1. Los Angeles, CA: Semiotext(e).
———. 2011. *Spread Anarchy, Live Communism*. Soundcloud. The Anarchist Turn, New School for Social Research, New York, NY: Anarchist Developments in Cultural Studies. http://anarchist-developments.org/index.php/adcs_journal/article/view/27/28.
———. 2013. "Spread Anarchy, Live Communism." In *The Anarchist Turn*, edited by Jacob Blumenfeld, Chiara Bottici, and Simon Critchley, 216. London, UK: Pluto Press.
'Til it Breaks collective. 2009. "Strategic Social War." *'Til It Breaks (Denver, CO)*, October.
Tilly, Charles. 1978. *From Mobilization to Revolution*. London, UK: Longman Higher Education.
Tiqqun. 1999. "Tiqqun #1, Conscious Organ of the Imaginary Party, Exercises in Critical Metaphysics." Tiqqun. https://tiqqun.jottit.com/.
———. 2001a. "How Is It To Be Done?" Translated by Tiqqunista. Tiqqun. https://tiqqunista.jottit.com/how_is_it_to_be_done%3F.
———. 2001b. "Tiqqun #2, Organ of liaison within the imaginary party, zone of offensive opacity." Tiqqun. https://tiqqun.jottit.com/.
———. 2010a. *Introduction to Civil War*. Los Angeles, CA: Semiotext(e).
———. 2010b. *Introduction to Civil War*. Los Angeles, CA: Semiotext(e).
———. 2011. *This Is Not a Program*. Translated by Joshua David Jordan. Los Angeles, CA: Semiotext(e).
———. 2012a. *Theory of Bloom*. Translated by Robert Hurley. Berkeley, CA: LBC Books.
———. 2012b. *Preliminary Materials for a Theory of the Young-Girl*. Translated by Ariana Reines. Los Angeles, CA: Semiotext(e).

Toros, Harmonie. 2012. *Terrorism, Talking and Transformation: A Critical Approach.* New York, NY: Routledge.

Torres-Soriano, Manuel R. 2014. "The hidden face of jihadist internet forum management: the case of Ansar Al Mujahideen." *Terrorism and Political Violence* 28 (4): 1–15.

Trotsky, Leon. 1911. "Why Marxists Oppose Individual Terrorism." Translated by Marxists' Internet Archive. Der Kampf. www.marxists.org/archive/trotsky/1911/11/tia09.htm.

Truth, Sojourner. 1851. "Ain't I a Woman?" Speech. Akron, OH.

Tsakalos, Christos. 2013. "The Direct Urgency of Attack." Parabellum (republished by Inter Arma). https://interarma.info/2014/02/13/ellada-amesh-anagkaiothtaths-epithsis-chts/?lang=en.

Tsakalos, Gerasimos, Olga Economidou, Haris Hatzimichelakis, Christos Tsakalos, Giorgos Nikolopoulos, Michalis Nikolopoulos, Damiano Bolano, Panayiotis Argyrou, and Giorgos Polydoras. 2012. "The Sun Still Rises." Untorelli Press. http://destroybristol.files.wordpress.com/2012/02/ccf_0.pdf.

Tucker, Kevin. 2009. *Revolution And/Or Insurrection: Some Thoughts on Tearing This Muthafucka Down.* Seattle, WA: Wormwood Distro.

Tuman, Joseph S. 2009. *Communicating Terror: The Rhetorical Dimensions of Terrorism.* 2nd edn. Thousand Oaks, CA: SAGE Publications, Inc.

United Nations Office on Drugs and Crime. 2012. "The Use of the Internet for Terrorist Purposes." Report. Vienna, Austria: United Nations Office on Drugs and Crime.

Untorelli Press. 2012. "Dangerous Spaces: Violent Resistance, Self-Defense, & Insurrectional Struggle Against Gender." Untorelli Press. http://zinelibrary.info/files/dangerous.pdf.

UpprorsBladet. 2011. "UpprorsBladet #3." UpprorsBladet. http://zinelibrary.info/files/UpprorsBladetX.pdf.

van Buuren, Jelle, and Beatrice de Graaf. 2013. "Hatred of the system: menacing loners and autonomous cells in the Netherlands." *Terrorism and Political Violence* 26 (1): 156–184.

Van Deusen, David, and Xavier Massot, eds. 2010. *The Black Bloc Papers.* 2nd edn. Shawnee Mission, KS: Breaking Glass Press/Alternative Media Project.

Vaughan-Williams, Nick, and Columba Peoples. 2010. *Critical Security Studies: An Introduction.* Taylor & Francis.

von Behr, Ines, Anais Reding, Charlie Edwards, and Luke Gribbon. 2013. "Radicalisation in the Digital Era." Washington, DC: RAND Europe.

Vonnegut, Kurt. 1999. *Player Piano: A Novel.* New York, NY: The Dial Press.

Waagner, Clayton. 2001. "Clayton Waagner's Message to the United States." Clayton Waagner Message Board/The Army of God. www.armyofgod.com/Claytonsmessage.html.

Wardlaw, Grant. 1989. *Political Terrorism: Theory, Tactics and Counter-Measures.* Cambridge, UK: Cambridge University Press.

Watson, Bruce. 2008. *Sacco and Vanzetti: The Men, the Murders, and the Judgment of Mankind.* Reprint edition. New York, NY: Penguin Books.

Weather Underground. 1974. *Prairie Fire: The Politics of Revolutionary Anti-Imperialism.* San Francisco, CA: Prairie Fire Distributing Committee & Communications Co. www.sds-1960s.org/PrairieFire-reprint.pdf.

Weber, Cynthia, Amy Lind, V. Spike Peterson, Laura Sjoberg, Lauren Wilcox, and Meghana Nayak. 2014. "The forum: Queer International Relations." *International Studies Review* 16 (4): 596–622.

Weber, Max. 1919. "Politik als Beruf (Politics as a Vocation)." Lecture presented at the Free Students Union, Munich University, January. www.ne.jp/asahi/moriyuki/abukuma/weber/lecture/politics_vocation.html.

Wedell, Noura. 2014. "Jean-Marie Gleize." *BOMB – Artists in Conversation*. 22 September. http://bombmagazine.org/article/1000259/jean-marie-gleize.

Weimann, Gabriel. 2006. *Terror on the Internet: The New Arena, the New Challenges*. Washington, DC: United States Institute of Peace Press.

West, Cornel. 1987. "Minority discourse and the pitfalls of canon formation." *Yale Journal of Criticism* 1 (1): 193–201.

White, Robert W. 2000. "Issues in the study of political violence: understanding the motives of participants in small group political violence." *Terrorism and Political Violence* 12 (1): 95–108.

Wibben, Annick T.R. 2011. *Feminist Security Studies: A Narrative Approach*. New York, NY: Routledge.

Wiberg, Håkon. 1974. "Are Urban Guerrillas Possible?" In *Urban Guerilla: Studies on the Theory, Strategy and Practice of Political Violence in Modern Societies*, edited by Johan Niezing, Proceedings of the 1st international working conference on violence and non-violent action in industrialized societies, 4:11–19. Brussels, Belgium: Rotterdam University Press/Polemological Centre of the Free University of Brussels.

Wild Reaction. 2015a. "Some Answers about the Present and NOT about the Future." War on Society. https://waronsociety.noblogs.org/?p=9588.

———. 2015b. "Wild Reaction MORTE." Translated by Anarchistnews. contra-info (republished by anarchistnews.org). http://anarchistnews.org/content/wild-reaction-morte.

Wild Reaction, Coyote-Skin Cloak group, Wild Reaction, Kill or Die group, and Wild Reaction, Infamous Aboriginals group. 2015. "A Short Message to the Distant Tribes from Wild Reaction." Translated by War on Society. contra-info (republished by War on Society). http://waronsociety.noblogs.org/?p=9382.

Wild Reaction, "Kill or Die" Group. 2014. "First Communique of Wild Reaction (RS)." Translated by War on Society. War on Society. https://waronsociety.noblogs.org/?p=9225.

Wild Reaction, Nocturnal Hunter Faction. 2014. "Detonation of Explosive Charge at the Mexico Teletón Foundation." Translated by War on Society. Instinto Salvaje [republished by War on Society]. http://waronsociety.noblogs.org/?p=9287.

Wild/terrorist Behaviors. 2015. "First Words from Wild/terrorist Behaviors." Translated by War on Society. contra-info (republished by War on Society). https://waronsociety.noblogs.org/?p=9307.

Williams, Leonard, and Brad Thomson. 2011. "The allure of insurrection." *Anarchist Developments in Cultural Studies* 1: 265–289.

Winfield, Nicole, and Derek Gatopoulos. 2010. "European Anarchists Grow More Violent, Coordinated." *The Huffington Post*, 28 December. Online edition. www.huffingtonpost.com/2010/12/29/european-anarchists-grow-_n_802277.html.

"With Egypt's New Choices, The Burden Of Democracy." 2012. *All Things Considered*. Online: NPR. www.npr.org/2012/12/29/168269594/with-egypts-new-choices-the-burden-of-democracy.

Wolf, John B. 1981. *Fear of Fear: A Survey of Terrorist Operations and Controls in Open Societies*. New York, NY: Plenum Press.

Wood, Alden. 2013. *The Cultural Logic of Insurrection: Essays on Tiqqun and the Invisible Committee*. Berkeley, CA: Repartee/Little Black Cart.

Woodcock, George. 1962. *Anarchism: A History of Libertarian Ideas and Movements*. 2nd edn. Cleveland, OH: Meridian Books.

World Health Organization. 2014. "Ambient and Household Air Pollution and Health." NGO. *WHO*. March. www.who.int/phe/health_topics/outdoorair/databases/en/.

Wright, Austin L. 2011. "Why Do Terrorists Claim Credit?" Unpublished manuscript. Princeton University Department of Politics. www.princeton.edu/politics/about/file-repository/public/Wright_CreditTaking_11.3.2011.pdf.

Young, James D. 2001. "Eric J Hobsbawm: 'Communist' Historian, Companion of Honour and Socialism's Ghosts." *New Interventions* 10/11 (3/4). www.marxists.org/history/etol/writers/young/hobsbawm/index.htm.

Zeskind, Leonard. 2009. *Blood and Politics: The History of the White Nationalist Movement from the Margins to the Mainstream*. New York, NY: Farrar, Straus and Giroux.

Žižek, Slavoj. 1997. "Multiculturalism, or, the cultural logic of multinational capitalism." *New Left Review* I (225). www.newleftreview.org/?view=1919.

———. 2002. "A plea for Leninist intolerance." *Critical Inquiry* 28 (2): 542–566.

———. 2008. *Violence: Six Sideways Reflections*. London, UK: Macmillan.

Zulaika, Joseba, and William Douglass. 1996. *Terror and Taboo: The Follies, Fables, and Faces of Terrorism*. New York, NY: Routledge.

INDEX

affinity group 54, 59, 61, 68, 82, 116–119, 127–128, 170, 178–180
Agamben, Giorgio 141, 209, 215
"anarchist wave of terrorism" 39–55
Animal Liberation Front (ALF)/Earth Liberation Front (ELF) 9, 11, 26, 37, 56–57, 61, 75, 109, 111, 120–122, 130, 132, 179
anti-abortion 111–112
anti-assimilation 154–157
Anti-Capitalist Convergence (ACC) 60
"anti-globalization" movement 58–62, 176, 181, 186
At Daggers Drawn ... 101, 104, 134, 157, 161, 163, 165, 166, 170, 172, 175, 178, 179, 180, 183, 188, 191, 192, 194
autonomous zones/temporary autonomous zones (TAZ) 97, 170–171, 207

Bakunin, Mikhail 41, 43, 44, 57, 70, 137, 145, 164
Bash Back! (BB!) 7, 141, 154–157
Berkman, Alexander 46, 113, 137
"biopower" 141, 143, 152–153, 203, 205–206
black bloc 57–59, 61–62, 66, 160, 176
Blanqui, Louis Auguste 41–42
Blanquism 134–137
Bonanno, Alfredo 58, 65, 66, 139–141, 149, 162

Bond, Walter 8, 111
Bonnot Gang [La Bande à Bonnot] 47–49, 50, 63, 160, 193
Bookchin, Murray 66, 198
Bresci, Gaetano 43, 50, 63
Buda, Mario 51, 52, 63
Butler, Judith 151, 157, 210, 216

Camenisch, Marco 76, 95
canonization 4, 26–27, 134–135, 138, 151, 154, 157–160, 161–197, 198–201
Caserio, Santo Geronimo 44
Ciancabilla, Giuseppe 52, 137
"civil anarchists" 29, 182, 184–187, 220
"Civil War" 142–143, 151, 168–171
claiming responsibility 3, 9, 12, 56, 75, 84, 86, 91, 92, 109, 116–124, 124–131, 211–215
Clausewitz, Carl von 167–169
Coming Insurrection, The 61, 98, 99, 104, 126, 141–143, 170, 183, 205
communiqués 6–11, 124–131, 199, 211, 214–222
Conspiracy of Cells of Fire (CCF) 36, 67, 70, 75, 76–81, 82, 91, 93, 94, 109, 123–124, 129–130, 144
  Imprisoned Members Cell, CCF-FAI/ IRF 29, 75, 79, 80, 81, 110, 111, 117, 128, 130–131, 147, 173, 174, 178, 185, 204
Cospito, Alfredo 50, 71, 72, 74, 109, 124, 179

Critical Security Studies (CSS) 11–14, 20–26, 60–62, 115–116, 207–209, 222–224
Critical Terrorism Studies (CTS) 4–14, 17–26, 102–103, 211–215, 221–225
Czolgosz, Leon 46, 50

Da Silva, Gabriel Pombo 76, 95
Debord, Guy 24, 141, 168, 215
Deleuze, Gilles and Felix Guattari 62, 141, 160, 202, 209
deterritorialization 27, 37, 62, 71, 74–75, 78, 81, 88, 90–93, 120, 125, 142, 145, 202–203, 217
Dondoglio, Nestor 50, 63
Di Giovanni, Severino 53, 109, 137
digital networks 6, 9–11, 19–20, 30, 159–160, 185–187, 218–222
discourse 22, 33–34, 161–197, 216–222
"dual use" 23–24, 26, 49

ecological crisis 189–190
"Empire" 141, 143, 160, 203
Evan Mecham Eco-Terrorist International Conspiracy (EMETIC) 110, 133
expropriation 47–48, 49–50, 54, 95, 99, 137

Fagotto, Alfonso 50, 63
false flag attacks 128–129
Federal Bureau of Investigation 48, 51, 60, 122–123
feminist research methodology 4–6, 20–23, 222–225
Filippi, Bruno 53, 137
foco/focalism 163, 171
"forms-of-life" 141, 142, 152, 203, 209
Foucault, Michel 2, 33–34, 141, 143, 152–153, 167–169, 171, 202–203, 205, 206, 218–219

Gai, Nicola 74, 144
Galleani, Luigi 49–50, 51, 137
Galleanists 49–55

Gallo, Charles 45, 164
Gelderloos, Peter 112–113
genealogy 32–37, 65–70, 94, 134–135
Gilbert, Doug 177–178
Girault, Jean 44
Global War on Terrorism 12–13, 19–20, 62, 214–215
Goldman, Emma 46, 50, 55, 195
Gramsci, Antonio 6, 14, 20, 221
green anarchism 84–90, 148, 187–191, 211, 220
guideline model 118–124, 129

Halandri Case 79–80
Haymarket bombings 45
Henry, Émile 46

Iberian Anarchist Federation (F.A.I.) 54
identity politics 150–151, 153–157, 196
illegalism 15–17, 29, 33, 43–49, 51–53, 63, 136–137, 154–157, 184–187, 192, 194–195, 196
immediacy 119, 140, 161–167, 178, 189
individualism 52–53, 69, 159, 191–195, 197
Individualists Tending Toward the Wild (ITS) 84–90, 110, 162, 188
Informal Anarchist Federation (FAI) 3, 37, 71–76, 90–93, 109, 116–117, 124–127, 144
informality 33, 49, 68, 83, 118, 127, 178–180
Institute for Experimental Freedom, The (IEF) 20, 99, 138, 144, 168, 174, 175, 180, 183, 205–207
intersectionality 150–154, 171–174, 196, 201–207
Invisible Committee, The (TIC) 58, 61, 98, 99, 104, 126, 141–143, 169, 170, 171, 183, 191, 202, 205

Kaczynski, Theodore 88–90, 131–132, 176–177, 187–188, 190, 197, 211
Karakozov, Dmitry 41
Kravchinski, Sergei 42–43

"leaderless resistance" 118, 130–131, 173
Leftism 176–178
Lenin, Vladimir Illyich 136, 178
lifestyleism 66, 68, 105, 176, 195, 198
Lombardi, Michele Angiolillo 44
Luccheni, Luigi 44
Luxemburg, Rosa 136, 145

Malatesta, Errico 43, 52, 137, 164
Marx, Karl 42, 57, 135, 136
method 17–26, 207–209, 216–225
"monopoly on violence" 113, 156
Most, Johann 44, 46, 50, 137

Narodnaya Volya 40–41
Nechayev, Sergey 41, 94, 111, 134, 137
"negative peace" 207–208
Negri, Antonio and Michael Hardt 31, 141, 143, 202, 203
nonviolence (critiques of) 102, 112–115
Novatore, Renzo 52–53, 137, 197

Obsidian Point Circle of Analysis (OPCAn) 87, 193
Obsidian Point Circle of Attack (OPCA) 87, 94, 110, 190–191, 193
"organic intellectuals" 6, 14–15, 143–145, 200
"othering" 5, 220

Pallás, Paulino 44
Passannante, Giovanni 43
performativity 39–40, 172, 201, 209–216
Phoenix Project 80, 90–93, 126–127, 182
poststructuralism 26–27, 33–34, 70, 102, 132, 141, 143, 146–147, 171–172, 175, 200–203, 206–209
"power/knowledge" 34, 203, 205, 219
Práxedis G. Guerrero Autonomous Cells for Immediate Revolution (CARI-PGG) 82–84
Primitive Rebels 15–17
"propaganda of the deed" 39–46, 53, 114, 164–165, 209

Queer theory 150–157, 203–204

recuperation 24–25
Red Army Faction (RAF) 18, 35, 37, 58, 130, 150
Red Brigades (RB) 37, 116, 182
Reinsdorf, August 43
representative democracy 180–184
Revolutionary Cells (RZ) 10–11, 35, 120, 122
Revolutionary Cells – Animal Liberation Brigade (RC-ALB) 121–123
"rhizome" 62–63
Romanos, Nikos 68, 94, 96, 100
"rupture" 106, 162, 166–168, 194, 195–196, 209, 215

Sabaté, Francisco 54, 63
Sacco, Nicola and Bartolomeo Vanzetti 51, 53
Salvador, Santiago 44
San Diego, Daniel Andreas 121–123
securitization 21–22, 23–26, 207–209
Serge, Victor 63, 137, 160, 184, 185, 193
social change (theory of) 97–99
social movement theory 19, 174–176
"social war" 148, 154, 167–172, 207
Spanish Civil War 16, 54, 117
"spectacle" 109, 126, 127, 141, 146, 168, 173, 209–216, 223
Stirner, Max 52, 53, 194–195
strategy (of insurrection) 96–107, 119, 140, 142–143, 147, 161–171, 178–180
"structural violence" 17, 33, 119, 169, 203–209, 211, 222–225

tactical dissemination 44, 45, 50, 81
targeting 101–102, 131–132, 173, 188, 212–213
temporality 118, 165–166, 178–180
terrorism 2, 11–13, 17–18, 20–23, 36, 40–41, 102, 105, 107–116, 148–149, 210–215, 217, 221–225
Terrorism Studies 2–4, 11–14, 17–18, 21–23, 213

Tiqqun 58, 98, 141–143, 148, 151–153, 168, 202–203
"the totality" 143, 148, 153, 171–174, 203–207
"total liberation" 171–174
Towards the Queerest Insurrection 153–154, 203–204

urban guerrillaism/guerrilla warfare 35–37, 68, 79–80, 97, 100–107, 125–126, 148–150, 164, 171, 199

Vaillant, Auguste 44
vanguardism 41–42, 104, 135–137, 150, 178–180

Weather Underground Organization (WUO) 118, 150
Wild Reaction (RS) 86–90, 127–128

Zalacosta, Francisco 42–43
Zapatista Army of National Liberation (EZLN) 55–57, 61, 63